AF305040

REASONABLE DOUBT

EXAMINING THE CASE OF LUCY LETBY

Christopher Morris

Published July 2026
ISBN 978-1-917447-48-5

Published by Cinto Press (an imprint of Bath Publishing Limited)
27 Charmouth Road, Bath, BA1 3LJ
Tel: 01225 577810; email: info@bathpublishing.co.uk
www.bathpublishing.com
Bath Publishing is a company registered in England: 5209173
Registered Office: As above

EU RP (for authorities only)
eucomply OÜ
Pärnu mnt 139b-14, 11317 Tallinn, Estonia
Email: hello@eucompliancepartner.com; Tel: +3375690241

For Keiko

READER NOTE

Queen's Counsel and King's Counsel: the acronym KC has been used throughout the book to reflect Counsels' status at the present time.

Judgment and judgement: court judgments which have been referred to are spelt 'judgment'; all other uses of the word have been spelt 'judgement'.

First names, surnames and titles: first names have sometimes been used where the author has a personal connection to them. Surnames have generally been used elsewhere and the author means no disrespect towards those individuals. Sometimes, people are referred to interchangeably by both first name and surname, for example Michele Worden has been referred to as Michele and Worden. Titles have been used generally to introduce a person but not always retained; for example Dr Michael Hall is referred to variously as Hall and Dr Hall.

American and English spellings: where American research papers or books are referenced, the American spelling has been retained; for example Pediatrician has been retained in preference to the English spelling Paediatrician.

Sources: links to all the sources used in this book can be accessed at https://www.cintopress.co.uk/reasonable-doubt-lucy-letby-case.html.

CONTENTS

PREFACE

On 18 August 2023, Lucy Letby was convicted of 14 counts of murder and attempted murder. The presiding jury at Manchester Crown Court decided that the neonatal nurse was guilty of using an array of murder methods, including air, milk and insulin, in order to fatally harm babies at the Countess of Chester Hospital. The verdict profoundly changed the life of Lucy Letby forever. And, in some small way, my life changed forever as well.

At the time her conviction was announced, I was entombed in my study, writing a completely unrelated book. I'm not sure if I believe in destiny, but if fate does exist then it decreed that I would plod down the stairs to my kitchen and encounter the news of Letby's conviction via a radio report.

Initially, I was shocked to my core. I couldn't understand how a neonatal nurse could engage in such abhorrent and aberrant behaviour. But as I continued to absorb the chilling disclosure of the various anchors and reporters, an intuitive thought steadily lodged itself in my conscious mind.

This is all highly disturbing. *But I haven't heard any evidence for this.*

A few more minutes passed without evidence. Then a few more. And then a few more. By this time, I had already resolved to seek out the evidence for myself.

At the absolute onset of this process, I encountered a note that was exhibited almost universally by media at the time of the conviction. I was informed that this handwritten note represented a confession by Lucy Letby. This will surely put my concerns to bed immediately, I reassured myself, as I prepared to download and look at the note for the first time.

If I were to be particularly generous, I would state that it took me about 10 seconds to see that this was clearly *not* a confession note. It was laughable, in fact. This incoherent scribbling on lime green paper was a key artefact from the court case, yet it starkly stood up to no scrutiny whatsoever.

This was the initial spark that prompted me to probe further. And the more I probed, the more problems I encountered. It became crystal clear to me rather rapidly that there was another side to this story. And it also became obvious that it was of paramount importance for me to see this through to its conclusion. The consequences were too great for me to invest energy or attention in anything else.

Over the last three years, I have left no stone unturned in my pursuit of information about the conviction of Lucy Letby. I have read every accessible report, article and document, and pursued every conceivable avenue. I have sought out and spoken with as many experts as possible; over 60 by the time of publication. (I should mention that dozens of other experts have contacted me, but it was impossible to include everyone). These experts encompass such fields as neonatology, paediatrics, vascular surgery, radiology, obstetrics, biochemistry, psychiatry, statistics, nursing, plus too many more to mention.

Along with my research, I have watched what began as a whisper of disquiet grow into a roar of discontent. Television producer Stephen Phelps is adamant that the response to the Letby case has never been seen before. Phelps is uniquely qualified to comment, having spent 12 years making television programmes investigating miscarriages of justice, most notably *Rough Justice* on the BBC and *Trial and Error* on Channel 4. Stephen told me that "there is no previous miscarriage of justice case that has received the response that we've seen with Lucy Letby. Every single mainstream newspaper, and many other media outlets, have raised doubts about this conviction. This is absolutely unprecedented."

This book is published at a time in which miscarriages of justice have repeatedly made headline news. Peter Sullivan suffered the most horrendous fate – 38 years in prison while completely innocent – and Justin Plummer was exonerated after 27 years of incarceration. The case of Andrew Malkinson broke at around the time of Lucy Letby's conviction; he spent 17 years behind bars for rape, and was refused three appeals. In this case, exonerating DNA evidence, which eventually resulted in Malkinson's conviction being quashed after he had served his entire sentence, was withheld from the Court of Appeal.

And the overarching debacle of the Post Office scandal retains an indelible impression on the nation. Over 900 subpostmasters were prosecuted, with 236 imprisoned. Over £1 billion paid out in compensation. 13 people involved are known to have committed suicide.

These disturbing cases are, nonetheless, only a mere scintilla of reality. In November 2025, at the Westminster All Party Parliamentary Group on Miscarriages of Justice, an assembled audience of MPs, academics and journalists heard that there are estimated to be between 2,000 and 10,000 innocent British people currently residing in prison.

Throughout the process of writing and researching this book, I have been conscious of the feelings of the parents of the babies who died or were harmed. They have clearly experienced great trauma and, like everyone else, I feel a great deal of sympathy for them. This has led to many people asking me why I am shining a light on this issue given it may only serve to prolong their trauma. My answer is that I would not be doing so if I wasn't absolutely certain that something has gone terribly wrong in the conviction of Lucy Letby. A very different story than the one set out in court is emerging and it is important this story is told, both to right a possible miscarriage of justice and to highlight that serious mistakes made in the management and care of their infants may not have been properly addressed.

Recent precedent and overwhelming evidence indicate that the criminal justice system is not always correct. It can get things very, very wrong. It is with this understanding that I therefore ask readers, as they embark on this journey of examining the conviction of Lucy Letby, to never forget the following five simple words:

This could happen to you.

CHAPTER 1: PRIOR CHARACTER OF LUCY LETBY

There has been no suggestion of any psychological illness or disorder in the case of Lucy Letby. Indeed, she is universally regarded by those who have encountered her to be psychologically healthy and happy, with many close friends, prior to the police investigation of the Countess of Chester Hospital (CoCH). Many of her nursing colleagues praised her conduct and professionalism. One Cheshire Police detective commented: "This is completely unprecedented in that there doesn't seem to be anything to say about why Letby would kill babies. There isn't really anything we have found in her background that's anything other than normal."

In the process of their investigation, Cheshire Police dug through the life of Letby, scouring every aspect of her existence for any evidence of wrongdoing, including excavating her garden. Despite this, a remarkably minuscule amount of dirt was found. Dr James Phillips, former Prime Ministerial advisor and now a critic of Letby's conviction, noted: "If you trawl through the life of virtually any person, you will find something amiss. Maybe they've got a gambling habit, or a tendency to swear at their colleagues. Yet despite an extensive search, with the full force of Cheshire Police, the authorities have come back with absolutely nothing."

Close friend Dawn Howe described Letby as the "most kind, gentle, soft friend; she is the kindest person that I've ever known. She would only want to help people." Howe stated in a BBC documentary that Letby had dedicated her entire life to working as a nurse after being saved herself by skilled nursing when an infant. She noted that Letby had shown steadfast and singular determination to succeed in nursing from an age that even preceded adolescence. Another school friend similarly insisted that "being a children's nurse was all [Letby] ever wanted".

Michele Worden, who worked at the CoCH for 20 years, latterly as an Advanced Neonatal Nurse Practitioner (ANNP), reflected that view. She told me a little more about her background, and how it was indelibly connected to the case. "In 1992, I was seconded to Southampton University under Mike Hall, who was the uncalled defence witness in Lucy's trial. At the time, he had started the first advanced neonatal nurse practitioner course in the country. Nurse practitioners are quite common these days, but they weren't back in the early nineties, and neonates were one of the first areas to introduce them under my call. When I qualified and obtained my degree, I worked on the neonatal and paediatric medical rota under the consultants, and I continued in this role for 13 years."

While Michele never worked with Letby, she was closely acquainted with her social circle. "I know lots of Lucy's friends. Based on their accounts, she was a very happy part of the team. They went out. They socialised. She wasn't odd in any way. She loved her cats. She was focused. She wanted her own house. A lot of the nurses, including Lucy, went on holiday together. Lucy was as normal as can be."

It is not disputed that Letby was well-adjusted and sociable, with close friendship groups both within the hospital and outside work. When I spoke with a Cambridge-educated psychiatrist and mental health practitioner, he told me that speculation about Letby's character was "unfair and unfounded". The practitioner further asserted that "there is absolutely no evidence of borderline personality disorder. And the same goes for speculation about psychopathic traits. There is absolutely no evidence for this. She was known as someone who is very kind, caring and good with animals. There is nothing macabre about her personality." This human side of Letby was evident in a Netflix film released in February 2026 which included footage of her arrests. During this traumatic experience, she was seen bonding with her cats in what was evidently an emotional farewell.

Dr Thea Gumbert, a psychologist and expert on criminal justice who has worked extensively with both perpetrators and victims of sexual and violent offences questioned the often tenuous comments that have been made on Letby's psychological constitution. "Lucy has been psychologically assessed, and what they found was that she had PTSD as a result of the ordeal that she'd been through. They didn't find any evidence of any prior dysfunction, even the police confirmed this in a statement. They couldn't find anything that would be a red flag. When people make these comments that she has borderline personality disorder – on what evidence are they making that assessment? It seems so easy to start throwing around unfounded accusations of people having personality disorders."

Nicola Lightfoot, deputy ward manager on the children's unit at the CoCH said at the Thirlwall Inquiry that she had found Letby "quite cold" during her placement as a student nurse. "I did not find a natural warmth exuding from her which I expect from a children's nurse." However, Karen Rees, the head of nursing for urgent care at the CoCH, saw things differently. "[Lucy] was quiet, [but] a normal 28-year-old. But when under stress, I can see she goes catatonic almost…People say she's not emotional. Trust me, she is emotional." Dr Lucy Beebe also recounted Letby crying following the death of Child I, while Occupational Health and Wellbeing Manager, Kathryn de Beger, remembered Letby being "upset and distressed", but having also expressed her concern regarding "how much more distressed and upset the parents must be feeling because they had lost their babies".

While preparing this book, I was approached by Ruth Sadik who was Lucy Letby's tutor at the University of Chester and had known her since 2008. Ruth told me that "Lucy was incredibly shy at that age" but that "once Lucy was on the neonatal unit with Eirian Powell [neonatal unit manager and Letby's line manager], it was like meeting a different person. Lucy flourished in the whole unit ethos that existed." Ruth believed that this shyness could have been a contributing factor in Letby's results.

This impression was further corroborated by one nurse from the CoCH, who had wished to appear in court as a character witness, but was discouraged. The nurse in question spoke to Sarah Knapton at *The Daily Telegraph* regarding the professionalism and human qualities of Letby. "Lucy was always very quiet with people she didn't know, but she adored looking after those babies and building that relationship. She got on really well with families and children and she used to get a lot of thank you cards from the families. She was always very good at building rapport and looking after babies was her passion, you could tell as soon as she walked on the ward she loved it." Similarly, Letby's colleagues describe her as reliable and conscientious, as well as very happy in her job.

The head of the paediatrics department at the CoCH, Dr Ravi Jayaram, who would later be part of the 'gang of four' consultants that reported Letby to Cheshire Police, told journalist Rachel Aviv at *New Yorker* that "there was an element of 'Thank God Lucy was on' because she's really good in a crisis", describing Letby as "very popular" among her fellow nurses. Dr Stephen Brearey, possibly the most prominent member of the 'gang of four', was head of the neonatal unit at the CoCH. When speaking with Rachel Aviv, he conceded that at the time of Letby's first arrest in 2018, a "significant cohort of nurses [at the CoCH] felt that [Letby] had done nothing wrong".

As acknowledged by *The Guardian* in July 2024, in Letby there was also "no psychological background that matched a serial killer", along with "no apparent motive". When Letby was initially blamed for an apparent spike in deaths on the neonatal unit at the CoCH, her good character and standing on the ward resulted in her being defended by hospital management. Karen Rees also shielded Letby against accusations of inappropriate conduct before there was police involvement. Rees stated that "Lucy Letby does everything by the book. She follows policy and procedure to the letter", and later elaborated on this, indicating that there had been no "sound reason" to remove her from the section.

When the Royal College of Paediatrics and Child Health (RCPCH) later spoke with Letby during an investigation into the spike in deaths on the neonatal unit, the team tasked with interviewing her described her as "an enthusiastic, capable and committed nurse" who was "passionate about her career and keen to progress". Parents of children that Letby cared for were also effusive in their praise, even after her arrest. Kate Walker from Chester informed *The Guardian* that Letby had advocated for the transfer of her premature son to the neighbouring Alder Hey Hospital during his treatment at the Countess of Chester, and had told

Walker "every step of the way what was happening". Walker concluded: "I can't say anything negative about her." Another mother from North Wales also received assistance from Letby with her premature son and described her as a "great nurse", informing *The Times* that "she helped me give my son his first bath. I could not have asked for a more caring and helpful nurse."

Commenting during a press conference related to Letby's appeal, Dr Richard Taylor noted that "nursing is an altruistic profession – people don't go into it for the money. They go into it because they want to help other people, almost universally. And I think that applies to her. She has no past history of any anti-social behavior, any criminal behavior, any psychiatric problems at all. There is no motive. Her friends are all completely astounded, flabbergasted by the accusations that were made against her. That immediately, for me, brought up red flags." Similarly, Dr Roger Norwich, previously CEO of Medico-Legal Consultancy Plc with lengthy experience in paediatrics and as a locum consultant, told me that he had "spoken to numerous people among her social circle, and they all think she's completely normal."

Documentation produced for the Thirlwall Inquiry, set up to investigate the circumstances which led to Letby's arrest and conviction, has further underlined the esteem in which Letby was held. Yvonne Griffiths, who was deputy ward manager of the CoCH neonatal unit in 2015 and 2016 and later the neonatal unit manager, provided a witness statement to the inquiry, saying: "Lucy was more than capable and fully trained in looking after babies in ITU. She was very competent, meticulous, and always attended any necessary training or study days. She was not as experienced as the Band 6 nurses but she ticked all the boxes…I did not personally suspect that Lucy had caused any baby to collapse or come to harm." Griffiths also considered the standard of work, attitude and documentation produced by Letby to be "excellent", and conveyed when questioned as part of Letby's grievance procedure that "the feedback from the unit has reflected there were no concerns with [Letby's] clinical competence and no red flags". In the same report, deputy director of nursing, Sian Williams, commented that "the feedback was that [Letby] was excellent".

Far from having any qualms about Letby's clinical practice, her direct line manager, Eirian Powell actively "wanted her on the unit, I really did". Powell had, in fact, noted the proficiency of Letby before she even began working professionally at the hospital. "When students come through the system, you are almost able to hand pick the crème de la crème and she was one of those." When Letby was removed from the unit, Powell was "adamant" about her return. "I want her back", Powell was quoted as commenting in a report dated November 2016. Yvonne Griffiths further observed that it "would be easy for [Letby] to walk away", but expressed her "hope she returns to the unit…we would be delighted". Karen Rees also marvelled at the tenacity of Letby under the fiercest of pressure and scrutiny, asserting that "her resilience was amazing, considering she could have just gone off sick with stress".

Griffiths noted that neither herself nor Powell "had any concerns at the time to believe [Letby] was causing any harm. There were no complaints from nursing staff or parents about unsafe practice or suspicions with regard to practice. No one reported any unsafe practice." Director of nursing at the hospital, Alison Kelly, similarly commented that everyone in the nursing team thought "highly of [Letby], and how she works and responds when the transport team are involved". Kelly further noted that "all [are] happy with [Letby's] practice, record keeping, and competencies", also describing her as "perfectly nice", and "good in a crisis". In fact, when statements from nurses who worked on the neonatal unit at the CoCH were finally released by the Thirlwall Inquiry in February 2025, they were almost universally supportive of Letby, with none of her colleagues having experienced or suspected any wrongdoing. While the remit of the Thirlwall Inquiry is narrow, it is notable that these comments were excluded from the public inquiry, having been submitted many months before they were finally published.

When reports surfaced that Letby had been described as "cold", much was also made of the then University of Chester student failing the final year of her placement. However, Letby's second mentor from this period, Sarah Jayne Murphy, told the Thirlwall Inquiry that she had met the three proficiencies on which she was assessed. Murphy added: "Also, I would like to reiterate that I sought feedback from other members of staff that she worked with and so I had no reason to believe that she was performing well only just during my assessments."

Ruth Sadik told me more about that period in Letby's career, explaining that "of about 300 candidates that we interviewed, Lucy was one of just 15 that were successful. She had all the qualities we looked for in a student nurse, in terms of being kind, caring, and compassionate, but she also had the tenacity and strength that is required. To endure some of the things that children's nurses have to go through, you need that inner core dedication that we just felt Lucy had."

In a neonatal review of the CoCH conducted in May 2016, Eirian Powell "found [Letby] to be diligent and have excellent standards within the clinical area". Later that year, when Dr Christopher Green conducted Letby's grievance procedure, Griffiths noted that "Lucy's documents are excellent; the standard of her work is excellent", and stated effusively that those working on the unit "would be delighted to have her back". During the same process, Powell described Letby as "amenable and flexible, one my best nurses. Her practice is second to none." Even staff that Letby worked with during a placement at Liverpool Women's Hospital were noted to be complimentary. "[Letby] has also worked in a Level 3 unit in Liverpool who said how good she was", Powell commented. "Transport team have commented on [Letby's] professionalism."

Ruth Sadik also recounted Letby "triple-checking everything. She was so careful and conscientious." When I asked Ruth if Letby would be in a position of seniority on the neonatal unit by now, she was unequivocal. "Oh, absolutely. There is no doubt about that. You only have to read what people say about her. Read the documents from the Thirlwall Inquiry; you can see the way that people spoke about Lucy – doctors, nurses, everybody about her competence, commitment and personal qualities. The people who knew Lucy best were gushing about her."

During the compilation of this book, I interviewed many nurses, including several from a neonatal background. There was universal agreement among them that Letby was a capable and conscientious nurse.

Others questioned why Letby had suddenly developed into an apparent serial killer, after several years on the unit with no concern whatsoever. "It's very strange that she went from being a good nurse for several years to suddenly supposedly changing, and there doesn't seem to be a precipitating event", another neonatal nurse told me. Another interviewee with a nursing background, who has since completed a PhD in mental health, also queried this. "If you look at Beverley Allitt [a former nurse convicted of killing and harming patients], I think the first murder was within two weeks of her starting on the ward. But with Lucy Letby, she is working for over three years before anything happens, with no red flags, being held in the highest regard by colleagues. You would have to say that seems really, really odd."

It is also notable that Letby was particularly co-operative after her arrest and throughout the following police and court proceedings. BBC journalist Judith Moritz described Letby as "well-spoken and unflustered, thoughtful and co-operative". Detective Chief Inspector Nicola Evans was quoted as deeming Letby to be "calm, compliant and co-operative". Letby herself told prosecutor Nick Johnson that she "tried to be as co-operative as I could be" during the police interviews. Letby indeed fully co-operated with the police, agreeing to be interviewed no fewer than 30 times, and the transcripts of Cheshire Police interviews that have been released indicate that Letby answered questions fluently and conscientiously. In the 166 pages of police interview transcripts that are available, there is no sign of evasion or deceit.

This was despite the fact that one childhood friend of Letby commented she was in a state of "terror and confusion" following her arrest. "I could tell from how she was acting that she just didn't know what to say about it, because it was such an alien concept to be accused of these things." Parents of the infants involved in the court case had also garnered a positive impression of Letby. "That's what confuses me the most", one mother said. "Lucy presented herself as kind, caring, and soft-spoken."

It was already evident that Letby's life had been turned upside down by the time she filed a grievance in September 2016 about being removed from her post. "My whole world was stopped", she said later. "From a self-confidence point of view, it made me question everything about myself. I just felt like I'd let everybody down, that I'd let myself down, that people were changing their opinion of me." Letby was diagnosed with depression and anxiety and began taking medication.

It is over nine years since Lucy Letby's grievance procedure. This neonatal nurse has been through a nine-year nightmare. Having spent several years dutifully co-operating, there is a distinct possibility that Letby has plummeted into a state of learned helplessness. This is defined by *Medical News Today* as "a state that occurs after a person has experienced a stressful situation repeatedly. They believe that they are unable to control or change the situation, so they do not try, even when opportunities for change are available."

Letby's demeanour can be seen as the behaviour of a deeply traumatised woman, not a guilty one. This is not difficult to deduce anyway, but it is also consistent with everything that has been reported in the media. Letby was suffering with PTSD, barely able to speak, at the beginning of the court case. She had, quite understandably, suffered a severe breakdown. In any other situation, she would have received extensive care and medical attention. This might perhaps explain why Letby seemed a little listless in court; something for which she has been, yet again, roundly criticised. "Criticism of her demeanour is ludicrous," Michele Worden asserted. "This is a girl, then only aged 25, removed from the job she loves, accused of the most horrendous crimes, who has been placed under house arrest, completely excluded from all of her friends. She was totally isolated. How would you expect her to react?"

While the tone of reporting has shifted recently, the initial media coverage of the Letby case was focused on assassinating her character. Absurd sophistry and nitpicking generated headlines, while comments such as the following, from Janet Cox, a Band 4 nursery nurse who had worked at the CoCH from 1986 to 2022, passed largely without comment or publicity. When asked by the Thirlwall Inquiry to submit a statement, Cox considered Letby to be "an exemplary nurse who is completely innocent of all the alleged crimes…I did not think this at the time, nor do I think now, that there was anything sinister about the increase in the number of deaths/collapses." Cox was not invited to be questioned at the inquiry.

Dr Philip Hammond wrote in *Private Eye* that "none of Letby's fellow shift workers gave evidence against her". Hammond also noted that some of Letby's colleagues had "given written evidence to the Thirlwall Inquiry supporting Letby and saying they do not believe she is a murderer. They have been told they won't be called to give oral evidence. The stench of cover-up grows stronger."

Finally, another psychiatrist who wishes to remain anonymous told me that there were no apparent "criminogenic factors" in the case of Lucy Letby. I was told that major criminal offenders can almost always be associated with these lifestyle and causative factors, such as drug use, addictions, mental health problems, personality disorders, financial pressures and relationship issues. Developmental trauma is extremely common in serious offenders, and yet there is "no behavioural trail" in the case of Letby, nor any conceivable motivation. There is also no feasible motive for the crimes, which run contrary to everything that we know about her as a person.

Before we examine any of the evidence presented in court, we can be certain that there is absolutely nothing in the prior character or conduct of Letby that would be even remotely consistent with her carrying out such heinous crimes. As the psychiatrist told me, "There is no evidence of any background or behaviour consistent with a serial killer, or even anything remotely suspicious. There is no history of harm to others, interest in macabre topics, or any indication of malicious or violent fixation, even in her internet history." Despite enormous efforts, Cheshire Police failed to identify anything incriminating in Letby's character.

"It's not merely that there's nothing in Letby's background to suggest that she would be a serial killer. The evidence points the other way", Dr James Phillips told me. "If anything, she is further away from the kind of person that would do this than your average person. That's reflected in everything that has been reported on her, and how she was regarded prior to falling under suspicion. It's there in the very compelling testimony of her friends, and it's reflected in the fact that nurses on that unit are still standing by her."

Until accusations suddenly began to circulate in 2016, Letby was deemed an admirable, even exemplary, nurse by her colleagues, many of whom demonstrably retain this impression to this day. This support was exemplified by a text message sent to Letby by Karen Rees herself in May 2017, in the very same month that Cheshire Police were contacted for the first time. "Hang on in there girl. Your nursing team are fully behind you. We will get through this."

Sadly, neither of these nurses knew what lay ahead.

CHAPTER 2: ACCUSATION WITHOUT EVIDENCE

The term 'gang of four' will be familiar to anyone who has followed the trial of Lucy Letby with even a passing interest. This phrase references four consultants at the CoCH, namely Dr Stephen Brearey, Dr Ravi Jayaram, Dr John Gibbs and a fourth doctor who was granted anonymity by the court.

We have prosecuting barrister Nick Johnson to thank for the proliferation of this phrase, as it was he who first introduced it during court proceedings on 18 May 2023. It was widely reported at the time that Letby had accused the consultants of a conspiracy, but, again, this concept was, in fact, voiced by the prosecuting barrister. Letby did state that they had "apportioned blame" onto her, and that a possible motivation for this could be "to cover up things at the hospital".

In the immediate aftermath of Letby's conviction, the four doctors were almost universally lauded as heroes. Detective Superintendent Paul Hughes, who led the investigation for Cheshire Police, told the *Observer* that the 'gang of four' had been "very brave in coming forward and they've put this ahead of their careers, in my view. If it wasn't for their ongoing determination, would there have been more [murders]? I don't know. It's difficult to answer or speculate on the future. But they've done well."

Brearey in particular focused on Letby as a potential cause for suboptimal patient outcomes at the CoCH. His interest pre-dated the existence of a spike of deaths at the neonatal unit. Yet email correspondence between Dr Jane Hawdon, a consultant neonatologist who was asked to perform pathology reports at the hospital, and Ian Harvey, former Medical Director of the CoCH, in February 2017, indicates that even at this stage of proceedings, the suspicions of consultants were "based on coincidence and 'gut-feeling'".

Dr Brearey, though armed with little substantial evidence, had begun to investigate his coincidence theory nearly two years before the police were contacted. In an email dated 22 June 2015, Dr Brearey informed Dr Jayaram that the infant who became known as Child D (each of the infants was anonymised and assigned an identifying letter before Letby's trial began) "is most likely to have suffered from early neonatal sepsis which she showed signs of from 12 minutes of age and she continued to be unstable". This conclusion was further advanced by emails between Brearey, Gibbs and paediatrician Dr Elizabeth Newby, in which Brearey states that "Child D's death appears to be due to early neonatal sepsis after PROM. She was symptomatic from 12 min of age."

This is mooted as the most likely cause of death, and there is some further clinical discussion, before Dr Brearey makes what, at the time, may have seemed like a fairly innocuous comment: "There does not seem to be any staff (medical or nursing) members present at all three episodes other than one nurse, who was not the nurse responsible for [Child D] on that shift."

Brearey even stated that "I would be very surprised if [Child D]'s death is linked in any way to the previous recent deaths of [Child A] and [Child C]." This was affirmed by paediatric registrar, Dr Andrew Brunton, who "did not make any links to the coroner in [his] statement regarding the deaths of Child C and D, and the collapse of Child B, as it had never been suggested that these incidents could be linked in any way".

Facere Melius, a healthcare improvement and investigation consultancy, was commissioned to investigate events at the CoCH, and its final report was entitled *Hidden in Plain Sight*. The report was later submitted to the Thirlwall Inquiry in November 2024. Unfortunately, we are not privileged enough to know the scope of that investigation, whether any medical information was submitted, or indeed anything that is contained within it as its entire contents remain 'confidential'.

We do, however, know that Facere Melius interviewed the neonatal unit manager, Yvonne Griffiths, in June 2020. At that time, Griffiths agreed that "Stephen Brearey picked out in July 2015 there was that commonality with Lucy". So just weeks after concluding that an infant who had died at the hospital was "unstable", and "is most likely to have suffered from early neonatal sepsis", Brearey was already seemingly focused on Letby as the possible cause of problems on the unit. There was no evidence to support this at the time; even Brearey's email of 22 June 2015 concedes this.

In her witness statement to the Thirlwall Inquiry, Griffiths further noted that "Dr Brearey did speak to me [in October 2015] of his concern that Letby seemed to be the common denominator to all the incidents which all seemed to happen on nights…I did not change allocation because I had doubts in Letby's practice but more to stop finger pointing." This was further underlined by a letter from the Director of Human Resources and Organisational Development at the hospital, Sue Hodkinson, who told Letby that "a decision was taken to take you out of the unit to protect you". When the RCPCH reported on the CoCH, the professional body found that Letby "had been moved to an alternative position around 10 weeks previously without explanation nor any formal investigative process having been established". Karen Rees noted that accusations levelled at Letby left her feeling "frightened…shocked and bewildered".

Dr James Phillips has been present for many high-level Whitehall meetings and has observed numerous collectives veering off on an undesirable tangent. "Groupthink has often been central to this process", Phillips observed, "and I keenly sense the same signatures infecting what occurred at the CoCH." James outlined his experience in this area:

"Essentially, with any issue, one position can develop to such an extent that it develops a kind of gravitational attraction. And then if there isn't a critical mass of people who enter into the process with a different view, the prevailing view becomes cemented. This is particularly dangerous when the incentives of those in the group are highly similar, and even more so when the people doing the thinking are highly similar themselves. And both of those things appear tangible in the chain of events around the consultants, which is why I think this groupthink was such a danger, and why some of the consultants appear to have determinedly followed a certain course without seemingly having any evidence to support their view."

James also explained why groupthink was particularly incentivised in this situation. "When you've got this cluster of deaths, even if it's not statistically significant, this could put the consultants in a difficult position. Ultimately, that would be their responsibility. There is a natural concern that the impression of a nurse acting malignantly becomes the common element that the consultants gravitate around. It's clear that Letby being a serial killer would enable other issues, such as potential medical malpractice, to go away, and that obviously, in itself, creates a danger for groupthink. And that could prevent the consultants from letting anything else into their bubble or adequately investigating other credible explanations."

Further emails between Alison Kelly, a former nursing manager at the CoCH, and Karen Rees indicate that the situation on the neonatal unit still hadn't changed by May 2016. Kelly was concerned at this point that activity on the unit could represent discrimination against Letby.

In an email chain between various consultants in June 2016, Dr Gibbs openly named "Lucy" as the person under Brearey's suspicion. Gibbs was more hesitant than the others about launching an investigation. Another doctor at the hospital, Dr Murthy Saladi, similarly expressed his reluctance to make such correlative links: "We have investigated these deaths as much as we can, which included seeking clinical input from outside. The only thing which came out of it (as I understand) is one member of staff was working in the unit (not necessarily with the baby who passed away in each incident but might have cared for the baby during the staff breaks) at the time of all these deaths.

"This is highly unreliable information and further outside clinical input is unlikely to help shed more light on the relevance of this information. However, we seem to be acting on this unreliable information… This is unfair to the staff under suspicion, unfair to parents and other staff who are unaware of the situation and unfair to the staff who are aware of the situation."

As the situation at the CoCH escalated, Letby found herself in an invidious position. Email correspondence in September 2016 between Tony Millea, a union representative at the CoCH, Karen Rees and Alison Kelly acknowledged this: "As a result of this, I now believe our member has grounds to action a grievance" wrote Millea. "Given the gravitas of what is being alleged by the organisation, I believe our member has a right to be fully consulted and a full and frank explanation is given by the organisation into my concerns. The allegations that have been made by the Trust could have a detrimental effect on our member's career. Which may constitute professional slander resulting in our member being constructively dismissed from the organisation."

One might infer from this that some form of solid evidence had been produced, but nothing could be further from the truth. Dr Christopher Green, Director of Pharmacy at the CoCH, was one of the personnel tasked with conducting Letby's grievance procedure, which was instigated in September 2016. Green interviewed Yvonne Griffiths on 17 October 2016, and it was clear from her comments that nothing had changed from 16 months previously. "Steve Brearly [sic] wanted to go to the Chief Exec and we said you can't just do that on a gut feeling", Griffiths noted. "We had looked at the information and the only thing seemed to be that [Letby] was on duty. They said that if they didn't go to the Chief Exec they would be going straight to the police. We were very uncomfortable. We told them to take their concerns to Lucy but they were adamant. I think they wanted her fired immediately. I found it very difficult to act on something I didn't believe in – it was a witch-hunt. I hate the secrecy. I think they were frightened she would go to the police herself about the allegations." Griffiths further noted that "Steve Brearey was concerned and wanted to grasp at anything that might be linked, to 'point the finger'…Steve Brearey was the only one with concerns prior to the triplets."

Before we go any further, consider the following – why would someone who had been deliberately harming babies on a neonatal unit choose to draw attention to themselves and their conduct in this manner? If you knew yourself to be guilty, and it was also clear that you were under suspicion, surely you would attempt to slip away quietly? Pursuing a grievance procedure does not seem to be the act of a guilty person.

The next chapter will deal with reviews of the CoCH. Nonetheless, it must briefly be mentioned here that a Neonatal Unit Review in 2015/16 prompted further discussion of the 'evidence' the consultants had on Letby. This review came to the following conclusion:

"There is no evidence whatsoever against [Letby] other than coincidence. [Letby] works full-time and has the Qualification in Speciality (QIS). She is therefore more likely to be looking after the sickest infants on the unit. Letby also avails herself to work overtime when the acuity or unit is over capacity. I have found Letby to be diligent and have excellent standards within the clinical area. Whilst our mortality rate has risen in the January 2015-January 2016 we have had x3 mortalities from January 2016 to date (May 2016) x2 died due to congenital abnormalities. Dr H and Dr G (Consultant) appear to be involved in many of the mortalities."

Understandably, Letby's nursing colleagues were somewhat perturbed about the allegations being made against her. An undated discussion between Brearey, Anne Murphy, Lead Nurse of Children's Services, and Eirian Powell saw the following concession made: "Karen Rees requested that we discussed exactly what the issues (if any) were other than coincidence that was evident. Despite highlighting the usual factors there was not real evidence or statement that could confirm whether there was an issue here."

Nonetheless, the conjecture continued into 2017. On 7 March 2017, Brearey demanded a further review of eight babies (six of whom were to become part of the eventual indictment), during communication with Ian Harvey and several consultants. During this discourse, Dr Nim Subhedar, a neonatologist based at Liverpool Women's Hospital, expressed what became an unchallenged conclusion: "Other network local neonatal units are working at similar levels of occupancy and staffing and CoCH is not an outlier in this regard. Since these units are not reporting an excess in neonatal mortality, it suggests that there is a different explanation for our increased number of unexplained deaths."

This is a fairly extraordinary assertion, considering that Dr Subhedar has, firstly, conducted no investigation into these unevidenced claims, and, secondly, he is contradicted by considerable evidence that will be outlined in forthcoming chapters. In my opinion there seems to be a reluctance on the part of Brearey to accept any other explanation other than to identify someone who was on duty all the time.

Brearey has accused management of "bullying" and "intimidating" both himself and other "senior doctors", despite the fact that every single point of Letby's grievance was either fully or partially upheld. The concluding document from the grievance notes that the behaviour towards Letby on the unit "has directly resulted in a junior colleague feeling isolated and vulnerable, with her reputation in question. This is unacceptable and could be concluded as victimisation."

During the writing of this book, I was approached by Dr Fiona MacRae who worked as an anaesthetist at the CoCH for 27 years, only leaving the hospital in 2022. Fiona indicated that whenever she "raised an issue" at the hospital, complaints would be made against her. "Eventually, I went through a list of bullying behaviours", Dr MacRae told me, "and I could tick off virtually every one. The consultant body is a powerful body, and I think the executives just cannot accept that there is a bullying culture."

I further spoke with a senior diagnostic radiographer, who wishes to remain anonymous, on the subject of the typical culture at NHS hospitals, and he had the following to say: "I have experienced first-hand the power dynamics and bullying that goes on every day in the NHS. Consultants rule the roost, without a doubt. They are not to be questioned or challenged. The story of consultant doctors being bullied by anyone in an NHS Trust doesn't ring true at all. Good and approachable consultants are admired and respected generally, but some can be tyrannical. In fact, the idea that consultants would be bullied is so absurd as to be quite surreal! Feel free to ask any other healthcare professionals with a significant amount of experience in the NHS – I'm certain you will hear a similar story."

Another experienced NHS professional, Ashleigh Tavoulari, enlightened me further on the culture of the NHS. Tavoulari has worked within the NHS in radiotherapy and oncology for 14 years, while also possessing experience of healthcare systems in Greece and Spain. "My experience is that the majority of the consultants in the NHS have an ego. There are very few consultants, certainly that I've worked with, who managed to rein that ego in. There is an inherent hierarchy in these organisations, with the consultants at the top. I've seen this hierarchy with many of the consultants that I've worked with, and this kind of integral superiority would completely negate the idea that they're being bullied." Whistleblowing authority Eileen Chubb, founder of the charity Compassion in Care, similarly told me that "one of the most common themes that we encounter all the time is that nurses are very rarely believed above doctors. We hear about this every single day. There is almost without exception an authority bias in favour of doctors."

And what was said about the consultants during Letby's grievance procedure? Annette Weatherley, chair of the grievance panel, commented that "it is clear that the two consultants call the shots and have put pressure on the Exec team in making this decision". Karen Rees also commented that unit managers on the unit "allow the consultants to dictate too much", while Annemarie Lawrence, who was the clinical governance lead at the hospital in 2016, told the Thirlwall Inquiry that there was a "definite hierarchy" in the unit, with nurses rarely challenging the medical team even when they strayed from established "process or guidance".

Dr Jane Hawdon had a somewhat more generous view of the consultants but still noted their resistance to objectively assessing conditions on the neonatal unit. "I perceive a combination of understandable professional pride regarding standards of care on the unit along with concern over unexpected and unexplained events, both of which are entirely reasonable reactions, but both of these should not prevent accepting and learning what could have been improved." Hawdon added that there had been an "apparent failure to accept things could have been improved" on the unit and was critical of "some of the behaviour" from the consultants after raising concerns. At an extraordinary board meeting held on 14 July 2016, it was recorded in the minutes that "there are strains in the system and as the neonatal lead, [Dr] Brearey could not see that any of the apparent changes in acuity or staffing levels can account for the increased mortality".

When statements of several nurses who worked at the CoCH during this period were released by the Thirlwall Inquiry in February 2025, it immediately became clear that many of Letby's colleagues were neither unduly concerned nor surprised by the increase in deaths, due precisely to the clinical picture discussed at the board meeting. Neonatal nurse Caroline Oakley cited a "very busy year" with "more vulnerable babies" and did not consider outcomes on the unit to be "unnatural". Fellow nurse Christopher Booth concluded that "the collapses and deaths could all be rationally explained" due to "an unprecedented level of acuity". Another neonatal nurse from the CoCH, Laura Eagles, mentioned "an increase in activity on the unit", along with "more sick babies than is usual". Nursery nurse Cherryl Cuthbertson-Taylor who worked on the neonatal unit observed that the unit was "short-staffed", while dealing with "a high influx of very sick babies". Neonatal assistant Valerie Thomas "was aware that the unit was very busy, especially with more premature [and] complex babies…some of which had complex needs". And the anonymised Nurse X observed that there were issues with staffing, while "the unit was much busier than it had been when I first started working there." This level of activity led Nurse X to conclude that "with an increase in patient numbers, it did not surprise me that the number of babies dying had also increased. I considered that the increase in acuity had increased the mortality rate further." Dr Fiona MacRae suspects that "Lucy was whistleblowing about the staffing levels on the unit".

It is evident that throughout this period, while accusations were being made against Letby, her nursing team and colleagues were largely supportive. I do not think this is out of some partisan tendency; nurses simply spent more time around Letby than any consultant could have, and thus have a much more nuanced feel for her competence and character. It is just as likely they would have turned against her if there were significant reasons for suspicion.

Several nurses I interviewed also had views on NHS culture and the atmosphere that can contaminate neonatal units. A mental health expert had previously worked as a nurse for several years but had left the profession "because of cultural issues". She explained: "My unit experienced several very nasty referrals to the Nursing and Midwifery Council, and I found this to be hugely distressing for the person involved. There was very little justice for them, and no voice for them either. I saw exactly how things can become distorted, and I immediately saw a parallel here with the treatment of Lucy Letby." Another neonatal nurse told me that units can be "gossipy", and that it is quite easy for someone to "decide that they don't like you", and suddenly "everyone is finding fault with everything that you do. Confirmation bias can lead to others finding fault in that person, even when they've done nothing wrong. It actually speaks volumes that Lucy was so obviously supported by nursing colleagues, because it would not be unusual for them to turn on her rapidly if they had the slightest suspicion, even if this wasn't particularly rational."

Returning to Dr Green's interview of Yvonne Griffiths, Griffiths told Green told that she pulled Letby off the unit "for protection for Lucy and partly to pacify those casting aspersions…I didn't want Lucy to be on the ward and Steve Brearey to come and say things to her…all the nursing staff are behind her and she is one of the most experienced B5 [nurses]." This is highly important as media coverage following the trial often stated explicitly that Letby had been removed from the unit due to suspicions about her conduct.

Yvonne Griffiths also "did not personally suspect that Lucy had caused any baby to collapse or come to harm", and went on to explain that Child I in the court case had been reallocated because they liked to give nurses breaks from particularly demanding or high-risk babies, not due to any suspicion of Letby. There was some initial discussion on the involvement of Brearey in this reallocation, involving Yvonne Griffiths, but this was later rebuffed by both parties.

When the RCPCH reviewed the CoCH, the organisation noted that there were no suspicions of "foul play" on the unit. "None of the reviewers considered that this was more than an "assertion", and it was not reflected in the interviews with nursing staff who considered that Letby was a good nurse."

By April 2017, nearly two years after Dr Brearey first raised suspicions and just weeks before Cheshire Police were contacted, the Trust went to the trouble of hiring a barrister, Simon Medland KC, to investigate. He told the CoCH board he could see "no evidence of a crime". Notes of the Trust's meeting with senior police quoted Assistant Chief Constable Darren Martland as saying: "There is nothing in the reviews, as a non-clinical expert, as to the direct allegation or suggestion of significant negligence or act that could constitute as a criminal act." It was further stated that "there is no specific allegation at this point to suggest a criminal act. We do not have any reasonable grounds to suspect or believe this may have been the case." Several months earlier, the CoCH commissioned a case review by Dr Jane Hawdon. Again, this discovered absolutely nothing untoward.

While every point of Letby's grievance against the hospital was upheld following a lengthy investigation, Dr Green wasn't quite so complimentary about the consultants, saying: "I was disgusted by their behaviour. It is likely that they lied." Dr Green's statement should have been a headline-generating comment across the country, but has, for some reason, not really attracted much attention. *The Daily Telegraph* has continued its excellent coverage of the case by making a specific point of highlighting it and the quote was also mentioned in *The Independent* but that seems a little on the light side. Janet Cox would later state that "certain consultants appeared to be trying to make Lucy a scapegoat".

The apparent determination of the consultants to 'investigate' Letby was further revealed by the grievance investigation interview of Karen Rees. During this interview, Rees noted that Dr Jayaram had also "raised major concerns with [Letby] purposely harming babies", which had been "highlighted" by Brearey. Rees later confronted Brearey, requesting what his "exact concerns" with Letby were, and for any evidence to be revealed. At this point, Brearey stated that he had a so-called "drawer of doom" in his desk but refused to reveal any further information, as reported in November 2024 by Sarah Knapton in *The Daily Telegraph*. This certainly appeared to be passive-aggressive behaviour – a term used by Rees specifically. She felt that Brearey "tried to bully me/putting pressure on", while still having "no concrete evidence".

Rees wrote to Alison Kelly in September 2016, stating that the "decision [to keep Letby off the unit] is wrong and immoral", as it was still "based on a senior clinician having a 'gut feeling' with no evidence". Rees asked the rhetorical question of why "a senior clinician [is] allowed to destroy someone's career, without any clear evidence". Rees went on to express concern about Letby's well-being and that "a clinician is being listened to and supported, with potential devastating consequences for a nurse without any evidence that there was any wrongdoing". Rees also referenced an unnamed consultant, noting that "senior nurses on that unit do not even want to answer the telephone to that particular consultant, who is making these allegations and making clear his personal view". Again, in my view, this does not really paint a picture of consultants being the bullied party. In an interview with Facere Melius, Rees again noted following Letby's grievance procedure that "consultants have got the power" at the CoCH.

An email from Brearey sent to Ian Harvey on 15 July 2016, and which Brearey himself described as 'angry', read: "I will look into the cases from 2010 to 2014 as soon as is possible, between all my clinic duties and without any of your help which hasn't been offered anyway…I have copied this email to others as I am completely underwhelmed by the support your department has provided this year…Naturally, I have not had any feedback directly from you about this ever…The feeling in the department is that our efforts are being hindered and that you are giving us work to do and distracting us from clinical duties. Your email below is an example of this."

Does this sound like someone who was intimidated by Ian Harvey, who was then the Medical Director at the CoCH? This email was sent only a couple of weeks after Brearey had made the following statement to Eirian Powell: "Just to confirm then, Ian and Alison are happy for LL to work on NNU in the same capacity as last week despite the paediatric consulting body expressing our concerns that this may not be safe and that we would prefer her not to have further patient contact? Furthermore, they are happy to wait til Friday before we can discuss this in person?" In September 2016, Dr Jayaram wrote to chief executive Tony Chambers, essentially apologising for Brearey's behaviour at a meeting – "he was perhaps less restrained than he might have been".

Perhaps the most damning indication of the behaviour of consultants at the hospital, though, is contained in the interview of Eirian Powell by Dr Christopher Green, which was conducted on 28 October 2016. In this interview, Powell stated that Brearey had attempted to force her to sign a letter while at a stakeholder meeting. Powell indicated that "our only issue was the way they were treating [Letby]. Believe she is 100% innocent."

The interview further outlines the fact that, in an urgent meeting, Brearey "alluded to [Letby] being responsible". The consultant obstetrician and gynaecologist, Dr Jim McCormack, then reportedly stood up, pointed to Powell, and said: "You are harbouring a murderer." There is some dispute over this, but McCormack later wrote a letter of apology to Letby. One can only imagine what had occurred behind the scenes for such an outburst and accusation to be made during a work meeting, but it is notable that Powell opined that the other consultants on the unit had been "brainwashed".

Powell made further extraordinary comments about events on the unit in the same interview. She recounted that Dr Jayaram had stated in outpatients that "somebody is causing these deaths on the unit", while Powell had also asked Brearey: "What if [Letby] goes home and kills herself – she has elderly parents, they might die?" His response? "I don't care." In this context, it is hardly revelatory that a Neonatal Unit Action Log dated February 2017 notes that "inappropriate behaviours of relevant doctors are addressed and discussed". This comment mentions Dr McCormack but also introduces a new consultant, Dr V (a paediatrician whose identity had been protected); thus, another consultant was now joining in.

Despite all that has been documented in this chapter, in an interview with Dr Christopher Green which formed part of the investigation into Letby's grievance procedure, Dr Jayaram made the following claim when asked whether there was a push to "move Lucy" among consultants: "All that was said was that we had concerns. We noted the association with Lucy being present. Decisions made were entirely those made by Senior Management – no clinicians were involved in the decision to remove Lucy from the unit. It was a board decision."

The consultants were instructed to write a collective letter of apology to Letby but Dr Roger Norwich was sceptical: "Essentially, they were forced to apologise to Lucy, and then they went running off to the police. That should never have happened. They should instead have been seeking an epidemiologist and the RCPCH to come back and look at the whole situation."

In any normal context, what occurred at the CoCH could be seen as the systematic bullying and removal of what is a relative underling by consultants. Even the very measured neonatologist Professor Colin Morley told me that "the consultants were ganging up on Lucy". The outcome of Letby's grievance procedure, which upheld five of the seven complaints fully and the other two partially, ruled that Letby had been subjected to "victimisation", and that "the movement of Lucy from the unit was orchestrated by the consultants with no hard evidence to support this action". The final report of Dr Green notes "significant concerns around the behaviours reported to have been exhibited by Stephen Brearey and Ravi Jayaram", with Green recommending that "the Trust takes action to investigate…in line with the Trust Disciplinary Policy".

Consultants at the CoCH even declined the possibility of supervision, as noted by the RCPCH: "The Director of Nursing considered supervised practice for [Letby], but the consultants would not accept this and required the nurse be removed from the unit." It was further observed that "senior operational staff on the unit reported being very upset at the situation". In itself, this would have been highly troubling and embarrassing for Letby, but preferable to what ultimately occurred. Under the circumstances, the observation made in the grievance procedure verdict that the "behaviours and comments [from the consultants], as witnessed by a number of Senior managers and Executive staff, all fall far short of what is expected by the Trust and professional standards" seems entirely accurate.

Among the documents released by the Thirlwall Inquiry is a note of a discussion that took place among Cheshire Police on 5 May 2017 following receipt of a letter from Tony Chambers. This letter from Chambers had requested the police to "exclude unnatural causes". At the end of this police document, there is a brief mention of the purported statistical relationship between Letby and collapses on the unit, before the following bald statement is made:

"There is no evidence other than coincidence."

CHAPTER 3: PREVIOUS REVIEWS AT THE COUNTESS OF CHESTER

As alluded to previously, the RCPCH reviewed the CoCH neonatal unit following a "higher than usual" number of baby deaths – the RCPCH review followed a Neonatal and Stillbirth Review conducted at the CoCH, examining cases from January to November 2015. It involved a multi-disciplinary review in the form of Perinatal Mortality/Morbidity Review, Obstetric Primary/Secondary Review and Level 1/2 NPSA Review and included an external reviewer.

The Neonatal and Stillbirth Review was prompted as there had been four deaths on the neonatal unit at the CoCH in 2014, which had jumped to 10 in 2015. Such neonatal deaths are not uncommon. The CoCH was one of 21 hospitals examined as part of the *Mothers and Babies: Reducing Risk through Audits and Confidential Enquires across the UK 2015 Report*, which is based on the widely adopted MBRRACE standards. The Neonatal and Stillbirth Review found that "although there had been an increase, many related to foetal abnormality or prematurity". There were no murder inquiries conducted at any of the other 20 hospitals that were reviewed at that time.

The RCPCH report was completed in November 2016 and received considerable media coverage in the months that followed, most of which was focused on what the report deemed to be "inadequate staffing". There were some positive findings, including the nursing team being "well-led and supportive". Consultants at the CoCH were also praised for being a "cohesive group", and the overall picture painted was of a unit staffed by professionals who were thoroughly committed to their important work.

However, criticisms of the unit and hospital were considerable, far-reaching and much greater in volume than the praise proffered. The RCPCH report also made a huge tranche of recommendations, noting that "recent events have put pressure on inter-team relationships". Summaries of positive and negative findings, along with recommendations are also easily accessible.

Michele Worden attempted to draw the report to the attention of Cheshire Police, without success. "I phoned the police in 2018 when Lucy was arrested", Michele told me. "I spoke to an officer and asked him if they had read the RCPCH report. He replied: "No, why?" I told him my background, where I'd worked, and I explained that, in my professional opinion, the report is extremely relevant. I even explained specific details related to its importance, and how they related to Lucy's case. The police were not interested at all. All they wanted to know was whether I had spoken to Lucy, and whether I had any evidence against her."

The unit at the CoCH was also extremely busy and often did not meet British Association of Perinatal Medicine standards, which mandated one-to-one care for babies in Neonatal Intensive Care Units (NICUs). The RCPCH review found there had been "higher activity and lower admission birth weight than average during the period corresponding to an increase in mortality". As referenced previously, there were also what was deemed a concerning number of stillbirths at the maternity unit in 2015.

While the RCPCH report should have generated significant concern at the CoCH, it appears that consultants at the hospital were too preoccupied with Letby to adequately consider these matters. But one of the repercussions of Letby's conviction has been an increased scrutiny on the hospital, which has revealed that reports published at the time catalogued numerous concerns.

In September 2024, Felicity Lawrence and David Conn from *The Guardian* reported on the "many failings in the unit", which were documented in an array of sources close to the hospital, as well as leaked documents and emails. The picture revealed was one of "a hospital unit operating beyond its skills and capacity" that was clearly "lacking the expertise to deal with babies with serious needs". The article also discussed the potentially lethal pseudomonas bacterium and sepsis that were circulating on the unit.

Reports submitted at this time highlighted "serious concerns about the state of care at the hospital". Incidents recorded included evidence of the ward being under-skilled and understaffed, along with ongoing shortages of doctors and suitably trained nurses leading to paediatrician Dr Alison Timmis to complain that staff on the unit were "chronically overworked" and "stretched thinner and thinner".

The pressure of the shortage appears to have been taking a serious toll on morale. Dr Timmis said: "Over the past few weeks I have seen several medical and nursing colleagues in tears…they get upset as they know that the care they are providing falls below their high standards…When things snap, the casualties will either be children's lives or the mental and physical health of our staff." This email from Timmis had, in fact, been in the public domain for some time, as it was originally reported by *The Times* in August 2023.

A leading neonatologist told Lawrence and Conn that "the overall impression" was one of a "neonatal unit that was out of its depth". Perhaps most tellingly, the neonatal expert noted that "they were a Level 2 unit that found itself having to provide Level 3 care". This was a struggling unit within a suboptimal organisation, dealing with the most critically ill and particularly premature babies, which had essentially bitten off more than it could chew. This was reflected in the quality of care delivered by the CoCH at the time, which the neonatal specialist noted included "poor recognition and management" of serious medical episodes, "delays in instituting treatment", along with "repeated occurrence of failed intubations". Collectively, these factors "cause further deterioration of already compromised infants and increase the likelihood of death".

There was one final point raised by the neonatologist, which is particularly important, namely that "there were delays in realising babies were in difficulty". I have interviewed numerous healthcare professionals, the majority of whom had experience on intensive care units, and they were united in their view that neonates can deteriorate rapidly and become vulnerable quickly.

This matters because in the court proceedings that led to the conviction of Letby, the jury was presented with the impression that babies collapsed suddenly, in a manner that was completely unexpected. However, the supposed unexpected nature of these collapses could be rather more reflective of the lack of monitoring, experienced staff or simply satisfactory numbers of personnel.

It is important to note that the prosecution case is entirely based on medical notes. None of the expert witnesses involved with the prosecution ever examined an infant, unlike the authors of the pathology and post-mortem reports which were seemingly discarded without reference or consideration. It is therefore entirely possible that vital warning signs were missed, and do not form part of these medical notes on which vital testimony was based. Dr Jane Hawdon recognised this and told Ian Harvey, the former Medical Director of the CoCH, that "there were insufficient details in records…to determine for each whether collapse and impossible resuscitation…subtle signs are missed or not escalated or responded to".

When the Care Quality Commission reported on the CoCH in June 2016, it specifically cited the level of neonatal nurse staffing as being a major concern. Michele Worden had written to several newspapers warning that both the removal of nurses and a deficit of top-grade neonatal nurses posed risks for the hospital and its patients.

"When you had ANNPs and senior nursing sisters with decades of clinical experience, the fact the consultants weren't there enough didn't matter so much. We recognised problems, we'd seen them before. But it became an accident waiting to happen", Michele commented when interviewed by *The Guardian*.

I spoke with Michele extensively, and she told me that "a lot of these babies had clinical signs that indicated issues, which goes back to having inexperienced staff, and those present not recognising that these babies are subtly deteriorating. They were not sudden collapses. As an example, night staff reported that one of the infants in the case had an increased heart rate and an increased respiration rate, and it also had a loopy bowel. Lucy is accused of striking the baby in the liver, at a time when she wasn't even on duty. When the doctor reported for the ward round, he examined the baby and considered it fine, but subtle clinical signs and signatures had been missed all along. It is then presented to the court as being a 'sudden' collapse, when, in reality, this isn't an accurate assessment."

Many nurses explained to me that the monitoring of infants is critically important, particularly in a neonatal unit. Staffing is therefore vital, and Michele gave me some fascinating insights into personnel issues at the CoCH, and how this can impact on clinical outcomes. "When I worked at the Countess, the whole medical roster was completely different to Lucy's time on the unit. We had very senior nursing staff and competent paediatric registrars. We had senior house officers (SHOs), split into two groups – one group comprised GP trainees, and the other was training to be paediatricians and neonatologists."

Michele then explained that financial and political decisions ravaged staffing on the unit. "I think it was in 2013 that the Dean of the University of Liverpool School of Medicine pulled paediatric SHOs off the medical rota, which greatly depleted the experience. And then, because the whole training system had also changed, paediatric registrars were coming through earlier, so they didn't have the same level of experience. You end up with a situation where your expertise and numbers are seriously reduced. Consultants were doing only two ward rounds per week, which is way down on what it should be.

"When I was in Chester, it wasn't as imperative, because we had experienced medical staff. We had experienced neonatal nurses, so we carried the load really. But when Lucy was working there, Lucy didn't have the experienced senior staff, because we had all been dispensed with. They didn't have the experienced paediatric registrars. They didn't have any paediatric SHO trainees. They only had GP trainees. One of the GPs commented during the trial that he was out of his depth.

"Lucy was deemed to be one of the most senior nurses. But I cannot think of any profession where, after three years of being out of university, you will be deemed senior. You wouldn't be a consultant. You wouldn't be a barrister. You wouldn't be a headteacher. So it's the system that was at fault, and the RCPCH, rightly, criticised the consultants for the lack of ward rounds. There is a perfect storm, where they're not delivering anywhere near the level of care needed for what are the most vulnerable infants". Indeed, the minutes of a board meeting at the hospital held on 14 July 2016 noted that Letby was "one of the unit's highest trained staff".

Michele had been employed as an ANNP at the CoCH until being made redundant. It was acknowledged in a Senior Clinicians' Meeting at the hospital on 29 June 2016 that the absence of ANNPs was a significant problem. Eirian Powell highlighted the inadequate "skill mix on the neonatal unit". The importance of this cannot be overstated, as the ANNP is an integral part of the neonatal team in NHS units of all levels throughout the UK. There is considerable evidence indicating that the culture of monitoring and reporting at the CoCH was far from satisfactory, while the unit was also understaffed and under-skilled. This can then lead to signs of deterioration and degeneration going unnoticed and unreported, which impacts on the clinical outcomes of infants. Furthermore, if such signs do go unreported, they do not form part of the clinical notes, and, as we will see, the prosecution case is largely founded on these notes.

Several neonatal experts wrote to the Thirlwall Inquiry, indicating their belief that the process should examine the situation at the CoCH more holistically. Professor Jane Hutton, a highly regarded academic at the University of Warwick, and consultant at the Royal Statistical Society, was one such signatory. She asserted that there were several factors that could contribute to both the collapses and deaths of infants, including prematurity, genetics, the fact that twins and triplets figured prominently in the cases discussed in court, along with the overall picture of staffing mentioned. "All the potential alternative explanations need to be considered", Hutton commented.

The Thirlwall Inquiry has, of course, had to assume the guilty verdicts stand but many documents collected in the process contradict what the court found. This has required surreal contortion to avoid contrary subject matters and facts, while enormous pressure has also been placed on all those giving evidence. With this in mind, the Thirlwall Inquiry has attempted to curiously downplay the RCPCH report, dismiss its criticism of the unit and suggest that it shouldn't even have interviewed Letby herself. Throughout the discussion of both the RCPCH report and the Hawdon case review, a running theme has been the assertion that those conducting the reviews should have been made more aware of the opinions of the consultants who accused Letby, even though they had absolutely no evidence whatsoever.

For example, there was considerable discussion at the Thirlwall Inquiry of how management at the CoCH should have informed the RCPCH staff that Letby was under suspicion in advance of the review. It is noted that Ian Harvey had spoken with RCPCH reviewer Sue Eardley, advising her "that a nurse had been suspended and she had been told that there was a spate of unexpected deaths with no conclusion". It was conveyed at this time that Letby's "pattern of attendance" was the sole reason for this suspicion, and Dr David Milligan, the lead clinical reviewer, remembered these terms of reference, telling the Thirlwall Inquiry that he had written "in advance of the review having seen the staffing schedule to identify that Letby was the focus of concerns of some paediatricians".

That should be considered perfectly adequate, particularly, as we will see later, the "pattern of attendance" cited was utterly flawed, and there was no other evidence for the conclusions of the paediatricians. Logically, a review of any institution should be unbiased and objective. The role of the RCPCH is to clinically assess the quality of care for infants on the unit. This should not take into account unsubstantiated allegations. If there is evidence to support those allegations, this should be uncovered during medical reviews.

Even voicing these concerns potentially introduces bias into the review. Nonetheless, the RCPCH interviewed Letby, providing a glowing review of her character and work. The RCPCH found that Letby was "passionate about her career and keen to progress", and that she "regularly volunteered to work extra shifts". The review further noted that Letby's "nursing colleagues on the unit were reported to think highly of her and how she responded to emergencies and other difficult situations", and that Letby was, ultimately, "very professional…demonstrating an enthusiasm to lead along with a high level of professionalism".

The issue regarding extra shifts was also noted during court proceedings related to Child I, when a statement from an unnamed nurse noted that it was "mainly Lucy doing a lot" of extra shifts, since she was certified to deliver emergency care when needed. The nurse added: "Lucy was young, living in a doctors' halls of residence, and saving to buy a house. She was single and was willing and wanting to do extras." Thus, the RCPCH review both praised Letby and criticised the standard of care at the neonatal unit, which has not been reflected in a public inquiry whose remit had to assume Letby's guilt.

As a consequence of this, the RCPCH statement to the Thirlwall Inquiry oddly asserts that "had the full information been provided to the whole review team and the IR Programme Board, it is likely that the review would not have been allowed to take place by RCPCH". But the 'full information' *was* available. There was nothing else that could conceivably have been provided at this time. There was no medical evidence and no one on the unit was a statistician or mathematician, so there was no analysis available of their crude statistical observation. As the Thirlwall Inquiry acknowledged, the police hadn't been called; thus, there was no criminal investigation. It is hard to know what specifically they would have needed to know, how this information could have been provided when it didn't exist, and what meaningful impact this would have had on the process, considering that the RCPCH was informed of everything that was known at that time.

At one point at the inquiry, Richard Baker KC raised the fact that the full report by the RCPCH wasn't provided to the families of those infants that came to harm. Baker commented that redacting the report and removing references to Letby was a "blatant lack of candour", and he went on to assert that the "families believe the management of the hospital were dishonest and covered up what happened, possibly to protect reputations". A noble effort from Baker, which perhaps overlooks the fact that the report defended and effusively praised Letby.

This was referenced in the opening statement submitted to the Thirlwall Inquiry by the RCPCH, which described the support for Letby among the nursing and executive teams as "staunch". This is somehow presented as being fallacious, but as seen in the previous chapter there was simply no objective reason for any other response. In fact, any other response would have been inappropriate and unprofessional.

Dr James Phillips was critical of the direction and agenda of the Thirlwall Inquiry: "The management of that hospital essentially did everything right in my opinion. They called in the most relevant and senior body in the country, with the expertise to deal with this case, and that body then concluded that there was no reason to suspect malign activity by the nurses. In fact, they acted according to the conclusions of the most senior relevant medical body in the country."

Several healthcare professionals indicated their belief to me that the RCPCH review should be given considerable credence. Dr Colin Ferguson, a highly experienced vascular surgeon who worked alongside primary prosecution witness Dr Dewi Evans at Morriston Hospital in Swansea, suggested that the RCPCH report painted an unduly favourable impression of the unit: "While the RCPCH review was correct in its underlying assertions, I think they possibly understated the problems a bit. Clearly, the staffing was inadequate, and the skillset was also inadequate for the tasks they were trying to do."

Another commentator with some important remarks to make about the RCPCH report is the pseudonymous Sloane Spade, a highly experienced, certified neonatal nurse, with many years of experience working on neonatal units. Spade reviewed numerous infants involved in the Letby case in great depth, and believes it is "interesting that the RCPCH report identified several areas of weakness that the CoCH had in their neonatal unit", and that this "confirmed the impression I have formed from my own research. The ratio of properly qualified nurses to patients on this unit was nowhere near acceptable. It was clear that there was a pressing need to improve fundamental procedures. Considering that nurses were often reported to be out of ratio, dangerously overworked, and bypassing safety measures, this report should have carried a lot of weight."

However, Judge James Goss ruled that all references to the RCPCH report should be excluded from Letby's trial.

Considering the spike in deaths on the unit and given that this would be natural and expected anyway, several of the babies that Letby was ultimately convicted of murdering had post-mortems at Alder Hey, a children's hospital located in Liverpool and a centre of excellence for the region. There has been no indication that any secondary post-mortem was requested. Speaking with Channel 5, Dr Philip Hammond, the physician, journalist and broadcaster, noted that none of the post-mortems "picked up any foul play", and that he couldn't understand why "they were turned on their head and changed completely during the trial".

Professor Carola Vinuesa, an immunogeneticist with the Francis Crick Institute, provided more background on this, telling me that "most of the post-mortems from this case did suggest plausible causes of death, and those findings certainly need to be taken seriously. These causes were reasonable and some would have been difficult to diagnose clinically." Vinuesa also suggested that the appropriate response to an 'unexplained' death would have been further investigation, possibly including genetic testing: "For example, a cerebrovascular accident due to thromboembolism could be suspected in a child born to a mother with antiphospholipid syndrome (Baby A), and a post-mortem MRI could help establish this as the cause of death."

Dr Colin Ferguson also wished to highlight the importance of post-mortem reviews: "The post-mortem reports by the paediatric pathologists should have held much more weight than anything that Dewi Evans had to say. Particularly in the Liverpool area, they have a very strong paediatric pathology setup, and the fact that quite natural causes were cited for almost all of the children should have taken precedence. That should have been the bottom line, not the views of a retired paediatrician." Senior coroner's officer, Stephanie Davies, who worked on the Cheshire Police investigation of the CoCH, told me that "paediatric pathologists are incredibly detailed with their post-mortems. They have forensic awareness and know how to identify deliberate harm."

Other experts shared this view. Professor Jane Hutton, who has 25 published papers in paediatric epidemiology, could not understand how "a review by a neonatal pathologist, who had conducted a post-mortem at the time, can be overturned by a long-since retired paediatrician". Stephanie Davies felt that the pathologist deserved a right of reply: "Certainly, I would want that. I'd want to make my own statement. They have a right to respond. It's almost as if this whole established process is just tossed away and treated as meaningless."

The Thirlwall Inquiry has attempted to diminish the importance of these clinical reviews, while elevating the completely unsubstantiated suspicions of the consultants. "A dominant impression that I get from this inquiry", Dr James Phillips told me, "is that the most novel, interesting and frankly disturbing information coming out of it is not being amplified and questioned by the inquiry from the standpoint that it should be, because all of the questions have to proceed from this assumption that Letby is guilty. This just taints the entire process."

It was just three days after the recommendations of the RCPCH were published, on 5 September 2016, that Ian Harvey contacted consultant neonatologist Dr Jane Hawdon and exactly one month later, on 5 October 2016, sent a letter of instruction requesting her to conduct a detailed case note review. At that time, Hawdon was the lead consultant neonatologist at the Royal Free Hospital in London, and she consequently examined the cluster of deaths and collapses. *The Guardian* reported that in 13 of the cases reviewed by Hawdon, she found that babies had received suboptimal care, and that the "death/collapse is explained, but may have been prevented with different care".

Hawdon then called for a deeper forensic review. Dr Jo McPartland, a consultant paediatric pathologist at Alder Hey hospital, reviewed the cases that were unexplained, finding no suggestion of any foul play or intentional harm. Dr McPartland concluded that the death of Child A was unascertained, but there was no evidence of the air embolism explanation that would be bolted on to the case by the prosecution. A cause of death was attributed to Child O and Child I, while McPartland noted significant abnormalities in the organ systems of Child I. Finally, McPartland found that the cause of death for Child P could be submitted as unexplained, recommending that the family be referred to specialists in order to discuss potential genetic causes of sudden unexpected postnatal collapse. There is evidence that this never occurred adequately in many of the indictment cases which will be discussed later.

During questioning at the Thirlwall Inquiry, Dr Hawdon hinted she may have approached the review differently if she had been briefed about the suspicions over Letby. However this could have introduced a conscious bias into the process as she herself acknowledged.

Dr Colin Ferguson suggested that the Hawdon review should never have been sidelined in the first place. "The conclusion of Dr Hawdon seemed to be that for the majority of the cases, she couldn't see any particular problem or issue. There were about four cases that were somewhat indeterminate, and she recommended a further examination of them. That seemed to be a fairly cogent, coherent outcome. I think the RCPCH got it pretty much right, but they could have perhaps rung alarm bells slightly louder regarding the conditions and competence of the hospital." Since Dr Ferguson spoke with me, details of a further review conducted in 2020 by Dr Grenville Fox, a consultant neonatologist at Guy's and St Thomas' NHS Foundation Trust in London, has been viewed by *The Guardian*. This review found that for three infants in the case, Children B, N and Q, collapses could have been expected for premature babies with their medical conditions, and this presupposes optimal clinical conditions, which we know definitely did not exist at the CoCH at that time. Despite presumably having access to this information, the Crown Prosecution Service (CPS) charged Letby on these cases anyway.

The prior review that was conducted concluded there was "major or significant suboptimal care" in 14 cases, with no mention of any method of murder or deliberate harm that were later introduced by the prosecution. While Cheshire Police mentioned the review in their initial documentation of Operation Hummingbird (the name they gave to the criminal investigation) it is not known whether Cheshire Police contacted Dr Hawdon or made significant effort to understand her report.

Hawdon did not merit a single mention during any available court transcript or reporting of the trial. It is also notable that Letby was charged on only nine of the 17 supposedly troubling cases that were identified. This is significant because it demonstrates that babies deteriorated unexpectedly when Letby was not present. Dr Philip Hammond highlighted in *Private Eye* that substandard care would be a likely explanation for their deterioration. Hammond also asserted that the work of

Dr Evans achieved a "statistical miracle" and posed the following rhetorical question: "When prosecution expert Dr Evans screened the notes "blind", all his suspicious cases turned out to involve Letby, but when Hawdon did it "eyes open", eight of them didn't. Why not?"

Ian Harvey had quite clearly outlined the purpose and terms of reference for the Hawdon review in October 2016. It is therefore difficult to understand why the Thirlwall Inquiry claimed that there is a legitimate question as to whether the RCPCH and Hawdon reviews "would have been capable of adequately investigating" the observed spike in deaths.

Thirlwall lawyers asserted that the medical reviews should have "address[ed] concerns of the type raised by the consultant paediatricians". This latter statement is particularly strange, as, firstly, specifically "addressing concerns" in any form of medical review obviously immediately subjects it to bias. Secondly, the so-called concerns of the consultant paediatricians were completely lacking in substance. As we saw in the previous chapter, even by the time Cheshire Police received a referral from the CoCH, there was still "no evidence" against Letby, aside from what they accurately described as "coincidence".

It is therefore a bit odd to ask someone who is reviewing cases to take into account the concerns of consultants at the hospital. This might be justified if there was some concrete evidence of wrongdoing, but even then, it's hard to imagine why an unbiased and unprejudiced investigation into the cases wouldn't be preferable.

With regard to the supposed inadequacy of the RCPCH and Hawdon reviews, one might not unreasonably ask what should have occurred instead. The RCPCH is a highly regarded body, and it's hard to imagine any organisation more qualified to investigate. Similarly, it would be considered perfectly normal practice in the case of unexpected deaths for them to be reviewed by a neonatologist and pathologist. There were some curious suggestions during the Thirlwall Inquiry that the case should have been referred to the police as soon as there were suspicions, but the first thing that the Cheshire Constabulary stated is that they were not medically qualified. Hawdon's review uncovered a pattern of "major suboptimal care" at the hospital which was even referenced in the opening statement of the parents of children that suffered harm at the CoCH.

Professor John Ashton, former Regional Director of Public Health for North West England for 13 years, has "extensive experience of dealing with clinical service failures in the NHS". He told me he was in no doubt that systemic issues contributed to poor performance at the CoCH: "It was obvious from the earliest moments of the trial that something crazy was happening. This had all the hallmarks of a dysfunctional hospital."

When I asked Professor Ashton to expand on this, he explained how his understanding had germinated: "I was in the Leppings Lane end at the Hillsborough disaster in 1989, when 97 people died. I ended up being involved in the triage of casualties, and ultimately had to certify seven people dead. I learnt lessons from that, which I then witnessed being repeated in my clinical and NHS career. If you have one or two issues, you might get away with it. But when you have a whole series of problems lined up, it's almost inevitable that something will go wrong. This situation at the CoCH was a systemic failure – a unit that was poorly run, and which had obvious environmental issues and clinical governance problems."

Nursing practitioner Sloane Spade similarly asserted that "several instances that were brushed off as not holding significance toward the well-being of the neonates were concerning to me, and this speaks of a systemic issue".

Professor Ashton continued: "I think the root of this is in the whole movement, emanating in the 1980s and 90s, seeking to either privatise, or make hospitals much more like private sector organisations, and then encourage them to compete with each other rather than cooperate. There was a political agenda in the early years of this century to encourage hospitals to take on Foundation Trust status, and the Countess was one of the first to achieve this. But then, after an initial boost in funding, the money dried up, leaving the hospital in this invidious position of having financial ambitions beyond its clinical capability. They simply couldn't cope with the babies that they were assigned." Several other experts cited both the potential motivation of extra funding, and multiple infants requiring Level 3 care being assigned to a failing Level 2 unit.

Once the spate of reviews at the hospital were completed, Ian Harvey wrote to the board reporting that "there was an unsubstantiated explanation that there was a causal link to an individual, this is not the case and the issues were around leadership and timely clinical interventions". The board then received a further update from Tony Chambers, noting that "the Hawdon review did not identify a single causal factor or raise concerns regarding unnatural causes". And a document authored by Stephen Cross, Director of Corporate and Legal Affairs at the hospital, on 3 April 2017 concludes that "the RCPCH review…did not identify a single causal factor for the deaths…A further independent in-depth review…did not identify a single causal factor or raise concerns regarding unnatural causes of death…12 of the deaths have been subject to post-mortem, but there have been no suspicious findings…A secondary review of four deaths, by pathologists at Alder Hey Children's Hospital, did not raise any concerns regarding unnatural causes of deaths."

At the time of writing, the Thirlwall Inquiry has yet to release its final report or recommendations. Nonetheless, the tone of the public inquiry has strongly implied that Harvey and Chambers should somehow have acted differently. It is difficult to understand, though, precisely what they could have done when consultants at the hospital had not presented any evidence of wrongdoing. Why should they go to the police in these circumstances? If the process of engaging the RCPCH, Hawdon and other medical reviews wasn't acceptable, what process would have been better?

None of these questions came within the remit of the Thirlwall Inquiry which many would argue renders the entire process essentially worthless, as predicted by the 24 experts who wrote to the inquiry, and whose letter was seemingly completely ignored.

None of the parents of Child C, Child D and Child H from the eventual court case were informed that Hawdon's review had criticised the care provided to their child, or that Dr Hawdon had concluded that suboptimal care had contributed to their deaths. In particular, the delay in providing an additional dose of intravenous antibiotics to Child D was considered critical. In February 2018, the case of Child D was discussed at a meeting with Margaret Bowron KC, with the actions of the CoCH and its neonatal division described as "indefensible". The statement from families attending the Thirlwall Inquiry noted that "there is no evidence that proper candour was shown even at this stage".

The inquest into the death of Child D was adjourned in November 2020 when the coroner was informed of the decision to prosecute Letby. A review of the coroner's file revealed no correspondence from the CoCH to inform him that major failings had been identified in the care provided to Child D, nor to disabuse him of the impression that he might have reached upon reviewing statements from the hospital and case reviews from 2016, describing the care provided to Child D as in line with accepted practice, and stating that "antibiotics were commenced within the recommended time limit". Considering that this comes verbatim from a written statement submitted to the Thirlwall Inquiry, it is fair to say that some considerable explanation is required for these events.

Many people, including Dr David Harkness, were not invited to speak at the inquiry despite being centrally involved in several of the cases. Similarly, Dr Lucy Beebe, Dr Sally Ogden, Dr Alison Ventress, Dr Andrew Brunton, Dr Kaliyilil Verghese, Dr Katherine Davis, and Dr Katherine Lyddon, all of whom provided statements stating that they had no concerns about working with Letby, were not invited. Fellow nurse, Christopher Booth, who spoke highly of Letby during the original court case, was also not required to speak at Thirlwall. And another nurse, Joanne Williams, who gave forthright evidence contradicting the original prosecution, was also not required by the Thirlwall Inquiry.

Medical experts who conducted principled reviews of infants treated at the CoCH have been forced onto the defensive by lawyers who could never possibly understand them. It is entirely unsurprising under such intense public scrutiny that self-preservation and the avoidance of blame might have been a motivating factor throughout cross-examination.

After of Letby's conviction, the general public was told consistently that bureaucrats are to blame for the failings at the CoCH. One can only feel great sympathy for Ian Harvey, who has been castigated in the media. Such has been the outpouring of anger he has even been forced to abandon his own home due to the threat of violence and retribution.

Thankfully, despite its absurdly narrow scope, the Thirlwall Inquiry has published many documents that completely contradict its narrative. This was noted by Sir David Davis MP who commented that "the Thirlwall Inquiry will keep throwing up evidence that is inconsistent with the thrust of the prosecution's main argument. From what I know alone, this is going to happen time and time again."

One such example was the statement submitted by Professor Neena Modi who later appeared as part of the expert panel assembled by Dr Shoo Lee. In her statement, Professor Modi commented: "It is my opinion, based on my experience of having worked in neonatal intensive care in tertiary referral centres for almost 40 years, that plausible alternative explanations exist for certain of the deaths and sudden deteriorations of the babies at the CoCH, but the cases were not investigated adequately at the time and subsequently, and this may have had an impact on the exploration of causality during the trial." Modi is one of the most respected neonatologists in the country, as well as being past President of the British Medical Association, UK Medical Women's Federation and UK Royal College of Paediatrics and Child Health. Her statement was only revealed in February 2025, after the public sessions of the inquiry had finished.

The Thirlwall Inquiry is a contradiction in terms. It is unable to actually inquire into what occurred at the CoCH, due to being fundamentally hamstrung by its own terms of reference which simply assume Letby's guilt. Lady Thirlwall could have paid heed to the 24 experts who wrote to her. Instead, she rather inappropriately, in my view, decided to dismiss this as "noise". I wonder if she regrets that comment now.

What would be concerning is if the inquiry recommends that any suspicions medics have should be quickly reported to the police. In 2015, this would have meant that all 21 hospitals identified in the *Mothers and Babies: Reducing Risk through Audits and Confidential Enquires across the UK 2015 Report* would potentially be referred to the police for further investigation.

The previous chapter examined the lack of evidence for assertions made by the consultants that they were bullied by the hospital. Let's pose that question in reverse – if a nurse made accusations of deliberately harming infants, without evidence, against a consultant at any NHS hospital in the United Kingdom, would this be taken seriously? No one I have spoken to, across the range of specialisms and vast amount of vocational experience accumulated in the dozens of healthcare experts, believed that it would. Similarly, none thought it plausible that consultants would be bullied in any NHS institution. It is therefore hard to wave away the stench of classism and distinct whiff of misogyny at the heart of this case.

It should finally be noted that very little of the information in this chapter formed part of the evidence presented in court. The jury was provided with almost no meaningful context on the neonatal unit at the CoCH, nor was it provided with any of the related reports.

"I cannot understand why the Hawdon review and other reports were not put before the jury, even with caveats given", Dr James Phillips told me. It is impossible to gauge precisely what influence this absence of information and context had on the decisions of the jury but I suspect the impact must have been considerable.

CHAPTER 4: PROBLEMS AT THE COUNTESS OF CHESTER

This book has already established that the standard of care for neonates at the CoCH was suboptimal. But there is considerably more evidence available that conditions on the neonatal unit at this hospital were far from ideal for the treatment of babies. It must be emphasised that the CoCH was dealing with vulnerable infants that required optimal care.

In the aftermath of Lucy Letby's sentencing, many working in healthcare, and particularly the nursing profession, began to feel uneasy, not just about the case, but also their own vocation. One nurse I spoke with told me that she had shelved her ambitions to work as a neonatal nurse solely because of this case and conviction: "Originally, I wanted to be a neonatal nurse. That was my passion and my drive. I was offered a staff nurse post on a neonatal unit early in 2023, and I accepted it. That's where I saw my career going, that's really where my heart is. And then, following the conviction of Letby in August 2023, I decided that I couldn't take up that position. I felt very vulnerable. Anybody in that position, especially someone newly qualified, there is a huge amount of risk of being blamed for something you haven't done."

Professor John O'Quigley, an experienced statistician, similarly asserted that "you are at great risk now working in that environment". This climate of fear was reflected in a BBC *File on 4* programme which featured the campaign group Nineteen Nurses delivering a letter to Downing Street calling for a review of the Letby case. At the time of publication, this letter has been signed by over 700 healthcare professionals. The BBC interviewed one nurse who stated that professionals working in every area of nursing were frightened. "They feel that they've lost their voice. It is important that they are able to speak out and raise concerns,

[but] they feel that they are no longer the patient advocate." Other nurses have described being fearful of sending cards, or even developing bonds with parents, for fear of being labelled the next Lucy Letby.

The culture of the CoCH, and the general atmosphere following the charging of Letby, could be viewed as rather repressive. One nurse from the hospital offered to be a character witness for Letby but was told "it would be better not to, as it could hurt my career". The nurse expanded on this, speaking with *The Daily Telegraph*, commenting on the dysfunctional operation at the unit, practical jokes played on nurses by senior staff and examples of low-key bullying. The nurse asserted that "Letby is innocent…I think there should be a retrial…I think there has been a miscarriage of justice."

The *Daily Telegraph* article also makes plain the veil of silence that has now been drawn around the CoCH. The quoted nurse talks about staff "wanting answers" but being warned not to speak about the Letby case. Elsewhere, doctors and registrars had been warned not to talk about Lucy Letby or her trial. The nurse gave her view on the functionality of the CoCH. "It sounds like it was short staffed and they maybe shouldn't be looking after babies that were that sick and premature." This comment was reflected in the fact that the CoCH neonatal section was downgraded to a Level 1 unit after Letby was removed from her previous role. After this decision, the unit was then only permitted to deal with babies that did not require intensive care – a fundamental change in operation that could account for the reduction in problems. Two new consultants were also added to the roster at this time, relieving pressure on the unit and reducing understaffing.

Writing in *Private Eye*, Dr Philip Hammond highlighted a 'rule 9 questionnaire', a statutory request for documents and witness evidence, regarding the Letby case. One of the staff nurses rostered during the 2015/16 period had stated that "my view of the Trust and so-called medical 'professionals' is prejudiced by the horrendous way they treated Lucy". The nurse further comments that the consultants "appeared to be trying to make Lucy a scapegoat for the increased number of deaths/collapses". Commenting on the increase in deaths, the nurse noted: "I did not think at the time, nor do I think now, that there was anything sinister about the increase in the number of deaths/collapses. I do not see how you can set a figure on how many deaths are acceptable in one particular timeframe. The babies required admission to an NNU…because they had a high chance of dying or collapsing."

Hammond asserted that it is "vital that the voices of all of those who worked most closely with Letby are heard at the inquiry, even if they contradict Thirlwall's preferred narrative". This has not occurred. A nurse who wrote to the Thirlwall Inquiry saying: "Lucy did not commit any crimes. If there had been CCTV the footage would have proved her innocence" heard back: "We can confirm that you are NOT currently named on the list as an individual from whom the inquiry wishes to hear oral evidence."

On 16 June 2017, David Semple, Associate Medical Director with a remit for Quality and Safety, sent a group email to numerous departments in the hospital, which stated that he had "inherited a mess". Semple went on to recount a laundry list of problems which included poor leadership, training and staffing issues, a "general lack of communication", an array of issues with feedback, "no dissemination of learning from incidents", a lack of liaison around incidents, "clinicians being named in Action Plans without being informed", and a disjointed structure related to reporting and escalation.

Many of the problems regarding staffing were thoroughly documented well before this email was sent. In March 2016, an internal synopsis of the CoCH noted that "staffing on the Neonatal Unit has been and is currently understaffed and under-skilled compared to other LNUs [local neonatal units] with[in] the Operational Delivery Network (ODN) in Cheshire and Mersey region". This had already been documented in a business case for neonatal staff nursing, published in December 2015, which outlined "a number of differences in staffing the Neonatal Unit compared to other wards that present a challenge to delivery in high quality neonatal care".

The document went on to discuss how the CoCH remained open when failing to meet British Association of Perinatal Medicine (BAPM) standards, which was not common in the surrounding region. It was noted that the CoCH was significantly understaffed with registered nurses – the figure below 75% being the "lowest proportion of NMC registered nurses in the North West Delivery Network". Other problematical staff practices would be "difficult to sustain in the long term, and are detrimental to the staff's well-being and staff retention", according to the synopsis.

It was reported that throughout 2014 and 2015 there was a 21% shortfall of nurses at the CoCH, with agency staff frequently recruited on a temporary basis in an attempt to plug gaps in the rota. This reliance on "bank staff", particularly at "night time", was recorded by the Care Quality Commission (CQC) – the health and social care regulator – on 26 May 2016. This is particularly important, as the prevalence of collapses and deaths at night was cited in court although, as discussed in Chapter 8, this is a known phenomenon anyway. The shortage of staff was further acknowledged by the anonymous Dr ZA who told Thirlwall on 7 October 2024 that "there weren't enough consultants for the workloads that we were doing", while also noting a shortage of junior doctors. Dr Paul Jameson, a consultant anaesthetist at the hospital, asserted that its paediatric service "was almost at breaking point and needed support before it hits the point of burn out".

The problems on the neonatal unit had been common knowledge for many years. As Michele Worden has already explained, the situation was similar during her time at the hospital but an experienced phalanx of nurses was able to paper over the cracks. As early as 2004, a letter signed by 12 nurses outlined the "continual excessive workload" at the CoCH, which was "causing serious concerns about the increased risk of clinical incidents". The problems continued for many years, with eight registered nurses having left the unit by 2011.

Michele had written to the *Chester Chronicle*, outlining her concerns about the "decision to dramatically increase the ratio of unqualified to qualified" nurses. She told me that staffing on the unit had been systematically downgraded. "We used to have specialist registrars, far more senior house officers (SHOs), and then we had two Neonatal Nurse

Practitioners (NNP). You have to understand what an NNP does. They are critical. If you look at Liverpool Women's Hospital, they have about 18 NNPs. They run that unit. They know the protocols, they know the guidelines, they know about important clinical indicators. They know everything. And they're doing the same procedures as doctors – intubations, lumbar punctures, infection screens, siting arterial lines. So much of this was removed at the CoCH. The unit being downgraded was only a reflection of this downgrading in care."

I asked Michele why this had occurred. "It seems that, beginning in around 2000, there was a drive to save money and make the Countess a hospital Trust. By 2002, it appeared that when a qualified member of staff left, they were either not replaced or they were being replaced with a nursery nurse. It got to the point where, in 2004, the qualified nurses wrote to management outlining the dangers. Nursery nurses are not qualified for the job that they're doing. It's not their fault, but neonatal work is completely different. I recognised the problems and dangers on the unit over a decade before this spike in deaths that began in 2015.

"But things got a lot worse. The manager at the time was asked to take voluntary severance. She refused, so they downgraded her to a Band 7. They gave her protective pay for two years before leaving, and one of the Band 6 nurses was internally promoted into the manager's role. The two Band 7 nurses were encouraged to retire early – one left under an early retirement scheme and the other was sidelined into another department. The other ANNP on the unit was told that she was not being given a new contract and so she moved to another hospital, while I was served with compulsory redundancy. And there were two more Band 6 nurses who were also removed. In total, there were about eight very senior staff who were eliminated from the unit without being replaced."

Michele told me that the final senior nurses left in 2009, and anaesthetist Dr Fiona MacRae, who worked at the hospital for 27 years, agreed with this timing: "The loss of senior staff, from 2009, was crucial. The hospital was focused on a cost-reduction strategy. They also had the 'brilliant' idea of deciding that Band 7 jobs should become Band 6 jobs. And then they required staff to apply for lower banded jobs where they would perform the same duties as before. You might not be surprised to learn that senior staff left!"

"Then, in 2012", Michele continued, "they employed two newly qualified registered nurses, one of whom was Lucy, straight out of university. When I read the RCPCH report, I laughed because one of the recommendations was that the hospital needed two ANNPS. Well, they had two ANNPs and they got rid of both of us!

"The consequence of all this cost-cutting is serious. There is no time, space or opportunity to mentor junior staff. They're not going to pick up the phone at 2am, phone a consultant and argue with a registrar, which is what I would do if I thought we needed consultants on the unit. But if you're junior and you've never witnessed anybody having that knowledge or confidence, you're just not going to do it. Ultimately, you cannot run any neonatal intensive care unit with no senior nursing staff. It is an accident waiting to happen. I told the hospital that in 2004, 14 years before Lucy was arrested."

Problems on the neonatal unit were a matter of common knowledge. In board meetings throughout 2015 and 2016, it was noted that the neonatal unit had the most 'red' ratings for staffing levels of all hospital departments. An urgent care risk register submitted to the Thirlwall Inquiry later outlined the catalogue of risks associated with various units, with neonatology being the most prominent.

When the RCPCH investigated the CoCH, it stated in its report that nurses were stretched thin, expected to help out on the maternity unit, and give antibiotics to infants on other wards, alongside their normal neonatal duties. Shortly before the cluster of deaths emerged, in March 2015, Eirian Powell had recorded on the hospital's internal register of risks that the neonatal unit was "currently understaffed and under-skilled". A further entry from Powell in October 2015 noted that there was no senior doctor present on the unit overnight.

"Nurses who are running off to give intravenous medications, including antibiotics, to babies from outside the neonatal unit, for example on the post-natal maternity ward, have the potential to bring back infection to those vulnerable babies", nurse Julie Yates told me. "They were stretched too thin already, and then they have extra jobs because other people wouldn't have been trained to give antibiotics, intravenously or through central lines, and they would have been leaving the unit when the unit needed them. Those nurses should have been dedicated to that unit."

In December 2015, Dr Alison Timmis, a paediatrician at the CoCH, emailed Tony Chambers, the hospital's chief executive, indicating her view that the neonatal unit at the hospital was chaotic, overstretched and unsafe for both patients and staff. Timmis noted that staff were visibly upset due to being responsible for more babies than the unit could safely accommodate. "Over the past few weeks, I have seen several medical and nursing colleagues in tears…they get upset as they know that the care they are providing falls below their high standards", Timmis commented.

Timmis further noted that staff at the CoCH were "chronically over-worked" and she felt "no one is listening". The paediatrician also explained that the conditions she was reporting were nothing out of the usual. "This is not an exceptionally busy week. This is now our normal working pattern and it is not safe. Things are stretched thinner and thinner and are at breaking point."

An inspection of the CoCH by the CQC found the neonatal unit was understaffed and "lacked storage space and resources for the care of patients who required strict infection control measures". This entirely tallied with a statement made by the anonymous Nurse ZX which was submitted to Thirlwall in June 2024. "I distinctly recall a stretch where nurses found themselves managing the ward and unwell patients for prolonged durations due to doctors being occupied in the NNU overnight. I recollect that senior house officers or GP trainees seemed unfamiliar with certain practices, treatment plans or policies, adding to the stress of these night shifts." The nurse further observed that this correlated with a "notable increase in collapses" during night shifts – a time associated with several of the collapses of infants in the eventual court case.

Another major issue on the unit was the significantly diminished number of ward rounds from consultants. In usual practice, these vital monitoring missions would occur once or twice daily. At the CoCH, this number slumped to once or twice weekly. The lack of ward rounds had been a major point of criticism in the RCPCH report and the anonymised Nurse X asserted that this made it "hard to get decisions on care at times". This is critical as the rounds are an important link between doctors and nurses, while providing vital information on infants that is central to the detection of problems. The parents of Child J from the court case were among those critical of a lack of monitoring, while a paediatric doctor questioned why infants were "constantly" left on monitors on the unit.

When I told an experienced neonatal nursing practitioner about this vast deficit of ward rounds, she was aghast. "I'm sorry…they were only rounding on the babies twice a week?!" she exclaimed. She then explained to me why this is so important. "During rounds, your nurse practitioner or a lower-level consultant examine the baby's vital signs for the last 24 hours, their intake and their output, how they're feeding, how they're progressing towards discharge. And then your supervising neonatologist will go over that, ensuring everyone's talking and thinking, because sometimes there are slow declines that you don't notice. Babies are great at compensating, until the moment that they don't. They may be struggling and struggling and struggling and just keep chugging along. That's when they collapse, and they really go fast. I've seen babies go from fine to deceased within 24 hours many times. That's why you have ward rounds. If you're doing such an inadequate number as was the case here, you're getting no meaningful impression of the well-being of any given infant."

Another neonatal nurse told me that "babies should be rounded on daily. At the very least. We do one big round set of multi-disciplinary rounds every morning. In our unit, we have the pharmacist, physical therapy, occupational therapy, dieticians, neonatal nurse practitioners, fellows, registrars, everyone, as well as the parents, talking about how their baby has been doing in the last 24 hours. Then we have other abbreviated rounds, and then the night providers do another set of rounds, checking in with the nurses."

Another neonatal nurse described this as "shocking to hear", continuing: "In all my experience, there has been one ward round a day at a minimum, and usually two. That shows that those senior clinicians, those consultants, were out of touch with what was happening on that unit on a day-to-day basis, and they were leaving that to more junior colleagues to run that unit. That is very concerning for patient safety, particularly as they didn't have experienced nursing staff."

Julie Yates, a retired nurse with more than 27 years of experience including specialist training in Intensive Care and Cardiology, told me that she could not "imagine working on an intensive care unit of any description without open communication with a consultant whenever necessary. Specialists on the unit should be seeing such vulnerable babies at least a couple of times a day, and they should be there immediately on a phone line if there are any problems. We know from some of the indefensible delays in basic care that this wasn't the case. There should be a neonatologist supervising a unit of that nature at all times – they didn't even have a neonatologist working at the hospital! It also appears that there was no consultation with neonatologists from other hospitals when they experienced difficulty.

"A big part of the problem was junior doctors, lower than consultant grade, were working unsupervised some of the time and they didn't have the knowledge, skills or technical expertise to manage patients effectively in this kind of environment. And then they were also required to cover paediatrics and maternity. And consultants should have been doing rounds at least twice daily. It's not even the same consultant doing these once or twice weekly rounds! It was whoever was on call. A consultant might not actually see the patient for two or three days, which is clearly suboptimal. The consultants should know what's going on with all of their patients every day. Ultimately, there was a complete disconnect between nursing and medicine on this unit. It was delivering nowhere near the level of care required for these often extremely vulnerable infants." The anonymised Nurse X had cited issues with registrars on the unit, noting that they "had differing levels of neonatal experience and were not always keen to make decisions".

Dr Roger Norwich told me that when he worked with neonates, "I would be doing at least two formal ward rounds every day, and I would be bouncing in and out, seeing what was happening, particularly if there was a child that was unwell. You need that constant presence." Dr Norwich described the situation at the CoCH as "absolutely ridiculous that they were doing one or two ward rounds per week", continuing: "The consultant should be there to monitor the babies on a regular basis, but also to be teaching all the time. That's the point of having untrained junior doctors in the unit, so that you can teach them. Well, if you're there for one ward round a week, you're not teaching them a lot! It's really a dereliction of duty."

Professor Colin Morley, a neonatal expert, similarly informed me that "any neonatal intensive care unit around the country would have at least two ward rounds a day and have somebody there most of the time", and obstetrician Dr Martyn Pitman asserted that "three ward rounds per day" should be considered requisite. Professor Morley explained the rationale for this: "Neonates can deteriorate very quickly. If you don't keep a very close eye on them then you can miss the signs of deterioration." Finally, by way of comparison, the CQC report recorded that the adult critical care unit at the CoCH "had a twice daily, multi-disciplinary ward round"; thus, another important department was seemingly run as would be expected.

Dr Margaret Ferguson, a doctor with several decades of NHS experience, has a particularly interesting perspective on the Letby case, having previously acted as a whistleblower in the organisation. "I initially thought this was an example of whistleblowers being denied a voice in the NHS. That's why I became interested", she told me. This was precisely the experience of Dr Philip Hammond, who was "initially very convinced by the whistleblowing paediatricians who were convinced that Letby was harming babies". But as she examined the evidence, a different story emerged for Dr Ferguson: "The more that I examined this case, the more it became obvious to me that something was very wrong with this conviction."

Dr Ferguson agreed with the opinions of nurses that I'd spoken with. "The babies were being left in the hands of inexperienced nurses. There were few experienced nurses on the unit, alongside junior house officers and registrars who had variable experience. So to say that these infants collapsed suddenly, or that they were stable, as was asserted in court, is meaningless if they were not being observed properly, or those working on the unit didn't have the skills to recognise deterioration."

The consequences of this were evident in comments that Professor Morley made to the BBC. He noted that Child C had received a demonstrably poor level of care and attention: "This baby certainly should have had higher level of care. They're tricky and they deteriorate, and you need to be able to keep an eye on things to see what's going on."

There is also evidence of cultural problems at the CoCH with consultants. Annemarie Lawrence, the clinical governance lead at the hospital in 2016, told the Thirlwall Inquiry that consultants were not "open and transparent" about clinical problems in neonatology, asserting that the "consultant body" as a whole "stuck together", and conferred before reporting problems. "They wouldn't go against one another. So even if they thought somebody had made a clinical omission, rather than report it, they could have a conversation first, consultant to consultant." Lawrence also mentioned an incident in which an infant had collapsed when Letby wasn't on duty, and admitted that she "wasn't aware of a collapse, because…at the time there were some challenges around whether we were reporting them."

Furthermore, Dr Philip Hammond noted in *Private Eye* that the consultants "had a statutory duty to contact the coroner after every unexpected death", so that "a full forensic post-mortem – including definitive insulin testing – could be done", which did not occur. A CoCH internal paper on neonatal mortality from 2016 observed that "external escalation was not always as timely as it could have been", and that "nurses did not feel empowered to participate".

This should be considered troubling, as reflected by comments from coroner Alan Moore, speaking at the Thirlwall Inquiry on 4 December 2024: "The coronial process is a judicial process. It demands complete candour from healthcare professionals, clinicians, nurses and from hospital staff and also from Trust management…Failure to disclose to the coroner any information which may have a material bearing on a coronial case…is to mislead the coroner and to mislead the court." Echoing this view, one medic told me that "the safety and the overall outcome of any patient is the direct and ultimate responsibility of the consultant. There has been this bizarre emphasis during the Thirlwall Inquiry of apportioning blame to administrators. There is no legitimate way for consultants to palm this off on management. Patient safety is the responsibility of consultants – it's as simple as that."

Anecdotal evidence also supports the general theme of a unit that was struggling to cope. As an example, Letby noticed three missed calls having attended a salsa class in November 2015 – nurses on the unit had called her because they didn't know how to give a baby intravenous immunoglobulin treatment. "Just can't believe that some people were in a position when they don't know how to give something, what equipment to use and not being supported by [a] manager", Letby texted to her best friend. "Staffing really needs looking at." Letby further described the unit at that time as "chaos" and a "madhouse".

Michele Worden filled in the background of this incident. "Yvonne Farmer, who was the practice development nurse, was involved with trying to train and update everyone on the unit with procedures. At the time, Lucy had just come back from a placement in Liverpool and had administered immunoglobulin there. At CoCH they apparently didn't know how to give it – I can't understand why! – so they phoned Lucy up. And when Lucy next came on duty, Eirian Powell, Yvonne Farmer and Lucy got together, and Lucy wrote the guidelines on how to give or administer immunoglobulin for the unit. That's actually quite frightening because they should know this. They should definitely know how to give immunoglobulin. Yet they've got Lucy, who's three years out of university, writing a guideline – there is no way they should be reliant on her."

Mirroring this sentiment, a neonatal nurse, who wished to remain anonymous due to her current employment, suggested that "Lucy was the most junior grade you can be. She was not a senior member of staff and shouldn't be treated or portrayed as such. She should be receiving support, not being the one supporting others." Other nurses that I spoke with were equally baffled and scathing about standards on the unit. One neonatal nurse commented: "That is so inappropriate. How is she the only one that knows this protocol? And it's not that difficult to give, so the fact that they don't know how to give that is disturbing and shows their lack of experience and knowledge base." Julie Yates told me that "it was simply not a functioning unit. There should be a clear line of communication from nurses, through the registrars, to the consultants. They should be on the phone to them, not to Lucy." Another nurse indicated that this account "suggests that they couldn't do any intravenous medicines. I can't see any significant difference between immunoglobulin and other IVs."

Radiographer Ashleigh Tavoulari asked rhetorically: "If trained nurses could not do this, what else did they not know?" Dr Roger Norwich told me that "the hospital had systematically removed skilled staff from that department and largely replaced them with nursery nurses. It's a complete anathema to imagine nursery nurses taking a clinical role in a neonatal intensive care unit. I find it absolutely extraordinary. This is why there is this evident and highly significant skills gap."

Elsewhere, the mother of triplets involved in the Letby trial noted her alarm when a doctor was sat at a computer "Googling how to do what looked like a relatively simple medical procedure: inserting a line into the chest." The surviving triplet was taken to Liverpool Women's Hospital, and his mother felt that the clinical staff there were more competent and organised. "The two hospitals were as different as night and day", she commented.

The mother of Child N had also lodged a formal complaint against Dr A (allowed to be anonymous), while *The Guardian* interviewed a mother who described the experience of giving birth at the Countess. "They had no staff and the care was just terrible", the mother stated. She'd developed "an infection which was due to negligence by a member of staff", she explained. "We made a complaint at the time but it was brushed under the carpet."

As an example of both the recurring nature of elevated incidents within healthcare, and some of the issues that the CoCH has faced across multiple sectors, the maternity unit of the hospital experienced a spike in adverse events during 2021. Over this period, five mothers required unplanned hysterectomies after each losing over two litres of blood. An inspection from the CQC led to the conclusion that the unit was not keeping "women safe from avoidable harm". Twenty one incidents involving 13 patients were investigated, much as when the RCPCH had examined the neonatal unit. The report asserted that the hospital had not done enough to investigate the circumstances.

This medical report attributed the incidents to a combination of more commonplace factors than a serial killer, including staff and equipment shortages, a lack of training, a failure to follow national guidelines, poor record keeping and a culture in which staff felt unsupported; the same sort of issues that were flagged up by the RCPCH regarding the CoCH neonatal unit.

As mentioned earlier, figures released by the CoCH indicated that there was an elevated number of stillbirth deaths in 2016, which was actually 50% more than the number of neonatal deaths in the same calendar year. An interview with the Head of Midwifery at the hospital, Julie Fogarty, noted that there had been an "increased number" of both stillbirths and neonatal abnormalities. One neonatal nurse told me that "when you look at the rate in stillbirth, and then you look at the rate in neonatal deaths, you see actually there is an increase in both. That highlights a wider systematic failure." None of this was ever treated as suspicious.

Professor Colin Morley commented that the resuscitation of Child C was just one example of "suboptimal" practice on the unit. "The skills [on the unit] were not up to the job of resuscitating a tiny baby like this. And that's not surprising. This sounds very critical, but this was a hospital that wasn't really set up for a baby as small and sick as this. They just were out of their depth." He later told me that "the court often heard that a baby collapsed and couldn't be resuscitated. But that was simply because the doctors were unable to resuscitate them, and the reason for this was they did not have the experience." Dr Margaret Ferguson similarly highlighted to me that "junior staff were mostly doing resuscitations, and if they were inexperienced in resuscitating a neonate of this gestation and size, it would be very easy to get it wrong. CPR on a tiny premature baby is extremely delicate, with minimal force needed. It would be very easy for somebody who'd never done it before to get that wrong. A failure to resuscitate successfully cannot possibly be deemed a criterion for diagnosing air embolism."

Other evidence points to deficient infrastructure and inadequate resources at the CoCH. The allocation of cots on the unit was a constant challenge, which was amplified by the closure of an intensive neonatal care unit in a neighbouring hospital in North Wales, creating heightened demand throughout 2015 and 2016 – the time of Letby's alleged crimes.

An email sent in June 2016 by Dr Stephen Brearey acknowledged numerous issues on the unit, shortly before it was downgraded. Brearey wrote that helpful measures "would include a deep clean and reducing the number of allocated cots on NNU at least temporarily. Two ICU cots and three HDU cots (rather than three and four) would improve nursing staffing ratios and reduce the risk of nosocomial infection by making the space around the cots closer to BAPM standards." It was well-known at the hospital that the neonatal unit failed to meet these standards, as noted in a service review from the RCPCH which stated plainly that "staffing levels are inadequate when mapped to the actual activity and acuity of an LNU under the BAPM standards, both from a nursing and a medical perspective". The anonymised Nurse Y later told the Thirlwall Inquiry that the "intensive care and high dependency care cots [on the unit] were occupied on a regular basis", which led to the hospital "breach[ing] BAPM standards".

This is important for two reasons. Firstly, this proximity makes it easier for infection to spread, and therefore more likely for spikes in collapses and deaths to occur. Secondly, it is interesting to note that even after these mooted improvements, the unit would only be 'closer' to BAPM standards; there was no proposal that it would actually be possible to meet them. Brearey was responding to a report by the CQC which indicated that "nurse staffing levels on the neonatal unit did not meet standards recommended by the BAPM". The CQC further noted that 11 incidents were recorded that related to the acuity of patients and staffing breaching BAPM standards, and on seven occasions in that period the neonatal unit had been closed to admissions.

Babies were also often inappropriately allocated to the CoCH when NHS guidance states that they would have been better suited to specialist hospitals. Intensive care cots in Liverpool were often unavailable, while specialised regional transport teams, required to move ill babies across Merseyside, also experienced gaps in availability. Nursing manager Eirian Powell had recorded transportation as a 'red' factor in the risk register, and even Dr Stephen Brearey noted in an email dated 26 November 2015 that Child I had been "transferred five times between Chester, LWH and APH before she died", asserting that "I don't think so many transfers helped her care at all". The "significant capacity pressures" on this service were also discussed in the RCPCH service review of the hospital. This review found that there was "inadequate liaison between CoCH clinicians and the transport team…and no mechanism to trigger closure of a unit when it has reached capacity". The same document further noted that there was "confusion about the protocol" involved with transferring patients, and that a surgical review in April 2016 had "made six recommendations for service providers and five for the network including a communication improvement plan and a single surgical model to reduce confusion and delays".

As accusations regarding Letby began to grow, Eirian Powell forwarded a "neonatal unit review assurance" document to other managers, highlighting the fact that the "Cheshire and Mersey transport service have been involved in a few of these mortalities and they may have survived if the service was running adequately". A shortage of intensive care cots at Alder Hey had contributed to the mortalities, and the report included one case in which "if there had been a bed sooner, the infant may not have died".

When investigating the grievance procedure initiated by Letby, Yvonne Griffiths told Dr Christopher Green that "we have had equivalent deaths in previous years", but that the situation on the unit had deteriorated over her 10 years of working there. "Now we have more older mothers, increases in fertility treatment and less termination of care.

Some outcomes are not fantastic." Caroline Oakley would later inform the Thirlwall Inquiry that 2015/16 "was a very busy year, and we had babies coming in from the labour ward". Oakley did not consider the mortality results on the ward to be overly concerning, due to "the increase in the number of vulnerable babies we were caring for".

This impression was later confirmed by email correspondence between Dr Jane Hawdon and Ian Harvey from February 2017 which included the observation from Harvey that the neonatal unit was running "very hot", with "significantly more cots and higher intensity than it has the space or staff for" on what he described as a "regular" basis. Harvey posed Hawdon the "probably rhetorical" question of "how time critical is responding to a collapse or impending collapse, and how often, in your experience, is this sparked by clinical observations and how often by alarms going off?" The implication here is obvious; observation is *critically* important to clinical outcomes, and even the recording of accurate patient data.

"The experience of nurses is so important", a neonatal practitioner told me. "There are a lot of very subtle signs babies can give that they're having trouble, or declining, becoming septic, for example. New nurses don't know what that looks like. It's therefore critical that they have experienced nurses around them, who can assist with these situations. If you don't have experienced neonatologists, neonatal nurse practitioners or nurses to help you then it can be potentially fatal."

It is clear that the process of monitoring on the unit was malfunctioning. Key incidents that could have raised alarms sooner were not noted. Unexpected collapses of infants were not adequately recorded on the Datix reporting system and often were not recorded at all, while individual case reviews were also neglected. According to the opening statement of Ian Harvey, Alison Kelly, Tony Chambers and Susan Hodkinson to Thirlwall: "The significance of not following established governance systems cannot be overstated...Objective abnormal clinical findings and near-miss incidents were not recorded or escalated." A critical baby monitor at the CoCH was also broken during the spike in deaths, further amplifying problems in this area.

When the RCPCH reported on the CoCH, the professional body wrote in desultory fashion of a crumbling hospital that was poorly lit, cramped and underfunded. This was then compounded by staffing cuts which left the neonatal unit chronically short of experienced personnel, a major factor in the consistent presence of Lucy Letby.

No one would reasonably doubt the determination of those working at the hospital to deliver an adequate service, but it was, as former neonatal nursing practitioner Michele Worden put it, an accident waiting to happen. It could be argued that the perpetual underfunding of the NHS generally has made such sub-par performance inevitable. As mentioned previously, 20 other hospitals in the UK were investigated due to excess stillbirths and neonatal deaths in 2015; just one example of a looming maternity crisis that has made headlines recently.

It should be reiterated that the situation at the CoCH was reflected in the downgrading of the neonatal section to a Level 1 unit, shortly after Letby was moved into an administrative position. After this decision, the unit was then only permitted to deal with babies that did not require intensive care, a fundamental change that could quite feasibly account for the reduction in harm. The unit has remained at this level ever since.

Dr Colin Ferguson told me that "it's clearly the case that the cohort of sicker babies had not been managed in that unit previously. The consultants are mostly general paediatricians, not trained neonatologists, and had little expertise of looking after sicker babies. They were under-staffed and under-skilled in terms of nursing according to the RCPCH. And they're dealing with the most vulnerable babies. It's hardly surprising that they had poor outcomes and were downgraded on the advice of the RCPCH". Similarly, Professor Colin Morley believed that a unit with "more than an occasional sick baby does need a neonatologist." In support of this apparent shortage of qualified staff, nurse Christopher Booth wrote in a statement to the Thirlwall Inquiry that this was "an incredibly busy period with high acuity", and that requests for "more registered nurses…did not seem to be forthcoming".

During the trial, the prosecution emphasised the cessation of incidents on the neonatal unit after Letby was removed, and this was widely reported in the press. This is reflected in the number of casual observers and commenters who reference this as being a critical component of Letby's guilt, or even that this alone proves that she was guilty. But the downgrading of the unit seriously diminishes the merit of this insinuation, making it yet another red herring. Furthermore, as has been discussed previously, spikes in deaths do happen across the NHS system. The whole concept of a 'spike' is, in fact, predicated on the notion of something increasing for a short period of time, and then returning to normal levels; if this does not occur then there is no 'spike'.

Even the fact that deaths on the ward increased and then declined can be, in itself, merely a statistical anomaly, which occurs across trusts, regions, and hospitals throughout the NHS system in any given year. The prosecution provided no evidence on the statistical significance of this, nor its prevalence or rarity. The precise cluster associated with the Letby case has even been difficult to identify, with the CoCH providing differing accounts of the number and dates of the deaths on different occasions when requested for information.

Those who are familiar with healthcare in the UK or who have studied the NHS system in particular, will probably conclude that such problems, or 'spikes', are nothing out of the ordinary. Rachel Aviv noted in her *New Yorker* article that the UK had four highly publicised maternity scandals in the preceding 10 years. And in October 2025, the total liability for negligence in the NHS reached £60 billion, with a rise in childbirth injury cases cited as being particularly significant.

These reports would be disturbing under any circumstances, but it is important to emphasise once more that neonatal units are dealing with the most vulnerable infants. Contrary to what was stated in the trial, collapses are commonplace, and many babies born prematurely, with serious healthcare conditions, simply do not survive, even if they receive optimal care. Everything that is known about the CoCH, from reports, official reviews, the accounts of those that worked there, and anecdotal evidence indicates that this was a unit operating at nowhere near any level that could be deemed optimal. It was, essentially, a failing unit, reflected in the stark reality that it had to be downgraded. Naturally, this inadequacy would place what are already endangered babies in an even more precarious position.

Speaking with *The Guardian*, a leading and practicing neonatologist who had examined the deaths in the Letby case asserted that there were plausible alternative causes of death and deterioration in the case of each death, with "delays in realising babies were in difficulty, poor recognition and management of [serious medical episodes], failed intubations… these factors cause further deterioration of already compromised infants and increase the likelihood of death."

Having examined some of the cases that were heard in court, Professor Colin Morley is adamant that the unit was inadequately staffed. Morley pointed to basic errors with intubation and other processes that "were actually easy to recognise", concluding that these failures occurred because staff were "unskilled" for a neonatal unit. "That sounds like criticism", Morley told me, "but that's just reality. They may understand what to do in principle in some cases, but in the heat of the moment it's rather different."

It is clear that some of these infants required Level 3 support and care, while being treated by a unit that had to be downgraded from Level 2 to Level 1. This is considerably unsafe and unacceptable. Also writing in *The Guardian*, leading neonatologist Professor Neena Modi noted that "it is legitimate to ask why these babies were born at the CoCH when best practice would have been a transfer to a Level 3 centre prior to delivery", and that the unit plainly was "not staffed or equipped to deal with the most seriously ill babies". CoCH anaesthetist Dr Fiona MacRae concurred with this: "It was common knowledge that staffing on the neonatal unit was poor. There was always talk in obstetrics that admitting babies took a lot longer because of poor staffing levels."

While *The Guardian* has spoken with numerous neonatologists, Dr Philip Hammond has communicated with several, Mark McDonald's appeal team features nearly 20, and this book has cited and quoted a multitude of expert practitioners, neonatologists were conspicuous by their absence at the CoCH. Numerous healthcare professionals expressed their dismay at the level of knowledge on the unit.

"The first thing is that they didn't have a neonatologist", the neonatal nursing practitioner commented. "That is very important. Smaller NICUs will often just have a paediatrician, and they haven't been trained in a lot of the unique issues for preterm babies. In my experience, they can become overconfident, especially if babies are well for a while. I remember speaking with a paediatrician once, and he told me that a certain infant was doing well because it was not breathing as fast. Whereas I knew that breathing was slowing down because the baby was about to have a cardiac arrest. Neonates are entirely different from every other section of medicine. That's simply why neonatologists exist in the first place."

Neonatal nurse Sloane Spade also highlighted this issue. "Having no consultant neonatologists is lacking the specialised knowledge needed to care for these babies. Newborn infants require intensive care for a few reasons – prematurity, congenital defects (birth defects), failure to transition from foetal physiology to neonatal physiology such as in immature homeostasis, and, over time, learning to eat and gain weight. Not all neonatal conditions can be treated on a standard paediatric unit. Specifically, surgical and failure to transition concerns, such as blood shunting away from the lungs in persistent pulmonary hypertension, are mostly seen in neonatal units and need to be managed by experts in neonatal medicine. Neonatology is not the same as paediatrics, and these patients deserve to be cared for by consultant neonatologists."

Dr Roger Norwich mentioned the lack of neonatologists on the unit, while dealing with the most vulnerable infants, while Dr Colin Ferguson questioned if the ward should be considered a Level 2 neonatal unit. "You probably need seven or eight consultants dedicated to that purpose – that's what they will have in Liverpool, and in other major tertiary centres. At that time, the consultants were also performing two ward rounds per week. There is quite a lot of discussion in medical circles regarding whether this sort of intermediate Level 2 unit has any place whatsoever." Julie Yates informed me that "it was bizarre to have a speciality within the hospital without a specialist consultant and a dedicated team", while another experienced nurse suggested that relying on general paediatricians was "dangerous".

Perhaps not surprisingly, considering this picture, several infants in the court case were acknowledged to have suffered from suboptimal treatment, and Letby was cleared on some counts and cases, with this poor treatment being a contributing factor. This begs the question of why this wasn't communicated during the trial as a whole, and why the lead prosecution witness continued to claim that the CoCH was delivering a "high standard" of care.

In addition to the many healthcare professionals and experts cited in this chapter, there are numerous others who share concerns about the conviction of Lucy Letby. "I have talked to some of my colleagues who think exactly like I do, but they fear repercussions from the NHS", Professor Carola Vinuesa told me. "They know other doctors are involved, and I respect and understand why they feel worried about talking publicly. I have the luxury of not working actively in a hospital, so I'm able to speak freely." Similarly, Dr James Phillips said that "it is very clear to me that a substantial number of people from inside the CoCH, some who know Lucy Letby and who worked with her, believe that she is innocent. For the Thirlwall Inquiry judge to begin proceedings by criticising any dissent strikes me as highly inappropriate."

A neonatal nurse who wished to remain anonymous concurred with this: "You have a unit that is caring for babies that are sicker than they should be, nurses who are less experienced than they should be and doctors who are less experienced than they should be, with less oversight that they should have, they have more infants that they can deal with, so they're trying to multi-task more on other units, and they're more vulnerable and unwell than they're used to…and then they have the most fundamental sanitary issues overarching this. Sub-par outcomes are bordering on inevitable."

It must be emphasised again that the post-mortems of these infants revealed nothing out of the ordinary, as did Dr Jane Hawdon's review of 13 cases. When speaking about the general climate among neonatal units in the UK, Dr Philip Hammond commented that "our maternity units and neonatal units, across the UK, are under extreme pressure".

This was echoed by the consultant neonatologist, Dr Svilena Dimitrova: "I've worked in more than 15 hospitals in my career, and I've worked on five surgical neonatal units, and these issues are endemic. We can see issues that have not come to light, with regards to the circumstances at the CoCH, that we suspect have played a very big role in the increased incidence of deaths in those years."

Yet when Dr Evans spoke to the BBC, he commented: "And in this hospital in Chester it was clear that the doctors and nurses and the service in general were of a high standard, missing out on hardly any baby. The treatment the babies were receiving, before Lucy Letby disrupted everything, was of a high standard. The standard of service for newborns in Britain is generally very high, it is important to say that." He repeated these views to Sky News at a later date.

In the forthcoming chapter, "The Curious Case of Child K", the tragic death of Noah Robinson at the CoCH in 2014 is discussed. At around this time, the National Neonatal Research Database supported a national research programme, which was led by the University of Wolverhampton and Royal Wolverhampton Hospitals NHS Trust. The purpose of the research was to assess, for babies born between 27 and 31 weeks gestation and admitted to a neonatal unit in England, whether care in a neonatal intensive care unit versus care in a local neonatal unit affected survival and key morbidities. The CoCH was the only hospital to decline participation, when it seems that this is precisely the sort of exercise the troubled hospital should have fully embraced.

The picture that emerges of the CoCH is a neonatal unit in a state of semi-chaos. Even Letby herself described it that way. Staff on the ward, whether nurses or medics, were clearly trying their best, and genuinely invested in the outcome of babies under their care. But it is evident that this was a hospital with major issues. When coupled with the fact that the neonatal unit was being extended beyond its capabilities, as evidenced by its subsequent downgrading, this was potentially fatal. Internal documents of the time recognise this reality as outlined in a neonatal summary, authored by Ian Harvey, on 3 April 2017: "Between March and December 2015 there was a higher than average number of babies born with a birth weight below 2,000g [just under 4.5lb] in all but two months. This correlated with the increased demand for high level care over the same period."

This was all omitted in a document seemingly authored by consultants, which purported to outline "reasons for a possible criminal cause" of deaths on the neonatal unit. "When this member of staff was no longer working on the unit…there have been no neonatal deaths on the unit and no unexpected or unexplained sudden deteriorations", the document notes, never once referencing the fact that the unit had been downgraded, nor that the number of ward rounds was increased following criticism from the RCPCH. Dr Stephen Brearey didn't mention it in his testimony in court on 15 March 2023, saying that there were "no more events" after Letby was moved to an administrative position, and that this "was the same staff doing the same job and there were no sudden collapses".

Dr Roger Norwich summed up the issues at the CoCH succinctly: "Lots of those babies should never have been in that department because the level of incompetence, that you can understand by reading the trial transcripts, was quite unbelievable. Actually, it was beyond incompetence. It was negligent, in my view."

This would be problematic enough in itself, if the unit was shown to have the most exemplary standards of sanitary conditions. But as we will see in the next chapter, this wasn't the case at all.

CHAPTER 5: SEWAGE, SEPSIS AND SUPERBUGS

As the former producer of BBC's *Rough Justice* and the Channel 4 programme *Trial and Error*, Stephen Phelps has observed many miscarriages of justice at close quarters. Stephen cited the "true facts about what was going on in that dysfunctional hospital" pointing to "sewage coming up through the sinks, sepsis, pseudomonas, necrotising enterocolitis…even if you take away the deaths for which Letby is accused of deliberate harm, there were many others that also occurred during that period. But Thirlwall has claimed that she was using the troubles of the hospital as a cover for killing babies. Absolutely absurd."

This chapter will deal with the first tranche of issues mentioned, beginning with something that needs no further explanation – raw sewage. It is difficult to imagine any occupied retail or residential building in which raw sewage wouldn't pose significant health risks. And it is equally hard to conceive of a worse place for this substance to be present than the neonatal unit of a hospital. But that is exactly the situation that not only arose at the CoCH but which was a persistent presence for an extended period of time.

This is precisely why Letby's defence barrister called Lorenzo Mansutti, an estate manager at the hospital during the period of Letby's alleged crimes, who provided testimony to the court on the unsanitary conditions present on the neonatal unit. No one has disputed the testimony given by Mansutti in court; it was instead downplayed by the prosecution, and perhaps not meaningfully understood by the jury. It is well established that there were major sanitation issues at the CoCH, and that these issues are well known and common sources of some highly lethal disinfectant and antibiotic-resistant pathogens.

Letby commented during the trial that "we used to have raw sewage coming out of the sinks [and] coming out on the floor in nursery one", noting that it was an "important thing to know there were often plumbing issues" in the room where one infant was being treated. "It's a contributory issue if the unit is dirty and staff were unable to wash their hands." Letby also noted that plumbers were often called into nursery one – the intensive care room for the most vulnerable babies – to deal with "backflow" through the sinks from a separate theatre. "That's not a safe working environment. I'm not sure what impact that could have on a poorly baby", she added.

This was confirmed by Mansutti, and never denied by the prosecution. In fact, the court heard that plumbers were called out on a weekly basis to address drainage problems. Mansutti confirmed that "foul water" had come out of a sink in the intensive care suite – as Letby had claimed – and that 11 other major plumbing incidents had occurred in the year to June 2016, and it is now known that the extent of the problem was worse than indicated in court. Sewage pipes at the hospital were constructed from cast-iron, and had been in use for nearly 50 years. Rusting and cracking was common, which would in turn create blockages, and as a consequence of this the sinks and taps in the unit were frequently polluted with foul water. Considering what else is documented regarding the neonatal unit, it is also quite possible that further incidents were never noted, despite claims from the prosecution that "there would have been a record made at the time".

In a statement to the Thirlwall Inquiry released in February 2025, nurse Christopher Booth also cited "extremely low" water pressure in the sinks on the unit, which amounted to "essentially a dribble". This was "experienced by everyone working on the [unit] for a significant period between 2015/2016", and, in the opinion of Booth, "was not ideal for hand washing in a nursery containing potentially extremely sick and vulnerable babies". Booth later "reflected upon it and saw it as a potential factor in perhaps cases involving sepsis".

Dr Roger Norwich was adamant that this was a serious issue. "It's not normal, or indeed healthy, for hospital neonatal intensive care units to have sewage and infected water running around. It wouldn't happen in normal residential buildings. It wouldn't be allowed anywhere else. Imagine allowing it in a neonatal intensive care unit. It should have been shut down immediately, and that didn't happen." But sewage wasn't the only extraordinary presence on the unit.

"When I was there, we had an outbreak of black insects on the ceiling, and they had to bring in an exterminator one time", Michele Worden told me. "They came through the ceiling. At one point, we ended up, like a Greek restaurant, where they've got those fly zappers in the tavernas. They put one of those up by the nurses' station." The bottom line according to Michele was that "the hospital was not fit for purpose. It was falling down. It was built 40 years ago now, and it was old. It was cramped. This was one of a legion of problems."

I had a lengthy conversation with Professor David Livermore, an esteemed microbiologist who headed the National Reference Laboratory for Antimicrobial Resistance (NRLAR), for what was then the UK government Health Protection Agency (now the UK Health Security Agency), over a period of 14 years. As a professor of medical microbiology, working with Public Health England and the University of East Anglia, Professor Livermore has published over 500 academic papers.

"During my career, I worked alongside the NRLAR's Laboratory of Hospital Infection, which used to investigate such outbreaks. And that occasionally included nasty outbreaks in neonatal intensive care units. So I've seen such things and how they can develop", Professor Livermore told me. "And I then read Mr Mansutti's evidence that they'd had sewage leaks into this wretched unit. And I sat there thinking: 'Well, this is an outbreak of infection'. And let's be clear – infection can kill small infants. Particularly premature babies on a neonatal unit. A sewage leak is appalling. That sewage is guaranteed to contain vast numbers of gut bacteria, particularly Escherichia coli, which can cause opportunistic infections. It may also contain enteric viruses. Sewage is the very last thing that you want leaking into a neonatal intensive care unit."

Criticism from experts and healthcare professionals seems inevitable when there was raw sewage in the vicinity of the neonatal unit, and this was not properly addressed during the trial. "Those babies were likely born into a contaminated environment, and they might have had viruses that the mothers weren't showing symptoms of, but the babies may well have picked up along the way", nurse Julie Yates told me. When I asked Julie if the unit should have been closed down, she was quite emphatic in her response. "Absolutely. Remember that Lucy also raised this specifically."

This is one area in which there is agreement between Letby and lead prosecution witness Dr Dewi Evans. During his interview with John Sweeney, Evans was horrified by the prospect that sewage could ever have been present in the hospital where he worked in Swansea. When asked what the response would have been should this event have occurred, Evans opined that "we would have closed the unit down. We would have demanded that the management sort out the problem altogether, sort the plumbing out, and would not admit any babies until it was dealt with." When pressed on why the unit would have been shut down, Evans was quite blunt. "It's an infection risk. It could cause infection and septicaemia in babies." Professor Livermore also agreed, saying, "By definition, a normal, healthy infant is not in a neonatal intensive care special care unit. That is where extremely vulnerable babies are placed. Many of these infants were very premature. They were tiny and had immature immune systems. They were at risk from underlying conditions, and that is greatly magnified by the infection hazard."

It is interesting to note that not only was the unit in Chester never closed down, but also that Dr Evans was adamant sewage poses such a risk of infection that he would have insisted that a comparable unit in Wales was shut immediately. And yet, as we will see later in this chapter, he is also, conversely, resistant to the notion that any of the infants in the Letby case could have been affected by this. It is further notable that the significance and importance of this presence of sewage was never satisfactorily conveyed in court. The jury were never made contextually aware of the pathogenic threat that was almost inherent at the CoCH.

"Raw sewage is an obvious health risk", a doctor who wished to remain anonymous commented. "In all clinical settings, hand washing is essential in limiting the transfer of pathogens to people and objects, where they can proliferate and cause serious health problems. It is hugely significant that the sewage was present in the very place that hands should have been cleaned, essentially magnifying what was already a massive risk to patient well-being."

It was later claimed that the hospital attempted to deal with sewage by arranging nappies in a roof cavity as former estates management staff informed *The Daily Telegraph*, although this cannot be independently verified. This was lambasted by Professor Livermore, who said that "the sewage leaks – and their infection risk – do not even seem to be acknowledged in any meaningful way by the hospital". Senior coroner's officer, Stephanie Davies, wondered if coroner Nicholas Rheinberg had been made aware of the critical sanitary problem. "Normally, Mr Rheinberg would be all over that. He would want a proper investigation conducted into conditions on the unit in case this had contributed to any deaths."

Medical literature repeatedly points to the role of pathogens as an instigator of the condition of sepsis. This is important because there is considerable evidence of such unwanted and dangerous pathogens circulating at the CoCH, and indeed the presence of sepsis in several of the infants that Letby was alleged to have harmed. Sepsis is a life-threatening medical emergency that occurs when the body's immune system has an extreme response to an infection. This response can injure the body's own tissues and organs, leading to organ dysfunction, shock and multiple organ failure. Sepsis is caused by many organisms including bacteria, viruses and fungi.

A neonatal nurse practitioner stated that it was a "running joke" on her unit that "every single differential diagnosis you have includes sepsis, because every single possible symptom a baby can have is also a sign of sepsis". Another neonatal nurse told me: "It's the silent killer for a reason. It can be very difficult to detect, and sometimes it isn't detected until it's too late. Neonates are particularly vulnerable because they don't have a developed immune system. They don't have the protection in place." This was also pointed out by Professor Carola Vinuesa: "The lungs of premature infants are immature. They are hugely vulnerable, even in an ideal environment, and we know how important it is for sepsis to be treated early." Another nurse who I interviewed agreed: "Anything that goes wrong could be sepsis. You always do a septic workup. It's a very high-risk thing, and something we are always worried about because the immune systems of neonates are very weak."

There is considerable evidence that sepsis was a common presence on the neonatal wards at the CoCH. On 2 August 2015, Dr John Gibbs recorded during ward rounds that Child F was recovering from respiratory distress syndrome, and was being treated for "suspected sepsis". This was also noted on 4 August. On the following day, Gibbs still queried sepsis and recorded that Child F had signs of decreased circulation, which was likely due to "stress, dehydration or an infection". The treatment for suspected sepsis was later discounted in court testimony.

"This is important because deadly bacteria are often water-borne", another neonatal nurse told me. "If staff were washing their hands in contaminated water and then coming into contact with these very vulnerable neonates straight away, that's a massive infection risk. It's highly dangerous, very hazardous for the infants." Another nurse explained that "most sterile procedures" will also take place in this potentially infected location. "That includes putting most Total Parenteral Nutrition (TPN) bags [feeding bags for young infants] up, quite a few drips up, inserting lines, and anything else they're doing – these are all going to be sterile procedures. How they've managed to wash their hands adequately before sterile procedures must be considered a major concern."

It should be noted that other babies involved in the court case had been considered as having, were diagnosed with, or were treated for, sepsis. Indeed, sepsis was mentioned more than 70 times in one single quality account report for the hospital. Yet when giving evidence in court in relation to Child A, Dr Evans ruled out sepsis, as well as a lack of fluids or hypoxia, as a contributing factor concluding that there was "only one" explanation – "air had somehow got into his circulation". This opinion has since been roundly discredited, even ridiculed, by countless neonatologists.

Child G was another child who was suffering with suspected sepsis.

In the early hours of 8 September 2015, Child G was moved to Arrowe Park Hospital in Liverpool, where she had been born weighing only 1lb 2oz (510g). She required ventilation support at all times, with 100% oxygen. It is notable that this child's condition improved at Arrowe Park, before deteriorating again when she was returned to the CoCH.

Providing further background and context to the occurrence of sepsis on the neonatal ward is the important revelation that there was a confirmed case of sepsis at the CoCH neonatal unit on or around 14 June 2015. The child in question, Jacob Evans "became very poorly with septicaemia, and his arms, leg and tummy all swelled up".

Almost immediately, Jacob was transferred to Liverpool Women's Hospital where, according to his mother, "he recovered quite quickly". After a four-day stay at the hospital in Liverpool, Jacob was then transferred back to the CoCH where he began to deteriorate again. Jacob developed an infection so severe that it led to sepsis – possibly twice. The unit, in turn, was so ill-equipped to treat him that it twice had to transfer him to another hospital. At the same time, between 8 and 22 June, Children A to D were observed to be suffering with suspected sepsis, suffered multiple collapses and three of the infants sadly died. Jacob's case raises the distinct possibility that sepsis was a factor in the collapses and deaths of infants involved in Letby's trial.

A post-mortem examination conducted shortly after the death of Child D identified the cause as "pneumonia with acute lung injury". Before these results had been received, the doctors caring for her had no idea that she'd even been suffering with pneumonia. And although they had suspected the presence of infection, the infant had been started on antibiotics over four hours later than should have been the case. This delay was inexcusable but also characteristic of the hospital's suboptimal standards at this time; indeed, a nationwide investigation had already revealed problems at the CoCH, which was deemed to have been the fifth-worst performing hospital in the NHS when it came to treating sepsis in a timely manner. An investigation found that only 33% of the hospital's patients who needed treatment for sepsis were given antibiotics within the appropriate timeframe. In a statement to the Thirlwall Inquiry, nurse

Caroline Oakley would later report sepsis as being instrumental in the clinical picture for Child D. Furthermore, during the trial, it came to light that Letby had told a friend on the neonatal unit that Child D had a rash which looked like "overwhelming sepsis", and the infant had later collapsed.

"If you don't spot sepsis quick enough, you can rapidly lose infants", an experienced neonatal nurse told me. "This is a monitoring issue. There is also evidence that mistakes were made with hydration at the hospital, and dehydration will magnify the impact of sepsis. There is a symbiotic relationship between dehydration and sepsis – dehydration can be caused by sepsis, and it can also increase the risk of sepsis." When I inquired further about the unit, I was told: "We know there was sepsis on the unit, and yet I didn't see anything presented in court regarding the typical methods of monitoring. Shallow breathing, over-breathing, arterial blood gasses, hydration, bradycardia desaturation [drop in heart rate] – they could have spotted signs of sepsis if they had their eyes open to them. But I haven't seen any of this, despite sepsis being mentioned in documents, which suggests that they just weren't aware of how to spot it."

It is undeniable that babies in the neonatal unit at this time were at an especially high risk of serious infection, which would also have been exacerbated by the cramped premises. The unit, in turn, was ill-equipped to provide these newborns with the care they needed. These problems were known to Dr Brearey himself – when profiled by the *Chester Standard* in 2013 as part of the Babygrow Appeal charity drive, he gave the following explanation for why the hospital was in dire need of a new neonatal unit:

"The nurses on the unit do wonderful work and are very professional despite the lack of space around the incubators. Neonatal intensive care has improved in recent years but requires more equipment which we have very little space for. In addition, the risk of infection for the babies is greater, the closer they are to each other."

However, during the interview of Dr Elizabeth Newby at the Thirlwall Inquiry, cross-examiner Nicholas de la Poer KC attempted to suggest that sepsis had been ruled out as a potential contributing factor of both collapses and deaths. But the reasoning behind this, that negative blood test results had been noted, is no meaningful indicator once infants have been started on antibiotics. Sepsis is diagnosed by clinical signs, inflammatory markers and blood cultures. It is extremely common for septic infants to return a negative blood culture; for example, in a recent study in the *Journal of Clinical Sciences*, 48% of suspected neonatal sepsis cases tested culture negative. Ruling out sepsis by blood cultures, as Dr Evans has apparently done, could be regarded as flawed.

The evidence of sepsis affecting infants on the neonatal unit is mentioned in many documents submitted to the Thirlwall Inquiry. A business case for neonatal staffing written in 2015/16 and submitted to the inquiry noted that the administration of intravenous antibiotics to babies on the post-natal ward due to neonatal sepsis was having a huge impact on what was deemed to be the already limited skill mix, resources and staffing levels on the unit, meaning that more personnel were required. And Dr U also discussed with Letby herself the possibility that the triplets from the case were suffering with adenovirus – a contagious pathogen that can cause sepsis.

In the email thread of 2015 referred to earlier, Brearey stated that Child D "is most likely to have suffered from early neonatal sepsis which she showed signs of from 12 min of age". On the very same day, Brearey emailed Dr Ravi Jayaram saying: "It appears that neonatal GBS sepsis following prolonged rupture of membranes is the most likely cause for death". Brearey is quoting the patient Datix (an internal hospital note-taking system) form for Child D, which notes, identically to Brearey's email, that "it appears that neonatal GBS sepsis following prolonged rupture of membranes is the most likely cause for death".

As early as May 2015, there was discussion on the unit of risk factors for sepsis. A Level Two Root Cause Analysis Investigation Report from June 2015 acknowledged that Child D "had two risk factors for sepsis" from birth. It should also be noted that the report states quite clearly Child D was born in poor condition – something that was repeatedly played down in court as we shall see in later chapters.

On 3 July 2015, a report concerning Child D was made on the NHS England Strategic Executive Information System regarding the delay in recognising signs of sepsis when Child D was born on 20 June 2015. When Dr Jo McPartland conducted the post-mortem on Child D, her initial reporting submitted on 26 August 2015, she considered that there was a possibility of early onset sepsis, with pneumonia with acute lung injury being recorded as the primary cause of death. This is reflected in the Datix for Child D, which spoke of "neonatal GBS sepsis" and "early neonatal sepsis".

A Senior Clinicians Meeting had earlier noted that standardised processes around medication should be put in place, in order to deal with the threat of sepsis. A later thematic discussion at the CoCH in February 2016 noted that "one baby had a significant congenital heart disease and probable sepsis…two babies (possibly three pending PM result) died of sepsis despite timely antibiotic treatment". A neonatal review in 2015-16 also discussed "overwhelming sepsis" in some cases.

Sepsis was still being discussed as a cause of death in email correspondence between Dr Brearey, Ian Harvey and Sue Eardley, following the publication of the RCPCH report, in November 2016, when Brearey wrote of NICE guidance on early neonatal sepsis. The parents of Child D were informed that overwhelming sepsis was the likely cause of death. In his witness statement submitted to Thirlwall, Dr Brearey notes that there were signs of sepsis in Child D, and that "the doctors at Arrowe Park Hospital felt at the time that Child G had collapsed due to sepsis and I agreed with them at the time". Further Datix records for Child C and Child D also explicitly reference sepsis as the cause of death.

An extensive witness statement from the mother of Child G was read at the Thirlwall Inquiry, during which numerous references were made to neonatal sepsis. The same comments and diagnosis had been made at neighbouring Arrowe Park Hospital following a transfer.

Despite the evidence collated here, the prosecution witnesses assembled for the court case have repeatedly denied the existence of sepsis. When Dr Evans was interviewed by John Sweeney, he rejected the existence of sepsis at the CoCH. Dr Evans had previously passed 25 further 'suspicious' cases to Cheshire Police, for which it can be presumed that infection and sepsis were ruled out. Of the 17 supposedly stable infants involved in the Letby case, evidence now points to nine of them having either confirmed or suspected sepsis.

Similarly, during the court case, Dr Rachel Lambie, a former paediatric registrar at the CoCH, said that, in her opinion, the rash observed with Child B was inconsistent with meningococcal septicaemia (a type of sepsis specific to the meningococcus bacterium), and that the diagnosis didn't fit sepsis, while the child recovered too quickly for this to be the case. Furthermore, in the case of Child D, which appears overwhelmingly to involve sepsis, the prosecution asserted in its closing statement that "another medical expert, Dr Marnerides, had ruled out sepsis, and concluded Child D was killed by an air embolus". Dr Philip Hammond, barrister Mark McDonald and myself have been unable to find any professional support whatsoever, for this conclusion, despite collectively consulting several dozen medics.

It is also important to briefly mention at this point that sepsis can have an impact on C-peptide and insulin levels in critically ill patients, as cited by a scientific paper published in the journal *Critical Care and Resuscitation* in June 2019, contributing to inaccurate insulin test results.

Another worrying aspect of the clinical picture at the CoCH was the presence of pseudomonas aeruginosa. Pseudomonas is a bacterium that can cause severe infections in neonates – a threat which is amplified within neonatal intensive care units. The existence of this pathogen at the hospital is particularly well documented, with evidence indicating that this was a 'red' threat on the unit for over a year. Professor Livermore told me more about this bacterium: "Pseudomonas aeruginosa is not a sewage organism, unlike Escherichia coli; it's a water organism that's good at colonising pipework. It forms a biofilm, that same sort of scummy layer that can develop on the bottom of a washing-up bowl, for example. Then, as the water flows out of the tap, it becomes contaminated. It's particularly dangerous for neonates, and vulnerable groups generally."

Professor Richard Gill provided some interesting background on the NHS and healthcare, explaining that "alarm bells were starting to sound in around 2015 and 2016 about infections and bugs in hospitals. It was only then that the NHS realised sepsis was a huge danger. The first NHS advisories were sent out at around that time because many doctors wouldn't recognise the signs of sepsis if they saw it. So, it's not surprising they missed it at this hospital which was performing suboptimally anyway." Professor Gill also informed me that "forensic science was destroyed in the UK in 2012, when it was privatised, and the FSS [Forensic Science Service – a government-run organisation that provided forensic services to police forces] was closed down. If Cheshire Police had access to quality forensic science, and, of course, knew how to use it, this case could have been investigated quite differently, and to a much better standard."

At the same time as the FSS closing down, the budget for forensic science services was cut by 60% in real terms, and a far greater degree when accounting for inflation, in just 11 years between 2008 and 2019. There are countless articles that are critical of this decision, but perhaps the most telling manifestation came in 2017 when 10,000 criminal cases were reviewed after it emerged that data at a forensic laboratory in Manchester had potentially been manipulated.

The dangers of pseudomonas in healthcare settings were already clear by 2015 as the bacterium had contributed to deaths at Southmead Hospital in Bristol and the Royal Jubilee Maternity Hospital in Belfast in the years leading up to Letby's alleged crimes. On both occasions, sink taps were found to be the source of infection, and this was precisely the area in which pseudomonas was recorded at the CoCH. Professor Livermore expanded on the importance of the Belfast cases: "That led to an inquiry, and it was found that three babies had been washed, again in an intensive care unit, using tap water, from which they picked up pseudomonas infections, and sadly succumbed."

Professor Livermore told *The Daily Telegraph* he was sceptical about the "superimposed clusters" that were reported at the CoCH. Livermore instead suggested that "they died for the usual problems why small babies die: haemorrhage, infection, congenital problems. It is simpler to believe that we are looking at a single spike of fatal infections in a chaotic unit." Equally, the US Centre for Disease Control's Prevention and Response branch informed *The Daily Telegraph* that "in our experience mortality rates during pseudomonas aeruginosa outbreaks can be high. As neonates have little capacity to compensate for additional stresses, infection can cause other problems in these patients that are not directly related to the infection."

One mother whose baby was at the unit in 2016 told *The Trial of Lucy Letby* podcast, that "a matron came upstairs to me while I was an inpatient for two weeks and said that there was a virus on the unit and all the babies have got to stay in the rooms that they're in and we're not accepting any new babies. She seemed very panicked and it left me thinking at the time, 'Oh my gosh, what is going on?' [My son] was the only one that apparently didn't have this virus. They didn't want him getting it because he was so small, he was still on the oxygen at the time."

Livermore further noted in discussion with Sarah Knapton of *The Daily Telegraph* that this outbreak wasn't even included in the RCPCH report. "Although the pseudomonas colonisation was known at the time of the RCPCH report, it is not mentioned. Why, especially given the Belfast deaths? Were they told? Did they speak to the infection control team, given that infection was such a plausible cause of clustered deaths? These are yet more questions that the Thirlwall Inquiry needs to address."

Professor Livermore provided more important background to this issue. "At the CoCH, there was a water supply potentially contaminated with pseudomonas, plus there was a sewage leak which would be full of Escherichia coli. This is a huge microbiological risk. And yet, I've not seen one clear statement about what those in charge of this unit did to liaise with the microbiology department at the hospital, which has an overarching responsibility for infection control and for checking potential sources of infection, nor how they pressured facilities management who are responsible for the plumbing.

"Here in Chester, there were 17 deaths scattered over the period of a year. Someone conducted an environmental investigation to detect the pseudomonas in the taps and get mention of that on the risk register. But what else did they do, considering that infection is a likely cause of collapse and death? There are several cases where infection is cited as a cause of death by the original pathologist, and at least 10 of the indictment babies were on antibiotics. So where is the microbiology department? What did they find? They should be intimately involved when infection is suspected, and particularly when there is a raised number of suspected infections."

When I asked Professor Livermore how the hospital should have responded, he explained that "they should have reviewed and documented all infections and microbiology results from infants in the unit. What infections were recorded from other infants? Is there any pattern? Is there anything indicating an outbreak organism? Infection is prominent in the index of suspicion here, and I would therefore want to know every scrap of detail about what was found in the infections of all babies within that unit. This should be central to any investigation or understanding of that neonatal unit."

At the time of writing, the Thirlwall Inquiry has not meaningfully addressed this. Despite the fact that pseudomonas appears in the risk register submitted to Thirlwall, and is referenced on several other occasions, it wasn't discussed in the inquiry.

"The important thing to note", Dr Roger Norwich informed me, "is that the risk report for pseudomonas was hidden from the court. How that could have happened, I don't know. We don't know if Dr Evans knew about that report, but if he didn't know about it then he definitely should have done." Similarly, Professor Carola Vinuesa noted that "pseudomonas colonisation of the taps is not in the individual notes of the babies. There are also other signatures and indications of infection that have clearly been missed, and this all contributes to an unclear clinical picture". Vinuesa pointed out that the pseudomonas colonisation was not mentioned in clinical notes, yet notes of a hospital meeting between clinicians and executives from 29 September 2016 indicate that there was full awareness of pseudomonas on the unit.

One note-taking template submitted to Thirlwall does give us an intriguing insight to events at that time. On 4 March 2016, the CQC specifically highlighted pseudomonas and sepsis in its assessment of the neonatal unit in Chester. The document also mentioned BLISS, a charity for premature babies involved with ensuring that all premature babies have the best chance of survival, and NEWS, an acronym for National Early Warning Score, which is essentially a scoring system for the detection and response to clinical deterioration. The NHS England website particularly highlights the efforts of the NEWS system to tackle sepsis, noting that it was developed by the Royal College of Physicians in 2012.

It is clear from this that both sepsis and pseudomonas were being actively discussed in March 2016, yet there is very little reference to either of these critical factors in the CQC's June 2016 report. It is briefly mentioned that "for admissions with severe sepsis or pneumonia, the unit mortality was generally higher than for comparable units". But there is no mention of pseudomonas whatsoever in the report, and neither sepsis nor pseudomonas managed to make the final cut in the CQC's statement that was submitted to the Thirlwall Inquiry. The CQC, rightly, criticised the neonatal unit with regard to staffing, but these were the only recommendations made in its 2016 report. It seems highly curious that such an important aspect could be excluded, particularly as it was discussed at the time, has been acknowledged in CoCH documents submitted to Thirlwall, and the link between sepsis and pseudomonas is both extensively established and understood to be particularly deadly for neonates.

When I showed Professor Livermore the documentation from the CQC, he was apoplectic. "It's unbelievable. This evidence and the original notes regarding pseudomonas and sepsis should have been worked up into a full report. This unit had 13 or 14 deaths in the 12 months prior to this document being produced, yet the report glosses over them. The much more critical RCPCH report was commissioned – due to deaths on the unit – a few months later, and looked back to the same period. Did the CQC inspector not recognise that something was amiss?"

Eileen Chubb, founder of the whistleblowing charity Compassion in Care, has had repeated dealings with the CQC, and her opinion on the organisation was not exactly favourable: "The CQC are responsible for an awful lot of problems within healthcare. Whistleblowers tell us frequently that they provided a wealth of information to the CQC, and that was in no way reflected in their inspections or reports. It seems that they're incapable of acting on concerns.

"At Compassion in Care, we conduct undercover inspections of care homes and hospitals. And the last time that I checked, 93% of calls to our helpline about hospitals and care homes that were demonstrably bad were regarding establishments that have been officially rated as good or excellent. That data should tell you immediately that there is something very wrong with how these inspections are being carried out." Chubb also provided me with a raft of *Private Eye* articles illustrating fundamental failings in responding to standards of care, spanning the years 2001 to 2018, in multiple locations. Many of these cases involved the CQC, with one report related to Gateshead asserting that "the CQC appears either unaware of neglect, poor care and worse, or ineffective at dealing with it".

Professor Livermore pointed to some sections in the report that he found particularly troubling. The CQC report states that between January 2015 and January 2016, 254 incidents were recorded by the children's unit, neonatal unit and paediatric outpatient's clinic, and, of these, 252 were reported as low or no harm. "This was in a place where allegedly healthy babies were dying in surprising numbers! Remarkable!" He also noted that the CQC had asserted that "the wards and clinical areas were visibly clean. Staff were aware of, and adhered to, current infection prevention and control guidelines such as the 'bare below the elbow' policy. We observed staff using personal protective equipment such as aprons when delivering care", yet had completely neglected to mention the pseudomonas contamination of the water supply. What's more, this was in a place where there were sewage leaks into the neonatal unit, and both the risk register and the inspector's notes mention pseudomonas contaminating taps", Professor Livermore observed. "The report bears so little resemblance to the situation on the ground, and even to the inspector's original notes regarding "additional deaths", "pseudomonas" and "sepsis", that one wonders if they confused the CoCH with another hospital!

"This was a unit with substantial problems and a substantial death rate. And what is the more likely cause of the substantial death rate – the general deficiencies of that unit, or one murderous nurse, whom nobody actually saw commit a murder, and whose murders were passed by the original pathologists as deaths from natural causes?"

This argument would be undeniably true anyway, were it not for the tragic case, in 2020, of Olly Stopforth. This toddler from Cheshire contracted a streptococcal infection due to mistreatment at the CoCH which led to sepsis and a viral infection. Olly sadly died two days after being discharged. It was accepted that the CoCH failed in their care of Olly. In the inquest into his death, it was noted that "the Countess did not follow NHS UK sepsis tool or NICE guidance which, if used, would have indicated the need for blood test and/or IV antibiotics". The CoCH accepted full responsibility for the tragic passing of Olly, and shortly after this incident switched to the updated NEWS2 system.

It is also notable that Olly had an observable rash that "was considered to be as a result of a viral infection". This is critically important because rashes were said to be major diagnostic factors in the Letby case. However, as will be discussed in more depth later, lead prosecution witness Dr Evans decided that these were 'unusual' rashes that couldn't possibly have been caused by infection. Staff at the time reported having never seen rashes of this nature previously, a common assertion throughout the trial. The jury was consistently told that phenomena observed on the unit had never been seen before. However, simply because such phenomena hadn't been encountered previously by those reporting them, it does not mean that they require some extraordinary explanation. Remember that Dr Evans never actually saw any of the rashes, or indeed any of the infants; he had to rely entirely on clinical notes.

One neonatal nurse I spoke with was concerned about the over-emphasis on phenomena that hadn't been encountered before during the court case. "In all the years that I've been a nurse, I've frequently encountered things that I hadn't seen before. Perhaps if there is a baseline level of competence, where the fundamentals are being done, you don't see new things. But if very fundamental things aren't being done, you do see things that are unusual. Of course you do!"

On top of the evidence provided already, there is no shortage of evidence that pseudomonas was circulating on the neonatal unit. During the Thirlwall Inquiry, Dr Murthy Saladi recounted that "for all the taps in the neonatal unit taps we had filters and there were growing pseudomonas from the taps". This was on a day when Saladi also noted that "we were being told the rise of acuity and busyness on the unit, that perhaps an increased number of deaths was inevitable". And emails in June 2015 demonstrated that registrars and consultants both believed that "we had some medical problem on the unit", as Dr John Gibbs put it, "superbugs or some nasty infection".

In 2017, the World Health Organization (WHO) listed pseudomonas as a bacterium that poses a particular threat in hospitals. It was one of only three pathogens that was listed as being a critical priority. The WHO noted that pseudomonas is an example of "bacteria for which new antibiotics are urgently needed". This is not discussed in the specific context of neonates – pseudomonas is potentially fatal for a wide variety of vulnerable groups, particularly those with weakened immune systems. It is therefore facile to state that the pathogen can be lethal when it comes to the most frail, premature, and vulnerable infants. One study of 2,177 neonates found that pseudomonas was fatal in 23% of cases. Without going into all of the complex biological data, there is also a close relationship between pseudomonas and sepsis. Another study of nosocomial pseudomonas found that of 11 mothers who were infected, three of their infants died of fulminant sepsis.

Infections and failures related to them are, frankly, also far too common in the NHS. Dr Philip Hammond noted in *Private Eye* that there had been a major scandal in the Derby and Burton NHS Foundation Trust which accounted for 168 perinatal deaths between January 2020 and March 2023. Similarly, 84 children were infected with water-borne bacteria at Queen Elizabeth University Hospital Glasgow. Both of these incidents happened before Letby was convicted. And in January 2026, NHS Greater Glasgow and Clyde, the largest health board in Scotland, conceded that contaminated water contributed to serious infections in four children that sadly resulted in their deaths.

Such was the picture at the CoCH, Professor Livermore told me that it was inevitable that other pathogens would be circulating. Within weeks of his comment, the expert panel cited stenotrophomonas maltophilia, a multidrug-resistant bacteria, as being critical in the case of Child I, and then an outbreak of the dangerous respiratory syncytial virus on the unit was also revealed. As fallout from the Glasgow NHS scandal became public, it was then discovered that an infant in that hospital had died after a tube delivering medication became infected with the stenotrophomonas maltophilia bug.

There have been suggestions from Thirlwall lawyers that infection had been ruled out, but, in the case of stenotrophomonas, blood cultures will only identify the virus if bloodstream infection is present. Instead, respiratory cultures are the appropriate method to diagnose pulmonary infection by this pathogen, and there is no evidence of any such test, or any test at all for that matter, having been conducted.

As a former regional director of public health, Professor John Ashton possesses a particularly acute insight into such problems. "For example, I had to deal with outbreaks of Legionella at some of the hospitals in the North West. I recall that there was one at Broadgreen Hospital in Liverpool, but we were told about it and were able to intervene." So how did things seemingly spiral out of control at the CoCH? "The real issue is: Who on the hospital board of management is responsible for monitoring and asking questions? Who is responsible for ensuring that these things are noted in the annual report of the hospital? I would suggest that this was a real weakness at the CoCH."

Professor Ashton outlined some of the broader underlying issues with hospital management: "As someone who is very experienced and has had a strong professional career, I have applied for probably 10 hospital boards to be a non-Executive Director, and have never been short-listed. Now I have a reputation for asking difficult questions, but the problem is that you need people on boards of management who *will* ask difficult questions. In my experience, hospital boards clone each other.

"They're all very similar people, and they're over-staffed with finance experts, because that's been the obsession of government and NHS for the last 40 years. How many of them have somebody with a public health and epidemiology background, or an environmental health background, or anyone with an understanding of the wider issues that impact on the outcomes of clinical practice? It seems to me that this was a major issue at the CoCH, and this is why these critical problems were never adequately addressed."

In summary, there is considerable evidence of both sepsis and pseudomonas at the CoCH. This is further recorded throughout documentation from the time, and the CQC noted this when it reported on the hospital – somehow this then didn't appear in their final report. In addition, this critical aspect of the clinical picture was almost entirely excluded from the Thirlwall Inquiry, even though both sepsis and pseudomonas appear in numerous documents.

Dr Evans was able to completely rule out infection, based on the clinical notes. It has been confirmed by Dr Evans that he was not present when sewage was discussed in court. When John Sweeney and Edward Abel Smith interviewed Dr Evans, they pointed out that Harry Clark, the second son of the wrongly convicted Sally Clark, had a potentially lethal infection, and yet every witness at the trial had completely missed this. Dr Evans apparently knew nothing about this either.

In December 2025, *The Daily Telegraph* reported that Evans had discounted infection in another infant. This baby was not included in the court case and had died at the Liverpool Women's Hospital from what examining neonatal experts concluded was respiratory infection; Evans had instead asserted that Lucy Letby had removed a breathing tube.

It is impossible to credibly discuss the spike in deaths at the CoCH without properly contextualising the staffing, organisational, professional competency, sanitation and virus-related issues on the neonatal unit, yet these issues was never adequately communicated to the court. The jury in Letby's trial were told repeatedly that this was a highly effective unit. Dr Stephen Brearey stated that "practices were going from good to better, the fact that we were working on a very good unit that normally had very good results, this all became very exceptional". Considering the jury weren't told that several children had died on the unit in both 2013 and 2014, this seems to me quite an extraordinary claim. This lack of context was a major criticism of the trial voiced by Professor Peter Green:

"The principal problem is the failure to account for other explanations.

There's also a sense that by summarising it in such a succinct way you are capturing the whole story, and that's very, very compelling. People like simple explanations. And of course, people also like to blame human culprits, not problems with systems."

A combination of under-skilled and under-prepared staff in insufficient numbers and specialities, inadequate sanitary conditions, pathogens circulating on the unit and a failure to address this overall clinical picture were far more likely to be the major contributors to the spike in deaths at the CoCH than the alleged crimes of Lucy Letby.

The case of Lucy Letby can be seen as one in which those investigating failed to account for a multitude of contextual factors. There could have been a different hospital, in another region, with an alternate police force and investigators, looking at exactly the same situation, and the outcome could have been wildly different. If that had been the case, none of us may even have become familiar with the name of Lucy Letby.

Unfortunately, as we will see in the chapters to come, the only too evident issues at the CoCH were seemingly trivialised by the investigation and judicial process in which Lucy Letby became unwillingly entangled.

CHAPTER 6: PROSECUTION AND DEFENCE WITNESSES

Having been arrested three times, Lucy Letby was denied bail on 10 November 2020, in the prelude to one of the most significant court cases in British history. We will return to the arrest and investigation of Letby in later sections, as this core component of the book will examine issues around the trial itself.

The primary expert witness in the Letby case was Dr David 'Dewi' Evans, while Dr Sandra 'Sandie' Bohin was tasked with reviewing the reports of Evans. It is reasonable to describe Evans and Bohin as prosecution witnesses, as Evans worked directly with the police, and Bohin reviewed the reports that Evans produced. Dr Andreas Marnerides, Professor Owen Arthurs, Professor Sally Kinsey, Professor Peter Hindmarsh, Professor Stavros Stivaros and Dr Simon Kenny also appeared in court as expert witnesses. Those last six names contributed relatively little to the prosecution case; in some cases, virtually nothing.

In fact, there is barely any reference to Stivaros or Kenny in any reporting of the case. Their names are also mentioned only once in the Court of Appeal verdict – simply to confirm that they were instructed by the prosecution. Stivaros submitted a statement to the court about Child G, in which he "defer[red] to my expert neonatal colleagues' opinions", stating that "the scans cannot determine a cause for this injury". As for Child M, Stivaros observed that "the imaging can only describe the brain damage resultant from this episode. It cannot determine the underlying cause of the collapse, about which I defer to clinical opinion". And for Child Q, Stivaros again commented that "I defer to my neonatal expert colleagues' assessment in regards to him having suffered a significant hypoxic ischaemic event at that time".

Stivaros offered no material support to the prosecution, while Kenny also made very little contribution to this case. In a witness statement read out in court, Dr Kenny did little more than provide the "opinion that Hirschsprung's disease did not account for [Child G]'s symptoms in September 2015". Furthermore, the main contribution of Professor Sally Kinsey was to tell the court that Child E had lost a large amount of blood, but that her observations did "not assist with what the cause of death actually was".

Some of the evidence presented by Professor Arthurs actually calls into question some of the diagnoses of Dr Evans, as we shall see later. The Court of Appeal acknowledged that the evidence of Arthurs was "consistent with, but not diagnostic of, air having been administered to Baby A". You could argue this is essentially meaningless, as no one disputes that air could have been present; the issue is rather how the air arrived there in the first place.

Similarly, Dr Marnerides identified the presence of an air bubble but stated that this was "not conclusive". As noted in court, Marnerides "could not or would not explain the mechanism by which air embolus causes death in a neonate". The Court of Appeal outlined the fact that "Professor Arthurs and Dr Marnerides were conspicuously careful not to go further than their specialist expertise would permit them". Marnerides also stated in court that air was injected into the stomach of an infant; a theory that Dr Evans has now abandoned as will be discussed in later chapters. It should finally be noted that Marnerides only appeared in court from 29 to 30 March 2023, two of 136 days of court proceedings, and that his contribution was largely prompted by reports from Dr Evans. The comments of Marnerides on Child O will be discussed in "Other Infants".

Professor Hindmarsh provided some support for the insulin hypothesis that was put forward in court, but certainly did not endorse it definitively. He stated in court that insulin could "potentially" have been added to feeding bags, as alleged by the prosecution case. He also agreed with Letby's defence barrister, Ben Myers, that there could have been other possible explanations for the readings recorded. The insulin aspect of the trial will be discussed in much greater depth in "Insulin Cases".

In March 2026, investigation by Felicity Lawrence and David Conn at *The Guardian* revealed that Hindmarsh had been under investigation by the General Medical Council (GMC) while giving evidence in the trial of Lucy Letby. The practice of Hindmarsh was restricted after his employer, Great Ormond Street Hospital, reported Hindmarsh to the GMC. The CPS informed the defence of Letby that it would oppose any attempt to inform the jury, due to the case having yet to reach adjudication. Consequently, the court never heard about issues with another key prosecution witness.

The GMC status of Dr Dewi Evans can also be considered concerning. Evans acquired a new licence to practice in July 2019, having allowed his licence to expire in 2015. When Dr Evans first arrived at Blacon police station in Chester, he could not practice as a medic, and this remained the case for the first two years of Evans writing countless reports for Operation Hummingbird, during which time Letby was arrested solely on the basis of his work. This latter point was confirmed by Detective Superintendent Paul Hughes, who led the inquiry, in conversation with Liz Hull and Caroline Cheetham. While having no licence to practice does not exclude Evans from giving evidence, it hardly marks him out as the optimal person to do this, particularly in such a fast developing and specialist field as neonatology.

Approximately 90% of the court proceedings dedicated to medical evidence was devoted to Evans and Bohin, with the other experts only appearing on 11 of 136 days collectively. The vast majority of the medical evidence which formed the prosecution case was provided by Dr Evans. "The whole case is an inverted pyramid sitting on top of Dewi Evans", Stephen Phelps told me. In my opinion, this case would never have ventured anywhere near a courtroom without the efforts of Dr Evans which explains why his name has been mentioned with some regularity already, and why he will remain a central figure in the remainder of this book.

Dr Sandie Bohin was tasked with peer reviewing the conclusions of Dr Evans. Paragraph 22 of the Court of Appeal judgment records the fact that Dr Evans reviewed 61 sets of clinical records, and paragraph 23 establishes that Bohin would "provide a robust clinical review of Dr Evans' opinions, setting out whether she agreed or disagreed with him and, as appropriate, to provide an alternative causation for the collapse". This is unequivocal evidence that the peer review was not blind, which immediately calls into question its objectivity. Bohin later confirmed that she had read all of the reports authored by Evans when speaking with Liz Hull and Caroline Cheetham. "This wouldn't be considered acceptable for an academic or scientific peer review", Professor Carola Vinuesa commented during our conversation. "It's not independent and the two reviewers are too close. It doesn't sound like a serious peer review from what I have read in the Court of Appeal document."

Dr Roger Norwich told me: "Any peer review should have been undertaken by somebody at massive arm's length from Evans' side of things. This clearly didn't happen. To just look at what he'd done previously is a complete travesty. They should have gone away with separate notes – it's highly illegitimate."

Dr Colin Ferguson agreed. "That's not a peer review at all. She should have independently scrutinised the case notes and drawn her own conclusion regarding causes of death, not see what Dr Evans said and then agree with him. This can so obviously introduce prejudice and bias into the process." Neonatal expert Professor Neena Modi wrote in *The Guardian* that "experts were not all asked to go through the cases in detail", as evidenced by the fact that, for example, Dr Marnerides didn't even view the clinical notes; he relied on the reports of Dr Evans.

This is a highly important aspect of the case, because Dr Evans tends to assert that several other experts agreed with him. In fact, the majority of them were involved in very narrow specifics and did not directly support his conclusions or diagnoses. Any checking or corroboration of the work of Dr Evans was conducted solely by Dr Bohin, and several medics have said this process was deeply inadequate.

Cheshire Police should have asked for a second opinion; indeed, as discussed in "Operation Hummingbird" (the name given to the police investigation), the National Crime Agency (NCA) made the constabulary well aware of this. The prosecution case was almost entirely reliant on the evidence of Dr Evans who wasn't a neonatologist and hadn't worked in a hospital since 2009. Seeking a second opinion is good practice, yet the only testing of the conclusions of Dr Evans came from Dr Bohin who was also on the roster of the NCA. The lack of a fully independent second opinion can introduce bias into an investigation and systematically diminish the value of its scientific assertions.

One paediatrician that I spoke with, who wishes to remain anonymous, told me that Dr Bohin had been working in Guernsey for over a decade, and that this is a particularly small unit, as would be expected for a tiny island with a meagre population of 64,000. She told me it was likely that Bohin had minimal contact with sick children, and added that she didn't think Bohin's work could be compared to the rather chaotic neonatal unit in Chester.

Since 2009, Dr Evans has frequently been called as an expert witness in various court cases. Dr Evans is not a neonatologist. This is not intended to diminish his work as a paediatrician; it is simply a fact that he never undertook the training and study required to qualify as a neonatologist. It is also not known whether Dr Evans has undergone any meaningful professional development since retiring, in what is a rapidly evolving field.

Dr Evans has employed a robust defence to any criticism regarding his qualifications, stating that neonatology is no more than a "label", as he told BBC journalists Judith Moritz and Jonathan Coffey. Evans has also made much of the notion that neonatology wasn't a separate field in Swansea when he began his career, but declares that his expertise at least equals, and in many cases exceeds, any neonatologist. Evans made these claims in court, and further suggested that "in the 1980s…neonatology was relatively new", and that other "consultants deferred to my interests in neonatology development".

The Neonatal Society, whose aim is to "promote neonatal science", was formed on 24 April 1959 at the Royal Hotel in Scarborough. The society notes that the pioneering work of Professor Robert McCance at the Department of Experimental Medicine in Cambridge had paved the way as early as 1938. An article published by the American Academy of Pediatrics asserted that 1960 was a "sentinel year" for neonatology, and Professor Alistair Philip wrote that "thereafter, an increasing number of pediatricians devoted themselves to full-time neonatology". Today, those qualifying for neonatology must undergo three years of specialist study. According to the British Medical Journal, the GRID program which neonatologists must undertake in order to qualify attracts "very high competition". All trainees are required to complete the RCPCH START exam for neonatology – a clinical examination encompassing 12 stations.

The notion that neonatology somehow did not exist in the 1980s could conceivably be given slightly more credence, as it first became possible to train as a neonatologist in the UK in 1982, even though neonatology had been an established field for 30 years by the end of this decade. Nonetheless, there is no evidence that Dr Evans chose to undertake this training.

It is possible that the comments of Dr Evans regarding the situation in Swansea at that time are accurate, but it is questionable for him to claim that he possesses the same level of expertise as a neonatologist, let alone someone who is currently practising. The nuances of this may be lost on legal professionals; Judge James Goss even apparently believed that Evans *was* a neonatologist, shortly before he began his summing up on 3 July 2023.

Sloane Spade, a highly experienced neonatal nurse, informed me: "Neonatology is a greater speciality of paediatrics. I describe it like this: if you needed brain surgery, you would want it to be done by a neurosurgeon, as they specialise in the brain, not a cardiothoracic surgeon. While both can perform surgery, you'd want the one who is the expert in the surgery you need. The kind of care required of intensive care infants should always fall on a paediatrician training to be a neonatologist, or a consultant neonatologist."

The international panel of experts, numbering at least 31 at the time of writing, possesses credentials and experience that far outweigh those of Dr Evans. Their career achievements read like the Dead Sea Scrolls of neonatal history, while they have collectively authored thousands of papers. It is universally accepted that Shoo Lee's panel massively outranks the prosecution; in the opinion of Dr Philip Hammond, "the prosecution experts at Letby's trial were clearly not in [the] league" of this newly formed group.

In a different case prior to his involvement in the trial of Letby, Evans was criticised for providing evidence lacking objectivity in court, with a judge describing his contribution as "worthless". The judge in that case, Lord Justice Jackson further noted that the work of Evans made "no effort to provide a balanced opinion". The judge also wrote that Evans "either knows what his professional colleagues have concluded and disregards it or he has not taken steps to inform himself of their views. Either approach amounts to a breach of proper professional conduct." Jackson continued: "The report [submitted by Evans] has the hallmarks of an exercise in 'working out an explanation' that exculpates the applicants. It ends with tendentious and partisan expressions of opinion that are outside Dr Evans' professional competence and have no place in a reputable expert report."

During the Letby court proceedings, Dr Evans claimed that the report referred to by Lord Justice Jackson was a letter, despite the fact that it was headed "Report of Dr Evans". In cross-examination, Dr Evans then attempted to claim that this was a matter of "semantics". It's hard to humour his view, considering that semantics is the branch of linguistics concerned with meaning, and 'letter' and 'report' mean fundamentally different things; no one ever reads a letter and mistakenly believes that they're reading a report. By the end of the discussion, Dr Evans conceded that it was a report, using the word 'report' to describe the document numerous times.

Following this exchange, Letby's defence sought to have the contribution of Evans removed from the process. The defence again made several criticisms of Evans during its application for appeal. These included the following: "Dr Evans had demonstrably established that he was not an independent expert...he had constructed theories designed to support allegations on the indictment rather than forming and presenting an independent opinion on the facts; he had been hostile and emotive, dogmatic and biased in his responses to questions on behalf of the applicant and that he was too closely aligned to the police having acted, in effect, as their investigator...he had stepped outside the proper boundaries of an expert witness."

There is some discussion of the decision to allow the opinion of Dr Evans to be heard by the court in the Court of Appeal judgment. But the critical aspect of this decision is really contained within paragraph 103: "Further, it was said, were the evidence of Dr Evans to be excluded, the appropriate course would be to discharge the jury, rather than carry on with the trial." This is a submission by the defence, but it is clearly true. Without Dr Evans, the prosecution case would have immediately collapsed. There was no other significant medical backing for the prosecution case, which was almost entirely predicated on the opinion of Dr Evans, opinion which has since found almost no backing from any other medical professional. It is therefore bordering on unthinkable that anyone else could feasibly have stepped in, and therefore the trial almost certainly could not have proceeded.

Sir David Davis noted during his parliamentary speech that Lord Justice Jackson had written to Judge James Goss from the Letby trial "with his judgement on Dr Evans attached, clearly indicating how unsuitable Evans was as an expert witness". On any objective level, this should have resulted in the immediate exclusion of Evans from any court case, especially one of this magnitude.

In May 2017, Evans directly offered his services to the NCA with whom he had already been affiliated since around 2014, having, according to his own account, read about Letby's case in a newspaper. The initial email of Evans to the NCA included reference to police involvement which indicates he knew the police suspected a crime. Two months later, again according to his own account, he travelled to Chester to meet with Cheshire Police, before deciding within "10 minutes" that infants in the case had been subjected to inflicted harm. Dr Evans told *The Slow Newscast* podcast that he decided one baby had been deliberately attacked "immediately…straightaway".

By way of contrast, comments made by Dr Jane Hawdon, the consultant neonatologist who performed a pathology review on the infants, paint a very different picture. Hawdon sent an email to Ian Harvey, former Medical Director of the CoCH, on 14 February 2017 in which she explained that "there were insufficient details in records, and [it is] unlikely to have been possible to record in anything but real time to determine for each whether collapse and impossible resuscitation [was]:

a)   purely out of the blue and unexplained;

b)   a slowly deteriorating baby, e.g. infection, shallow breathing, but signs missed until baby collapsed…If subtle signs are missed or not escalated or responded too, in some cases alarms going off is too late. Sadly, even alarms are missed or ignored on occasions, which is below an acceptable standard of care;

c)   sinister cause, which seems to be the concern of paediatricians. This could range from a member of staff who for some reason was not spotting or escalating the babies in b) to active harm."

Bear in mind that Hawdon has conducted an extensive review which included examining the infants and has recorded gaps in information and numerous problems with determining the precise cause of death, while Dr Evans walked into a police station, and concluded "immediately" that there was inflicted harm.

Aside from the speed of his conclusion, Evans also made the curious statement to the National Crime Agency, writing: "I understand that the Royal College [of Paediatrics and Child Health] has been involved but from my experience the police are far better at investigating this sort of problem." It seems incomprehensible that a paediatrician would believe that the police are better at investigating medical issues than the Royal College of Paediatrics and Child Health (RCPCH).

Furthermore, Evans has offered his services to the National *Crime* Agency; he has told the National *Crime* Agency with whom he had been affiliated for three years that the *police* are better at investigating medical cases than the RCPCH, even though he has been a paediatrician throughout his career. He has then driven down to meet with Cheshire *Police*, he has told Cheshire *Police* in the Blacon *police station* "immediately", in his own words, that a child has been deliberately harmed, but has since claimed that he had no idea that a crime had been committed!

For example, when interviewed by Raj Persaud, Evans recounted telling the police: "I've got no idea what's going on here". Conversely, when speaking with TalkTV on 18 August 2023, Evans recollected that "I was aware that some criminal activity was suspected, obviously". And when I queried why he had shown preference to Cheshire Police over the RCPCH, Evans explained that "police are better at investigating incidents where a crime is suspected." According to his own accounts, Evans advised the police that it would be better for them to investigate than the RCPCH because a crime was suspected, but he also had "no idea" what was going on. He would then decide in 10 minutes at most that inflicted harm had definitely occurred.

We will return to the subject of Dr Evans shortly, but it's important to discuss the conspicuous lack of defence and character witnesses in favour of Letby. The fact that Letby's defence only called a plumber has become infamous, and in the immediate aftermath of the trial many stated that this was a reflection of the unwillingness of experts to speak in her favour. But this position is untenable; many experts now doubt the evidence and verdict presented in this trial.

What is even more puzzling is the failure of the defence to call neonatologist Dr Michael Hall to the witness box. Dr Hall is highly experienced, having been involved in the Ockenden Review, a public inquiry into maternity services. Hall was readily available to the defence and yet was never called. I spoke to Dr Hall in January 2026, and it quickly became evident that he had expected to be called: "My name was mentioned over 30 times on day three of the court case, clearly with the intention that I would be called as a witness." Had Dr Hall been disappointed that he hadn't had the opportunity to give evidence? "I was frustrated because I heard things that I would have challenged. Not only things said by Dr Evans and Dr Bohin, but also by Professor Arthurs and Dr Marnerides. I heard things said which were medically implausible."

Could the decision not to call him have been because Dr Hall would have supported the prosecution case? "All I can say in response to that is I didn't at any point assert or suggest that Lucy Letby had killed any of the babies. At no time in my reports did I say that I thought Lucy Letby was guilty of anything." I asked Hall whether he thought Letby had received a fair trial. "No, I don't think it was a fair trial. The jury should have been given the opportunity to hear evidence given by the prosecution being challenged. I don't think the trial met the expectations of natural justice." Not only was Hall not called, his reports were never seen by the jury. Dr Philip Hammond told Channel 5 that "to not let the jury read the expert reports seems very unfair".

It has become apparent following press conferences related to Letby's appeal that highly respected neonatologist Professor Neena Modi reached out to the defence but was not asked to give evidence in court. Others who wished to speak in favour of Letby were actively discouraged. One of Letby's childhood friends told Rachel Aviv at the *New Yorker* that she had asked Cheshire Police if she could serve as a character reference. "They weren't interested at all", the friend commented. This is consistent with a similar account provided to me by Michele Worden, who, as mentioned previously, found that the police were completely unreceptive when she approached them.

This was not the only incidence of positive character witnesses being discouraged. An NHS hospital informed a nurse who tried to support Lucy Letby that she shouldn't give evidence as it would harm her career. This nurse spoke glowingly of Letby to *The Daily Telegraph*, noting that Letby "got on really well with families and children and she used to get a lot of thank you cards from the families. She was always very good at building rapport and looking after babies was her passion, you could tell as soon as she walked on the ward. She loved it." Such testimony could have countered accusations and allegations made in court, yet it was actively discouraged by the nurse's NHS Trust. The nurse further described Letby as a "scapegoat", declared her belief that Letby is "innocent", and was bemused why "her defence doesn't seem to have called some of the witnesses that could have helped", declaring the case to be a "miscarriage of justice."

The *Daily Telegraph* article expanded on the wall of silence that continues to be shrouded around those that worked at the CoCH. One doctor who had worked alongside Letby indicated that he had been advised not to comment by the hospital. "Yes, I did work with Lucy, but I'm afraid I just can't say anything. I still work at the hospital and we've been asked and advised not to say anything about the case." Sir David Davis told *The Daily T* podcast on 4 February 2025 that he had encountered four nurses who wanted to give evidence in favour of Letby, "but they were told by their managers that it would not be good for them". Unit manager Karen Rees was another person who wanted to give favourable evidence, but she was never called to the trial.

Considering the failure to call defence witnesses, the acceptance of critical insulin allegations that are far from bulletproof and some meek arguments in court, there have been question marks regarding the defence that Letby was afforded. As criticism of the trial continued to proliferate in the mainstream press, *The Times* reported that friends of Letby were unhappy with the quality of her defence team and spoke to her about hiring different representation before her appeal application. It is, of course, supremely difficult for Letby to make that decision, given her situation.

Psychologist Dr Thea Gumbert offered some interesting insight on narratives in court and the lack of defence witnesses, drawn from her vast experience of working in the criminal justice system, including authoring over 1,200 psychological assessment reports for diagnostic and medico-legal purposes. Dr Gumbert has also written a PhD thesis on the behaviour of juries and explained her findings: "In my thesis on models of jury decision-making, the evidence shows that juries tend to favour one story over another. As the trial unfolds, they are persuaded to opt for one version of events, and that usually informs their decision-making. In this case, they were provided with a compelling story, delivered in a very persuasive manner, and when that wasn't countered then it can look very damning for the defendant because there is no counter-narrative."

Both barrister Mark McDonald and Dr Philip Hammond have spoken about the difficulty in attracting expert defence witnesses for potentially contentious court cases, particularly those involving children. Professor Carola Vinuesa provided some further insight: "During the Kathleen Folbigg case [Folbigg was wrongly convicted in Australia of murdering her children], efforts were made to find experts who would comment on cardiac genetics. But none of the local experts approached wanted to take part in a court hearing. Some of them had done it before and promised themselves that they'd never do it again. It's extremely taxing. It's often poorly remunerated, and sometimes not at all. You risk reputational damage. It takes an enormous amount of time to prepare and write the reports. There is huge pressure. In addition – and this is, of course, entirely understandable – doctors are often reluctant to speak out against their colleagues." It's interesting to observe that, in the second Folbigg legal inquiry, most experts who volunteered their services were international, in common with the panel of experts who have submitted reports related to the Letby case.

There has been significant criticism of the methodology Dr Evans employed to identify suitable cases for court. This will be discussed in following chapters, but it can be noted here that Evans "told police that if you harm a baby, it will deteriorate there and then…So I also identified a time and date when each had probably been harmed and told them they needed to find out who was on duty. If they found the same person was there *during lots of incidents* [my emphasis], they'd have a suspect." At this stage, it seems that Dr Evans didn't believe it was necessary for the same person to be on duty all the time, as was alleged regarding Letby during court proceedings; they merely need to be around during *lots* of incidents.

There are numerous problems with this, before we even examine the assertion that the deterioration of an infant can be almost automatically associated with deliberate harm. Firstly, by employing this methodology, no effort has been made to examine what the 'suspect' was doing. They may not have been assigned to the baby in question or even have been anywhere near it at the time of collapse or death, both of which did apply to Letby for some infants. The association can be entirely correlative, with no causality implied whatsoever. Additionally, Evans asked the police to seek someone who was around for "lots of incidents". This is, firstly, almost inevitable, meaning that the police would definitely identify a 'suspect', and, secondly, begs the obvious question of what would occur if no one was identified. What happens to all the so-called inflicted harm then? Is it then forgotten because the shift chart doesn't fit around it?

Also, the term 'lots' is undefined. In order for this to have any validity or credibility, a careful measurement of statistical significance is necessary; this bar was nowhere near met by the Cheshire Police investigation.

This approach to identifying a suspect is deeply concerning. "I think your use of the word 'inevitable' here is pretty much correct", Dr James Phillips told me. "The system for investigating this appears to be set up in such a way that reaching the conclusion of serial killer was far more likely than would be justified given the baseline probabilities." It is possible that if Letby had volunteered for fewer shifts at the hospital, and another nurse had done more than her, she would now be looking on in bemusement, still working at the CoCH, as the other nurse was prosecuted and then imprisoned.

It is also known that on several occasions babies collapsed or died when Letby wasn't even on duty, but the prosecution still argued that she could have been culpable. "The prosecution case is littered with incongruity and contradiction", I was told by a senior NHS professional.

Some of the medical testimony given in court by prosecution witnesses is now, since the involvement of Shoo Lee's panel, seen to be highly questionable. For example, in the case of Child J, Dr Evans claimed that there was no straightforward cause of the collapse, but instead of concluding that there was therefore no definitive explanation, he told the jury that it could be "consistent with some form of obstruction of her airways, such as smothering". This appears highly speculative, whereas Dr Evans was seemingly able to rule out what are clear clinical signs of natural deterioration, medical errors and infection across every infant in the court case. His explanation was always that Lucy Letby had deliberately attacked babies.

This lack of certainty likely proved critical when Letby was found not guilty of charges related to Child J. Yet the jury heard neither doubt from the prosecution, nor counter-argument from expert witnesses for the defence, in the overwhelming majority of cases. Elsewhere, Evans was unconditional in his diagnoses, even though other experts have since doubted, dismissed and even ridiculed many of his conclusions. For example, with regard to Child F who Letby was found guilty of attempting to murder, Evans told the court there were "astonishing" blood readings, and that "there's only one explanation for this; [Child F] had received insulin from some outside source". We know by now that this is contentious; many with more qualifications and experience doubt this conclusion. It appears far too definitive to state that there was "only one explanation", and this would surely have been contradicted if medical experts were available for the defence.

Evans has also changed diagnoses that were made in court since the trial took place. This is covered in some depth in "The Curiously Evolving Case of Child C".

Further post-trial comments from Evans have been rather curious. Evans told *The Slow Newscast* podcast that, "You should never, as a clinician, decide that you don't know the cause of death. What you should never do is to say, 'Well, this baby has died. I've no idea why he's died. It's all a bit unusual. But there we are.' That, to me, is not clinically acceptable." This is an extremely strange view, considering that a National Child Mortality Database Report, entitled *Sudden and Unexpected Deaths in Infancy and Childhood* found that "for sudden and unexpected infant deaths (under one year) that occurred during 2020, and had been fully reviewed by a Child Death Overview Panel…52% were classified as unexplained".

Professor Carola Vinuesa expressed a strong view on the assertions of Dr Evans: "The suggestion that babies are simple, and unexplained deaths must be due to murder once sepsis, haemorrhage and congenital abnormalities have been excluded, is simply not correct. Whole genome sequencing is recommended for infants and children with sudden unexplained death. In fact, now the NHS funds whole genome sequencing for cases of sudden unexplained death in infancy and childhood in England. Many of these cases are due to cardiac arrhythmias (irregular heartbeats). These cardiac arrhythmias can occur completely unexpectedly."

Michele Worden described the comments of Dr Evans as "scary", pointing out that pathologists were far more qualified to deem deaths unexplained or due to natural causes. Other medics also backed up the opinion of Professor Vinuesa. "It's not necessary to be an expert to conclude that the opinion of Professor Vinuesa makes a lot more sense than what Dr Evans said", one physician told me. "A large number of neonatal deaths, and even regular infants, are recorded as sudden and unexplained. I honestly have no idea what Evans is talking about." Dr Colin Ferguson also criticised Evans' view saying it was "ridiculous. It just beggars belief that you would say that."

Evans has, though, been fulsome in his praise for himself. He has told more than one interviewer that he enjoys a virtually unblemished record in the courtroom, furnishing John Sweeney with the information that he has "done over 40 cases for the defence and the prosecution – in relation to the prosecution every case I've supported involving murders, the death of children, has led to a prosecution", and similarly told Dr Philip Hammond that he has "never lost a murder, manslaughter or serious abuse case other than one when acting for the defence". It is interesting that he is apparently so proud of 'never having lost' a case, considering that his role should always be that of an independent witness.

Professor David Livermore told me that when he "was trained for legal work by Public Health England, it was emphasised that you provide factual evidence as best as you can. If you were asked for an opinion, you gave a balanced view. I've heard several interviews with Dr Evans, boasting about never 'losing' cases, when he'd been engaged as an expert. He clearly sees himself very much as partisan towards one side or another, rather than a professional trying to give a balanced opinion. He's acting more like a character witness for one side or the other."

Some may quibble slightly with the notion that his court record is blemish-free. Aside from the 'worthless' case discussed earlier, the contribution of Dr Evans was criticised in a case heard in the High Court of Justice in Northern Ireland. This case involved two young infants being "removed from the care of their mother" due to allegations of deliberate harm. Dr Evans had given evidence in this case, and the account of the appeal court does seem to indicate that he was rather hasty in his verdict, having changed his opinion seemingly entirely on the basis of seeing some photographs.

The trial judge at the time "was critical of Dr Evans, suggesting that his evidence should have been more considered and structured than in fact it was". It is notable that, according to the appeal verdict, Dr Evans, and a second expert, Dr Primrose, were "clearly unsure about expressing an opinion about whether the injuries were non-accidental but both did so because they had been asked to and were expected to do so". It was later noted in the verdict that "the trial judge in the present case was unimpressed by Dr Evans".

In December 2025, a new shaken baby syndrome case emerged, already a controversial diagnosis, in which allegations reported by Anouk Curry in *The Daily Telegraph* were made that Dr Evans had acted outside of his expertise. Philip Peace was jailed for life in February 2021 for the murder of his five-month-old daughter Summer, but both Peace and the mother of Summer maintain his innocence. This case also involved Dr Evans ruling out signs of pneumonia.

Medical witnesses required to give evidence should be circumspect in their views when there is any doubt, particularly when the potential consequences are serious. From what I've read, it appears Dr Evans is always certain that he is irrefutably correct, except when he changes his view, at which point his new opinion is correct. As an example, Dr Evans told Judith Moritz that Letby had "bloody murdered those babies" – when I spoke with Stephen Phelps, he described these insensitive comments as "disgraceful". Dr Evans also proclaims himself to have a virtually untarnished record of victory in court, and informed *Private Eye* that "had he been called in after the first unexplained death, he would have spotted it; Letby could have been stopped after one murder and many lives saved".

Evans is fairly withering in his views on those that question him. He told John Sweeney that "neonatologists who had nothing to do with the case" should essentially keep out of this matter because they "did not read the statements from the local nurses and doctors", although it's not clear why this matters or whether this includes the numerous statements that are supportive of Letby. He is critical of the experts who wrote to the Thirlwall Inquiry, stating that "none of the 24 people had anything to do with the trial". He told Dr Philip Hammond that the same group is guilty of "professional hubris of the worst order". He has been dismissive of statisticians and the Royal Statistical Society on several occasions, decrying them for both failing to understand the case, and for speaking from "ivory towers". He considers any criticism of his work to be "frankly astonishing", asserting that it is "led by people with the least amount of information about the cases". He is derisive towards anyone who questions him, describing them as "poundshop Poirots". And he even attacked the international panel of experts assembled by Dr Shoo Lee in a Channel 4 documentary, deriding them for being "hired guns".

Perhaps most bizarrely, Evans has attacked the more qualified Dr Michael Hall, the uncalled defence witness in Letby's court case, stating that he misunderstood his role in the case, and acted as Letby's advocate rather than an impartial expert. This is a fairly extraordinary claim, considering that Hall wasn't called by the defence, and the prosecution did not attempt to remove him from the process for lacking independence, as occurred with Evans himself. For Evans to make such accusations therefore seems a trifle hypocritical. In one slightly amusing exchange with Dr Philip Hammond, Evans states that he hopes a certain comment "doesn't sound partisan". It seems the ship may have sailed on that concern already…

Hammond himself notes that Evans "was first employed by the police to examine all the case notes", and "then employed by the Crown Court as an expert witness", a situation that should be a "clear conflict of interest" because it "gives a single expert witness huge power over a trial". Dr Colin Ferguson concurred with this view: "Dr Evans has been working on this by the time it came to court for over five years. And the whole idea of somebody coming up with a hypothesis and then driving it through all the way to conviction can't be right. He's been driving the whole process from the word go. The system should prevent that level of unnatural justice being perpetrated. Dr Evans should not have been the generator of the theory, the gatherer of the evidence, the chief witness – it's a one-man show. It's ludicrously inappropriate."

This is precisely why so much space has been devoted to Dr Evans in this chapter. Dr Evans is a significant factor in the conviction of Lucy Letby. As discussed previously, he provided the overwhelming majority of evidence in the case, and without him it's doubtful that Cheshire Police would have located an advocate.

Dr Svilena Dimitrova, an NHS consultant neonatologist, and Dr Roger Norwich were among five physicians who wrote to the GMC indicating their belief that Dr Evans had failed to provide balanced, impartial views, instead giving the court "opinions that would not be supported by most doctors". Dr Norwich also extended this assessment to Dr Bohin, while neonatologist Professor Neena Modi wrote in *The Guardian* that Dr Evans "drew selective conclusions which were not consistent with the full range of evidence". It is not known whether the GMC has provided a response.

If this seems unfair then consider the attitude of the system itself to fairness. Prior to the selection of Dr Bohin, Dr Martin Ward Platt was selected to work alongside Dr Evans. Ward Platt had previously presented evidence, notably supported by Professor Sir Roy Meadow, in the wrongful conviction of Angela Cannings. Ward Platt's evidence contributed to Cannings being convicted in 2002 of smothering her own children, but the conviction was rapidly overturned on appeal in December 2003. The name of Meadow may also be familiar to readers as he was principally responsible for the wrongful conviction of Sally Clark, who then, tragically, drank herself to death. Professor Carola Vinuesa told me that Meadow's work was also used in the wrongful conviction of Kathleen Folbigg. Ward Platt further gave evidence in the trial of Donna Anthony, also wrongfully convicted of murdering her own children.

Several healthcare professionals pointed out that Evans and Meadow were associates, most notably co-signing a letter to the GMC complaining about "frivolous complaints" against doctors. This is deeply ironic considering that criticism regarding Meadow proved to be anything but frivolous. Dr Ravi Jayaram also co-signed a different letter defending Meadow, which states that the signees "deplore the decision of the GMC to remove the name of Professor Sir Roy Meadow from the medical register". Dr Evans told Raj Persaud that Ward Platt was a "great guy" who was "highly regarded". I wonder if Angela Cannings and Donna Anthony, both of whom were convicted of murder and later exonerated in cases involving evidence provided by Ward Platt share the view that he was a 'great guy'? I guess the jury is out on that one.

During the interviewing process for this book, numerous credentialed and experienced experts called into question the contribution of Dr Evans to the conviction of Lucy Letby. Senior Coroner's Officer, Stephanie Davies, asserted that "had the coroner been allowed an active participation in Operation Hummingbird, he would likely have required someone more suitably qualified than a long since retired paediatrician". And neonatologist Professor Colin Morley stated plainly that Dr Evans was "not an expert neonatologist", and that he came nowhere near the standard of even one member of the expert panel, let alone the panel as a whole.

Dr Jonathan Moore was another medic who came to question the conviction of Lucy Letby when observing Evans speaking after the trial. This is significant as Dr Moore has been an expert witness since 2003. "Your duty to the court is to be completely impartial", Dr Moore informed me. "I therefore almost immediately concluded that something was very seriously wrong when I witnessed Dr Evans being interviewed on ITV's *Good Morning Britain*. I was shocked by his apparent boastful arrogance and his advocating what even initially seemed highly implausible personal opinions without any direct evidence. This seemed entirely unbefitting of a medical expert witness."

Since the conclusion of the Letby trial, the default reaction of Dr Evans to criticism has been to cite the fact that he saw the case notes, whereas none of his critics did. Evans repeatedly references the importance of the clinical notes but has yet to mention anything in public statements that isn't known already. If the clinical notes are so important, it should be possible for him to inform us of something in them of which we're not aware.

While emphasising the importance of the clinical notes, Dr Evans made the following statement in court: "An awful lot of the information that we now know is information that's come out in this trial, so therefore I think it is unrealistic to expect anybody to form a view that is absolutely correct in each of these cases. I wish I could. As I said, I've done these reports years ago, and the idea that I could get it all perfectly right simply from looking at notes is a little bit unrealistic…especially as I was not able to talk to any of the local nurses or staff. I had to rely on the notes completely…and I was never going to get everything 100% correct."

This seems an incredible admission, and also something which is practically the definition of reasonable doubt. Aside from the fact that Evans has conceded that he can't be expected to get everything correct from the materials provided – and remember that he never examined any of the infants directly – the Thirlwall Inquiry also noted that a detailed forensic case note review should constitute a "much broader inquiry [that] is taken into things that may not be in the case notes. They may be in unit records, staffing records, equipment records. There is more information available than just from the case notes themselves." However, Thirlwall attempted to use such information to question the reviews of pathologists whose work would usually be regarded as more relevant than that of Dr Evans.

There is so much that is deeply unsatisfactory about the trial of Lucy Letby and the prosecution and defence witnesses must rank pretty high on this lengthy list. Having corresponded extensively with the main prosecution witnesses in the Letby case, Dr Philip Hammond concluded that "experts can draw very different conclusions from the same evidence and it is important in these cases for the jury to listen to a range of experts – alongside all the other evidence – before a verdict can be fairly arrived at". Dr Hammond also stated that independent, and considerably more qualified, experts had arrived at completely different conclusions to Evans, as has become increasingly evident following the submission of reports from an international panel of neonatology experts.

Dr James Phillips likened the situation with Evans and Cheshire Police to scenarios he has witnessed in government bureaucracies: "There doesn't appear to be a serious effort to ensure that the case has been examined by an expert of the highest calibre, and certainly not a world authority, or someone that might be invited to a national conference. Instead, they have selected someone who appears to essentially just tick the boxes of having some qualifications.

"This can often happen when governments need a particular skill set. You can see some of this phenomenon in the composition of SAGE (Scientific Advisory Group for Emergencies) and bodies like Public Health England. While there were some very good scientists in there, a lot of them are people who happened to be in a particular bureaucratic position at the time the pandemic hit. For some of them, it has been many decades since they were actually involved in science. Equally, it should have been quite clear that Dewi Evans was not of sufficient calibre for a case of this magnitude."

It must also be reiterated that Cheshire Police should have actively sought a second opinion. It is one thing to have the evidence of Dr Evans acting as a plinth that supports the whole case; that is inappropriate enough in itself. But the failure to identify any conflicting opinions, or, indeed, any different views whatsoever can only be described as a massive and unforgivable failing. Even the chance for Cheshire Police to involve Professor Jane Hutton in the process was incomprehensibly spurned as will be discussed later.

In my opinion, the judicial process that resulted in the conviction of Lucy Letby bore very little resemblance to a fair trial. This would be concerning in any criminal case but must be considered far more serious when there are such enormous consequences for the convicted. The only thing that Letby's trial proved decisively is that the existing British criminal justice system does an extremely poor job of dealing with cases involving complex scientific and medical information, and that extensive reform is significantly overdue.

Furthermore, the parents of the deceased and harmed children deserve to know the truth. They have been carried along on a tidal wave of emotion, and if this has all been for nothing then they are another hugely damaged party as a result of this deeply unsatisfactory process. It is critical for them, Lucy Letby, our collective notion of justice, the judicial system, and the moral and ethical fibre of the entire nation and society for this case to be reassessed in an environment that enables the defendant to have equal expert representation as the prosecution.

We know only too well from recent history that court verdicts are far from bulletproof. When interviewed by *The Guardian*, Dr Evans himself openly asserted that miscarriages of justice can be readily associated with the criminal justice system: "Wanting to shoot the messenger is not an unsurprising response, especially given the criminal justice system's record of miscarriages of justice."

CHAPTER 7: STATISTICAL CASE AGAINST LUCY LETBY

I t's always Lucy, isn't it?

These words spoken by Dr Ravi Jayaram, and reported to Rachel Aviv of the *New Yorker*, were seen as prophetic at the time and the jury in the trial of Lucy Letby were presented with a shift chart that seemed to strongly confirm Jayaram's suspicions. This aspect of the prosecution case was repeated relentlessly in the popular press, and in online commentary both during and after the trial. One BBC report from August 2023 states uncritically that "Letby was always on duty". Even during the Thirlwall Inquiry, Dr Elizabeth Newby commented that "the conversation was then around the fact that [Letby] was always on duty when these events had happened". And as one example of the countless exchanges in which this was asserted in court, prosecutor Nick Johnson at one point asked Letby why it was "always" her that was on duty when incidents occurred.

The prosecution of Letby leant heavily on two statistical arguments. Firstly, that there had been an unusual and statistically significant spike in deaths. And, secondly, that Letby had been on duty for all of the collapses and deaths discussed in court. This was not only utilised as a central aspect of the prosecution; it was presented to the court as a *fait accompli*. It was supposedly an established fact, one that proved Letby's guilt more than any other aspect of the case. After all, who else could it have been?

Professor Richard Gill was instrumentally involved in the exoneration of the Dutch nurse Lucia de Berk, and he explained to me that the methodology used in the Letby case was chillingly foreshadowed by the wrongful conviction of de Berk. In the de Berk case, suspicions had been raised at Juliana Children's Hospital in The Hague after an initial spike in deaths. Interestingly, Professor Gill informed me that this institution, perhaps in contrast to the CoCH, had a venerable reputation. "It was the premier children's hospital in the Netherlands", Professor Gill said. "Very high profile, prestigious place, with the best doctors, the best apparatus, and knowledge base."

Once the initial alarm had been sounded, the sights of prosecutors began to be trained on de Berk. "It was believed that she had been there too often when suspicious things happened. So, actually, there was already the indication of a statistical coincidence from the very beginning of the investigation", Professor Gill explained.

Statistics had also been central to the infamous wrongful conviction of solicitor Sally Clark. Professor Jane Hutton told John Sweeney during a podcast that the cases of Letby and Clark are "fundamentally the same", and that the "Court of Appeal judgment makes the same mistakes" in both cases. Professor Hutton criticised the verdict of the Court of Appeal, saying: "The Court of Appeal asserted that it's a surprising coincidence that twins and triplets were ill at the same time. It's not a surprising coincidence. The triplets were what is called monochorionic – that means they had one placenta. Anybody can go to the Royal College of Obstetricians and Gynaecologists, look up the guidelines for monochorionic pregnancies – they are very high risk, even twins before they're born. They're much more likely to be ill or to die." Professor Hutton further reiterated that "medical experts have told me that this concentration of twins and triplets should never have been born on this unit".

Even Dr Evans conceded during the same podcast that "the Sally Clark case was an absolute disgrace". Meadow was struck off (but later reinstated) after providing profoundly flawed statistics during the Clark case. Professor Carola Vinuesa explained that Meadow's involvement had also been important in the wrongful conviction of Kathleen Folbigg: "In Kathleen's case, the statistical approach introduced by Roy Meadow was relied upon. His followers gave evidence, and it was quoted that the chance of four children dying from SIDS [Sudden Infant Death Syndrome] in a family would be one in a trillion. Yet if, for example, the cause is a genetic condition with autosomal dominant inheritance, that probability could become as high as one in 16."

The statistician and mathematician, Professor John O'Quigley, has worked across Europe and the United States in numerous universities, most notably in the University of California, San Diego and the University of Paris Sorbonne in France. Professor O'Quigley has been an outspoken critic of Letby's conviction, and when I spoke to him he described his distress with the case: "It was shocking to me, because of everything being based on statistics. It's also put together by people who have no clue what they're talking about when it comes to statistics. No clue. These were not professionals. No professional statistician would have supported any of the evidence."

I asked Professor O'Quigley why statistics seemed to be so central in many similar miscarriages of justice, and particularly involving nurses. "You always see the same blueprint used. It's always the same – there's a spike", Professor O'Quigley explained. "Then there's the chart showing presence. And then there is the method that comes much later. And that always involves something completely extraordinary and bizarre."

Despite the apparent prominence of statistical arguments in the Letby case, Dr Evans, amongst others, has frequently dismissed the notion that statistics were involved, telling Dr Philip Hammond that statistics "weren't relevant" to the case and also complained about "statisticians in their ivory towers". But there are numerous statements and items of information which indicate clearly that the entire case is, in fact, absolutely founded on statistics. One of those emanated from Dr Evans himself, who told the *Daily Mail* that "if they found the same person was there during lots of incidents, they'd have a suspect". Ironically, that in itself is a statistical assertion.

During the promotional film that Cheshire Police made about Operation Hummingbird, it becomes apparent that the chart produced in court, and the data related to it, was an important turning point. It was once this was assembled that several officers became convinced of Letby's guilt – "the only obvious person was Lucy Letby", one remarks. This also became clear during the Thirlwall Inquiry, when it was recounted by Hayley Frame, independent chairwoman of the Child Death

Overview Panel for Cheshire, that Nigel Wenham, formerly of Cheshire Police, knew it was "very much a matter for his officers" when he learned that one member of staff was on shift for a series of baby collapses.

Furthermore, paragraph 27 of the Court of Appeal judgment notes that "the applicant alone was present on the unit at the time of all of the deteriorations and deaths and was the common factor in all of the cases". And the initial discussion of the Cheshire Constabulary regarding Operation Hummingbird confirms the statistical spike that was referenced by consultants from the hospital, particularly Dr Stephen Brearey and Dr Ravi Jayaram which was also referred to during the meeting between the consultants and Nigel Wenham on 15 May 2017 (discussed in more depth in later chapters).

Statistical assertions were not only the defining aspect of accusing Letby in the first place; they were central to her conviction. It is untenable to claim otherwise. "If you remove the statistics, what points to Lucy?" Professor John O'Quigley told me. "Let me tell you – nothing points to Lucy Letby other than the statistics. And since they're completely wrong, you can only conclude there is nothing pointing at Lucy." In short, without the roster chart that was presented in court, there is no basis whatsoever to convict Letby. Prosecuting barrister Nick Johnson highlighted the central importance of the shift chart during the trial: "If the jury conclude that a certain combination of children were actually attacked by someone, then the shift pattern gives the answer as to who the attacker was."

One of the many odd arguments made by Dr Evans was that "if statistics were relevant I'd expect the prosecution to engage a statistician". But *The Guardian* was the first newspaper to report that Cheshire Police *had* recognised the importance of the statistical aspect of the case, and commissioned a statistical study to be conducted by Professor Hutton. The Cheshire Constabulary had signed a consultancy agreement with Hutton and agreed fees but later reneged on this agreement after the CPS advised them not to proceed. Cheshire Police commented: "The prosecutor does not agree with our line of inquiry and has instructed us not to pursue this avenue any further at present". Peter Green, emeritus professor of statistics at the University of Bristol, described this as an "extraordinary revelation".

Dr Steve Watts, a former senior detective who was also the national lead for police investigations in healthcare settings, was similarly stunned: "This episode is astonishing. The constitutional position is that the police investigate and gather relevant evidence which they present to the CPS, who review it and decide upon whether charges should be laid. Importantly, the CPS do not become part of the investigation, and they certainly have no right to instruct the police to do, or not do, anything. In fact, the code for Crown Prosecutors states explicitly that Crown Prosecutors cannot direct the police or other investigators.

"As an investigator at all levels, I have had many interactions with CPS lawyers. Sometimes there have been heated professional exchanges when disagreements occurred, but I have never been given an instruction by a CPS representative, nor have I heard of a colleague being given an instruction. If a CPS lawyer had done so, I would have refused and reported the matter to the Chief Prosecutor.

"This account from Jane Hutton raises red flags as to the conduct of the investigation, and how it was being led. It was, undeniably, wrong for the investigation to ignore this evidence that challenged the narrative. The fact that this exchange was not disclosed to the defence is also troubling."

Professor Hutton told me herself that she was thoroughly expecting to work on the case: "I had an email on 22 March 2018 in which Cheshire Police indicated that they wanted somebody to help them understand and assess the chances of sheer coincidence." Professor Hutton confirmed to me that Cheshire Police had simply informed her in July 2021 that they no longer wished to explore that avenue, a decision that she found perplexing. "The Criminal Procedure and Investigations Act 1996 specifically states that no one can tell the police to avoid looking into evidence which might provide evidence of innocence. And yet, of course, that's precisely what this instruction by the CPS did.

"Furthermore, the Department of Health published material in 2011 on what should be done when there is a spike. You need the right quality data from the start, and you must involve a statistician from the start. That is the official Department of Health position", Professor Hutton explained. When I asked her what this would constitute, her response was crystal clear: "You must have very precise definitions of what is meant by unexpected, unanticipated or sudden collapses, which I never saw. I was drip fed things about more babies being included, but not actually information that was necessary. And I was very clear with Cheshire Police about what needed to be done." Professor Hutton then walked me through an extensive list of factors which should have been included, before concluding that "you must collect and consider all of these things, or the chart that you produce has no merit".

The internet commentator TriedByStats has been a tireless exhibitor of the myriad problems with the Lucy Letby case, and played an instrumental role in BBC and Channel 4 documentaries. TriedByStats explained to me why the statistical aspect of the case is so important: "The medical evidence is ambiguous. It's not slam dunk at all. There is always a more likely natural explanation or cause. And in each case, the prosecution claims: 'Well, if it was just this one, I would agree with that, but look at all of these cases together'. And that is at the heart of the statistical problem with this case."

Before addressing this aspect of the trial, it is important to examine the spike in deaths at the hospital. Such spikes are not uncommon. As mentioned in an earlier chapter, the CoCH was one of 21 hospitals examined in 2015 via the MBRRACE standards due to increases in deaths.

On the subject of spikes in deaths at hospitals, Owen Jones reported in *The Guardian* in January 2023 on the "excess death rate" in Britain, in the same month an investigation began into two spikes in neonatal mortality in Scotland; David Strain wrote for the *British Medical Journal* on excess deaths in April 2023; there was a spike in baby deaths at Royal Stoke University Hospital in May 2023; and two A&E departments in Shropshire were forced to address a spike in deaths in January 2024. Other historical spikes in avoidable maternity deaths occurred at Morecambe Bay, Shrewsbury and Telford, East Kent, Northwick Park Hospital, Nottingham University Hospitals NHS Trust and Leeds

Teaching Hospitals NHS Trust. Just months before the publication of this book, 55 'avoidable' baby deaths were documented in a scandal at the University Hospitals Sussex NHS Foundation Trust.

John Ashton was required to address several such healthcare failures in his position as Regional Public Health Director. "As an example, I had to suspend the breast screening service at Carlisle when some women were given erroneous breast cancer results due to failures by doctors on the unit," Professor Ashton recounted. But the notorious scandal at Morecambe Bay has the most obvious parallels with the CoCH, with the avoidable deaths of 11 babies and one mother involved. Ashton continued: "It was when I visited the medical director of Morecambe Bay that I began to notice fundamental failings. He had recently received notice of babies that had died three or four months before. It was incredible that this was only happening at that time, and not at the time of death. Then I recognised some of the communication problems, simple things that could have been addressed, but were not."

Random clusters of unexpected deaths can and do occur. In a letter addressed to the Thirlwall Inquiry, Dr Andrew Garrett, the president of the Royal Statistical Society, and Sarah Cumbers, its chief executive, warned of the dangers associated with inferring conclusions from such data: "It is far from straightforward to draw conclusions from suspicious clusters of deaths in a hospital setting – it is a statistical challenge to distinguish event clusters that arise from criminal acts from those that arise coincidentally from other factors, even if the data in question was collected with rigour." One example of this was Sherwood Forest Hospitals NHS Foundation Trust which was placed in special measures after death rates soared between 2013 and 2015. Professor Jane Hutton also divulged "messages from colleagues at the RSS" which indicated to her concern that the Letby case was "essentially a re-run of previous miscarriages of justice".

Professor John O'Quigley told *The Trials of Lucy Letby* podcast that "the inexplicable spike is entirely explicable". Having studied the issue in more depth, he later concluded that "there was in fact no evidence of anything extraordinary having taken place and that the belief in an inexplicable spike is based on an elementary, and very common, statistical misconception". O'Quigley indicated that the CoCH should have been compared with other poorly performing Trusts, rather than the NHS average, noting that "in 2014, one centre already showed a spike the same as that seen at the CoCH, while another suffered a spike far worse".

Professor O'Quigley continued: "Spikes in deaths can be attributable to conditions. They usually *are* attributable to conditions! The Royal College of Paediatrics and Child Health pointed out, as many others have, that there were very unfavourable conditions at the hospital. There are obvious risk factors, which I don't think anyone denies, they just haven't been included in any aspect of statistics related to the case.

"The units performing the poorest will change from one year to the next. But whichever one comes bottom – if you're going to start comparing the mortality there and rate of collapses with the average, it's going to be wrong. It will tell you there's a spike, obviously, compared to the average. It will look very far removed from the average. Any spike must be assessed in a meaningful context. The poorest performer is explicable in terms of a lot of risk factors."

When I put it to Professor O'Quigley that if you were to perform an experiment where you put millions of cases into a statistical model, then, inevitably, the dataset would produce similar spikes to the CoCH, and indeed worse, he responded emphatically: "Yes, that is absolutely certain. Everything you said is correct. If you look at the analysis of MBRRACE, you see a lot of variability year in, year out, from within a centre. A given centre is not stable across time. It's not in stasis. It jumps up and down.

"However, if you look at 2015, the CoCH was the worst performer within the NHS system. But it was close. The gap between worst and second worst was very small. So that suggests we are not looking at what statisticians refer to as an 'outlier'. The situation at the CoCH looks entirely compatible with all of the rest of the information across all of the other hospitals. We're not seeing something so strikingly unusual that we would have to conclude that the CoCH is really out on a limb. This applies to other years as well – there was a very similar result from another hospital in the previous year."

Similarly, TriedByStats produced research examining MBRRACE data, which indicated that the CoCH wasn't even in the top 10 hospitals for excess deaths in 2014-15. "This indicates that hospitals, unfortunately, have spikes in deaths", he informed me. "And the data actually makes it very clear that hospitals are very rarely stable. Very few hospitals have no change from one year to another, they actually do vary, almost inevitably, quite a bit. And you would expect that because you're looking at an immensely complex scenario with many different variables, and the circumstances are never the same.

"There is also indication from Thirlwall and elsewhere that the hospital did have an increase in babies with more serious conditions. There is evidence from court that the hospital ordered more insulin tests because the hospital was going through twice as much insulin as it was the years before. And one of the notes from Dr Gibbs indicates that, in prior years, they would send sicker babies away. So I don't think you can even compare that year to the previous years." Indeed, a draft CoCH report from July 2016 records "increased acuity within the second half of 2015", and that "a sustained increase in low birth weight admissions (less than 2,000g) also corresponded with the increase in mortality levels".

The notion, therefore, that the situation at the CoCH was some unimaginable spike is extremely poorly founded. But it's also important to note that there were many more collapses and deaths than those which ultimately appeared in the court case. The official figure of neonatal deaths at the CoCH has fluctuated depending on the reporting mechanism, but one chart submitted to the Thirlwall Inquiry indicates that there were ultimately 18.

Letby was found guilty of seven murders, so it is immediately clear that over 60% of the deaths on the unit are attributable to other reasons. As discussed elsewhere, poor care was described in relation to some of the infants in the trial, and Letby was found not guilty on several of these counts. It is clear from Thirlwall documents that the original intention was to charge Letby with more cases than ultimately appeared in the court case. It is therefore extremely difficult to extricate such explanations from the infants that Letby was found guilty of harming, particularly when a statistical case has been advanced that Letby was 'always there', but then a picture emerges where she cannot be linked with the vast majority of collapses and deaths on the unit.

There were 11 deaths associated with the unit for which the prosecution and investigation concluded that Letby was not to blame. Several of these infants featured clinical conditions that are either linked with those babies who were part of the court case, or that have even been asserted by the prosecution in court. Extreme prematurity, pneumonia, sepsis, hypoxic-ischaemia and respiratory distress are also in the original post-mortem in relation to infants that were not part of the court case. Similarly, widespread hypoxic/ischaemic damage to the heart and lung immaturity were reported for Child C, and there was a very similar prognosis for Child I, pneumonia for Child D, necrotising enterocolitis for Child E, prematurity for Child P and rupture of subcapsular haematoma coupled with prematurity for Child O. It was only the death of Child A that was considered 'unascertained' and it is now known, as will be discussed in coming chapters, that this infant's mother was suffering with the immune system disorders antiphospholipid syndrome and systemic lupus erythematosus, the infant struggled with severe respiratory problems from birth and there was a catalogue of failings in care as well.

In short, when the unit as a whole over the time period associated with the case is adequately examined, it is impossible to produce a chart that in any way resembles the one presented in court. The distribution of collapses and deaths is completely different, and Letby is certainly nowhere near as ubiquitous as is implied by the fallacious material used by the prosecution.

With this in mind, the selection of cases for the court case has inevitably come under scrutiny. In September 2024, it was reported that 25 further "cases of concern" had been passed to Cheshire Police but no further action was ultimately taken. This can be added to the additional 4,000 cases the constabulary has since examined, and the countless collapses and deaths that occurred which have been conceded are not remotely related to Letby. It's suddenly looking quite a lot less as if it was 'always Lucy'.

Another problem is that the name of Lucy Letby was, undeniably, written all over the medical records that were used to select cases. This would be problematic anyway, but we also know that Dr Stephen Brearey had been actively involved in passing cases to investigators, as reported by *Vanity Fair* and many other sources. It is difficult to see how this selection of cases could do anything other than steer the investigation; as noted by Professor O'Quigley the chart "was put together initially by the consultants – the accusers of Lucy Letby".

Dr Evans has always maintained that he was unaware of Lucy Letby's name when he began working with Cheshire Police. When we questioned him on this, Evans wrote that he was "unaware of Letby's name until July 2018", and was keen to emphasise that this was after what the prosecution described as his "sift reports" on all cases other than the second insulin case.

However, when Evans spoke during a podcast with John Sweeney and Edward Abel Smith, he conceded that Letby's name was "in a good number" of the case notes, but that it "didn't stand out". Evans also submitted his witness statement to Cheshire Police on 3 July 2019; by this time Letby had already been arrested twice, and yet Evans still wrote more reports, some of which altered or introduced new methods of inflicted harm, even after this date.

Another problem noted by Professor O'Quigley is that "we have no definition of what constitutes a suspicious case. If you're trying to show who is present when a suspicious event occurs, you need to define what you mean by a suspicious event. And the only definition we seem to have is Lucy's presence. So if her presence is defining an event that is 'suspicious', we're not looking at all the events. We're looking at a small subset of the events – only the ones involving Lucy Letby."

Professor O'Quigley expanded on this important concept: "My feeling is that the starting point was not whether the event was suspicious, the starting point was Lucy. Evans has always maintained that he didn't know about Lucy's presence. But in his interview with John Sweeney, he backtracked and recognised that her name was everywhere, so he knew exactly which cases she was involved with. And, of course, the majority of the cases had been given to him precisely because she was there, by someone who had long since suspected her. That changes everything." Professor O'Quigley similarly told John Sweeney that "Unconscious bias is, by definition, unconscious. But [Letby's] name is all over the place, and it will be in the documents he's looking at, certainly in most of them. The police will know her name – that will have been conveyed via the consultants. So there's no way that the chart has any value."

TriedByStats further exposed a fascinating exchange that was recounted in court, during which Dr Evans makes the following statement: "Which room is the baby in at the time the nurse was on shift?" before then asking, "What other medical staff were in the room for the duration of the shift?" This points to two things: firstly, it is crystal clear that Evans has been told that this is an investigation into a nurse. Secondly, this is made even clearer by the separation of "other medical staff". This exchange, again, makes it clear that the 'other medical staff' are not being considered; they are neither suspects in the investigation, nor of any real relevance. All that matters is the activities of 'the nurse'. As confirmation of this, it was recounted in court on 23 March 2023 that Evans had written in his second and third reports for Child P that "it is necessary to scrutinise nursing care during the night shift of 23 and into 24 June". There was no mention of any doctors.

Documents submitted to the Thirlwall Inquiry demonstrate that the selection of cases prior to any police investigation was problematic. The very first day of Thirlwall revealed that the deaths originally deemed worthy of suspicion and further review did not overlap perfectly with the cases that Letby was ultimately charged with. It's important to remember here that many of the infants in the trial, and the so-called non-indictment babies, featured very similar symptoms, clinical traits and recorded causes of death.

During a neonatal review held in January 2016, Eirian Powell informed Dr Stephen Brearey that she had "amended the last list to ensure that we have included ALL of the babies that have died on the unit within this timeframe". And when Dr Jane Hawdon was interviewed during the inquiry, she confessed that when she conducted her examination she had no notion of why cases had been passed to her: "I did not know why they were selected other than they were the deaths and near misses that [Ian Harvey] had referred to in the first email."

An email chain from February 2017 involving Dr John Gibbs outlines a somewhat befuddled Gibbs attempting to explain how he collaborated with Children's Unit Manager, Anne Martyn, and other consultants to select cases involving unexpected collapses. The main problem expressed in this email is that none of the lists corresponded, and no one could even agree what constituted an unexplained collapse: "Although I thought we had highlighted about six inadequately explained patients, the attachments contain 17! But I thought the number was closer to 30 (or even more)."

Under these circumstances, it is not at all surprising that statisticians have been critical of the methodology used by Cheshire Police. Professor Jane Hutton told David Conn and Felicity Lawrence that any proper statistical inquiry should not have concentrated on one member of staff from its onset, and should instead have included "all possible explanations for any increase in babies collapsing including their medical conditions and prematurity, as well as the performance of the unit".

Professor Richard Gill told me: "You have to ask why, how, when and by whom these events were classified as being suspicious. And, actually, we know. Because it was the consultants that collected the events. So the stack of paper which went to the police was already biased against Lucy, and it had been prepared by her accusers at the hospital. The police spreadsheet was just the latest version of the chart that Brearey had already started compiling when he concluded that it was odd that Lucy was present again."

A statistical paper that Professor O'Quigley shared with me, entitled *Use of roster charts in the investigation and prosecution of nurses suspected of inflicting deliberate harm on patients*, concluded that "any such study, in order to claim validity, would require the implementation of a carefully constructed experimental design. A considerable amount of training and experience in epidemiology and statistics would normally be required." It hardly needs to be stated that no one from Cheshire Police quite met this level of expertise.

Another O'Quigley paper published in October 2024 found that even if 100 of the world's top neonatal pathologists had reviewed the full complement of 61 case notes, the chance that any of them would have produced a roster associating Lucy Letby with 25 cases would be 0.1%. This indicates there is a 99.9% probability that the roster included a non-trivial number of cases where Letby's presence was the primary factor used to determine whether a particular case was to be viewed as suspicious. O'Quigley notes that "all other explanations were quickly dismissed with little or no further investigation of any kind".

If one was similarly selective with other nurses who worked at the CoCH, it is perfectly possible to produce an equally damning chart for several of them which, equally, would have no statistical or evidential merit. This was observed by Dr Alexander Coward, a former maths lecturer at the University of Oxford and University of California Berkeley: "You could make a chart like that for any nurse in any hospital. All you would have to do is only focus on the times when something went wrong when that nurse was on duty and ignore all the times that nurse was on duty and everything was fine. You don't need a PhD in statistics or maths to know that this is dreadful."

Additionally, doctors on the unit were never considered as suspects. This may be logical on certain hospital units, but on a neonatal unit consultants should be considerably more hands-on. There is also, clearly, far more likelihood of sudden collapses, and so it is therefore far more feasible that medics will be around when babies deteriorate. Yet it is clear, as will be seen throughout this book, that the doctors on the unit were never suspects. This is despite the fact that staff raised concerns about a doctor who "features in a number of cases of babies who collapse", as reported in *The Daily Telegraph*. The Thirlwall Inquiry later revealed this conversation to have occurred in an email chain between Sian Williams, Sue Hodkinson and Eirian Powell, with the doctor in question being named in the document. Two months before this, the anonymised Dr G and Dr H were observed in a neonatal review authored by Eirian Powell "to be involved in many of the mortalities". I am not for one second suggesting that any of these doctors engaged in malicious acts – the odds are massively against this – but if there was to be a criminal investigation, it should not have zoomed in on one nurse; it should have been all-encompassing.

During the Thirlwall Inquiry, on 5 November 2024, Dee Appleton-Cairns indicated that a wider-reaching shift chart had previously existed. "The spreadsheet that I saw…did not look like the one that was presented to the jury, it was far more comprehensive, there were far more dates on there, there were far more babies on there, there were far more staff on there, including doctors as well." Letby herself observed in a letter following her grievance procedure that she was "disappointed to have discovered within my grievance that analysis tables relating to the mortality rates had columns 'amended'…with information relating to the involvement of medical staff being 'removed'."

The next problem with the shift chart presented in court was that Lucy Letby worked more shifts than any other nurse on the unit. This was stated explicitly during the court case; for example, on 26 January 2023, an anonymous nurse outlined the following: "We had massive staffing issues where people were coming in and doing extra shifts. It was mainly Lucy that did a lot as she was one of only three Band 5 nurses that had done the neonatal course. Lucy was young, living in halls, saving to buy a house, she was single, able to swap, willing and wanting to do extras."

Speaking at the Thirlwall Inquiry on 7 October 2024, the anonymised Dr ZA agreed that Letby "did more shifts and she was one of the few nurses with the intensive care qualification who wasn't a shift leader, so was more likely to be looking after the sick babies". Ten days later, on 17 October, Eirian Powell reported to Thirlwall that "when we got busy [Letby] did the overtime, so she was there more often. There was a lot of staff that did part-time so they were [there] less so. But she was there more often by working full-time and overtime." Nurse Margaret Kitching also included in her statement to Thirlwall that Letby "was full-time, and that there were a lot of part-time staff". A neonatal unit review authored by Eirian Powell, and published on 5 May 2016, noted that "LL works full-time and has the Qualification in Speciality (QIS). She is therefore more likely to be looking after the sickest infants on the unit. LL also avails herself to work overtime when the acuity or unit is over capacity." In a later statement submitted to the Thirlwall Inquiry, the anonymised Nurse X noted that "our ratio of QIS trained to non-QIS trained staffing was poor compared to other units". Similarly, nurse Laura Eagles observed that Letby "was a full-time member of staff with QIS, therefore it would not be unusual to be involved with the sickest babies". This was again referenced by Eirian Powell in a report related to Letby's grievance procedure in November 2016: "They had assigned the sickest babies to LL because of the high standard of her care."

Lucy Letby was simply one of the few adequately trained and full-time nurses on the unit, despite being relatively inexperienced. This was once again acknowledged by the CoCH's former director of corporate and legal services, Stephen Cross: "The nurse is one of a few who are full-time and regularly worked overtime…The nurse is highly qualified, so tended to look after the sicker babies." In fact, it was revealed during the grievance procedure for Letby that she didn't seem concerned by her "commonality" in certain incidents: "LL didn't seem concerned as she was full-time plus overtime". Eirian Powell had clearly rated Letby's nursing skills very highly, and during the same meeting with Dr Christopher Green informed her that "because you're good at your job, you get put in the position of looking after the sickest babies". The message here for nurses is simple – don't earn qualifications, don't undertake training, don't be good at your job and don't work hard!

All of the criticism in this chapter would apply if Letby was actually on duty and in attendance during the times when the prosecution claimed suspicious events occurred. But that is simply not the case. Way back in 2016, it was acknowledged by Stephen Cross that "the allegation against [Letby] was based on her having been present on the unit disproportionately frequently, not necessarily caring for the baby, at the time of the collapse". Similarly, during the grievance procedure meeting between Dr Green and Yvonne Griffiths on 17 October 2016, Griffiths explained that "in some of the cases, Lucy wasn't providing care and the baby had already deteriorated before she was present". Griffiths further explained one possible reason for this: "If a nurse goes on a break they do everything before they go, but then someone else is assigned in case the bell goes and so names are attached."

Anyone encountering this for the first time might assume that such infants and cases were eliminated from the case before it went to court. Well, don't make such rash assumptions! Infants C, D, H, I, J, M and N all experienced incidents outside of the hours that Letby was even working, there are countless examples of Letby being accused of deliberately harming infants at times when she wasn't the designated nurse for a baby and she also wasn't present when Child F was allegedly poisoned by her. As has been established, if there was a scenario in which a baby collapsed, and Lucy Letby couldn't be shown to be present (although, as will be demonstrated in "Swipe-Card Data Falls Apart", the methodology for achieving this was, at best, highly suspect), it simply didn't feature in the court case. It *couldn't* feature in the court case because the prosecution placed considerable emphasis on the notion that Letby was always present when things went wrong and cross-examined her numerous times on this basis. Another example of a basic error in the roster chart involves an unexpected collapse for Child J on the day shift of 17 December 2015, when, it is now established, Letby wasn't on duty.

As discussed previously, if everything related to all infants who died on the unit during the period was added to the shift chart, each of the collapses were included, all of the incidents where Letby wasn't present were incorporated, incidents where it was logistically impossible to commit an attack were excluded and it was made clear that Letby wasn't even working when certain things occurred, then the shift chart that was presented in court would look completely different. It would, as Professor O'Quigley has stated, be impossible to recreate the chart that was used during the trial.

"The shift chart is simply a physical manifestation of their flawed procedure, and it's also flatly wrong", TriedByStats commented. "Letby is not there many times when they identified a so-called suspicious event. As an example, for one of the insulin poisonings, it is claimed that she poisoned a bag of dextrose. But as she supposedly put insulin in it, the people who hung up the bag are marked as not present on the shift chart – I believe it was Caroline Oakley and Samantha O'Brien. They're the ones that gave it to the baby. The people actually administering the supposed poison are marked as not present. Yet the person who through this elaborate theory, they claim, put the poison in the bag, is marked as present. It's completely contrived. It's not objective data. The data is cherry-picked, twisted, and contorted, so that it leads itself to a pre-determined conclusion." In accordance with this, defence barrister Ben Myers noted in court that the chart "isn't a piece of evidence…it's a presentational aid designed by the prosecution for the prosecution to say what they want".

In November 2024, it was revealed that an audit of baby deaths at the CoCH discovered many of the most rapid deteriorations occurred when Letby was not on duty. This mortality data had been gleaned from multiple sources, including Freedom of Information requests. The data was then solidified by an exceptional piece of reporting in *Unherd* by the journalist David Rose, which established that Letby wasn't in the hospital when 10 of the 28 incidents described as "suspicious" took place. It later emerged that the information for this article had been derived from an actual shift chart of Lucy Letby sent to Peter Elston by none other than Dr Dewi Evans. And in his closing speech in court, Myers made reference to multiple collapses for which Letby was not on duty.

In the case of Child A, Evans found that the child began to deteriorate at 5pm, prior to Letby's arrival at the hospital. For Child B, Letby had left the CoCH before the period at 9:30pm on which Cheshire Police were told to focus inquiries by Dr Evans. There is an extensive chapter to come on the prosecution case related to Child C, which includes the information that Dr Evans changed the day on which Letby supposedly attacked the infant during the trial, as she wasn't working on 12 June 2016. Dialogue with police indicates that Evans had cited an errant UV line which occurred when Letby wasn't working. In fact, she hadn't even been on duty since the birth of the infant.

Child I deteriorated overnight on 22 October 2015 in common with many of the other infants in the case, but not while Lucy Letby was working. Similarly, Letby was not on duty for the key incidents associated with Child O, although there are serious question marks regarding whether these alleged incidents have any validity whatsoever. And when she was around, "just because a chart states she's on duty, it doesn't mean she's anywhere near a particular baby", Professor Colin Morley observed.

This information is critically important. Firstly, it means that for several incidents outlined in the court case, there would need to be at least two serial killers on the loose at the CoCH for this version of events to be logistically possible. Secondly, several cases and incidents that were discussed in court were entirely predicated on the assertion that Letby was always on duty. As has been established, no one witnessed her commit any of these alleged acts, and all of them are completely hypothetical. The ubiquitous presence of Lucy Letby was used throughout the prosecution case and cross-examination of the defendant as supposedly damning evidence of her guilt. But actually, this simply doesn't stand up to any scrutiny.

Any claim related to statistics not forming part of the prosecution case in the Letby trial is baseless to the point of being absurd. This was the centrepiece of the prosecution's argument; it was the keystone around which their entire case was constructed. In an interview with *Times Radio*, Professor O'Quigley observed: "If you look at the opening statements of the chief prosecutor, Nick Johnson, and his closing statements, he leans very, very heavily on statistics." As an example, Johnson asserted: "These rapid collapses and deaths always happened when Lucy Letby was in close proximity", which we now know not to be the case. This supposedly statistically consistent presence of Letby was also referenced repeatedly throughout court proceedings, and particularly strongly in the cases of the first few infants discussed.

It would therefore make sense for statistics to be used competently. In accordance with this, a report by the House of Lords Statutory Inquiries Committee, entitled *Public inquiries: Enhancing public trust* asserts that "inquiries should make use of statistical expertise", while "an inquiry's terms of reference should include information about how statistical evidence will be investigated and handled". The Royal Statistical

Society primer on *The use of statistics in legal proceedings* asserts that "when conclusions…are drawn from data, it is crucial that the data and the reasoning supporting those conclusions are transparent". There is no conceivable way that any statistician would endorse the methodology for the statistical case made in court, which is why so many professionals affiliated with the RSS have made scathing criticisms.

Professor Jane Hutton told *The Guardian* the shift chart used in court is "a large pile of crockery, much of which is broken. Such a pile does not hold water, however big it is." Professor Burkhard Schafer, a law professor at the University of Edinburgh who studies the intersection of law and science, informed *The Daily Telegraph* that "the weak statistical evidence 'shored up' or compensated for any concerns with the other evidence". And in May 2025, eight statisticians collaborated with Dr Philip Hammond on an article which made swingeing criticisms of three core aspects of the prosecution case.

Professor John O'Quigley informed me that "as soon as I looked at the chart, I thought: 'this is ridiculous'! This is not possible. There is no way they can possibly obtain a conviction here. But they did. It is clear to me that a roster chart like this should never be shown to any jury for the simple reason – they will not understand it. Most people don't understand, unless they're given time. I can only ever see such charts being used in an incorrect way, and leading to errors in justice.

"That single row of crosses against Lucy Letby's name has no value at all. It has no scientific value, it has no statistical value. However, there is other information in the chart, which is on the presence of other nurses during suspicious events, and that tells us a lot. What I have been able to derive from that is that if you look at those nurses working 33% more than the average then they are exactly the same as Lucy Letby. The probability of them being around for the same number of incidents as Letby is exactly the same. Essentially, with selectivity you could construct a similar chart for them."

Professor Peter Green, emeritus professor of statistics, and former president of the RSS, has also been strongly critical: "My concerns about these data are…what was the selection of an event as being suspicious?

Were all of these nurses actually on ward duty? Why are the doctors not visible in this chart? All of those things seem to us [at the RSS] to be potentially sources of bias. But the main thing is that there's no other information about all of these suspicious events, or other information about the infants concerned. When we're teaching statistics, we show our students good and bad practice. And this spreadsheet, as presented in the courtroom, is a lovely example of how not to do something!"

The inclusion of Professor Green is notable, as not only is he a statistician at Bristol University, but he was also part of a group that wrote the *Healthcare serial killer or coincidence?* report which was published by the RSS regarding the use of statistics in cases of suspected medical misconduct. This paper was partly prompted by the prosecution of Lucia de Berk, with its aim being to help legal teams present data correctly. Its chief executive at the time, Stian Westlake, noted that some members of the RSS viewed the Letby case as one that could replicate errors made in court previously. William C. Thompson, one of the authors of the RSS report and an emeritus professor of criminology, law and psychology at the University of California, Irvine, had previously told the *New Yorker* that medical-murder cases are particularly prone to errors in statistical reasoning. With this in mind, the RSS provided the prosecution with a copy of the report ahead of the Letby trial.

Unfortunately, there is little evidence the prosecution paid any heed to the report. Professor Gill told *The Guardian* that "the police investigation and CPS made all the mistakes the RSS warned about. Nobody studied the statistics in a professional way." Professor Gill cited the "eight recommendations on how to avoid bias in healthcare serial killer cases", and encouraged "everyone to read it".

When I asked Professor Gill if there was any evidence that the prosecution had read it, he answered in the negative: "No! I know that they paid no attention to it. I met somebody high up in the CPS at a meeting which the RSS held. And during a break, I spoke to a top guy from the CPS, and he told me that they are not using statistics in the Letby case because nobody understands them. So the CPS, the police, the defence lawyers, and the prosecution barrister, they all knew in advance about our report, and it's probable that none of them understood it. They probably don't even understand that they *did* make statistical arguments in the preparation of the case and in court!"

Speaking to *The Times*, Professor Green also stated it was clear that the standards the RSS had recommended were not applied in presenting Letby's shift roster to the court. "Whatever the truth here, it is clear that the investigation and prosecution did not follow the good practice laid out in our report."

Professor O'Quigley added that "the report did make a number of very sensible recommendations. I was very impressed by how well written it is, because it's carefully constructed in a way that is not technical. They really make it accessible. There is no reason for it not to be read. And had its advice been taken, we wouldn't be having this conversation, and we would never have heard of Lucy Letby.

"The chart does not show what it claims to show. That's one of the reasons I called the chart a fake at an RSS meeting. It has no validity as evidence. It is worthless. I said this at an RSS meeting, and no one disagreed with me."

It is not as if problems with the roster chart weren't raised before the case reached court. A service review for the CoCH included one anonymous commenter noting that "the significance of this one nurse being rostered on shift at the time of each of the deaths had not been investigated via a thorough process, and is only one individual senior consultant's subjective view…It's important that we recognise that these allegations were only hearsay, and have no substance."

When considering this catalogue of blunders, it is important to remember that Cheshire Police were initially asked to "exclude unnatural causes". In accordance with this, it has often been reported that deaths on the unit ceased when Letby was moved into an administrative role. But not only are the reasons for this understood – the unit was downgraded, and so was no longer dealing with the same level of vulnerable infants – it was even anticipated at the time.

Legal representative, Corinne Slingo, had told numerous key personnel from the CoCH in July 2016 that "there is a likelihood that, having changed the admissions criteria to remove the highest risk of sub 32-week neonates…that the mortality rate will drop significantly in any event, and that could easily be interpreted as being due to the removal of the individual, as the timescales coincide. That may make life much more difficult for her, and also for the Trust in trying to identify the true cause of the spike in mortality for this group of babies." Echoing this argument, Ian Harvey informed Dr Jane Hawdon in February 2017 that the consultants "are being selective and disingenuous in that there is no comparison between the intensity of the workload before and after we downgraded the unit and we believe that they are trying to suggest that the only significant change has been reassigning the member of staff (which we did to protect that member)."

There was also one dissenting voice among the consultants that ultimately pushed for the situation to receive a police referral. Dr John Gibbs doubted the statistical validity of concerns raised primarily by Dr Stephen Brearey on several occasions. In commentary at the Thirlwall Inquiry on 1 October 2024, Gibbs observed that "there were some deaths and collapses that I knew she wasn't around at the time", and even more tellingly that "I felt sympathy for Letby at that time because I felt she had been unlucky to have been involved in a number of incidents. It can happen to any of us, and it's happened to me during my career." Similarly, when cross-examined by defence barrister Ben Myers, Gibbs conceded that it was "difficult" to contact the police because "Nurse Letby seemed to be involved in all the cases that involved me!"

In an email conversation with numerous key personnel from the CoCH in July 2016, Gibbs demonstrated that he was astute enough to at least attempt to understand the probabilities involved in the concerns being expressed by Dr Brearey in particular, while also conceding that "my stats isn't good enough". Nonetheless, Dr Gibbs attempted to argue why "the increase in neonatal mortality that we have experienced over the last 18 months might be within 'expected' statistical variance", and also that "using Chi-squared analysis the difference is NOT statistically significant".

Later, in February 2017, Dr Gibbs again questioned the statistical coincidence that underpinned the suspicions of consultants: "Lucy did not feature prominently in the staff correlation analysis of those collapses." The assertions of Gibbs were further reflected by comments made in relation to a service review in September 2016: "I am not convinced this was anything other than a random fluctuation which has almost certainly occurred in previous years."

While extensive, this chapter is by no means an exhaustive account of the statistical problems associated with the Letby case, nor of the expert condemnation of what was allowed to be presented in court. It is in my view quite surprising that Dr Evans has argued, repeatedly, that statistics are unrelated to the case, while he has also stated that the police should find someone who was around for "a lot" of collapses, as the foundation for how the police should identify a suspect.

With the Thirlwall Inquiry seemingly crafting a narrative that could lead to recommendations that similar spikes are reported to police more quickly, the stakes couldn't be higher for those working in the health-care system, particularly nursing. This case has become about far more than Letby. In the simplest terms possible, this will happen again. There will be more spikes. Some hospital will always be bottom of the table. There will be more pronounced spikes than occurred at the CoCH. If police constabularies are assigned to investigate all of these spikes, it is hard to see anything other than utterly disastrous outcomes on the horizon. A nurse in Birmingham was arrested in May 2022, initially in relation to supposed poisoning. Over three years later, in August 2025, West Midlands Police had yet to charge her, but she remained "under investigation". One wonders how long it takes to investigate the alleged 'poisoning' of one child; this bears the hallmark of the approach to the Letby case happening all over again.

"We know there's a blueprint for these cases now, and, by the sounds of it, this poor woman in Birmingham is having the same blueprint applied to her", Professor O'Quigley told me. "It's becoming so clear now what a travesty of justice the Letby case has been, and that Lucy should be allowed to regain her freedom very quickly. This would absolutely apply if she had been on duty for the cases used in court, but considering that we know she was not, it is, frankly, beyond a joke."

It's always Lucy, isn't it? Well, no. It's not always Lucy. Not at all.

CHAPTER 8: CLAIMS REGARDING THE CONDITION OF BABIES

Throughout the trial of Lucy Letby, a core contention of the prosecution was the rapid deterioration of babies at the CoCH. Infants were presented as being stable, with undesirable events and collapses depicted as completely unexpected. It is also clear that this was the impression conveyed to the police, because shortly after Letby was sentenced, Detective Superintendent Paul Hughes who led the investigation commented: "What we found out was in neonatal infants, if a child collapses, it is usually expected. And even with the outside chance of it being unexpected, it is always explainable. What separated this collection of events was they were unexpected and unexplained."

Many infants die in unexplained circumstances, and neonates are extremely prone to collapse. "A baby can destabilise very, very quickly", Professor Carola Vinuesa told me. "To say that this is predictable is very difficult to justify. For example, infections can be difficult to diagnose in a neonate because they can present with higher or lower temperatures. Neonates also don't readily express symptoms."

As an example of the fragility of neonates, a study of approximately 1,000 infant deaths in southeast London, published in *The Journal of Maternal-Fetal & Neonatal Medicine*, found that the cause of mortality was unexplained for about half the newborns who had died unexpectedly, even after an autopsy. Another more recent review of neonatal mortality, encompassing 51 studies from 36 articles and over six million births, concluded that "newborns experience high mortality throughout the entire postnatal period, with the highest mortality rate in the first week, particularly on the first day".

There were instances of multiple births in the Letby case, and data from the charity BLISS indicates that "multiple pregnancy is also associated with an increased risk of neonatal death. The neonatal mortality rate for twins is 3.5 times higher than for singletons." This is further acknowledged in the *MBRRACE-UK Perinatal Mortality Surveillance Report*, published in September 2023, which reveals what the charity Twins Trust describe as a "concerning rise in stillbirths and neonatal deaths among pregnancies of twins, triplets or more", which is "now five times greater for someone who carried two or more babies than someone carrying one baby".

Professor Carola Vinuesa expanded on this: "You need to ask the doctors and witnesses in court: 'How many times have they looked at triplets that are premature?' Prematurity already means that there is either placental insufficiency, or some other factors, could be genetic or maternal, that have made that pregnancy difficult." Placental insufficiency was described by midwives as a contributing factor in the deaths of Child O and Child P. "These infants are not just early", Professor Vinuesa told me. "They're not just immature. They are born immature, but they've lacked vital nutrients, appropriate oxygen, so they are compromised immediately, while also being very low birth weight, which is a further complication. And very low birth weight and premature infants are susceptible to pseudomonas and sepsis."

Throughout the research for this book, the topic of monitoring was repeatedly brought up, and Dr Margaret Ferguson explained that this is potentially important in the way that collapses were presented in court. "If you're claiming that a baby is stable and then suddenly collapses, considering the clinical picture that we know about these infants, it does raise the question of whether the babies were being properly monitored. It is quite feasible that these babies were increasingly unwell and the staff around them didn't recognise the signs. It is definitely possible that some of the subtle changes that occur in neonates were simply missed."

It is also pertinent that not all infant deaths are explained, particularly in the case of neonates. ONS figures indicate that the number of unexplained infant deaths was not unusually high during the period of Letby's alleged crimes. The figure was slightly higher than for 2015, but significantly lower than had been the case, for example, in 2006. It is also notable that unexplained infant deaths are not uncommon; the ONS report in fact delineates that unexplained infant deaths accounted for 8.3% of all infant deaths that occurred in 2016, and that this figure is routinely above 7.5%. A statistician hired by the ONS to comment asserted that "while unexplained infant deaths increased in 2016 for the first time in three years the total remains low in historical terms. However, due to the low numbers involved the overall increase in unexplained infant deaths is not statistically significant." Professor Carola Vinuesa told me: "It should be emphasised as well that the jury won't know that triplets are more vulnerable than a baby born on its own as a solitary infant. All of these things must be stated clearly in court, and there is no evidence of this having occurred."

This does not mean that unexpected spikes should not be investigated, nor does it mean that there weren't very real and troubling problems at the CoCH. The issues discussed in the earlier chapters of this book can clearly contribute to infant deaths, making them predictable rather than unexpected. But the important thing to note is that little of this critical context was provided during criminal proceedings against Letby.

In addition, and overwhelmingly, throughout the trial the prosecution insisted that the babies who had died or been harmed at the CoCH were in relatively good health. Infants were variously described as "in good condition", "stable", "all observations normal", "doing well", and even "excellent". Professor Vinuesa was highly sceptical of such appraisals: "One of these babies, just 12 minutes after being born, was collapsing. How can you say that this baby was stable? The idea that collapses are always predictable, let alone in neonates, doesn't stand up to any scrutiny, even if the infants are being monitored really carefully in a superb hospital, which wasn't the case."

Dr Evans informed Raj Persaud that, "In most situations, getting a baby to start breathing again is relatively straightforward", and that babies died in Chester "despite what I considered outstanding resuscitation efforts". This gives the impression that resuscitation works almost inevitably, and the impression was once again conveyed to the jury, but many other experts disagree. "The idea that it's easy to resuscitate a baby is complete nonsense", Dr Roger Norwich asserted. "That was never the case in any paediatric or neonatal unit that I worked in. Everybody was absolutely terrified when one of these babies went off in a bad way. The situation is scary because you know they can die. The way it was spoken about in court – give them a bit of oxygen and they'll be all right – is completely untrue." Professor Colin Morley was also dubious about the standard of resuscitation on the unit: "The doctors couldn't resuscitate infants because they didn't have the skills. That seems critical of them, but, unfortunately, they hadn't had experience at doing it, and opportunities to do so are becoming rarer."

One third of all neonates receive some form of resuscitation and, naturally, the success rate is high. If this was not the case, there would be a vast number of deaths on neonatal units. It is therefore reasonable to assert that resuscitation attempts are usually successful. But neonates do die, and with more regularity than other infants, so, by definition, resuscitation is sometimes unsuccessful. As an indication it should be remembered that 11 infants died at the CoCH in the four years preceding the indictment period.

Approximately 10% of all newborns require some assistance to begin breathing at birth, and about 1% require extensive resuscitation. It is known that resuscitation can result in death, while infants who survive are prone to developing complications in the immediate postnatal period, or even subsequently. Neonates are also attached to monitoring and breathing equipment precisely to keep them alive. They will not survive without this. With this in mind, guidance written for NHS Scotland discusses suitable approaches for dealing with unsuccessful neonatal resuscitation.

One of the interesting facets of resuscitation in neonatology is that it developed to a great extent during the 1970s. Even though quantum leaps were made during this period, procedures associated with neonatal resuscitation and NICU care are notably less successful in preserving brain functionality. This is important because Letby was also both accused and convicted of causing permanent injuries in children who survived.

It can be difficult to acquire accurate figures on the likelihood of death from resuscitation in developed countries as most studies have examined this study globally. There is no doubt that outcomes are much worse in lower income countries. However, it is therefore equally undeniable that inferior conditions significantly increase the likelihood of deterioration. It is likely that doctors are trying their hardest in developing countries, and equally probable that maximum effort was made at the CoCH. But if conditions are less than ideal, resuscitation attempts diminish in effectiveness.

When writing to Dr Jane Hawdon, Ian Harvey observed that "noting a failure to respond to resus is always going to be very subjective", and several nurses made similar comments in submissions to the Thirlwall Inquiry. Joanne Williams described neonates as "unpredictable", asserting that "nothing really surprised" her with them, as they can "deteriorate quickly". Laura Eagles noted that "it is very difficult to say if a child on the NNU collapsing is expected or unexpected…it is not uncommon for babies on the NNU to have profound desaturations". And Nicola Dennison observed that the CoCH "had a lot of babies who were very poorly, some of which were born to very poorly mothers and as such our statistics naturally increased…we also had a high incidence of congenital abnormalities which included heart conditions and gastroschisis".

Little of the context regarding the hospital, infants, or previous deaths was communicated to the court or jury. "The health of these babies was not accurately portrayed at all", Dr Roger Norwich commented. "That was probably because they didn't have a neonatologist, they didn't have neonatal nursing practitioners, they had diminished nursing at the hospital generally, and they were very reliant on junior doctors, who were mainly completely unsupervised. They probably didn't know enough about neonates to be able to recognise a sick one, as that sickness was developing."

The resuscitation dogma was later repeated by the Court of Appeal, which noted that "most concerning was that the infants failed to respond to resuscitation". The Court of Appeal did concede that "preterm infants are at increased risk of numerous complications: infections;

haemorrhage or feeding difficulties" but essentially dismissed the idea that those working at the CoCH failed to identify clinical signs of deterioration. Of course, in addition to that argument, it is undeniable that problems were spotted that haven't been acknowledged internally, by the Care Quality Commission regulator, in court, or as part of the Thirlwall Inquiry, even though they are present in countless documents submitted to Thirlwall.

The Court of Appeal emphasised the assertion made in the original trial that infants usually recover. The jury were told this, the police have recounted this perspective uncritically and the Court of Appeal repeats it. These claims featured prominently in the trial but many medics strongly disagree with them. Even simply analysing related statistics suggests that it is extremely hard to sustain this view. Despite diligently seeking it during research, no expert or qualified support for the assertion that the collapse of neonates is always predictable could be found.

Evans asserted in court that "resuscitation is usually effective". This is, of course, true, but 'usually' is the key word here. Obviously if something is *usually* effective, then sometimes it isn't effective. The word is used again in the next assertion made by Dr Evans: "If the infant fails to respond one usually can find a cause in the form of overwhelming infection, severe haemorrhage or total systems failure." One can usually find a cause, but sometimes you cannot!

Dr Philip Hammond noted that while Evans had walked into a police station and decided within 10 minutes that there was definitely inflicted harm, "a very senior neonatal pathologist, who looked at the notes blind, decided it was more likely to be a naturally occurring subcapsular haematoma" as was recorded by the original pathologist. One of the problems with the medical investigation that led to Lucy Letby being charged is that nothing occurred blind. Realistically, Dr Evans must have known that the police were investigating a crime and there was a possible subject, so that wasn't blind. There is significant doubt that Dr Bohin's review was conducted blind. While it was initially claimed that no one investigating knew anyone's name, there were probably names of staff all over the case notes. These are all potentially prejudicing factors, whereas when more qualified professionals than Evans or Bohin have examined the notes blind, they have drawn completely benign conclusions that do not point towards Lucy Letby.

Before going any further, it must be emphasised once more that both babies admitted to neonatal intensive care units and premature babies have an elevated prospect of death. There are various studies available which estimate the proportionate chance of death or injury for infants born prematurely; as an illustration, a study of children born at 22 through 34 weeks' gestation in France is a good guide.

The French study concludes that a total of 0.7% of infants born before 24 weeks gestation survived to discharge; 31.2% of those born at 24 weeks; 59.1% at 25 weeks; and 75.3% at 26 weeks. Survival rates were 93.6% at 27 through 31 weeks. This study assessed infants that would be officially categorised as very premature, and five of the indictment infants that died, and nine overall, would be placed in this category. They are as follows:

- Child A – 31 weeks
- Child B – 31 weeks
- Child C – 30 weeks
- Child E – 29 weeks
- Child F – 29 weeks
- Child G – 23 weeks
- Child I – 27 weeks
- Child K – 25 weeks
- Child Q – 31 weeks

All of these babies were at serious risk of collapse and death, even in an ideally functioning neonatal unit. Statistically, and without meaning to sound disrespectful, Child G and Child K would have been unlikely to survive. Other studies have indicated that the majority of children born at this degree of prematurity do not survive. Since the spike at the CoCH, there have been developments in neonatal care, but these are effectively irrelevant for this case.

Complications arising from premature birth is the leading cause of neonatal death in the UK. For babies born before 32 weeks, 6.5% die before being discharged, 6.2% develop necrotising enterocolitis (NEC), 7.5% experience intraventricular haemorrhage (bleeding in the brain), 5.4% have bloodstream infection caused by micro-organisms, 2.6% experience cystic periventricular leukomalacia (a debilitating brain injury), and 39.7% develop bronchopulmonary dysplasia (BPD) – a condition in which lung development is impaired – or die as a consequence of prematurity. One in 10 of all premature babies suffer with permanent disabilities, which rises to 50% for those born before 26 weeks gestation. One study found that 80% of infants born before 26 weeks ultimately suffered with significant disabilities.

A particularly authoritative study of 15 middle and high-income countries assessed 125.5 million nationwide birth outcome records between the years 2000 and 2020. This research found that premature birth and low birth weights were consistent predictors of an increased risk of neonatal mortality. The study noted: "Babies who are born preterm or [with low weight at birth] have an increased risk of complications including neonatal morbidity and mortality."

Infection is a major cause of neonatal deaths. The Neonatal Research Network has conducted rigorous research into neonatal units for nearly 40 years and has extensively documented that "newborn infants are at high risk of infection, particularly when born preterm. Neonatal infections are associated with increased risks of mortality as well as short-term medical morbidities and enduring neurodevelopmental impairment among survivors." Studies conducted by the network have repeatedly "highlighted the profoundly negative impact of neonatal infection on the most preterm infants".

This is critical because an infection of sepsis is highly dangerous and difficult to diagnose, especially in premature babies. Sepsis is heterogeneous, meaning that it can be present in many different forms, with its symptoms often mistaken for other infections. Diagnosis is often delayed, with blood cultures from laboratory tests often taking 48 hours to turn positive. In the case of a neonate, there often simply isn't enough time for such testing. There is no specific biological characteristic ("biomarker") that can definitively identify sepsis, which means that a combination of several biomarkers is required. Most determinants of sepsis can also be present in many other circumstances, which further complicates diagnosis, and it is common for there to be a lack of obvious symptoms generally. Additionally, inflammation from other diseases or prior antibiotic use can complicate diagnosis, meaning that the condition can often be overlooked until serious illness or death is already inevitable.

Even when sepsis has been identified, it is notoriously difficult to address. Pathogens that are resistant to antibiotics can make sepsis harder to treat, increasing mortality rates, and the management of sepsis therefore requires multimodal therapeutic approaches, which can be difficult to implement. Most septic patients also have co-morbidities – more than one medical condition – which can complicate treatment and affect outcomes.

The application of inappropriate antibiotics can lead to suboptimal outcomes. Antibiotic resistance can further impact on the treatment of sepsis; a phenomenon that has been notably increasing in recent years. This is particularly problematical for neonatal infants who suffer with weakened immune systems and susceptibility to illness. Sepsis can develop rapidly, which contradicts assertions made by the prosecution in court that collapses were completely unexpected, and that there is always ample warning of deterioration in any infant.

All of these factors collectively indicate how dangerous sepsis, and other infections, can be for neonates. This is true in the most efficient and well-staffed hospital unit, but, as we have seen previously, the CoCH was unsanitary, beset with problems and significantly understaffed and under-skilled.

The dangers of understaffing are extensively documented. A study published in the *American Journal of Infection Control* outlined the fact that understaffed hospitals have higher rates of infection. Another study published in the *British Medical Journal* discovered a "statistically significant association between the fill-rate for registered nurses and inpatient mortality". Research in the journal *JAMA Pediatrics* noted that nursing shortfalls "are associated with higher rates of nosocomial (i.e. originating in a hospital) infections among infants with very low birth weights".

An analysis of 92 cases by the *British Maternity and Newborn Safety Investigations* programme found that "staff shortages are a key contributor to baby deaths". A further study published in the *British Journal of Surgery* found that "nurse understaffing is associated with adverse outcomes for surgical admissions". A literature review conducted by the Royal College of Nursing concluded that both the skill mix and numbers of nurses on any unit has a direct impact on mortality and morbidity. Finally, a House of Commons Committee report recently warned that the persistent understaffing of the NHS poses a serious risk to patient safety.

All of this information is incredibly important because it was conveyed to the court and jury in the Letby case that all of the collapses and deaths involved were completely unexpected. The impression presented was that babies were healthy and stable, inexplicably collapsed, and that this is both completely incomprehensible and something that would not usually occur. Furthermore, the jury was not informed adequately about conditions at the hospital, or how this could directly impact on patient outcomes.

Yet it is crystal clear that many of the babies were born desperately early, had extremely low body weight and, from birth, were besieged with numerous complications. The majority were admitted to the intensive care unit, and most required assistance with breathing, with many suffering from medical accidents which were unrelated to Letby. As mentioned previously, an unusually large proportion of the indictment babies were also twins and triplets, both of which are associated with hugely elevated risk of complications and premature death.

Several of the babies experienced medical accidents while on the ward, including four incidents where umbilical venous catheters were placed wrongly or fell out – a mistake that can sometimes lead to deadly clots. "It is clear from both the trial and the Royal College report that the skill sets of both the consultants and junior doctors were not up to spec", Dr Colin Ferguson told me. "Simple procedures failed, often several times. I have a lot of experience of examining units that have poor outcomes, and that's a very common theme – clinicians aspire beyond their skills, and try to do things that they're really not up to doing. This case has all the hallmarks of that."

In the case of Child A, staff failed to give fluids for four hours, there was an unforgivable delay in the administration of antibiotics for Child D, while Child H had breathing difficulties from birth and the prosecution accepted that she received "suboptimal" treatment on the unit. But other babies were regarded as having been treated adequately, as if the issues that befell these infants somehow existed in isolation. In reality, these problems were all-encompassing, impacting on the unit as a whole and on all infants treated there. They were certainly not outlier cases.

Despite this, when speaking with the BBC, Dr Evans once again made the claim that "babies don't suddenly drop dead". He further dismissed criticisms from other medics, stating that all assertions made by anyone other than himself are "completely flawed and indicate either that the people making them have not seen the clinical evidence or that they are unaware of what constitutes well-being in a premature baby". Since a panel of 14 international neonatal experts have submitted reports, supplemented by 17 further experts, having examined all available information related to the case, such claims from Dr Evans have died down somewhat.

Dr Michael Hall was critical of evidence provided in court for Child A. Born at 31 weeks, Child A faced increased morbidity and mortality risk and was receiving CPAP. His breathing rate was abnormal throughout the 24 hours before collapse; the increased rate suggested possible respiratory distress syndrome. This requires surfactant therapy but he never received it. Dr Hall told me: "Although his respiratory rate was high, the heart rate was in the low-normal range. Usually you would expect the heart rate to be relatively high if there was a significantly high respiratory rate. One explanation of the incongruously low heart rate is that his mother had been treated with a beta-blocker medication, labetalol, during the three weeks prior to his birth. It is known that this can cross the placenta and affect babies in the newborn period, both in terms of heart function and in causing the blood sugar to be abnormally low."

Dr Martyn Pitman further cited the potential for labetalol to induce hypoglycaemia, while Dr Hall explained that "the high breathing rate seems to have been missed by the doctors involved in the care of Child A", based on accounts submitted to the Thirlwall Inquiry.

As mentioned earlier, Child A went at least four hours without IV fluids (only 2ml of breast milk) and was kept under a heat lamp while staff attempted IV access. That prolonged heat and lack of fluids raise the risk of fluid deficit and electrolyte disturbances which can affect brain and heart function; infants of this size and gestation should not spend more than one hour without fluid and beneath a heat lamp. Child A also had an elevated lactate, linked to higher morbidity and mortality.

Chest compressions can introduce free air into the body, which could explain the air noted in front of the spine where compressions occur. The skin discolouration and rash seen in Child A can indicate a cardiorespiratory event – blood seeping away from the skin to internal organs – and CoCH staff, being relatively inexperienced with intensive care patients, may not have recognised these patterns.

During treatment the long line was judged too deep by both the inserting doctor and the consulting radiologist but was never corrected. Taken together, these facts point to suboptimal care and serious questions about stability – points raised by Dr Hall in discussions with Judith Moritz and Jonathan Coffey. Furthermore, Dr Hall informed me that the respiratory rate of Child A was elevated above a normal and stable level in 19 of the 22 observations made (86%). Nevertheless, prosecution witnesses claimed that Child A was "stable" and "doing so well" that feeds were given, a claim repeated by the Court of Appeal in paragraph 52 of its judgment, despite evidence that Child A should have been delivered at a tertiary unit because of extreme illness in mother and infant.

"For Child A, we need to look at the umbilical venous catheter (UVC) placement", a neonatal nurse told me. "There are multiple attempts. Research will tell you that every single attempt heightens the risk of collapse and illness. Other than that, the child crashed 15 or 20 minutes after having fluids put up a UVC line that they had not established was patent [correctly positioned], and they then just shrugged and decided they would use it.

"The line was coming out repeatedly. I believe that they forgot to prime the lines with fluids, so that there wasn't a line of air. Because otherwise you can place a line of air into somebody. This, of course, then feeds into the whole venous air embolus diagnosis. The other thing is two attempts – then you pass it on. You don't ever continually do something like that over and over again. They were so messy with the lines in this case, it was truly poor practice." Much of this information was corroborated by the Child Death Overview Panel form for Child A that was submitted to the Thirlwall Inquiry.

Child B was born at 31 weeks, increasing her risk of mortality and morbidity. She required immediate resuscitation and was placed on a ventilator indefinitely because her body could not support breathing. Her mother had an auto-immune disease that can increase clotting risk.

A decision to extubate Child B was made prematurely which can cause diminished oxygenation, organ and blood-pressure problems, an increased risk of brain bleeds, and/or the need for reintubation – which can scar the trachea and stress the neonate. Death is also an inherent risk.

Child B was placed on CPAP, which was removed so she could be held. This was substandard practice; CPAP should not be removed from infants requiring respiratory support as they are vulnerable to respiratory and metabolic stress. When the CPAP prongs were removed, Child B desaturated, indicating the need for support; she later desaturated further and required reintubation.

Her skin was observed to turn purple with white patches, a sign of blood shunting away from the skin during hypoxia. There is evidence of an apnoeic event consistent with apnoea of prematurity (an exclusionary diagnosis once infection is ruled out). Child B continued to have desaturation and apnoea during her NICU stay, yet these collapses were excluded from the indictment.

"When independent experts state that Child B could not have apnoea of prematurity due to being on caffeine, when caffeine does not prevent apnoea 100% of the time, it raises red flags regarding what else was said with certainty", expert neonatal nurse Sloane Spade told me. "Most of the deaths and collapses seem to have explanations that match the actual clinical states of the infants. Since air embolism is so rare to see, it would be hard to conclude that it was definitely the cause of these incidences due to other potential, and more common, neonatal complications."

Child A and Child B were also twins, with Child B actually being born first. Experienced obstetrician Dr Martyn Pitman has examined all of the available documents for the infants in the Letby case, and cited the "unusually high number of multiple pregnancies". As an illustration of this, the ONS recorded 1.38% of all births being multiples in 2024, compared with 58.8% of the infants included in the Letby trial. This is significant, Dr Pitman explained to me, because "the risk for those pregnancies is incomparable to singleton pregnancies".

This should have been a matter of some importance in both the hospital and the court case, yet the obstetric picture of these infants barely featured during the trial. This is not hugely surprising as Dr Evans informed the police at their first meeting on 10 July 2017 that "no maternity" information would be needed. "When there is full reflection on the CoCH and the Letby cases, I think there will be significant question marks about the obstetric and maternity management side as well," Dr Martyn Pitman reflected. Dr Michael Hall had raised this issue before court proceedings began, indicating "that a neonatologist starts assessing a baby from conception, or even before". But maternity, obstetric and foetal medicine information was not made available, despite it being requested. This would have provided critical insight into several infants, not least Child A and Child B.

A close working relationship between obstetrics and neonatology should also be considered essential and yet Dr Martyn Pitman told me that he hadn't "seen anything that would indicate a close working, questioning, challenging relationship between what should be intimately related specialties". And there was a good reason for this: "There *was* no interaction between obstetrics and paediatrics, and there was certainly no familiarity there", Dr Fiona MacRae, who worked at the CoCH for 27 years, told me.

The autoimmune disorder antiphospholipid syndrome (APS), which was a major issue for the mother of Child A and Child B, will be discussed in "Injection of Air Hypothesis". But there was another condition of significance that somehow slipped under the radar and was even redacted from Thirlwall Inquiry documents and possibly those disclosed for trial. Several documents from the CoCH indicate that systemic lupus erythematosus ('lupus' for short), another chronic autoimmune disease, was recorded for this mother. And yet, in a pattern that will continue as this book unfolds, the jury never heard of this. "There is no medical confidentiality associated with lupus. There is no reason for this not to be declared", Dr Pitman explained. When I asked him what the consequences would be for mother and children, he provided an extensive response:

"The mother had two very serious autoimmune illnesses. And lupus can cause congenital heart blocks in babies, which is a significant problem as antibodies can attack the heart. There are major blood clotting risks from APS. There are also placental problems. Dr Shoo Lee mentioned that with APS the placenta can get gummed up with thrombi, and that can cause problems.

"It was essential for the hospital to take a detailed history from the mother, and a full history of her care should have been obtained. I would have ensured that the mother was kept on anticoagulants, but assiduous monitoring was also essential – regular scans and checking out placental function. Lupus is a multi-system disorder for the mother. It's extremely serious, even in the absence of other issues, which definitely was not the case here!"

There are three important points in relation to this. Firstly, lupus is noted in an internal document from the CoCH, and then, curiously, disappears from any discussion. Secondly, it appears that the hospital had badly mismanaged this infant. Thirdly, not only was all of this discounted by the prosecution and the jury never furnished with this information, but no obstetric or maternity input was even thought necessary at the trial.

The background to Child C will be discussed in "The Strangely Evolving Case of Child C".

Child D lost colour and became floppy in her father's arms within 12 minutes of birth, later showing signs of respiratory distress and infection. The mother did not receive antibiotics while suffering premature rupture of membranes (PROM) which increases the risk of early onset sepsis and pneumonia, an error for which the hospital was criticised. Despite complications, Child D was not assessed by a doctor until three hours after birth, and only after her parents begged. She was not treated with antibiotics until an hour later.

Child D had a low oxygen saturation rate of 47% for a prolonged period, with no record of when this ended (levels of 85-95% would be normal after 10 minutes in a child responding to resuscitation). The infant was first on CPAP, then intubated, then extubated to room air, and then returned to CPAP after an event required Neopuff PPV. This all occurred within the first day – an excessive amount of respiratory weaning in a very short time.

There were prolonged indicators of adverse reaction to weaning, including acidotic blood gases that impair respiration, yet the child was trialled off respiratory support more than once. Child D showed signs of requiring increased support, including desaturation events, but was removed from CPAP immediately after an event that required 100% oxygen to recover; another event then followed 45 minutes later. Compounding this, a resuscitation order was conducted incorrectly: chest compressions were performed prior to an endotracheal tube (ETT) being placed, and potentially even before Neopuff breaths. Public trial records contain no statement that an ETT was ever placed.

Following autopsy, the cause of death was pneumonia with acute lung injury, entirely aligned with the infant's clinical status, and there appears no rational reason to overrule this post-mortem finding. The mother's concerns were dismissed by unit doctors. There is further evidence of sepsis: Dr Brearey and Dr Elizabeth Newby both noted sepsis (with PROM a possible contributor), and Dr Michael Hall referenced pneumonia and the need for breathing support. In a Thirlwall Inquiry statement (February 2025), paediatric registrar Dr Andrew Brunton said he "was contacted by Dr Newby via an email stating that the post-mortem for Child D had shown congenital pneumonia", noted the "concerns raised by the family", and that the case was being investigated as a Serious Untoward Incident and by the coroner. In court, Ben Myers asserted Child D was "very unwell indeed", but Dr Sandie Bohin disagreed.

The background to Child E and Child G will be discussed in the chapter "Other Infants", and the background to Child F will be outlined in "Insulin Cases". It can also be noted that Dr Michael Hall informed me that prosecution claims regarding Children C, D, E and G being stable were simply inaccurate.

Child H had breathing difficulties at birth and required intervention for desaturations. She was later found to have a collapsed lung (pneumo-thorax), which can cause rapid desaturations and bradycardia because the infant could only use one premature lung. After the initial difficulty, she had multiple desaturations and bradycardia episodes related to the pneumothorax.

Two chest drains were performed, one of which was not placed or draining properly. The lung re-accumulated air, and a full resuscitation was carried out, resolving in 20 minutes, before more air was removed with another drain. Less than 24 hours after that resuscitation, and being off ventilation, Child H required resuscitation again following a dramat-ic heart rate drop and desaturation. She was eventually transferred to Arrowe Park Hospital, where her parents believed she received consid-erably better care.

Child H, for whom Letby was charged with two counts of attempted murder, is actually a key child in the case as Letby was not convicted on either count. This infant suffered collapses, despite the fact that she was significantly healthier at birth than virtually all of the other infants discussed here, indicating that babies could and did collapse when this would have been less likely. The prosecution was unable to come up with a plausible method of inflicted harm, and there seems to be no rational reason why this infant was even included in this court case, except for the fact that Letby could be tangentially linked with it. The same could be said for other children in the case who Letby was found guilty of harm-ing, even though in these cases there was increased prematurity, exces-sively low birth weights, catalogues of negative health conditions, and an overall picture that pointed to an obviously increased risk of collapse and death.

Child I was another particularly premature infant, weighing under 1kg at birth, increasing her risk of mortality and morbidity. She had repeated bowel concerns, with suspected NEC which has a potential mortality in neonates of 50%. She also had chronic lung disease, reducing lung capacity and making her prone to respiratory collapse; any added external stress could trigger a respiratory event.

During her brief life, Child I experienced multiple deteriorations requiring immediate response, both at Liverpool Women's Hospital and the CoCH when Letby was not present. In court, Caroline Oakley had recounted that her parents had expressed dismay that Child I was not accepted by Alder Hey. Staffing and monitoring issues on the unit have been discussed previously, and the mother of Child I also reported a lack of monitoring.

On one occasion a large vomiting and apnoea event required resuscitation: manual breaths via masks likely increased stomach distension. X-rays then showed a distended stomach with pneumatosis in the bowels – a definitive sign of NEC. Child I was made nil by mouth and started on antibiotics per NEC protocol, but enteral (tube) feeds were restarted after 24 hours despite NEC guidance that neonates remain nil by mouth while on antibiotics (typically five to seven days); her antibiotic course was seven days.

Two weeks later, while unmonitored, Child I had a large apnoea requiring positive pressure ventilation (PPV), again risking gastric distension. Her stomach appeared distended and, given her NEC history, antibiotics were recommenced. She suffered another end-of-shift event requiring intubation and transfer to Alder Hey, where she had a further cardiorespiratory event and needed a new ETT because of a blood clot at its tip; likely from a traumatic intubation at the CoCH.

Further resuscitations, intubations, apnoeas and cardiorespiratory events followed. Shortly before death, Child I's ETT was removed and she immediately had a resuscitation. For an infant with her respiratory history, extubation immediately after neonatal resuscitation can be deemed inappropriate. Neonatal nurse Caroline Oakley observed that the "neonatal journey [of Child I] over her 10 weeks of life had been complicated".

In summary, Child I's recurrent NEC and bowel issues led to on-and-off nil-by-mouth status and antibiotics, alongside repeated cardiorespiratory events. She developed BPD and had limited physiological reserve. Dr John Gibbs commented that Child I "had serious collapses, and consultants had been called in each time, so a little like Child G, I had gained the impression that Child I was quite a vulnerable, very premature baby". In fact, Gibbs made similar comments about several other infants involved in the Letby case and overall didn't find the collapses of the babies unexpected or unexplained at the time. It was only with the benefit of hindsight when he had been told Letby was guilty of inflicting harm on them that he somewhat revised his opinion, even though he retained the view that numerous infants were unwell and vulnerable.

The background to Child O is discussed in "Other Infants", but it's important to understand that both Child O and Child P were monochorionic (sharing a placenta) triplets, which significantly complicates both their delivery and care. Dr Fiona MacRae was one of many healthcare professionals who believed that the infants "should have been transferred to Alder Hey and managed appropriately" in what was a higher-grade unit. "There is a huge question mark regarding why the CoCH took on so many complex cases, who was driving this and why that decision was made", Dr Martyn Pitman added. "This is a rare event – you would expect to see triplets perhaps once every three years in a unit of this size."

When I spoke with Dr Pitman, he walked me through all of the issues with Child O: "This was, immediately, a high-risk pregnancy. The babies are sharing a placenta, which puts this scenario at the apex of obstetric risk. The pregnancy would have been monitored with very regular Fetal Medicine Ultrasound scans to check the growth of the babies and to rule out the development of twin-to-twin transfusion syndrome. Planning and close inter-specialty discussion is therefore essential here. This mother was initially informed that her infants would likely be born at another hospital. The change of plan, landing them with three premature, potentially complicated infants on their unit, is an enormous undertaking, with huge logistical considerations.

"Significant concerns remain regarding the caesarean section delivery of these triplets, particularly the seniority of the operating obstetrician. The parents recount a traumatic delivery, with blood spraying over the drapes and splattering against the wall behind them. This is astounding, incredible. And then there are numerous troubling clinical signs. There was a significant delay in the baby passing meconium, in common with Child C. There were concerning markers in the baby's blood, indicating that the baby was becoming acidotic, which can be a reflection of respiratory issues.

"That's not all, though. Sequential blood samples taken either end of the final resuscitation indicated that this infant's haemoglobin level had plummeted, to such an extent that it was indicative of life-threatening blood loss. That was documented by the consultant who undertook the paracentesis procedure. Despite this, the resuscitation was terminated without giving an urgent blood transfusion.

"It is therefore not surprising that when staff on the unit conducted a debrief, they concluded that there was suboptimal care. Given what I've read, one has to wonder about the standard of basic neonatal resuscitation on the unit. This is another infant in the case where everything is pointing to several underlying chronic issues, contrary to what was suggested in court."

Michele Worden concurred with this verdict: "A lot of these babies had clinical signs, which again goes back to having inexperienced staff, not recognising that these babies are very subtly deteriorating. They were not sudden collapses. The opinion of Dewi Evans does not stand up to scrutiny. With Child O, from 1:30am there was increased heart and respiration rate, and a distended abdomen. At 7am, he accuses Lucy of hitting this baby in the liver. No one saw this, of course, not least because Lucy actually wasn't on duty!"

Documents from Thirlwall further cement this impression. A meeting related to a thematic review of neonatal mortality, held in February 2016, noted that "one baby had severe HIE" (hypoxic-ischemic encephalopathy – brain damage that occurs due to insufficient oxygen), another "had severe multiple congenital abnormalities with a very poor prognosis", while a third child "had a significant congenital heart disease and probable sepsis". The document concludes, as mentioned earlier, that two further babies, and possibly three depending on the result of post-mortems, "died of sepsis despite timely antibiotic treatment". While this diagnosis is fair, it is difficult to claim that all of the antibiotic treatment administered at the CoCH was 'timely'.

An email from Eirian Powell to Dr Stephen Brearey in October 2015 had already outlined that "each cause of death was different, some were poorly prior to their arrival on the unit and the others were NEC or gastric bleeding/congenital abnormalities". It remains incredible that this, further reviews and post-mortems have all been overturned on the basis of evidence produced by Dr Evans which had been almost entirely derived from case notes. Even taking this into consideration, post-mortems conducted at Alder Hey did not include systematic testing for toxicology, blood electrolytes, genetic factors or blood sugar after death, all of which could be hugely significant.

One paediatric doctor who spoke with me anonymously told me that events that can be associated with these infants happen "all the time" in neonatal units, and that there often isn't a "clear cut" cause for such incidents. The paediatrician further suspected that delays in recognition and monitoring could have been critically important, as has been suggested by a multitude of experienced NICU practitioners.

The 2016 thematic review also noted that "three [preterm] babies had delayed cord clamping when hospital guidance says this is only for term babies…the obstetric, midwifery and paediatric teams have not yet been able to ensure adequate temperature control for all preterm babies close to Mum during delayed cord clamping", indicating that known safety risks for neonates had not been reliably managed.

Another neonatal review from May 2016, submitted to Thirlwall, outlined a catalogue of issues on the unit, and with the infants involved in the Letby case. The document references several infants with congenital abnormalities, more with congenital pneumonia, a child with maternal syndrome, two with NEC, issues with overwhelming sepsis, problems with cot availability, issues with transportation and difficulties in liaising satisfactorily with Alder Hey. Powell also mentions that Dr H and Dr G "appear to be involved in many of the mortalities". She concludes the review by stating that "all the post-mortem results show there was no evidence of foul play".

One practising and registered nurse I spoke with indicated her belief that there are "many alternative non-malicious explanations for occurrences at the CoCH. At a certain point, it becomes ridiculous how many different scenarios branch off from a lack of care and prolonged periods of time with no monitoring and intervention. It is quite literally the opposite of beyond reasonable doubt. From my perspective, there is zero reason why experts in this case were so apparently confident about the specific scenario of inflicted harm." Dr Michael Hall agrees with this verdict: "It's my opinion that the prosecution medical expert witnesses exaggerated the degree of wellness of those babies to a significant extent. I would have thought it would have had a significant influence on the jury."

Every medic and healthcare expert I interviewed, which was dozens, was extremely sceptical about the way that the health and collapse of babies was presented in court. Neonatal expert Professor Neena Modi wrote in *The Guardian* that "the jury were told that the babies were mostly healthy and well and that the deaths and deteriorations were unexpected. This is not the case; the babies were either overtly unwell, or at high risk of developing complications." Even Dr Ravi Jayaram had conceded at an extraordinary board meeting on 14 July 2016 that "the nature of neonatal babies is that they are premature babies and by definition at higher risk".

Before concluding this section, it must be noted that this is not an exhaustive account of this subject, but it does establish the following: "The asserted causes of death or attack just don't line up compared to the clinical status of the infants and more common conditions", as neonatal nurse Sloane Spade told me. The impression that the prosecution communicated throughout the trial, that babies were essentially healthy and stable and then suddenly inexplicably collapsed cannot possibly be deemed accurate. It is unsupported by evidence to such an extent that it could reasonably be described as unfounded.

Remember that Dr Evans commented that those criticising his work "either have not seen the clinical evidence…or are unaware of what constitutes well-being in a premature baby", while Dr Bohin asserted that it was "outrageous" to suggest that the prosecution witnesses may have misled the court regarding the well-being of infants.

Conversely, Dr Michael Hall informed me that "all of the babies who died had some form of instability".

CHAPTER 9: INJECTION OF AIR HYPOTHESIS

Amidst all the allegations associated with the conviction of Lucy Letby, the information and reports related to air embolism requiring the purposeful injection of air are perhaps the most chilling. There is something especially disturbing about the notion that anyone could deliberately inject air into the anatomy of a vulnerable infant, let alone that a nurse had done this. It is therefore particularly important to examine these cases, as they arguably had the biggest emotional impact on those who observed the trial, whether jurors or simply interested parties.

The theory that Dr Dewi Evans communicated in court was that Letby had deliberately injected air into neonates at the CoCH which caused their physical condition to deteriorate rapidly, fatally in some cases. There were two alleged mechanisms involved; air was either injected with a syringe to cause air embolism, essentially bubbles of air that can in some cases impede the vascular system; or else air was administered via a nasogastric (feeding) tube, allegedly causing a splinting of the diaphragm, which would lead to respiratory issues. In this context, splinting of the diaphragm refers to the muscle at the base of the lungs being restricted and preventing normal respiratory function.

This chapter includes the word 'hypothesis' in its title, precisely because these allegations are entirely hypothetical. Speaking with Raj Persaud shortly after the verdict, Dr Evans noted that "injecting air into the blood circulation" was "very difficult to prove" and also "very difficult to diagnose". This latter point is undeniable, not least because none of the post-mortems, pathologists or experts who have examined the case since have drawn this conclusion. When Dr Evans was asked by the *New Yorker* about any existing medical literature regarding this process, he responded: "There are no published papers regarding a phenomenon of this nature that I know of." Similarly, Evans informed *The Guardian* that air embolism "was a phenomenon I had never encountered previously".

As the conversation with Persaud continued, Dr Evans outlined the underlying reasons for his hypotheses. It must be said that this was a rather stuttering explanation and even Persaud admitted that he was confused. But Dr Evans cited what he described as "this peculiar abnormality of the skin", particularly a "discolouration". According to Dr Evans, "the medical team clearly didn't appreciate the significance of this discolouration". This was then coupled with what Dr Evans considered to be a sudden deterioration. For many infants in the case, it is highly debatable whether their deterioration was either sudden or unexpected, but what is undeniable is that sudden collapse is not a meaningful diagnostic criterion. "In fact, the term 'collapse' is vague and emotive", Professor Colin Morley asserted when I spoke with him. "It would be much better to have a detailed description, such as 'apnoea' or 'bradycardia'".

The hypothesis of Dr Evans therefore rests entirely on this discolouration – "something that occurs in most babies with compromised cardiac function", as Professor Morley observed. In order to achieve this, Letby would need to inject a significant amount of air into infants on the unit. But the orchestration of this seems rather unlikely. Firstly, Letby was often surrounded by other nurses and demonstrably accompanied at the times identified for alleged crimes, even according to the prosecution case and its flawed swipe-card data (discussed in more depth in "Swipe-Card Data Falls Apart").

And, secondly, a host of medical professionals are incredibly sceptical of the logistics required to inject a sufficient amount of air. Many believed that it was practically impossible. "You would need a really large amount of air to cause a significant air embolism", one neonatal nurse told me. "More than just a small syringe. Because there are several cases in which the prosecution cited air embolism, but the baby recovered after positive pressure ventilation. If air is essentially blocking a blood vessel, and preventing blood from moving normally, it won't be resolved by someone just bagging a baby. That's not going to get rid of the air in the system."

Referring to similar evidence, neonatal nurse Sloane Spade told me that "if you have an IV line and there's a small air bubble in it, typically that will not cause harm. There are even instances where a full 10ml syringe of air given directly in the veins may not cause air embolism." Professor Colin Morley agreed with this opinion: "I doubt whether such a small amount of air would cause any problem."

Spade also pointed to various ways that air can be introduced accidentally. This was a primary contention of Dr Colin Ferguson, who wondered that "as the paper that Dr Evans relied on in court relates to accidental air embolism caused by high pressure ventilation, how did he conflate this with his hypothesis of venous injection, and how did he rule out all the alternative causes cited in other papers? There are a whole range of mechanisms by which air can be introduced ante-mortem." Professor Owen Arthurs agreed in court that "the presence of air may also be the result of medical procedures or placement" when prompted by Ben Myers.

Spade echoed this, noting that "gas present in the infants could have come from multiple things". A neonatologist made exactly the same assertion when interviewed by *The Daily Telegraph*, observing that "certainly, a small amount of air in a thin syringe will not make the difference". And Dr Philip Hammond encountered extreme scepticism when he spoke with neonatologists on the plausibility of air being deliberately introduced via a nasogastric tube, with these experts describing the diagnosis as "ridiculous" according to Hammond. The reason for this was quite straightforward – "the tubes are tiny, and to inject enough to cause some sort of catastrophic result, I think, firstly, would take far too long, and, secondly, almost certainly be absurd".

Several expert clinicians also told *The Guardian* that this alleged method of murder was "not practically feasible", due to the "tiny" nasogastric tubes, which would require several refills to inject a significant quantity of air. Dr Colin Ferguson therefore deemed the theory to be "complete nonsense", as if "there is high pressure developing in the stomach, for instance, it will just vent back up the nasogastric tube. Or the baby will either vomit or burp the air back up." Numerous experts cited precisely these methods of air leak, vomiting and burping when interviewed by Felicity Lawrence for *The Guardian*, as did Professor Colin Morley in conversation with journalist John Sweeney. Consultant neonatologist, Dr Svilena Dimitrova, also asserted that "injecting lots and lots and lots of air…would be actually quite technically difficult to do", but even if this did occur "a competent team would have gone in, aspirated it out within the first couple of minutes of the resuscitation of the baby".

It is also known that the process of resuscitation can trigger air embolisms, as recorded in several studies. Paediatric surgeon Dr Abid Qazi was the primary of three co-authors of one such published case report in 2015. Dr Qazi told *The Daily Telegraph* in July 2024 that he was "very sceptical about the diagnosis", citing that air embolism has "been reported in several cases through the natural course of illness". Dr Qazi had "been closely following" the Letby case, concluding that "she has been a victim of the poor NHS system".

Further research in 2015, published in the *Resuscitation* journal, concluded that "post-mortem [scanning] after prolonged resuscitation showed a high prevalence of intravascular air-embolism", asserting that this "needs further research". Another case report from 2016 discovered "frothy air dense material" after resuscitation, which suggested an air embolism. The significance of this froth will be discussed later in the chapter. Professor Colin Morley noted that "lots of these infants had multiple resuscitations, with drugs through intravenous lines and vigorous hand ventilation; it's very easy to accidentally introduce air".

Professor Owen Arthurs, who appeared in court during the Letby case, also conducted a review of infants at Great Ormond Street Hospital, finding that 25% of them had gas in the large vessels. This percentage was roughly consistent with those aged under two months, for which gas was present in eight out of 38 cases (21%). Professor Arthurs acknowledged in court that there could be other explanations for the air as opposed to its supposedly deliberate injection. In relation to this, Dr Colin Ferguson told me that "to translate the radiological presence of gas in the large vessels after death to an assumption that somebody has clearly injected it is just nonsense. It's patent nonsense."

This was echoed by Dr Michael Hall, who questioned the assertion from Arthurs that the presence of air was an "unusual finding", which he witnessed in court first-hand. "Air was present in 25% of the autopsies he found, but he also said this was 'unusual'. I don't think you need to be a statistician or epidemiologist to know that this figure is not unusual, it's well within a normal range." Dr Hall recounted what he'd heard Arthurs say in court about his use of source material: "He didn't do a thorough literature search. He said in court that Dewi Evans had done it, so he didn't need to. But there is a paper from Germany in which signs of air embolism were found in about nine out of 10 babies who had received resuscitation attempts. Professor Arthurs didn't emphasise in his evidence that this is often found in resuscitation, so the jury, which isn't medically trained, never heard this. The jury was given the message that there was no other explanation, but there are other explanations."

Dr Ferguson pointed out that "intravenous catheters are a potential source for air getting into infants". If tubes are not adequately flushed with liquid, or if there is a break in the line, such insertions can potentially cause air embolisms. Dr Qazi also noted this possibility when interviewed by *The Daily Telegraph*.

The stuttering commentary of Dr Dewi Evans has been notable, both during and since the court case. But he was also prone to introducing terminology which doesn't appear to be particularly scientific. One such occasion came on 23 March 2023 during discussion of Child P when Dr Evans was discussing a supposed incident involving Letby on 24 June 2016. Dr Evans suggested that Letby had given the child a "dollop" of air. This was ridiculed by the defence barrister, Ben Myers, and yet while prosecution barrister Nick Johnson defended the use of the term, he also acknowledged that it "originated from Dr Evans".

It is perhaps this sort of testimony that has led some medics to be so dismissive of the theories floated in court. One such consultant responded to the air injection theory by telling *Private Eye* that it was, quite simply, "bollocks". The consultant informed Dr Philip Hammond that "babies get too much air in the stomach all the time, with all the bagging and masking and CPAP, and all you do is take it out again". Two neonatologists spoken to by *The Times* were also critical, stating that a more plausible explanation of deterioration would be the use of vasoactive drugs, such as adrenaline, given to a collapsing baby during attempts at resuscitation. Rachel Aviv in the *New Yorker* also disclosed that several doctors she interviewed were "baffled" by the entire air embolism theory, and "struggled to understand how it could be physiologically or logistically possible".

In Letby's application to appeal, Ben Myers contended that the prosecution experts did not possess adequate clinical expertise in air embolism, and warned that their diagnosis had been given "on the hoof" without any scientific basis: "None of the experts who gave evidence of air embolisms had the knowledge to do so", Myers asserted. The Court of Appeal acknowledged that neither Dr Evans nor Dr Bohin had any significant direct experience of patients with air embolism, but the presiding judge rejected the suggestion that they were not qualified to give evidence on the issue. Similarly, Professor Sally Kinsey conceded when cross-examined that air embolus did not feature in her expertise but she was still permitted to provide evidence on the topic in court.

It is intriguing that Dr Evans described his theory of air being delivered via the nasogastric tube in court as a "clinically proven mechanism", especially considering that eight expert clinicians informed *The Guardian* that the theory was "rubbish", "ridiculous", "implausible" and "fantastical". Dr Evans himself then later conceded in conversation with Liz Hull of the *Daily Mail* that the injection of air via a nasogastric tube is "utterly bizarre" and something he'd never heard of before. "That doesn't mean it can't exist", asserted Dr Evans, but this is rather different from the assertion that this is a clinically proven mechanism.

Dr Evans dismissed criticisms of his air embolism diagnosis, saying that "these individuals are [not] in a position to comment objectively" because they haven't had "access to the clinical records". Since then an array of experts, with access to the clinical records, have rejected all of his work. Dr Evans responded by shifting the goalposts, informing the *British Medical Journal* that "I have not heard any criticism from any individual whose view I respect". A point has now been reached where Dr Evans can reject the view of any expert if he decides that he doesn't respect them. This new position requires Dr Evans to disregard, for example, Professor Neena Modi, past president of the British Medical Association, UK Medical Women's Federation, and UK Royal College of Paediatrics and Child Health. Professor Modi has also held, by election, the three leading national children's research positions in the UK.

The air embolism theory of Dr Evans was based on skin discolouration, something that he asserted "was not appreciated by the clinicians as something that you get with air embolus". His theory was based on a scientific paper published in 1989, entitled *Pulmonary vascular air embolism in the newborn*, authored by Dr Shoo Lee and Dr Alan Keith Tanswell. Dr Lee has become centrally involved in the Letby case, quite inadvertently, simply by virtue of his research being used so prominently by the prosecution, or "misused" as he has since asserted. Dr Lee, Director of the Maternal-Infant Research Centre at Mount Sinai Hospital, and an Associate Member of the Lunenfeld-Tanenbaum Research Institute, described the air embolism diagnosis as a "fundamental mistake of medicine". It is important to emphasise that neither Dr Evans nor Dr Sandie Bohin had any prior experience with air embolism, and both have conceded this.

Having further investigated the Letby case, Dr Lee assembled 14 renowned experts from six countries to assess the medical data in the case. "I wanted to have a panel that was highly distinguished, highly experienced, whose reputations and credibility were beyond reproach, so that they could say authoritatively what they thought was going on", Dr Lee told the *Sunday Times*. Letby herself was asked if she was happy for their findings to be released, even if evidence of foul play was discovered, to which she unequivocally agreed. Each infant assessed by the panel was assigned to two experts to independently review the case. Should their opinions differ, a third expert would be assigned to review the case in order to reach consensus, but this only occurred in two of 17 cases. Speaking at a press conference to disseminate the results, Dr Shoo Lee announced: "We did not find any murders. In all cases, death or injury were due to natural causes, or just bad medical care."

It was now damage limitation time for Dr Evans when he stated: "[Dr Lee's] paper from 1989 got a lot of publicity, but it was not a major factor in the prosecution case." Dr Evans also made a statement about babies responding differently to treatment in 2015 compared to 1989. This overlooks the fact that Dr Evans hasn't worked in a hospital or treated a baby since 2009, and also that he was entirely reliant on literature for this diagnosis.

The following chapter of this book discusses Dr Evans' support for the July 2024 verdict of the Court of Appeal. The judgment notes the "*Lee and Tanswell* paper featured prominently in the trial" so it is curious that Dr Evans later asserted that the *Lee and Tanswell* paper "was not a major factor in the prosecution case". Perhaps Dr Evans can add the Court of Appeal to the list of people and organisations that he doesn't respect.

The Court of Appeal further notes that Dr Evans "remembered reading the description of the skin changes in [the *Lee and Tanswell* paper], which made him feel 'quite cold and worried'". This paper was clearly diagnostically instrumental, and Dr Evans confirmed this again in conversation with Raj Persaud: "The most commonly quoted scientific paper was 30 years old, but it is a very good paper…the medical team clearly didn't appreciate the significance of this discolouration." Later in the discussion, Dr Evans talks about staff at the CoCH "overlook[ing] something that is very, very important and very significant, i.e. skin discolouration". Dr Evans is not only confirming that the *Lee and Tanswell* paper was central to his theory but also that discolouration was the decisive diagnostic factor. "Evans had no experience of this, and so cannot be so confident", Professor Colin Morley observed.

During court proceedings, Ben Myers questioned Dr Evans on the basis for his diagnosis of air embolism and asked him the following question: "You base [what you've asserted] upon what you've read, the description in the report by Lee and Tanswell, don't you?" The response of Dr Evans was as straightforward as is possible – he simply said "Yes". Dr Evans later praised the *Lee and Tanswell* paper in court, describing it as "the best known in relation to pulmonary vascular air embolism in the newborn", as referenced by the Court of Appeal in paragraph 45 of its judgment, and stated at the trial on 25 October 2022 that it was "the main paper we refer, the paper we refer most commonly to". The Court of Appeal judgment is almost entirely devoted to discussing the *Lee and Tanswell* paper, and its referencing during the court case.

Nonetheless, one of the many talents of Dr Evans is back-pedalling rapidly. Faced with the fact that he had based a central diagnosis in the court case on one particular academic paper, sung the praises of that study, and now the person who authored it was dismissing his work, Dr Evans relied on the assertion that he had "presented 18 papers" in making this diagnosis. This is pretty poorly founded anyway, considering that court proceedings make it explicitly clear that *Lee and Tanswell* was principally used as a diagnostic reference. But, as an example, in the case of Child N, other academic work was introduced making an association between air embolism and screaming: "I quoted these papers because of the association between air embolus in these two cases and screaming". In the Court of Appeal judgment, the *Lee and Tanswell* paper is referenced 41 times. All other scientific papers collectively are cited only once; in that single instance, Dr Lee doubts a case described in a 2009 Korean paper.

Professor Sally Kinsey referenced the *Lee and Tanswell* paper in court during proceedings related to Child A when confirming that she drew a parallel between the 1989 journal review and discolouration observed in infants. When Child B was discussed, Professor Kinsey again referenced the *Lee and Tanswell* study and its supposed proximity to skin discolouration observations seen in Child B. Dr Sandie Bohin cited the medical journal review as being instrumental in the diagnosis of Child D. And Professor Kinsey again confirmed that she was "drawing a parallel" between material in *Lee and Tanswell* and discolouration observed in Child E.

In reality, the *Lee and Tanswell* paper was a central pillar in the entire argument and diagnosis of air embolism, referenced repeatedly throughout the court proceedings and Court of Appeal verdict, while clearly having been utilised as a sole diagnostic source. The study was referenced repeatedly in the Court of Appeal judgment, and while Dr Lee featured in this appeal and his work was therefore of particular relevance, the court explicitly acknowledged that the paper was of critical importance in the original trial.

It is difficult to see how Dr Evans can downplay the significance of this diagnosis being completely discredited by the co-author of the paper itself which is ironic because, as Dr Mike Hall informed me, none of the cases from the *Lee and Tanswell* paper refer to air embolism in a neonate, contrary to what is stated in the Court of Appeal judgment. Dr Evans has also made claims of having referenced 18 papers for his air embolism theory, but, in fact, only two of them described venous air embolism (air in the veins), which is the method allegedly used by Letby to kill and harm babies.

Dr Colin Ferguson told me: "Dr Evans has a very sketchy idea of a whole range of issues relating to the pathophysiology of the hypotheses he has come up with. There are major deficiencies in his knowledge of cardiac and vascular physiology, the physics of gas absorption in blood, the blood supply to the skin and the physics of respiration. In addition, he has indulged in a clear misrepresentation of the medical literature that he relied on in court."

During the interview with Raj Persaud, Dr Evans explained that staff at the CoCH "overlooked something that is very, very important and very significant, i.e. skin discolouration". The comments of Dr Evans, in fact, make it clear that there is no air embolism theory without discolouration as the other criteria that he references, both in interviews and court, cannot possibly be considered diagnostic.

Dr Evans told *The Times* that "the presence or absence of skin discolourations neither ruled out or confirmed air embolism". But without discolouration there is literally nothing. There is simply a neonate deteriorating, which cannot conceivably be regarded as being caused by an air embolism. Yet this was seriously advocated in court: "Sudden collapse and a failure to respond to resuscitation were, he [Evans] observed, characteristics of several of the babies whose records he had reviewed for the police. These features were 'characteristic of the description of the babies in the studies described above whose death was attributed to air embolus'", the Court of Appeal recounts.

This seems a ridiculous assertion which I'm sure most medical professionals would agree with. "Sudden collapse and a failure to respond to resuscitation" are not *characteristic* of anything, let alone an incredibly obscure hypothesis. "In neonates, such issues could be due to many problems", Professor Colin Morley informed me. "The most common is sub-par ventilation from inexperienced staff; potentially a major factor at the CoCH. A lack of response can be due to the inflation pressure being too low."

One observer who did witness everything that was said in court was the uncalled Dr Hall. In a letter published in the *British Medical Journal*, Dr Hall was critical of the discolouration evidence used in court. He noted that the term 'skin discolouration' appears 48 times in the document submitted by the prosecution, while the *Lee and Tanswell* paper is referenced 25 times. Dr Hall pointed out several problems with citing this evidence, including the skin discolouration being more likely to be caused by circulatory impairment, associated with sudden collapse from various causes. Dr Hall had been able to locate only one paper that discussed the alteration in skin colour associated with the accidental injection of air, and the changes documented in this "were quite different to those described by *Lee and Tanswell*". Hall goes on to assert that "an experienced medical reviewer would have identified at least the first two points [that I have raised], enabling the judges to determine their significance".

Most importantly, Hall observed that the "*Lee and Tanswell* paper did not describe features of venous air embolism!" The *Lee and Tanswell* paper addresses pulmonary vascular air embolism, not venous air embolism. This completely discredits observations made in court, while Dr Philip Hammond, writing in *Private Eye*, also noted that "the skin changes described didn't even match [the] research findings".

This was elaborated on by Dr Lee when speaking at a press conference on 4 February 2025: "There is a difference between arterial and venous [air embolism] because the arteries carry blood to the body, to supply the organs and the skin, whereas the veins actually carry blood away from the skin to the heart and lungs." Dr Lee went on to reference supporting findings in his recently authored paper. It is important to reiterate that Dr Evans has described his diagnosis as a "clinically proven mechanism" in court, when, in reality, the author of the source he has relied on diagnostically has stated, and backed this up in a published paper, that "none of this actually has ever been described".

Dr Hall later told *The Daily Telegraph* that "both the barristers and the medical witnesses talked in terms of 'we've now established that these skin discolourations are clearly due to air embolism' but there is little evidence for that. Babies who are very sick can get variations of skin discolouration." An email from Dr John Gibbs to Dr Ravi Jayaram in June 2016 observed that no one had spotted an air embolism via chest X-rays taken at the CoCH.

A forensic pathologist told me that "blood can appear frothy in the heart in cases of air embolism at post-mortem". This was also cited by Dr Philip Hammond, who explained that "right ventricular activity churns the mixture of air and blood into a bloody froth". Unlike the method of murder described by Dr Evans in court, this genuinely is a clinically documented mechanism. A literature review of air embolism cases describes "the churning of the frothing blood within the heart chambers", air rising and being "churned into froth and mixed with blood", and "frothy blood and air bubbles [being] found in the pulmonary trunk, inferior or superior vena cava, and the coronary veins". Another study references the right ventricular activity mentioned by Dr Hammond, providing accounts of "frothy blood inside the heart" at autopsy. And a third, very recent study, also gives evidence of frothy blood. There are numerous other studies that also document this frothing of the blood.

No such froth was observed by the pathologists who examined the actual infants at the CoCH. In fact, Ian Harvey had written to Dr Jo McPartland, a consultant pathologist, requesting some specific details: "Just one query – the report states: 'A very small air embolism might not be detectable at autopsy'. Does this mean that a significant embolism would be evident?" And Dr McPartland answered in the only way that is reasonable: "Yes, a significant air embolism should be accompanied by froth in the vessels or lungs." Pathologists from Alder Hey Children's Hospital also informed Harvey that a significant air embolism would be detected at post-mortem.

The critical *Lee and Tanswell* paper notes that "a frothy mixture of blood and air [are] often obtained" with air embolism, which was even quoted by Dr Evans in his witness statement submitted to Cheshire Police on 3 July 2019. The submission from Evans also references a 2007 study co-authored by Sowell, Lovelady, Brogdon and Wecht, and its comment that "right ventricular activity churns the mixture of air and blood into a bloody froth well known to forensic pathologists". Yet despite quoting both of these passages and despite the conspicuous absence of any such frothy blood, Dr Evans still cited air embolism.

On 25 January 2017, Dr McPartland filed her report, having carried out a forensic review of Child A, Child I, Child O and Child P. McPartland found "no evidence of air embolism" in the case of Child A which was the only death that remained unascertained. McPartland observed that "at autopsy there was no evidence of air embolism…a very small air embolism might not be detectable at autopsy, but then would not be expected to lead to death". Similarly, a discussion between coroner Nicholas Rheinberg and the anonymised Dr S saw the latter confirm that "there have been cases of respiratory arrest followed by cardiac arrest where an air embolism would be present and normally one would see froth when the heart was opened up…however this had not happened in this case and there was also nothing in the brain to suggest any particular problems".

Both Evans and Bohin conceded that they have no expertise or experience with air embolisms, nor are they pathologists. This also applies to Professor Sally Kinsey, who confessed that she was not an expert on such mechanisms when speaking in court. Professor Kinsey relied on medical literature related to decompression in deep-sea divers, and when asked a question about nitrogen bubbles being in anatomical circulation longer than oxygen bubbles, she was forced to state "I don't know the answer to that question", and conceded that "there were many limitations to [the] findings [of the paper]". Dr Michael Hall informed me that the *Lee and*

Tanswell paper "was largely studying oxygen embolism, not air embolism. 78% of air is nitrogen, and this behaves quite differently if it enters the circulation. Despite the paper being cited on numerous occasions during the trial, the jury were never informed of this."

The many problems with using the *Lee and Tanswell* paper were already established before the involvement of Dr Lee himself. The paper was not directly related to the supposed link between air embolism and skin discolouration, with this phenomenon only being noted as an aside in less than 10% of the more than 50 cases reviewed. The subjects of the *Lee and Tanswell* paper were not comparable in age, medical condition or clinical circumstances with neonates. And the mottling and discolouration of the skin that was used diagnostically by Dr Evans cannot be used to make such a diagnosis as it is associated with numerous other clinical conditions such as hypothermia, sepsis, allergies, viruses and immune reactions. Dr Lee, in fact, explicitly told the Court of Appeal that "the only cutaneous sign which is itself sufficient to make the diagnosis in a baby is the bright pink blood vessels superimposed on blue skin".

Dr Evans referenced the condition of cyanosis during the introduction of his theory when being cross-examined by prosecuting barrister Nick Johnson on 25 October 2022. Unfortunately, the infants in the case don't show any actual signs of cyanosis. When cross-examined by Ben Myers, Dr Evans conceded that skin discolourations "written down" by the anonymised Dr B were "not the same as the *Lee and Tanswell* description. It's not the same."

Air embolism cases are extremely rare; at the time of writing there have only been 117 reported in babies globally. When I spoke to Dr Lee, he told me that he had "examined every case of air embolism that has been published to date and there has never been a case of venous air embolism that has exhibited skin discolourations similar to what was described in the trial". As an example of this, the highly experienced Professor Colin Morley told me that he'd never encountered a single case in a baby. In fact, there is no evidence that the criteria cited by Dr Evans has ever been used to diagnose venous air embolism. One medic told me that "it would fail peer review". Of course, the lack of a serious peer review was a major problem with the entire prosecution case.

The paper by Lee and Tanswell references an earlier study, *Post-mortem Gas Accumulation in Premature Infants* which was published in 1974. Dr Roger Norwich pointed this paper and its significance out to me: "What this study demonstrates is that if X-rays of a baby are not taken within 25 minutes of death, the build-up of air or gas in the body is completely irrelevant because it's nothing to do with the situation when the baby died." The study indeed concludes that "since physiologic gas accumulation can occur rapidly, the significance of post-mortem intravascular gas can be interpreted only if the interval between death and the radiographic exposure is known". This is yet another factor that weakens the evidence provided in court that air injection was the cause of collapse and death in infants.

During her cross-examination, Dr Bohin accepted that discolouration of the skin could be caused by conditions other than air embolism, and that it was not possible to say what pattern of skin discolouration is specifically distinctive of this. Conversely, Dr Lee described a very specific pattern of red vessels on a blue background in his original paper. But Dr Evans was so unyielding in his hypothesis that he claimed the ability to perform an incredible feat:

"We've since heard about the discolouration. But before I knew about that, I thought if you – if this baby has collapsed as promptly as that, and even more significantly, more significantly resuscitation was unsuccessful, that is an air embolus. That is an air embolus, in my opinion, and that was my opinion before I knew about the X-rays and the discolouration."

So Dr Evans doesn't require the X-ray, nor any evidence of air being present, even though this could be naturally occurring air. He also doesn't require any evidence of discolouration. He is able to diagnose air embolus purely because "the baby has collapsed as promptly as that... [and] resuscitation was unsuccessful". That is what he is using as diagnostic criteria for air embolism, in his own words. The baby collapsed, it wasn't successfully resuscitated – it's an air embolism, obviously!

There are, conservatively, hundreds of reasons why the condition of a neonate could deteriorate and then fail to resuscitate. Yet Dr Evans stated quite plainly in court that he was able to diagnose air embolus from these factors alone. He didn't even need to know about the discolouration, which, while utterly flawed, was the solitary diagnostic criterion of any merit whatsoever. Evans later doubled down on this absurd position, telling *The Guardian* in May 2025 that he "had reached a diagnosis of air embolus long before (re)discovering Lee and Tanswell's publication".

Another component that was discussed in court was the presence of rashes in some infants. This was introduced during the initial discussion of the overarching air injection theory that was of primary importance in court. Dr Evans explained that he "heard the descriptions of this rash" in the case of Child A and this was another contributory factor to this "diagnosis that his collapse was the result of an air embolus". It is important to observe that this element of diagnosis was based on the *Lee and Tanswell* paper: "[Dr Evans] later [became] aware that his colleagues were describing a rash, and so he had then undertaken a literature review and came across the *Lee and Tanswell* paper". This cannot possibly even be described as a diagnosis.

This was another highly tenuous aspect of the trial, which has been criticised by Dr Lee: "There were no cases that have been described where, in fact, these skin rashes have occurred", Dr Lee told assembled journalists at the February 2025 press conference. "The notion that these cases are air embolism because they collapsed, and because there were skin rashes, has no basis in evidence."

This assertion of Dr Lee was universally supported by a variety of medics and nurses. "Anybody who is undergoing a circulatory collapse will become mottled, and that mottling can take a range of appearances", Dr Colin Ferguson told me. "The descriptions of rashes and discolourations have varied quite considerably from patient to patient." The Court of Appeal has been informed of this by Ben Myers, who, rightly, asserted that "the prosecution expert evidence provided neither a research basis nor clinical experience sufficient to enable reliable identification of any specific cutaneous discolouration which would be diagnostic of air embolus. The witnesses, he argues, unjustifiably treated a wide variety of cutaneous discolouration as diagnostic."

Experienced nurse Julie Yates also cited these same evidential problems: "With air embolisms of the nature assumed, we are not seeing the required blue background reported with pink blood vessels showing up. It's very specific, and it simply wasn't described." Similarly, another neonatal nurse was of the opinion that evidence used in court was "floppy and indistinct", based on "a rash that a doctor can't adequately describe, which doesn't even fit the description from the paper used". Furthermore, many of these 'rashes' were not documented at the time, and only recalled several years later, which would obviously immediately call their accuracy into question.

Michele Worden also asserted that "babies often have rashes and mottling when sick. Consultants were seeing things that are quite normal in neonatal practice, if you're a neonatologist." In her statement to the Thirlwall Inquiry, neonatal nurse Minna-Maria Lappalainen observed that "mottled appearance of the skin in preterm or ill newborn is not uncommon. This can be due to a baby being ill with infection [or] poor blood circulation." Dr Jane Hawdon also explained at the Thirlwall Inquiry that Ian Harvey's questioning on mottling was not something she had expected: "I was surprised that he asked about mottling because it is such a common finding in babies that are unwell, and we were sadly talking about babies who were unwell. [Air embolism] is something that would not have crossed my mind at all at that stage when thinking about mottling. I would be thinking of common causes of mottling of the skin." Hawdon had informed Harvey in an email on 5 February 2017 that mottling in the infants was "variable", and that if it was "transient" then it was "probably not of significance".

The fixation with rashes or mottling at the CoCH was addressed similarly by two interviewees I spoke with. Dr Margaret Ferguson opined that "it's possible that there was mutually reinforced groupthink to some extent. These rashes seem to become such a significant piece of remembered evidence, with no real medical basis for this, since the descriptions were so variable and not deemed important enough to be recorded at the time." As an experienced operator in government, Dr James Phillips has been privy to certain perspectives becoming cemented within groups, and he told me that "it can become very difficult to reverse, or even slow down, the momentum created by a critical mass of people who hold a certain view. This seems to have occurred in this case." A study published in 2023 examined this phenomenon, noting that "there is increasing interest and awareness that health professional teams may be vulnerable to groupthink…One perspective is that health professional teams are typically homogeneous in background…and professional values, and may exhibit convergence in thinking that promotes group cohesiveness that leads to poor decision making."

What we do know for certain is that multiple infants involved in the court case were exhibiting signs of other illnesses. Neonatal nurse practitioner Sloane Spade highlighted the case of Child D, who was "struggling to breathe from birth…her mother then had prolonged rupture of membranes, which increases the risk of intrapartum infection [an infection of a mother's amniotic fluid], of which the pneumonia Child D presented with was a complication of the prolonged broken waters". Conversely, Dr Bohin stated that Child D "had been born in good condition".

Dr Evans accepted during the trial that pneumonia was present, but claimed that "the pneumonia was not responsible in any way for her death". When I put this to Professor Colin Morley, he told me plainly: "Evans simply has no basis for saying this." And speaking at the Thirlwall Inquiry, Dr Jo McPartland observed that "there was a clear pneumonia, but not only was there pneumonia; there were hyaline membranes which indicated acute lung injury, which you don't normally see. That did lead me to believe that there was more extensive lung injury from the pneumonia than you might expect, so that could explain then why the child didn't behave as the clinicians might have expected." Again, Professor Morley explained the significance of this: "Hyaline membranes at post-mortem indicate that the lungs had been damaged. There is no reason to suspect air embolism. Evans was simply wrong to rule out respiratory distress and has no basis to do this."

The hyaline membranes were also referenced in a case review of Child D in August 2015. This was a clear sign of respiratory distress, but it was ruled out by Dr Evans in favour of air injected into her bloodstream. In

September 2015, Dr McPartland had emailed Joanne Davies, consultant clinical lead for obstetrics and gynaecology, to inform her that, "As I said in my report, I think this could be a congenital pneumonia." Professor Carola Vinuesa highlighted this testimony from the pathologist, and also noted that Dr McPartland found no evidence of air embolism.

In the case of Child D, it is not contested that Letby had raised the alarm indicating that the child was unwell, and also that she was called to the nursery to assist having not been the designated nurse for the infant, as indicated by nursing notes. Dr Emily Thomas, who was on a six-month paediatric placement at the CoCH and had been alerted by Letby, told the court on 8 November 2022 that Letby was visibly upset by the collapse of Child D: "This is my second baby that this has happened to", Dr Thomas recalled Letby saying.

The prosecution claimed in court, with absolutely no basis, that the notes were inaccurate or that Letby was attempting to provide herself with an alibi. It was fully accepted by the prosecution that notes associated with Child D indicate that Letby wasn't present for the initial collapse. The allegations directed at Letby in this case were reliant on:

- Not trusting sources of data that in other instances the prosecution cited as proving its case;
- Coming up with hypothetical explanations for why this data shouldn't be trusted;
- Ignoring information about the movements of nurses at the time of the collapses;
- Ignoring the fact that Letby wasn't present for the initial collapses;
- Ignoring the fact that Letby raised the alarm;
- Overlooking the conduct of Letby, which in any reasonable context would be considered exemplary nursing, and certainly not suspicious.

That's before the unlikely diagnosis of Dr Evans is even examined. And then, on top of that, the prosecution used its trump card throughout this court case, citing that none of the medical staff on duty that night had also been present for the collapses of Child A, B or C. It's always Lucy, isn't it? Well, no, we've established that this aspect of the prosecution case is completely without foundation. It is important to note in this case that the prosecution has relied on the 'it's always Lucy' theory, because without that there is nothing to indicate that she committed any malicious acts against Child D. In fact, the evidence points to the complete opposite.

Dr Jane Hawdon observed at the Thirlwall Inquiry that there had been a "backing off of respiratory support on the day that [this] baby sadly deteriorated". Dr Hawdon cited this "change in respiratory management" as being significant in the "baby subsequently deteriorating again". The parents of Child D had observed that the infant was "limp" and "without colour – a bit grey, purple", making "grunting noises", and was "not responsive", which, understandably, made them "really worried". But Dr Sandie Bohin simply concluded in court that "I can't believe [the midwifery team] would have allowed…the baby to…stay on the post-natal ward in that condition." In response, Professor Colin Morley explained that the infant was "very sick with respiratory problems, based on easily observable signs".

There was a catalogue of failings in relation to Child D, while all clinical indicators pointed to this being an extremely poorly infant. There was considerable evidence of necrotising enterocolitis. The presence of sepsis was also noted. The infant had multiple collapses, and had to be moved to Arrowe Park Hospital in Liverpool; the parents of Child D were told that the CoCH "couldn't do any more for her". The infant was kept nil-by-mouth in order for a dye test to be conducted (this test examines the digestive tract), yet it was never carried out.

When challenged by Dr Lee on having never criticised care at the hospital, Dr Evans referred to a delay in the provision of antibiotics for Child D as his only example. But Evans never raised this himself during the trial. He was asked whether he had considered the delay by prosecuting barrister Nick Johnson, and responded: "I did – I'm not sure. Yes. Yes, I did. Yes. I – Yes". Hardly a convincing indication that this was even included in the four reports that he wrote on this infant, let alone Evans emphasising this in court. During cross-examination Evans asserted that the infant's "management was entirely consistent with what I'd expect of a modern neonatal unit".

Apgar scores (which measure Appearance, Pulse, Grimace response, Activity and Respiration) are conducted five minutes after birth. These scores were brought up continually during the trial by the prosecution as evidence that infants were stable and well. However, just 12 minutes after birth, Child D became floppy and collapsed, which completely overrides any relevance of Apgar scores. The jury are therefore hugely reliant on expert medical opinion, and they firstly heard Dr Bohin suggest that the collapse had occurred due to the father holding the infant incorrectly. Dr Bohin then attempted to claim discolouration as evidence of air embolism when this was observed to be reddy-brown in colour, not the "bright pink vessels against a generally cyanosed...background" cited in the 1989 *Lee and Tanswell* paper used for diagnosis.

Evans described Child D as being "extremely well". This has been treated with derision by every healthcare professional that I've spoken with. "It is stunning", experienced anaesthetist Dr Keith Wilkinson told me. "This infant was so ill towards the end of her life that if I had been present – and I've been in this situation in intensive care units many times – I would have told colleagues that the right thing to do is explain sensitively to the parents that the best thing to do is remove support, due to the inevitability of death." It should finally be mentioned that pathologist Dr Andreas Marnerides conceded in court that he had "not reviewed the medical records".

This is just one example of how flawed the original court case was. Lucy Letby is serving a life sentence for the murder of Child D, despite not being present for the initial collapses, not being the designated nurse and only being present because she was called to the scene, no one having been witnessed doing anything untoward or suspicious. And it is agreed by all parties contradicting the prosecution case that much of the medical evidence used in court is highly dubious, and that other more prosaic explanations for the tragic passing of Child D, such as infection, were discounted. All of this points to the conclusions of the original pathologist being correct, but, inexplicably, the pathology reports have been jettisoned in favour of the arcane theories of Dr Evans. Professor

Colin Morley asserted: "This baby had several collapses, which is not surprising for an infant with possible sepsis and respiratory difficulty. It is utterly illogical to say that the last collapse was caused by an air embolus."

Continuous positive airway pressure (CPAP) was also frequently discussed during the court case. CPAP is a form of ventilation used to provide respiratory support. A paper published in 2020 by doctors from the neonatal unit at Westmead Hospital in Sydney suggested that a condition called CPAP belly syndrome can sometimes occur in neonates, with similar symptoms to necrotising enterocolitis (this latter condition will be discussed imminently). Writing in the *International Journal of Clinical Paediatrics*, the authors described the case of a newborn suddenly developing a massively distended abdomen and feed intolerance, which led to a "crisis point" with extremely low oxygen levels and blue-purplish skin. They concluded: "In our experience, the clinical presentation of CPAP belly syndrome in extreme preterm infants can be dramatic, mimicking acute NEC scare, necessitating urgent diagnostic evaluation."

In the case report for Child C, the large amount of gas in the stomach prevented the infant's chest from rising meaning that the baby could not breathe, and needed immediate intubation. Similar breathing issues occurred in other indictment infants, but prosecution experts claimed this was due to Letby injecting air into the stomach. "Both the use and lack of CPAP contributed to a lot of the problems in these cases", Sloane Spade told me. "Excessive CPAP can cause CPAP belly which leads to loops of bowel filled with air, and there is explicit evidence of this in the case. The large abdomen while on CPAP can mask the abdominal distension seen with NEC. Furthermore, the lack of CPAP usage seen in several cases can lead to various respiratory difficulties."

During court proceedings, Professor Owen Arthurs opined that "marked gas dilatation" in the stomach has several potential causes, including CPAP belly, while also citing sepsis and necrotising enterocolitis. It is notable that Professor Arthurs offered very little support for the prosecution case despite appearing prominently in court. In the case of Child I, an infant who faced ongoing clinical problems due to her extreme prematurity, CPAP treatment was linked with CPAP belly in the baby, leading to the distended abdomen that was observed. And Child O, who was suffering with infection, also showed explicit signs of CPAP belly.

"If any of these babies had more than an average amount of air inside of their abdomens or stomachs, this was almost certainly due to the units of CPAP that are used these days", Dr Roger Norwich explained. "I personally believe that the injection of air is utter nonsense, and I've yet to meet a neonatologist who thinks it's anything other than total rubbish." Another paediatrician who wished to remain anonymous concurred that "CPAP belly is a very common and well known reason for neonates to have an excess amount of air in the gastrointestinal tract." The administration of CPAP was a prominent aspect of court proceedings, being discussed in relation to Children A, B, C, D, F, G, H, I, O and Q.

The serious intestinal disease necrotising enterocolitis was linked with several infants in the case. NEC has a particularly high mortality rate in premature infants, ranging from 20 to 30%, and elevating to nearly 50% in those born at 28 weeks or earlier. The association of this life-threatening illness with Child E will be discussed in "Other Infants", and Child C, the focus of the next chapter in the book, also showed signs of this gastrointestinal disease, as noted by neonatal nurse Joanne Williams, while the infant was suffering with serious intestinal problems.

Staff at the CoCH recorded that Child I was suffering with NEC, following an X-ray which revealed "moderately severe bowel distention". The situation was considered so serious that Child I was another infant who was transferred out to Liverpool Women's Hospital, with a focus on being closer to Alder Hey. An extraordinary proportion of these infants were either transferred, or considered for transfer, to other hospitals – 11 in total. This is hardly ideal considering the condition of these babies, although it is notable that many of them recovered once they were in a different environment. This would beg the question of whether Liverpool Women's, Arrowe Park or Alder Hey should have been caring for them in the first place.

Child I was given metronidazole, the antibiotic used if NEC is suspected. The parents of Child I were "not happy" that tests were not conducted to diagnose or rule out NEC in the infant, which could have informed future care. Further ward rounds on 14 October 2015 revealed that the child was still suspected of having NEC, and this was echoed when the infant was transferred to Arrowe Park the next day, with suspected NEC and inflammation of the gut – common conditions in pre-term babies.

Speaking in court, Dr Evans noted that staff at the CoCH "were concerned about NEC on a number of occasions". Professor Arthurs also provided radiographic evidence that indicated features of NEC with Child I. However, Dr Evans dismissed this, citing the post-mortem which had not given NEC as the cause of death. He didn't quite so readily mention that he himself had discounted post-mortem verdicts repeatedly throughout the court case, without examining any of the infants. Dr Bohin claimed that the condition of Child I was "compatible" with air embolism, which must be considered a fairly meaningless statement.

In the case of Child J, it is not contested that NEC was suspected, and the infant was treated for bowel and intestinal issues at Alder Hey, undergoing an emergency procedure. It is not really clear why Child J was part of the court case, considering that no specific form of harm was even identified by the prosecution, and Dr Bohin conceded that she was not able to identify an "obvious cause" for collapse. Dr Evans came up with a cause of inflicted harm, asserting that her brain had been deprived of oxygen, causing hypoxia. This was described in court by the defence as an "assumption of deliberate harm".

Child N was another infant linked with NEC as paediatric registrar, Dr Huw Mayberry, informed Cheshire Police. Child O was treated for suspected NEC and this was cited as a possible cause of illness and collapse in court by Professor Arthurs. In the case of Child Q, medical staff noted a "mildly dilated loop of bowel" on the left side of the infant and raised the possibility of NEC. This was recorded in the clinical notes for the infant, including by Lucy Letby herself, and again supported by radiographic evidence from Professor Arthurs.

Professor Carola Vinuesa discussed the importance of NEC, drawing my attention to an academic study called *Statistically significant association between NEC and pseudomonas infections* which found that 36% of infants with pseudomonas aeruginosa also suffered with NEC. "The gas present in infants could easily have been caused by NEC, and this is particularly heightened as a possibility by the presence of pseudomonas on the neonatal ward", Professor Vinuesa explained.

Other abdominal and intestinal conditions associated with NEC, including obstruction of the intestine and perforation, could help explain some of the phenomena observed in infants from the CoCH. And there are two other critical aspects of NEC, particularly regarding neonates. Firstly, NEC is an undeniably deadly condition. Depending on gestation, size and condition of the infant in question, NEC can have a mortality rate of 50%. In a study from 2021, the prognosis was found to be even worse than this; 52 neonates with NEC were found to have an overall survival rate of just 44.2%. This is then amplified on a unit where pseudomonas is circulating, considering that a 2020 study observed that 50% of extremely low gestational age newborns with pseudomonas succumbed to the infection.

Secondly, the early identification of clinical warning signs is extremely important in treating NEC, but the diagnosis relies heavily on the interpretation of abdominal radiographs. If this does not occur, and diagnoses are not made rapidly, the chances of survival are hugely reduced. One recent study notes that "prompt and accurate diagnosis [of NEC] continues to be a challenge for health professionals", and that "postgraduate training of paediatricians and neonatologists in neonatal abdominal radiography is scarce, and there is variability of radiological input to neonatal services". This tendency was quite evident in court proceedings, where diagnoses of NEC were made at the CoCH, but never tested or confirmed, let alone actioned adequately.

Neonatal nurse Sloane Spade was quite adamant that "any amount of bad bacteria colonising in a neonatal ward would speak badly for the unit and heighten such risks significantly". And another neonatal nurse recounted that "when there is a more silent onset of NEC, in my experience it tends to be more severe. It's very difficult to diagnose, this is documented, and I can't see how it can be ruled out as a cause, particularly when it was suspected in so many infants."

As discussed in Chapter 5, sepsis is also linked with pseudomonas. There was considerable evidence of underlying sepsis in numerous infants in the court case. In her statement to the Thirlwall Inquiry, Caroline Oakley specifically mentioned sepsis as a likely cause of a rash observed on the neonatal unit. Similarly, the very earliest emails available from the Thirlwall Inquiry record Dr Stephen Brearey, Dr John Gibbs and Dr Elizabeth Newby discussing sepsis in June 2015.

This can be contrasted with the insistence of Dr Evans that infection had no impact on any of the infants involved in the court case, and he also completely dismissed the possibility that infection had any significance, even when cited by pathologists. This is despite the fact that Children A, C, D, E, F, G, I, O and Q were all either confirmed or suspected to be suffering with sepsis, Children B, H, J, K and N were all noted to be suffering with other forms of infection, and some infants showed signs of more than one type of infection.

Another critical topic in the whole picture of the air embolism diagnosis is related to Child A and Child B, twins who were born prematurely. Child A died within 24 hours of birth, while an allegation of attempted murder was discussed in court with regard to Child B.

In both of these infants, antiphospholipid syndrome (APS) was considered crucial. This condition is an autoimmune disorder, described to me by Dr Martyn Pitman as "pretty horrible", which leads to an increased risk of blood clotting, often resulting in conditions such as thrombosis (the formation of clotting, which prevents the flow of blood). The APS observed in both infants was cited by the panel of experts that Dr Shoo Lee assembled. It was also indicated in clinical notes from the CoCH, which was mentioned in court reporting of the time.

A paediatric contact considered that "the impact of APS wasn't properly explored in the trial. It can affect the baby, especially when there are other factors involved such as repeat catheterisations, trauma and sepsis. And there were certainly both repeat catheterisations, where they attempted six times, plus evidence of sepsis." Dr Roger Norwich also cited APS as being significant: "It's likely that antibodies from the mother affected her infants. And one of the babies was subjected to incredibly poor treatment. There weren't enough blood tests done despite evidence that lactates were increasing alarmingly. And the child was deprived of fluids for a dangerously extended period."

When providing evidence in court, Professor Sally Kinsey appears to have dismissed these clinical notes, instead citing skin discolourations. She also conceded that she may not have sufficient expertise to recognise or diagnose air embolism but the impact on the jury of her citing this, and dismissing APS, could have been considerable.

The presence of APS is important as it left both Child A and Child B vulnerable to thrombotic events and inflammation, particularly as premature babies. One study published in 2010 found that mothers with "antiphospholipid positivity and/or previous thromboembolism seem to have a high probability of poor neonatal outcome". The condition was linked with both infants at the CoCH, and Letby herself noted during court proceedings that APS was discussed at the hospital. She also confirmed, which is not contested, that if the death of Child A had been established as air embolism – of course, this wasn't even suggested at the time, including by pathologists – then the air embolism itself must have been caused by the person connecting the fluids, which was not Letby.

Speaking in court, Professor Kinsey ruled out the possibility of APS, despite the presence of clinical notes suggesting the contrary. But ruling out the APS recorded in the notes would require a series of blood tests that search for antibodies, which have the exotic names of lupus anticoagulant, anticardiolipin, and anti-beta-2-glycoprotein. This requires tests to be carried out 12 weeks apart. It is essentially impossible to rule out APS based on a solitary blood test, when the relevant mechanism of action is the abnormal level of antibodies found in the baby's blood alongside a thrombus in the liver, which corroborates this impression. This is why APS is listed in the clinical notes for the infants in the first place.

The 12-week testing period is not a secret; it is required as the levels of antibodies in the blood can fluctuate due to infection and other factors. There are many sources that point to this requirement. In fact, the *minimum* 12-week diagnosis period is also a stipulated guideline of the British Society for Haematology. There is simply no way to rule out an APS diagnosis from one blood test. When I spoke with Professor Carola Vinuesa, I asked her about the way that APS was dismissed in court, and she raised an interesting point: "The baby had a mother with APS. The differential diagnosis of a potential cerebrovascular accident – thromboembolism causing neonatal stroke – should have been included." It is important to emphasise that I spoke to Professor Vinuesa before barrister Mark McDonald's panel convened, and made precisely this diagnosis.

Professor Vinuesa continued: "With regard to Child A and those claiming that the APS doesn't get passed on – the auto-antibodies that cause thrombi *are* passed on 30% of the time. Also, if there is repeated catheterisation, sepsis or trauma, there can be thromboembolic events." How did she feel about the way this was discussed in court? "The science presented in the trial regarding this subject was deeply disappointing", Professor Vinuesa replied.

In addition to this, it is also known that babies can inherit a predisposition to APS without showing the antibodies at birth. One study from 2020 notes that "it is not common to detect [APS antibodies] at birth, even in children born to mothers positive during pregnancy". The same study highlights the occurrence of the neonatal thrombosis in affected infants, while noting that "thrombosis episodes [are] not always associated with maternal antibody positivity". One medic I spoke with asserted that "there was a lack of clarity in the testimony of Dr Kinsey. The babies are likely to have been passed APS antibodies from the mother, which increased their risk of clotting."

Several medics also indicated that the rashes observed in Child A and Child B could easily be an indication of livedo reticularis – a skin condition that results from the disturbance of blood flow. This is the most common skin problem associated with APS, and it is also characterised by a mottled pattern of discolouration on the skin. Considering that we know the mother had APS, livedo reticularis is a far more likely cause of rashes and discolouration than maliciously administered air embolism. Professor Colin Morley explained that "this physical sign could be from many causes, of which air embolus must be the rarest and least likely".

Studies indicate that livedo reticularis affects up to 80% of patients with antiphospholipid antibodies, while the condition is a marker for predicting multi-system thrombosis in APS as confirmed by a comprehensive academic review which found that livedo reticularis is frequently observed in APS patients. As discussed in a previous chapter, there is also strong evidence that the mother was suffering with maternal lupus.

Another medic I spoke with pointed to "unusual rashes, which seem likely to be this condition called livedo reticularis". Again, in this instance, much was made in court of the fact that staff present had never seen this type of rash before. But this can simply be explained by the lack of experience on the neonatal unit, which has already been documented.

Also of relevance to many of the conditions discussed in the chapter is medication called ranitidine which is now banned in many countries. Dr Nim Subhedar, who had been the Clinical Lead at the Cheshire and Merseyside Neonatal Network, flagged this up as a concern to Dr Stephen Brearey in February 2016. This was just two days after the hospital itself recognised the potential dangers of the drug during a thematic review, and proposed to change its practice based on academic evidence. Nonetheless, the review also concluded that the CoCH was not an "outlier"; something that the consultants appeared determined to believe and assert.

The risks associated with ranitidine usage were already established by 2016, and these are particularly pertinent to this case. A 2012 study in the *Pediatrics* journal demonstrated "an association between the use of ranitidine and infections, NEC and fatal outcome in very low birth weight newborns". The study concluded that "caution is advocated in using ranitidine in newborns", owing to the six-fold increase in the incidence of the condition NEC and a higher mortality rate overall. Another study found that infants receiving ranitidine had a significantly higher incidence of infection and mortality versus a control group. A summary of ranitidine as a medication, posted on the Australasian Neonatal Medicines Formulary in 2017, warns that it "may be associated with increased risk of NEC in preterm infants", and that "the use of ranitidine in infants admitted to the NICU increases the risk of late onset sepsis".

There is one other final important medical component to discuss in this chapter, which is the fact that the original conclusion of air embolism was a diagnosis of exclusion. This term refers to any diagnosis made when other conditions have been ruled out. The notion that air embolism could be diagnosed by exclusion caused consternation in several interviewees. Professor Carola Vinuesa exemplified this: "How can anyone talk about a diagnosis of exclusion, particularly with premature and low birth-weight babies?"

Both during and since the court case, Dr Dewi Evans has attempted to deny that air embolism was a diagnosis of exclusion. But this position is completely untenable. One example of this denial emerged early in court proceedings, during discussion related to Child A. Barrister Ben Myers made the observation that air embolism was a diagnosis of exclusion, to which Dr Evans claimed that there was more to the case than that. He then made the extraordinary statement that he had made his original conclusion without knowing about the skin discolouration in Child A – once again stating that he was able to make this diagnosis without the only meaningful diagnostic criterion. If you were to "discover additional information", Dr Evans claimed, that would "simply firm up your diagnosis".

But during court proceedings for Child A, Dr Evans stated regarding air embolism that "in general, it's a diagnosis of exclusion". This was another moment when he emphasised that he didn't need any actual tangible information to diagnose air embolism, "but if you then discover additional items of information, discolouration is one, air on X-ray is another". Dr Bohin similarly stated that she had formed her view after excluding other possibilities. In discussion related to Child A, Dr Bohin also divulged that she had encountered one example of an air embolism in her entire career, and that she could not recall the specifics of the case. Similarly, Dr Evans was later asked whether he was "comparing [his diagnosis] against any clinical personal experience". What was the response of Dr Evans? "Good heavens, no!"

When questioned on Child A, Dr Evans was asked whether he had "to some extent relied upon what could be called a diagnosis of exclusion?" Dr Evans simply answered: "Yes". Child A was critical in the court case, as it established patterns and precedent that were then relied on throughout the remainder of the trial. This is seen in the Court of Appeal judgment, whereby it was noted that "the pattern of collapse was similar in both cases of Baby A and B", and it had been stated in court that "if the pattern is the same, it's more likely that the cause is the same". Effectively, the misdiagnosis of Child A is being transferred over to Child B in the 'chain link' practice that was previously used to wrongly convict Dutch nurse Lucia de Berk.

In the case of Child D, Dr Bohin indicated that she had examined the clinical picture before excluding the explanations that were commonly found. For Child I, Dr Evans commented that "what you do in clinical medicine is you look at all options, and once you've excluded every other option, then maybe you're left with – maybe you're left with just one explanation. And in my opinion, this is the explanation in this particular case…What is relevant to me is that I have excluded all the usual causes and that all of these events are consistent with inflicted injury. I have been consistent with that throughout."

Dr Evans again commented during court proceedings that "what we do as clinicians, we exclude those causes. We exclude those causes. And what's important is, when you are dealing with a baby or a patient who has deteriorated, you make sure that you exclude those causes…where prompt intervention makes a difference, and you exclude those causes where prompt treatment makes a difference."

Air embolism was established in court to be a diagnosis of exclusion, although Professor Colin Morley exclaimed that "there are a number of potential causes of collapse, and I have not seen any of these excluded". But Dr Evans has further expanded on this concept following the conviction of Lucy Letby. Dr Evans had conceded, when interviewed by Raj Persaud, that air embolism "is a very difficult diagnosis to make…it's not easy to prove at all", and he then explained how he had drawn this conclusion: "Having ruled out the usual cause of collapse, it's dawned on me that the only explanation was that these babies had suffered from an injection of air directly into the bloodstream, a condition called air embolus."

It seems surprising that this could have 'dawned' on him with no other supporting evidence having been established, Dr Evans having no previous experience of the condition and extremely minimal academic literature being available. Yet Dr Evans was still able to draw this conclusion without even knowing about air being present in X-rays or skin discolouration. Dr Evans continued: "These are cases where your diagnosis is made by ruling out other factors, and you end up with the diagnosis where this is the only explanation. You ruled everything out, what's left is the diagnosis." Dr Evans proceeded to provide a garbled commentary, which even saw Persaud state that he was "a bit confused".

Evans also indicated, in an interview with TalkTV, that his diagnosis of air embolism was a diagnosis of exclusion: "It's a matter of excluding the usual, sort of, collapse of babies…one could easily exclude those, when in addition to this, one also found…in addition…in addition to this…the only explanation was the injection of air into the circulation."

The BBC *Panorama* programme was another platform which Dr Evans used to explain his diagnosis, beginning with him stating that "the babies were stable beforehand, showing no signs of illness, and then underwent a sudden and catastrophic collapse. And that's vanishingly rare in the neonatal world, you just virtually never see it." This opinion was described by Professor Colin Morley as "simply untrue. It is common for premature babies to have episodes of apnoea and bradycardia." Dr Evans then continued: "So having crossed off all the likely things, you then have to look at unlikely and rare and unthinkable things like air embolism. I kept looking for alternative causes, and so, you know, I kept going back, what else could it be? What else could it be? But I eventually came to a conclusion, no, this, this, it must be this. It must be air." One might reasonably ask Evans how he 'crossed off' all of the conclusions that pathologists had drawn previously, all of the evidence of infection and everything we know about poor care at the hospital.

If there is any doubt that the citation of the injection of air in this court case was a diagnosis of exclusion, the Court of Appeal ends this immediately in paragraph 53: "[Dr Evans] accepted that the diagnosis of air embolus was a diagnosis of exclusion." The paragraph also references claims from Evans that "additional information" helped to "firm up" his diagnosis, including discolouration and X-rays, but Evans has already stated elsewhere that he had decided on his air injection theory before he even encountered that information.

It's also important to emphasise that the mere presence of air embolism isn't a diagnosis of deliberate harm; this has to be inferred. There is no particular reason to believe that air cannot be present accidentally even if air embolism was a credible diagnosis, and no reason was ever given to exclude this likelihood. This was confirmed in court by Professor Arthurs who told the court that the appearance of air bubbles was "consistent with, but not diagnostic of, air having been administered". In accordance with this, Professor Colin Morley concurs that "nothing presented by Professor Arthurs meant that the presence of air was deliberate".

The Court of Appeal notes in paragraph 52 that having eliminated the administration of noxious substances, Dr Evans "was therefore left with air embolus as the explanation". And in paragraph 58, the court observes that Dr Evans commented during the trial that he "could think of no alternative explanations for the collapse" (this seems to be the polar opposite of what Tony Chambers originally asked Cheshire Police to do, namely "exclude unnatural causes"). Dr Evans also told *The Guardian* that he diagnosed air embolism "by excluding other medical causes".

There is further evidence of Dr Bohin also using this process of elimination associated with a diagnosis of exclusion. Paragraph 54 of the Court of Appeal judgment records her "starting off with a list of differential diagnoses and then excluding things from that list left her with air embolus as the diagnosis". Dr Bohin did not dispute this, accepting that "her diagnosis was based upon excluding other conditions" and that "she made her diagnosis therefore by excluding other conditions". In paragraph 66, during a discussion of Child D, the Court of Appeal references Dr Bohin having "excluded conditions which featured on her list of differential diagnoses". This is again referenced in paragraph 74 which recalls that Dr Bohin had "gone through the list of what might have caused the sudden collapse…and then crossed them off as they had been excluded".

In the same paragraph, it is noted that Dr Bohin "said that there was no single diagnostic feature of an air embolus but that this clinical scenario fitted with a diagnosis of air embolus". Elsewhere in paragraph 54, Dr Bohin asserts that air embolism "[as an] explanation for the presence of the rash was the only plausible explanation for Baby A's condition". These are fairly extraordinary assertions, and Professor Colin Morley wondered "what indeed were the clinical, or laboratory, findings she used to be so confident that air embolism was involved?"

Overall, it is rather difficult for either Dr Evans or Dr Bohin to legitimately claim that air embolism was not a diagnosis of exclusion. Yet the idea of reaching this unlikely diagnosis via exclusion has been widely criticised. During a conversation between coroner Nicholas Rheinberg and the anonymised Dr S in October 2016, Rheinberg asked the medic "whether he would be able to reach any kind of conclusion by eliminating other causes of death". The doctor replied that "he would not really be able to do this as he would simply be hypothesising". Rheinberg then asked Dr S whether Child A had died of natural causes. Dr S observed that "they had not found anything to suggest a natural disease, but then there was no evidence that there had been anything unnatural either, and it would be very difficult for him to conclude that it was more likely than not natural causes because there is no evidence of it either way".

This is why medics such as Dr Tariq Ali, one of 24 experts who wrote to the government expressing concerns about the case, have been critical of the concept of diagnosing air embolism via exclusion. Dr Ali commented in a BBC *Panorama* documentary that air embolism "wouldn't be one of your likely diagnoses given the circumstances, and you certainly couldn't say it is air embolism years after the event. I would think that's impossible." Dr Colin Ferguson told me that "to make a diagnosis of air embolism, you have to have more than being unable to think of anything else. There has to be absolutely clear pathological and histological changes which are well described."

Even if a diagnosis of exclusion had been appropriate, this would require genetic causes to be excluded. This definitely did not occur; for example, Dr S told Nicholas Rheinberg that "there are other tests that can be run such as those for genetics, however there was nothing in this case to suggest that this would be necessary". Professor Carola Vinuesa considers this "ruling out the normal causes of death" as being "the most troubling aspect of the Letby case". Professor Vinuesa cited the condition of Sudden Unexpected Death in Infancy or Childhood, explaining that "any unexplained infant or child death in England is eligible for whole genome sequencing to analyse genes associated with sudden death. The fact that the expert witness claimed he could rule out all known causes of death and be left with murder by poisoning or air embolism is deeply concerning."

Professor Vinuesa explained why this was so important: "In neonates and premature babies there are many potential causes of collapse that cannot be easily excluded. Then there are around 10,000 rare diseases, including cardiac, neurological, mitochondrial and metabolic, many of which are difficult to diagnose clinically. Even a genetic post-mortem will identify only between 30% and 50% of Mendelian genetic conditions – the rest may lie in areas of the genome that we do not yet understand, or for which we still lack the tools for proper analysis. To claim in the 21st century that a diagnosis of exclusion can be made, without considering sudden death syndromes and rare diseases, simply doesn't make sense."

Genealogist Debbie Kennett had also raised the issue of genome sequencing on the social media platform X, while Child P had been recommended by Dr Jo McPartland to be referred on to discuss potential genetic causes of sudden unexpected postnatal collapse. But shortly after that, Dr Evans was beginning to draw his conclusion that the injection of air had splinted his diaphragm.

The standards of diagnosis and conclusion associated with pathology are much higher than everyday general practice, or even specialist, diagnosis. And this should especially apply in any legal setting, particularly when the case involved will result in life sentences. Using a highly tenuous diagnosis of exclusion for an incredibly obscure phenomenon in these circumstances, while citing the work of someone who hasn't been a practicing doctor for the best part of two decades and who has no experience with the air embolism theory, is, at best, deeply unsatisfactory. And that's being highly generous.

Chapter 7 discussed Letby not being present for various collapses cited during the court case, and earlier chapters have also outlined the multitude of problems at the CoCH. But there are other documented and practical reasons to doubt the diagnoses used in this court case, all of which were overlooked, ignored or downplayed by the prosecution.

Child A couldn't have her long line pulled back (withdrawing a catheter slightly so that it's located more safely) because qualified staff were busy with another child. Neonatal nurse practitioner Sloane Spade cited "prolonged dehydration, paired with risk of overheating under a heat lamp, while attempting to place a long line multiple times". There were also, even according to the prosecution case, multiple doctors and nurses in the same room as Letby at the time that she supposedly attacked Child A.

Letby was not cot-side when Child B collapsed; in fact, she could not see Child B at the time of her collapse due to an intervening screen. Again, in the case of Child B, Sloane Spade was "confused" that Dr Evans had suggested that situations related to Child B never happen. "Collapses requiring positive pressure ventilation, such as in her case, are common in premature infants – referred to as 'apnoea of prematurity'." In court, Dr Bohin cited this condition being treated with caffeine, but Spade told me that "this is not foolproof, and apnoeic events requiring manual ventilation still occur…This mindset and statements made by experts in court are misleading to the jury of laypersons." Professor Colin Morley also mentioned this condition, noting that "sudden collapse in premature infants is common; we refer to it as apnoea of prematurity. But, somehow, I couldn't find any reference to this from Dr Evans. It didn't seem to feature in his so-called 'differential diagnosis' at all."

There was a litany of incompetence with Child C, despite the infant being in a perilous state, and the catalogue of failures related to Child D have been discussed previously.

In the case of Child E, it was agreed in court that only two doctors were on duty that night and were stretched across two entire units. Dr Stephen Brearey told Nigel Wenham of Cheshire Police that Child E was "displaying typical signs of NEC", and that "as an isolated case, he would not have been considered suspicious".

The full background to Child G is discussed in "Other Infants", but this was a chronically ill and extremely premature infant.

Child I had an unexplained deterioration the day before readmission to Liverpool and then suffered another daytime collapse. Lucy Letby was not on duty during either of these incidents. The child then experienced a sudden cardiac arrest on 29 September 2015, again when Letby was away, and then there were further unexpected deteriorations of the child before 30 September when Letby was accused of destabilising the infant. None of these other collapses appeared on the shift chart used in court, and they were downplayed during the trial; it can be surmised that this was because Letby wasn't present. This infant alone entirely disproves the theory that collapses followed Letby around; they simply did not.

Pathologists provided a cause of death for Child I related to extreme prematurity which was disregarded by Dr Evans. However, the cross-examination of Dr Evans in relation to Child I was one of many surreal moments in the court case. Dr Evans initially made an accusation related to the nasogastric tube but then discovered that Child I did not have one in place, at which point he simply altered his diagnosis to smothering.

In the case of Child J, Dr Stephen Brearey told the Thirlwall Inquiry in a written statement that "electrolyte disturbance...might have caused a seizure. Other possible causes included sepsis or a collection of infection (pus) in the bowel." In court, Brearey had commented that "I do know hypoxia causes seizures so that would be possibly the most likely cause. There remains the question why was [Child J] hypoxic when two or three weeks beforehand she had been breathing normally in air and there was no suggestion of infection." It is not entirely clear how his opinion changed so much in the intervening period. As mentioned previously, Child J was a particularly strange case in which the prosecution was unable to even identify a hypothetical form of harm being inflicted.

A later chapter addresses the circumstances surrounding Child K.

The prosecution case for Child N involves a catalogue of absurdity which is discussed in more depth in "Eyewitness Accounts". And it is clear that chaos had ensued on the neonatal unit during the collapse and death of Child P, with the father of the infant describing a nurse "Googling a procedure", and that an image appeared on the screen of the device she was using depicting a lung drain, "with an arrow pointing to where the incisions should be". This made the father "angry", and he observed the assembled staff having "a word with each other, and [then they] did the procedure". Furthermore, there were three witnesses present in the nursery at the time the supposed attack on Child P took place, and during the trial the prosecution changed its opinion on the time of this attack as Letby wasn't working during the night shift. "It's like a game of chess with check, check, check, moving around. It's not the night before, okay, now it's the night before", defence barrister Ben Myers observed during his closing statement. This wasn't the only time that the prosecution engaged in such activity, as they were guilty of exactly the same shifting of days and incidents for Child C.

It should finally be reiterated that there were 18 deaths associated with the unit during the period Lucy Letby was alleged to have maliciously harmed infants (Cheshire Police investigated 17 of these), and Letby was only charged with seven of these deaths. There were also, undeniably, dozens of collapses for which she was never charged, and many of these occurred when it is known that Letby was either not present, or not even in the hospital.

The clinical picture between these 'non-indictment' infants and collapses is virtually interchangeable with those discussed in court; both collapses and infants were swapped in and out of what became the court case. One non-indictment infant who was ruled out of the court case was suffering with pneumonia, but in the case of Child D, Dr Evans seemingly ignored her pneumonia and infection. Other babies who died on the unit were full-term infants, born at 39, 40 and 40 weeks respectively, but these were excluded from the court case while severely premature babies were included, and Dr Evans and Dr Bohin repeatedly informed the court that they were "well" and "stable".

Considering this context, it is not surprising that the expert panel assembled by Dr Lee found evidence of numerous mistakes when they assessed the infants from the Letby case, drawing different, far more plausible and evidence-based conclusions than those of Dr Evans. The summary diagnoses for all infants are now readily available, but it is worthwhile to briefly recount some of the cases here.

In the case of Child A, the panel cited APS in the case of the mother, which triggers blood clots to form in arteries and veins. These antibodies passed through the placenta, leading to thromboembolism. In post-mortem, there was a non-occluding thrombus in the liver, indicative of an IV line penetrating a vein. The numerous insertions of an umbilical venous catheter were referenced which can cause trauma and clotting. Other factors were also mentioned but the conclusion for Child A was that he died from thrombosis, with no evidence of air embolism.

Child D was discussed earlier in this chapter, while Child I was a preterm infant with intrauterine growth restriction, respiratory distress syndrome and chronic lung disease. The child had repeated episodes of apnoea, desaturation and bradycardia, requiring frequent resuscitation. The baby also had an episode of lung collapse amid reports that there were thick, gelatinous airway and oral secretions present.

In this case, a surveillance culture of the infant revealed a bacteria called stenotrophomonas maltophilia which is highly resistant to antibiotics. And the doctors in the unit were duly notified that that was the case. This led to the endotracheal tubes of the infant being constantly blocked and replaced, interfering with ventilation.

Sepsis and lactose intolerance were also cited while repeated abdominal X-rays showing intestinal gaseous distension indicated that air was introduced via resuscitation. The panel also noted that a nurse had explained the reason why an alarm on the unit hadn't sounded; a 20-second period without breathing required to trigger the alarm had not occurred due to gasping from the patient.

Child I was not treated for stenotrophomonas maltophilia and the panel concluded the infant died due to respiratory complications caused by respiratory distress syndrome and chronic lung disease that were complicated by the stenotrophomonas maltophilia colonisation. Doctors on the unit failed to respond to routine surveillance warnings, did not recognise a key diagnosis and this was likely a preventable death. There was no evidence of air embolism.

The hypothesis of the deliberate introduction of air into babies, relied on for much of the Letby court case, is utterly bizarre and completely bereft of reliable evidential support. That is not an assertion made by myself; it is the opinion of every healthcare expert that I've interacted with, and is reflected in the view of the international panel of experts. In fact, as mentioned earlier, even Evans himself described the concept of introducing air via a nasogastric tube as "utterly bizarre". No serious or qualified person has come forward to offer any support whatsoever to Dr Evans or his theories, while his work has been strongly criticised and dismissed by numerous considerably more qualified people. There is no justification whatsoever for going against pathologists, post-mortems, the Hawdon review of cases, another neonatologist reviewing even more cases, the comments and observations of countless neonatologists and other medics and the author of the paper that was solely used diagnostically. This would require extraordinarily strong evidence, and this evidence simply does not exist.

Furthermore, the court case included a substantial amount of curious commentary from Dr Evans, not least the following exchange with Ben Myers:

MYERS: What's the evidence?

EVANS: Baby collapsed, died.

MYERS: A baby may collapse for any number of reasons. What's the evidence that supports your assertion made today that it's because of air going down the NGT?

EVANS: The baby collapsed and died.

MYERS [referring to X-rays]: Do you rely upon one image of that?

EVANS: This baby collapsed and died.

MYERS: What evidence is there that you can point to?

EVANS: A baby collapsing and where resuscitation was unsuccessful – you know, that's consistent with my interpretation of what happened.

There is no evidence to show that collapses and unsuccessful resuscitations are diagnostic indications of the malicious injection of air. When pressed by *The Guardian* on this topic, Dr Evans said the following: "Well without being too blasé about it, it's only difficult if you don't know the answer, OK. Once you know, you know…It's not very good asking me why I diagnosed air embolus. I think you should be asking other people why didn't they make the diagnosis."

Of course, the reason others haven't made this diagnosis is that there hasn't been a single medically qualified person who has agreed with it since the trial was completed. Nothing asserted in court related to the injection of air into infants comes even remotely close to being a valid diagnosis. Air embolism is not evidentially supported, while it also requires reams of evidence regarding infection, the clinically proven state of many of these infants, conditions at the hospital and medical mistakes that were made to be ignored. Furthermore, virtually everyone with experience or qualifications believes it to be logistically impossible. There are numerous collapses for which Letby has been accused of injecting air in which there are demonstrably other nurses around her, if she was even present at the time of the collapse which often wasn't the case. Letby frequently wasn't the designated nurse for the infant and there is no evidential basis to assert that she injected air, even if the data used to suggest this was accurate (which it wasn't, as will be discussed in "Swipe-Card Data Falls Apart").

Much of this court case and conviction was founded on hypotheses so questionable that Dr Evans was forced to change them. He spent years piecing them together in the first place, which seems, in itself, absurd. And yet all of these hypotheses still came to the conclusion that Letby is guilty. He changed the material details of them numerous times, while always coming to the same conclusion. The panel of experts convened by Dr Shoo Lee both rejected the assertions of Dr Evans and found no evidence of murder. Considering this, and everything that is presented in this chapter, how can what was presented in court possibly be viewed as credible medical or scientific evidence?

Earlier in this chapter the elimination of 'noxious substances' across all infants by Dr Evans was mentioned. There is just one minor problem with this – Dr Evans still cited "a noxious substance" in the case of Child M. This followed a lengthy cross-examination by defence barrister Ben Myers, during which Dr Evans stated that he had "dismissed" a noxious substance being involved, which indeed applied across all infants. But then later in the court case, Evans stated that observations he had made "beg[ged] the question whether [Child M] received some noxious substance prior to his arrest or a bolus of air via his long line". This was headline news on the BBC website on 23 February 2023. It is hard to understand why Evans has mentioned a "noxious substance" in court.

With regard to Child A, Dr Evans claimed to have conducted a differential diagnosis, whereas at other points during the court case he professed to have made a diagnosis of exclusion. But there is no evidence that he ever ruled out hundreds of potential conditions, and in the case of the supposed differential diagnosis, he appears to have never considered anything other than potential methods of murder – hardly a legitimate diagnostic model.

Furthermore, not only was this comment tossed casually into the trial in relation to an infant Letby was never accused of poisoning with any such "noxious substance", but the statement itself is palpably absurd. If Child M had been poisoned with a noxious substance, the clinical signs would have been completely different to an air embolism. The alleged deliberate harm therefore categorically *cannot* have been caused by one or the other.

Dr Evans, by his own admission, changed his mind during the court case, which was, admittedly permitted by the presiding judge. But Evans often denies that he has changed any of his diagnoses since the trial was completed. The next chapter of this book will examine this claim.

CHAPTER 10: THE ODDLY EVOLVING CASE OF CHILD C

While there are massive problems with the scientific evidence presented during the trial of Lucy Letby, and indeed with the trial as a whole, the case of Child C must be considered particularly egregious.

Child C was born in a precarious state which was acknowledged by those working at the CoCH. The consultant obstetrician from the CoCH, Dr Jim McCormack, told the Thirlwall Inquiry that "I never, ever considered that this death could have been from deliberate harm…when I saw the post-mortem result and the immaturity of the baby's lungs, I presumed that this was a death entirely consistent with prematurity…I knew that this baby was very sick…In Child C's case there was a post-mortem report that actually had a cause of death. It's not as if the pathology is saying this was unexplained."

Conversely, speaking in court, Dr Bohin claimed that "in his early days [Child C] managed very well indeed. A couple of times he had skin-to-skin contact with his parents and that is something you would not do if you had concerns. He was not only doing well but was actually improving. This was not a baby who was ill." This is striking because Dr Evans had initially concluded that the infant "was at great risk of unexpected collapse", and one wonders if something can both be at "great risk" of happening, and also "unexpected".

In reality, Child C was suffering with a catalogue of ailments as well as being significantly premature. He was born at 30 weeks weighing only 800 grams (1lb 12oz) after problems with the blood flow to the placenta. One nurse described him as "the smallest baby I have ever seen". The infant also suffered with pneumonia and breathing distress, while an X-ray taken the day before his death showed air in his stomach, indicating that his bowel was potentially blocked. Dr Michael Hall told me that he cited this issue in his report on Child C.

Child C had also suffered from intrauterine growth restriction, which occurs when the foetus is smaller than would be considered healthy for its gestational age. As a consequence of this, the infant had diminished ability to grow and develop fat on the body, meaning less ability to handle temperature changes, fluid imbalances and respiratory changes. This infant even declined over 10% beneath his already fragile birth weight, meaning that he fell below the minimum weight required for the CoCH to be responsible for his care. Neonatal nurse Joanne Williams referenced several of these issues in her statement submitted to the Thirlwall Inquiry, including the child's size, prematurity, the difficult antenatal period Child C had endured, nasal CPAP, reversed end diastolic flow and a heightened risk of infection.

Professor Colin Morley cited clear physical issues with this infant. "Child C was an extremely small baby, weighing only 800 grams", Professor Morley explained. "The infant was suffering with bile-stained vomiting within days, literally bright green in colour, and didn't pass meconium. These were signs of serious illness that were dismissed, which indicates a serious knowledge gap on the unit." The highly experienced neonatal nurse, Sloane Spade, similarly cited "bilious black gastric residual, and an episode of bilious emesis" in her extensive analysis of this infant, noting that Child C "was not properly treated for suspicion of NEC, outside of not receiving food [for a period]. With regard to this, abdominal X-rays, including a lateral X-ray which is the gold standard for NEC diagnosis, were not conducted."

Professor Morley asserted that Child C "had all sorts of problems". He had rising lactate and CRP (C-reactive protein) levels, with CRP being one factor used in diagnosing neonatal sepsis. He was being treated for sepsis, but was also weaned off respiratory support at the same time, contrary to studies on the best timing and methods for weaning infants off CPAP. He was also at least two weeks too young to manage without respiratory support, and showed increased work of breathing and elevated lactate levels. He was fed despite never having had a bowel movement and while still producing dark residuals. After being put back on respiratory support, he had two bradycardia/desaturation events shortly before being fed, before then experiencing his final cardiorespiratory event. There were three failed intubations resulting in at least 90 seconds without breaths during resuscitation, and chest compressions were given before a stable airway was established which is not recommended under neonatal resuscitation guidelines.

The clinical picture for Child C was extremely grim and offered considerable evidence that the infant was suffering with a bowel obstruction. Professor Morley confirmed when speaking with the BBC that the clinical signs for this infant were "absolutely classical of a baby who has got lower bowel obstruction". Professor Morley further commented in *The Trials of Lucy Letby* podcast that the bile-stained vomiting and aspirates were "a major sign of illness". Morley also questioned the quality of care and treatment that Child C had received. "The doctors should investigate the baby to see why it's vomiting bile, because it may be some sort of obstruction in the intestine of this baby. But they rather dismissed this, and they just said: 'Well, we'll keep an eye on it'. But they should have known that this needed urgent review by a paediatric surgeon and a lot of investigation…The baby was not in the right hospital." The mother of Child C had expressed precisely this sentiment to Ian Harvey, questioning whether he should "have been transferred to a more specialised centre".

In her analysis of this infant, neonatal nurse Sloane Spade informed me that, "Child C was a baby who was severely growth restricted – a more significant indicator of mortality and morbidity than weeks of gestation." In common with Professor Morley, Spade also pointed to sub-par care and treatment. "Child C was described as 'doing well' and had various moments where respiratory support was removed periodically, when per their gestational age and weight, the infant should have remained on support. Presenting Child C as 'doing well', when actions were made that increased the respiratory stress, on an already vulnerable infant, is contradictory." Again, the mother of Child C had questioned "whether the respiratory support given was sufficient", while the parent also queried if "his blood gases, electrolytes and blood glucose [were] monitored closely enough". Dr Michael Hall also cited prosecution expert witnesses describing the respiratory rate of this infant as "staying within the norm", whereas over the 24 hours prior to the passing of Child C, the hourly measured respiratory rate was abnormally high on 18 occasions and borderline normal just five times.

Professor Colin Morley further spoke with the BBC *File on 4* programme stating that he was "very confident" that Child C suffered with an intestinal obstruction, and that an X-ray taken which showed a distended bowel was symptomatic of this: "I don't see any reason to come up with a very strange hypothesis. There were plenty of other things going on that would mean the baby wasn't going to survive if he didn't have the proper treatment."

In accordance with this, Sloane Spade pointed out that "it is also known that, likely due to inadequate staffing on the unit, Child C was not seen by a consultant until the third day of his life". As has been stated in previous chapters, Spade's opinion was that there had been serious failings on the unit, and this was corroborated by Professor Morley when speaking with the BBC: "This baby certainly should have had a higher level of care. [Neonates are] tricky and they deteriorate, and you need to be able to keep an eye on things to see what's going on. The consultant didn't see the baby for the first three days. He was seen by nurses and trainee doctors. I also got the feeling that the resuscitation was suboptimal. The people's skills were not up to the job of resuscitating a tiny baby like this. And that's not surprising. This was a hospital that wasn't really set up for a baby as small and sick as this."

There were a multitude of risk factors for Child C that were far more likely to have contributed to his cardiorespiratory event than the various methods of murder that the prosecution conveyed both during and after the trial. Despite the complete lack of any criticism of any aspect of the court case during the Thirlwall Inquiry, consultant paediatrician Dr John Gibbs also stated that, "I was not suspicious of deliberate patient harm to either Child C or the other babies who died in June 2015." Documents from Thirlwall indicate that the mother of the infants had high risk factors for absent diastolic flow – a form of placental dysfunction – which in itself causes an increased risk of intrauterine death. The mother was also suffering with a condition known as oligohydramnios, which results in reduced amniotic fluid – too little for the baby's gestational age.

Child C suffered with a distended small bowel, and had been deemed high risk at birth. Child C was therefore one of several infants in the case linked with CPAP belly, and, during court proceedings, it was noted that paediatric registrar Dr Gail Beech had described the infant as "very gaseous" due to CPAP. In his concluding comments on Child C, Professor Owen Arthurs stated that the "marked gas dilation" in the stomach of Child C could be caused by CPAP belly, sepsis or NEC. In line with this, speaking at a press conference in December 2024, Letby's newly appointed barrister, Mark McDonald, said that reports compiled by practicing neonatologists indicated that "identifiable medical reasons" were responsible for the tragic passing of Child C, and that the infant had become unwell "due to problems caused by failing placental function".

This would all seem damning enough for the prosecution case if there had been one consistent diagnosis presented, but that was not the case. Dr Dewi Evans changed his mind about the diagnosis in court and since Letby was convicted. "Last week, I carried out a detailed review from the corrected case notes, only received by me in June 2022…" Evans began in his statement to *The Guardian* in October 2024. One might wonder why he required 28 months to do this. Dr Evans did not mention during the court case that he hadn't read accurate case notes, nor did he provide any of the new information in court that forms this so-called updated version.

Evans continued: "…and have now worked out what led to Infant C's death in more detail…" Dr Evans has provided a differing diagnosis based on completely different information, including elements that were not communicated in court. Dr Evans then informs us that he has "completed" his report. Typically, witnesses review their medical data before, or at least during the trial, not 14 months after someone has been committed to prison for the rest of her life.

Still, let's go out on a limb here, and assume that after 'reviewing' the new data Dr Evans has still concluded that Lucy Letby murdered the child. "I think that in my evidence I said that it was the result of air into the bloodstream (but I have not seen the transcript)". Asked by *The Guardian* to expand on this, Dr Evans commented that, in a perhaps not unsurprising move, Cheshire Police had now told him not to discuss Child C with the media, although Dr Evans struggled to comply with that request for an extended period. By January 2026, this request from Cheshire Police had extended to the entire case after numerous damaging media performances and outbursts from Evans.

Fortunately, the transcripts are openly available. When discussing Child G in court, Dr Evans explained the mechanism that he also cited for Child C: "One problem that can cause a baby to suddenly stop breathing is if the abdomen is filled with air or filled with oxygen. If you get a significant injection of air into the stomach, it will cause what we call splinting of the diaphragm…Therefore, his collapse is consistent with a volume of air injected into his stomach, it splints the diaphragm, stops breathing, he's less than 800 grams, so that's what happens." There is no mention of any other mechanism or cause. Professor Colin Morley also told me that it would be "impossible for any air in the stomach to be under such pressure that it would splint the diaphragm, as the stomach is attached to the oesophagus and excess air in the stomach is easily vented by belching. There is no evidence that a so-called 'volume of air' can splint the diaphragm."

When later cross-examined by Ben Myers, the pair had the following exchange:

MYERS: Dr Evans, you've explained today that your conclusion is that the cause of death in Child C's case arose from the splinting of his diaphragm.

EVANS: That is…the mechanics of that, yes, is correct.

MYERS: You've had the relevant clinical material and the statements relating to Child C for over five years or thereabouts, haven't you?

EVANS: Yes.

MYERS: You've considered other cases featuring in this trial where

you have provided reports giving the opinion that splinting of the
diaphragm is a cause of death, like Child G, haven't you?
EVANS: Yes.
MYERS: Before today, just now, you've never suggested that
splinting of the diaphragm on 13 June is the cause of death for
Child C, have you?
EVANS: That's correct.
MYERS: This is the first time we're hearing it right now, isn't it?
EVANS: Yes.

Commenting on this matter in *Private Eye*, Dr Philip Hammond noted that the theory of death by splinting had played a substantial role in the trial, being referenced 159 times, along with "detailed descriptions of how it kills, with support from other experts". As Hammond rightly asserted, "Evans has [since] disowned it, leaving a great hole in the prosecution case. But at least we don't have to argue about splinting any more." Even that theory of splinting represented Dr Evans changing his opinion in court, during the trial, having had a mere five years to propose something that could be relied upon.

One neonatal nurse that I spoke with was highly doubtful of this hypothesis: "If babies died from having air put into their stomachs, 99% of the babies in the neonatal unit would be dead. Many babies on CPAP experience CPAP belly. They made a big deal in court about how distended the stomachs were, but basically every baby who was resuscitated at the time of death will have that appearance."

As criticism of Dr Evans mounted, instead of defending his pre-existing opinion on Child C, he shifted the goalposts in what seems to be a direct response to that criticism. Evans told the BBC that his appearance on the *File on 4* programme had led him to "review the events leading up to Infant C's collapse and death". The BBC acknowledged that Evans told the *File on 4* programme that Child C had likely died due to "a combination of air and milk" administered via a nasogastric tube into the stomach, which "differed from what [Evans] had said in court when he only mentioned air".

This is fairly extraordinary. Not only has the key witness for the prosecution case changed his opinion in court, he has now changed it again, introducing an entirely new mechanism. Furthermore, not only is the alleged method of murder evolving, but the logistical challenge of administering this is becoming ever more unfeasible – Letby is alleged to have done something with air, and then something else with milk, possibly even switching between the two. Remember, no one on the unit has seen Letby do anything.

It is clear Evans has changed his diagnosis because he told *The Guardian*. Additionally, when Channel 5 broadcast its first documentary on the Letby case, at the end of the programme there was a quote from Dr Evans that gave one explanation, and when the channel aired an updated version there was a new explanation from Dr Evans: "Babies were destabilised by air injection into the stomach. The action likely involved fluid injection, not just air." This is simply not the same explanation as the splinting of the diaphragm that was provided in court, during which there was never any mention of milk in relation to Child C. Furthermore, there is no evidence for any such fluid injection.

When John Sweeney interviewed Dr Evans, he also noted that barrister Nick Johnson had specifically referenced air being injected into Child C's stomach in his closing statement. In relation to this, possibly realising that he had been backed into a corner having made clear statements in court that were consistent with this, Dr Evans stated: "It's not something I would rule out." Compare this to the assertion that Evans later made in a letter to Channel 5: "None of the babies were killed as a direct result of the injection of air, or fluid and air, deliberately injected into their stomachs."

Evans may have changed his diagnosis due to another article in *The Guardian* in which eight expert clinicians dismissed his diagnoses as "rubbish", "ridiculous", "implausible" and "fantastical". This was certainly the opinion of Dr Philip Hammond who told John Sweeney's podcast series that Evans had changed his diagnosis for Child C numerous times because "eight currently practicing neonatologists wrote to *The Guardian* and said that [his] theory is ludicrous…I think because currently practicing neonatologists appear to be laughing at him, he changed his position…the fact that he's changed his position so many times is pretty concerning."

Furthermore, in his statement to Channel 5, Evans claimed that "other paediatric experts shared his opinions", and that his "findings were confirmed by both a paediatric expert and a neonatologist". Dr Sandie Bohin performed a heavily criticised peer review on the diagnoses that he presented *before* the trial but I am not aware there has been any peer review of the new theories that Evans has presented since the verdict. This matters because one of the main defences Dr Evans employs when criticised is that other experts reviewed his work as he stressed when speaking with Liz Hull of the *Daily Mail* in July 2024.

As referenced previously, a leaked email written by Dr Evans to Channel 5 has emerged. Dr Colin Ferguson stated that he "cannot believe the arrogance of Dr Evans in the way he talks down to a lay audience". In this email, Evans writes "none of the babies were killed as a direct result of the injection of air, or fluid and air, deliberately injected into their stomachs". This seems to me an extraordinary claim as it appears to contradict his testimony in court.

On 21 June 2023, prosecuting barrister Nick Johnson conceded that Dr Evans had been "justifiably criticised" for failing to give a written cause of death for Child C, before making the following lucid statement: "It's as plain as the nose on your face that Lucy Letby must have injected air down the nasogastric tube [into Child C]. It was one of her favourite ways of trying to kill children in this case."

Johnson also asserted that "it's obvious what happened", perhaps in an attempt to make his closing statement more convincing. Nonetheless, it is crystal clear from court transcripts that Dr Evans had stated, quite explicitly, that the cause of death was "air down the nasogastric tube". And while Dr Evans has since attempted to squirm away from his original diagnosis, it was also reported in the *Chester Standard* on the day of the trial.

When speaking about Child C in court, Dr Evans was as emphatic as Johnson, describing his diagnosis as a "clinically proven mechanism".

It seems that Dr Evans has used elements of his air embolism theory to push this diagnosis, particularly the discolouration that the paper's author, Dr Shoo Lee, has since rejected. But Dr Evans also told journalist Liz Hull that injecting air in the stomach was something he had never encountered previously, "utterly bizarre", in fact, and that "there are no published papers regarding a phenomenon of this nature that I know of", as reported by Rachel Aviv in the *New Yorker*.

The Court of Appeal not unreasonably notes that "air forced down a nasogastric tube…was alleged to be the cause of the collapse and death of Baby C, Baby I and Baby P". Consistent with this is a table contained in paragraph 26 of the Court of Appeal judgment which lists the mechanism of death for each infant. The mechanism for Child C is listed as "air via nasogastric tube". A very similar table was later included in a document submitted to Thirlwall, entitled *All of the Neonatal Deaths Linked to the CoCH in 2015 and 2016*, which contained exactly the same mechanisms, described within as 'modes of attack/causes of death'.

As mentioned in the previous chapter, Dr Evans claims to have read the Court of Appeal judgment. For example, on 17 December 2024, Evans was quoted by multiple media outlets as stating that the Court of Appeal "provided a very thorough review of the evidence", and that he wasn't "in receipt of any information that indicates that the appeal court judges were mistaken", even though the Court of Appeal judgment lists methods of murder that he has since abandoned.

It must be emphasised that when writing to Channel 5, Dr Evans claimed that some bizarre combination of air and milk had destabilised the babies, but that this hadn't been the direct cause of death. Yet the Court of Appeal judgment lists the methods of murder cited in the trial as only including fluid in relation to Child G, starkly refuting the claims of Evans.

While the focus of this chapter is Child C, it is also important to briefly mention other infants involved in the case. Remember that Dr Evans has stated that "none of the babies were killed as a direct result of the injection of air…into their stomachs", even claiming that "an action sufficient to destabilise babies is more likely to involve an injection of fluid…and not air alone".

In opening comments made in court, prosecuting barrister Nick Johnson commented that "for other babies, some were 'harmed and killed' by the 'injection of air'…via a tube into the stomach."

With regard to Child I, Dr Evans commented that "my opinion was that [Child I] had been subjected to an infusion of air. In other words, air had been injected into her stomach." The prosecution went on to claim that air had been injected via a nasogastric tube, resulting in a 'splinted diaphragm'.

During proceedings for Child P, it was asserted that Child P died as a result of "excessive injection of air into the stomach". Dr Evans concluded that excess air in the stomach could have "splinted" the diaphragm of Child P, and Dr Bohin concurred with this verdict.

In addition to the previously quoted comments on Child C, Dr Evans stated that "if you get a significant injection of air into the stomach, it can cause splintering of the diaphragm".

Even with regard to Child Q, the comments of Johnson "that Lucy Letby had sabotaged [Child Q] and had injected him with air and a clear fluid into his stomach via the nasogastric tube. She was trying to kill him" are not consistent with the comments of Evans listed above. On Wednesday 5 April 2023, Dr Evans claimed that "there was enough clear fluid injected down into his stomach to make him vomit. He was unable to breathe properly because his tummy was full of liquid." While this does involve a combination of air and fluid, this is being cited as the direct cause of collapse, rather than a source of destabilisation. Nonetheless, Letby wasn't found guilty of the alleged attempted murder of Child Q.

As noted during the trial by defence barrister Ben Myers, Dr Evans had not provided this 'splinting of the diaphragm' conclusion in the eight previous reports which preceded his comments in court. But he then removed it from his diagnosis, according to comments in his letter to Channel 5, relying on a completely different mechanism, disowning what was stated in court.

Speaking at the December 2024 press conference, Mark McDonald noted that the "Court of Appeal said that Baby C died as a result of air going down the nasogastric tube". Virtually the entire Court of Appeal document is an extensive discussion of air embolus and mechanisms that Evans has now, according to his own words, abandoned.

In the Channel 5 letter, Evans makes a case for hypoxia being the cause of collapse. There were only two references to hypoxia in the Court of Appeal document, the main one being in relation to Child A during which it is stated that hypoxia would not cause the type of rash associated with this infant, as asserted by Dr Bohin in court. The other reference is preceded by Dr Evans commenting that "descriptions of the clinical features of infants proven to have died from the effects of air embolus and described in many of the enclosed publications show marked similarities to the pattern of collapse and death of many of the babies" in relation to Child A.

Hypoxia was only cited by the prosecution with regard to two infants – Child H and Child J. What did these two babies have in common? Letby was not convicted in either case. In fact, for Child C and Child I, the original post-mortem indicated hypoxic/ischaemic damage due to prematurity, which has since been refined by Dr Evans to air via nasogastric tube – there is some discussion of Evans *rejecting* hypoxia in Chapter 5 of this book. Unexplained hypoxia and rapid desaturation are also associated with an array of other conditions, all of which are considerably more common than air embolism.

It should be noted that in the case of Child I, the prosecution attempted to claim that this hypoxic damage was somehow caused by Letby, but the post-mortem is disowned in the case of Child C. Discussion in court related to Child C was almost entirely focused on the assertion by Evans that air had been used to somehow splint the diaphragm of the infant, and that this had directly caused hypoxia. During the cross-examination of Dr Evans, 25 references were made to splinting and 35 to diaphragm – "if you get a significant injection of air into the stomach, it will cause what we call splinting of the diaphragm", Dr Evans explained in court. "[Child A's] collapse is consistent with a volume of air injected into his stomach, it splints the diaphragm, stops breathing."

Furthermore, during court proceedings related to Child A, Dr Evans commented: "Hypoxia, lack of oxygen – there was no evidence of that." There is some further explanation from Evans regarding this infant having not become hypoxic, and he then outlines how he eliminated hypoxia from this case via differential diagnosis, along with several other conditions. Evans also discounted hypoxia for Child B.

The Court of Appeal verdict also invalidates everything that Dr Evans has stated in his letter to Channel 5 regarding hypoxia being significant. But Dr Evans modified his theory because his previous opinion has been discredited by his medically qualified peers. He has fallen back on this theory, even though it was, as the Court of Appeal notes, not referenced with regard to the vast majority of infants in the case, and certainly not to Child C. The claim that he made this diagnosis and proffered it in court is without foundation. Equally, the assertion that he hasn't changed his diagnosis is completely unsupported.

Under the circumstances, one might expect Dr Evans to be critical of the Court of Appeal judgment, or at the very least to reference the fact that the document had misrepresented his court hypotheses. But, instead, Dr Evans is an outspoken admirer. "I've read all 58 pages, all 209 paragraphs of her original appeal and it comes out very strongly, I'm pleased to say, in relation to the strength of the prosecution evidence and in relation to the evidence given by those of us acting as independent witnesses", Evans told *The Sun* newspaper.

The Sun published this statement on 25 October 2024, over two months after Evans had written to Channel 5 on 3 August. So after Evans has written a letter which contradicts numerous diagnoses and assertions that he made in court, he then reads a judgment that repeatedly refutes everything he has written in the letter, and then tells the national media that it is a wonderful document and "comes out very strongly… in relation to the evidence given by those of us acting as independent witnesses", without ever mentioning anything to the contrary.

Dr Evans has since confirmed that he has read the Court of Appeal judgment. How can it be that he read the judgment, but didn't notice the numerous references to mechanisms and causes of death that he himself has explicitly disowned? Perhaps he didn't want to draw attention to the fact that he has changed at least three diagnoses from those listed in the document, and several others are also now inconsistent with statements made in the letter to Channel 5.

In the remainder of the letter to Channel 5, Dr Evans asserts that "my opinion was shared by my fellow paediatrician and by the consultant neonatologist who reviewed my reports initially". The 'consultant neonatologist' referenced here is Dr Martin Ward Platt. While Ward Platt may have reviewed the original reports, he was not in a position to review the Channel 5 hypothesis as sadly he had died by then.

The other individual referenced is Dr Sandie Bohin, who was involved in the peer review of the cases. Again, Dr Bohin has not reviewed the theory discussed in the Channel 5 letter because, as has been established, Dr Evans had already changed his diagnosis of Child C to the splinting of the diaphragm, which he has since changed again, during the court case itself. Dr Bohin presumably peer reviewed the cases before the trial began. Or maybe everything, as it seems to me, was happening on the hoof in this case. Perhaps the prosecution witnesses were assessing evidence, making new diagnoses, peer reviewing them, and changing their verdicts on the fly, in real-time, as part of the court case. It would be traditional to complete your peer review before you take the case to the CPS and charge someone with multiple murders.

It appears to me a trifle presumptuous for Dr Evans to describe what was written in the letter as "our hypothesis" as this is, by any objective assessment, his theory alone.

The rest of the letter to Channel 5 is characteristic of Dr Evans' approach, for which he has been criticised in previous court cases. "The injection into the stomach of a large volume of fluid or a combination of fluid and air would interfere with the breathing of the baby causing hypoxia and collapse. An action sufficient to destabilise babies is more likely to involve an injection of fluid (or fluid and air), and not air alone." However, he made no such assertions or references in court. The court transcripts make this crystal clear. The extensive reporting online makes this crystal clear. The document from Thirlwall listing the causes of death makes this crystal clear. The Court of Appeal judgment makes this crystal clear.

The letter to Channel 5 continued: "It is possible to inject a significant volume of fluid (or fluid and air) through narrow nasogastric tubes within a matter of seconds. The injection of fluid and air leads to abdominal distension 'splinting' of the diaphragm and respiratory collapse. This was seen most dramatically in the case of Child G." It is illustrative that Dr Evans has referenced Child G, because the response to his assertions regarding that infant has been total derision by everyone that has reviewed it (discussed in the chapter "Other Infants"). Also, the implication of "most dramatically" is that the injection of fluid and air was also observed elsewhere, but, in reality, this possibility was not suggested for any of the other infants. A more accurate statement would be that it was asserted solely with regard to Child G. There were assertions of air and fluid being used in the case of Child Q, but Letby was not found guilty of attempting to murder this infant.

Note as well that Evans is stating here that "it is possible". Countless nurses that I've spoken with are sceptical that using air or milk alone to destabilise a baby is feasible, even if it is practical to do so. Now Dr Evans is stating that both are "possible". Again, one wonders why Letby took the risk of, naturally *hypothetically*, lacing feeding bags with insulin when she was already the first nurse in known human history to achieve hypoxia through the highly inventive combination of milk and air.

If Letby is in a normally functioning neonatal unit, how can she do all of these things without being seen? If she is on her own, why is there the need for this immensely complex and uncertain method of destabilising the infants, which Letby would have been extremely unlikely to know about and understand (not least because the person who came up with it has acknowledged that it's never been witnessed or recorded before)? Why can't she simply suffocate the infants? And then why would she switch from this murder method, which completely evaded pathologists, to one involving insulin that could potentially be detected? Could it be because the collapse and death of Child C was actually due to the rather more plausible combination of an obvious bowel obstruction, natural causes and poor care?

The case of Child C, too, has become increasingly hypothetical. Dr Evans is not unequivocally stating that Letby did inject the infant, just simply that "it is possible". Is the injection hypothesis really the most likely scenario at this point, especially for the highly unwell Child C who was demonstrating all manner of clinical signs? Of course all of Dr Evans' attempts to settle on a cause of death still result in Letby being solely responsible for deliberately harming the infant. Professor Colin Morley's opinion is that "gaseous distension of the stomach would be highly unlikely to kill a baby. Frankly, I don't know where Dr Evans gets that from. It's a wild hypothesis that is completely lacking in logic."

The court statements of Dr Evans are explicit; it is beyond any contest that he has changed his diagnosis since then. This is why, in his letter to Channel 5, Dr Evans has dug himself into such an absurd hole. In my opinion, from everything I've read, Dr Evans seems to be a man who has difficulty admitting he's wrong.

Anyone encountering this for the first time would surely consider it highly embarrassing for the police and prosecution. Letby's barrister, Mark McDonald, noted that Evans was "shifting his opinion regarding one of the most fundamental aspects of the case", and noted that he had "reports, from some of the most senior neonatologists in the country, and none of them has yet agreed with Dr Evans".

In court, Evans had been accused in relation to Child C of "introduc[ing] something new with the purpose of supporting the allegation rather than explaining the facts". Even Judge James Goss acknowledged that Evans "did step over the line in relation to one baby", namely Child C. Yet now Dr Evans has come up with new 'facts' that weren't even reported to the court. Remember that Lord Justice Jackson had previously decried Evans for making "no effort to provide a balanced opinion" and submitting a report that had "the hallmarks of an exercise in 'working out an explanation' that exculpates the applicants". In this case, Dr Evans can be witnessed altering the material facts of his diagnosis some 14 months after the trial has concluded, while always remaining aligned with the prosecution.

"You have a person who went before the jury, gave one theory, and has now said that he no longer stands by that theory", barrister Mark McDonald commented. And Dr Colin Ferguson similarly told me that "there is no doubt that Dr Evans has changed his view on this infant several times. There is no medical training required for this – any non-medic can see it quite clearly."

Furthermore, Letby was convicted of murdering Child C based on evidence from a day when she wasn't even on shift. Central to the prosecution case for Child C were X-rays taken on 12 June 2015, two days before he died. Dr Andreas Marnerides testified in court that someone injected air into the infant at a time when Letby was not on duty and had never had any contact with the infant.

The cross-examination of Dr Evans in court revealed that in a report filed one month before the trial began, he had indicated that there was a significant collapse of Child C on 12 June, while neither suspecting nor asserting that there was any collapse on 13 June. Dr Evans had written in this report that "the massive gastric dilation seen on the X-ray of 12 June was most likely due to deliberate exogenous administration of air via the NGT". Dr Evans reversed this view during the trial, and conceded this while being questioned. It was also established that Dr Bohin had approved the report related to 12 June, which was then shifted to a later date, with one incident that was previously considered benign suddenly becoming malign, and the previous day then becoming irrelevant in the diagnosis of Dr Evans. This is just one example of Dr Evans shifting incidents in and out of the court case, completely abandoning what were previously considered to be critical collapses which are then rendered irrelevant. It is an approach that is completely unscientific.

Dr Michael Hall told *The Guardian* that he felt "a particular sense of injustice about Baby C because all four main prosecution witnesses [who gave evidence about the child] either directly or indirectly led the jury to believe that part of the cause of the demise was evidence from an X-ray taken on 12 June 2015. Letby had never been involved with that baby prior to that X-ray." It is important to emphasise that Dr Evans had cited a supposed incident on 12 June as being instrumental in the death of a child. He then later removed this from the case completely, considering it to be of no consequence. This is an extraordinary action.

The BBC *File on 4* programme on Letby's case noted that the X-ray "was one of the key pieces of evidence in this case". In the same programme, Dr Evans himself cited the X-ray as being central: "The biggest concern was that the X-ray showed a huge, great bubble in the stomach, and also far more gas than I would expect." The X-ray that cannot have been anything to do with Letby was not only important in the case of Child C, it was the sole diagnostic criterion. This circumstance then required Dr Evans to shift to a different day, collapse and mechanism, as he was forced to concede in court.

Judge James Goss made an error in relation to the X-ray, conceding that he "did not make it clear" that the X-rays presented in court related to the date of 12 June when the X-rays were taken, rather than 14 June when Child C died. There is no mention during this correction that Letby wasn't actually on duty when the X-ray was taken, and, in fact, had not been involved with this baby whatsoever. "This is an inconvenient truth that the prosecution knew about", Dr Michael Hall told me. "It was not until the closing address that the prosecution counsel did concede that Lucy Letby had not been involved with Child C prior to 12 June, which was probably too late for the jury to understand the significance of this. What is more difficult to understand is that the defence counsel did not highlight this in the questioning of either the prosecution expert witnesses or the witnesses of fact."

Judge Goss had previously ruled that the prosecution was allowed to overrule the original autopsy report for Child C, which noted an abnormality, namely that the descending colon was on the wrong side of the baby's body. Somehow this was then allowed to be overturned completely, and for the interpretation of Dr Andreas Marnerides to supersede the original report, even though Marnerides wasn't present when the report was authored, and has never examined any of the infants. It is difficult to conceive of any possible rationale or justification for this.

It has further been asserted that Letby herself accepted that Child C had a distended stomach. But court proceedings indicate precisely the opposite. Letby told the court when directly asked about this by Nick

Johnson that she was "not accepting that [Child C] had noticeable gas between 23:00 and 23:15", instead citing Neopuff resuscitation as a possible cause of air at the time of death.

Since the trial of Lucy Letby was completed, seven of the eight prosecution witnesses have kept extremely low profiles and in my view the reason for this reticence is simple. This alteration in diagnosis "embarrasses all the expert witnesses" according to Dr Philip Hammond. "All the expert witnesses get together before the trial starts, and they try and decide what they agree on. They noticed gas in the stomach of Baby C, and they all came up with this theory, including the pathologist and the radiographer, that this was due to deliberate air injection crushing the lungs. And it wasn't until the trial started that somebody spotted that not only was [Letby] not on duty on this particular day, but she'd never, at that point, according to the swipe-card data and the duty records, ever met that baby, so couldn't possibly have been responsible for all that air."

In accordance with this, Marnerides cited "excessive injection/infusion of air into the gastrointestinal tract" in court, and agreed definitively with prosecuting barrister Nick Johnson that this had been introduced via the nasogastric tube. This is awkward considering that the creator of this theory, Dr Dewi Evans, has now disowned it. Dr Michael Hall also remembers Marnerides changing his mind on another infant after receiving the opinions of Evans and Bohin: "Originally, he said Child D died of pneumonia, but then when he heard what Dr Evans said, he changed his mind."

After Child C collapsed and died, a post-mortem examination at Alder Hey concluded the death was natural, exacerbated by the lack of blood flow in the womb. A coroner supported this finding. Several neonatologists have cited clinical signs and other far more plausible explanations. Any assertion that Child C was not at serious risk of collapse, health complications, and potential death is indefensible making it hard to see why this case was even selected as one involving inflicted harm. Both Dr Fiona MacRae and Professor Colin Morley felt that Alder Hey should have played a more central role with this infant. Dr MacRae indicated that Child C "should have been sent straight over to Alder Hey to be managed", while Professor Morley concurred that the infant "should certainly have been treated on a tertiary unit, and lack of space at Alder Hey seems to have been an issue. I think one of the problems is that ordinary paediatricians may only see bowel obstructions every few years."

The continual shifts in Dr Evans' views on the cause of death are monumentally important and indicates that he has provided inaccurate information to the jury which required him to change his diagnosis during the trial. By revising his opinions post-trial, Evans appears to be admitting that the opinions of other experts are correct, and that what he presented in court was not. The comment by *The Guardian* that the conviction of Child C has "become the subject of a mounting controversy" is entirely accurate.

When speaking with *The Guardian*, Evans "admitted he no longer stood by a key diagnosis he produced for the trial", and conceded that there are "probable medical causes for the air in the stomach seen on the X-ray, including that the baby had not had a bowel movement", as reported by both Professor Colin Morley and neonatal nurse Sloane Spade. Indeed, Child C never opened his bowels during the entire four days of his existence – again pointing to a bowel obstruction. Failure to defecate for this period of time, in the earliest days of an infant, is strongly indicative of serious health problems.

In a subsequent email, Evans said: "Air via an NG [feeding] tube is one explanation regarding [Baby C's] X-ray findings. [The baby's] lack of intestinal movement, and…treatment with CPAP, later Optiflow [breathing aids], offer a more realistic explanation." It is interesting that this is now a "more realistic explanation" because Dr Evans would have presented the explanation that he gave in court as being 'realistic', but, as Dr Evans told *The Guardian*, "Something must have happened", conceding that 'something' was "not a very scientific term".

For many months, Dr Evans denied that he had significantly changed his diagnosis, and issued a statement claiming that criticism of his conduct is "unfounded". He also claimed that the press conference had been "disrespectful" to the parents of the infants, although he himself had previously made the remark that Letby had "bloody murdered those babies"; hardly the most sensitive comment.

But then, in a 2024 BBC *Panorama* documentary, Dr Evans performed a curious about-turn. Suddenly, he conceded that he had changed his diagnosis, but that this didn't "matter". An interesting position to take considering that the two separate diagnoses would have differing clinical presentations.

He then topped even this when he wrote to various journalists following the broadcast of *Lucy Letby: Murder or Mistake* on Channel 4 in September 2025. In this letter, Dr Evans claimed that the dates mentioned earlier in this chapter "seem to have become confused, leading to the prosecution alleging that the assault took place the previous day. I recognised the confusion at the trial, reaffirming my original concern that the fatal assault was on 13 June. I believe that Cheshire Police, the CPS and the prosecution team should set the record straight."

There is one small inconvenience for this argument. The entire 1 November 2022 court transcript of Dr Evans being cross-examined on Child C is widely available, and he never made any such claim or statement. Evans was in the witness box for approximately four hours so he had plenty of time to inform the court that the police, CPS or prosecution had somehow mixed the dates up.

Responding to questions from *The Guardian* about Child C, Evans wrote in an email: "Lucy Letby murdered Baby C. Get that into your head." It seems that we are expected to accept the word of Dr Evans simply because he says so. Perhaps Evans should have written to the panel of international experts before they began their work and told them to get it into their heads that Child C was murdered.

"I almost admire the gumption of Dr Evans, because he's standing his ground", the former prime ministerial science advisor, Dr James Phillips, told me. "But it's not going well for him."

CHAPTER 11: INSULIN CASES

In her exceptional summation of the Letby investigation and trial, Rachel Aviv argued that the insulin cases for which Lucy Letby was convicted were a locomotive that pulled all of the other cases behind them like carriages. Reflecting this view, when prosecuting in court, barrister Nick Johnson argued that "the fact that there were two deliberate poisonings with insulin will help you when you are assessing whether the collapses and deaths of other children on the neonatal unit were because somebody was sabotaging them, or whether these were just tragic coincidences." It has indeed been argued that the case would never have reached court without the alleged insulin poisonings due to the weakness of other charges levelled at Letby during the trial.

The first thing to note about these supposed poisonings is the logistics involved. In order for Letby to carry out the poisonings, she would need to have injected insulin into a bag that had been chosen randomly from the refrigerator by another nurse. This is not only implausible, but also illogical. If Letby had been successful at causing death by injecting air and milk, it seems odd that she would attempt this much more arbitrary method.

Consequently, there was considerable discussion in court regarding the fact that Letby could not possibly know which bags would need to be spiked, in order for her alleged attacks to be successful. Letby was found guilty of spiking the total parenteral nutrition (TPN) bag of Child F and the dextrose bag of Child L yet both children, it is acknowledged, had their nutrition bags changed when Letby was absent. Advocating for Letby in court, Ben Myers KC not unreasonably asserted that Letby would have required a "Nostradamus-like" ability to see into the future if this was to be deemed a targeted attack: "It's incredible to maintain [Letby] is responsible for this. How can Miss Letby be held responsible for that second bag on any fair or logical basis? A high level of insulin in a bag that no one could have foreseen would have been used which comes into play hours after she has left."

Evidence which arose during court proceedings indicated that there were five stock maintenance bags at the time in the neonatal unit's fridge. With regard to this, Myers asserted that "even if somebody guessed that a maintenance bag may be needed in an unexpected way, they are not to know what bag would be taken", describing the prosecution case as a "series of Russian dolls of improbability…There is no sensible way of claiming that Miss Letby could have been responsible for putting insulin in the second bag. That fundamentally undermines the accusation she put it in the first bag." Feeding bags were also wrapped in a plastic exterior, with a tamper-free polypropylene cap, which would be bordering on impossible to breach undetected. A consultant radiologist that I spoke with described the prospect of tampering with the bags as "impracticable".

It's also important to emphasise that the assertion Letby tampered with feeding bags is entirely hypothetical. There is no supportive eyewitness testimony for any malicious acts. There is no tangible evidence that Letby ever deliberately contaminated the bags referenced, nor were these bags ever examined; in fact, she wasn't even on shift when Child F was supposedly poisoned. Tests were never carried out on the content – the prosecution relied on blood samples from the babies. There is no evidence provided of missing insulin on the neonatal unit, no hospital records that provide any usable evidence, and no suggestion that Letby was the only person who could have accessed insulin. Notes from a meeting at the CoCH on 20 July 2016 mention "feeding bags for analysis", but for some reason the same note immediately states "agreed retain – do not send for analysis". Thirlwall testimony from Dr Chris Green indicated that these bags related to Child O and Child P, but it is clear that the hospital could have both retained bags and sent them for analysis; they simply declined to do so – they were "disposed of a long time ago," as Ben Myers recounted in court.

Professor Alan Wayne Jones, a forensic chemist, highly published academic and one of Europe's foremost experts on toxicology and insulin, has been a critic of both the conviction of Lucy Letby and evidence used in other similar serial killer nurse poisoning cases. He told me that he had a "strong objection" to the evidence provided in court because "the contamination of intravenous feeding bags with insulin was pure speculation. There was no evidence that this actually happened. There was no analysis done of the bag contents and/or the tubing by any form of analytical technology."

In the spring of 2025, I met with Professor Matthew Johll, a forensic and analytical chemist who has been a consultant for the LaSalle County Coroner since 2017, to discuss the insulin cases. He was also critical of the court case citing "increasingly ridiculous scenarios" in order to assert that Letby was guilty. "You should always start with the most probable scenario, not begin with poisoning as a hypothesis. Which is a more probable cause for an increase in deaths at a hospital – a rogue nurse murdering babies, or understaffed, under-trained, overworked nurses with consultants not trained in neonatal medicine taking critically ill patients beyond their ability to give proper care? In a web of increasing absurdity, they desperately tried to link Lucy to each child's death, and this is unsupported by any actual evidence."

The prosecution case was, as it had been consistently throughout, entirely hypothetical, and based on the utterly flawed statistical assertion discussed in a previous chapter that it could only have been Letby that carried out these acts. The insulin cases again completely disprove the argument that the prosecution didn't rely on statistics. The insinuation that Letby definitively poisoned insulin bags is absolutely dependent on the assertion that she was always present when suspicious events occurred. The prosecution maintained this 'guilty-by-presence' notion throughout the court proceedings and made this argument a central pillar of its closing statement. It was explicitly communicated to the jury that it could only conceivably have been Letby who tampered with feeding bags, despite the fact that no physical evidence exists that anyone did indeed act this way. Furthermore, as is agreed by all parties, Letby did not fetch or utilise the feeding bag from the refrigerator which she had allegedly spiked. This assertion is entirely dependent on the shift chart data which has since been decimated by statisticians.

Another illogical aspect of the allegations is that, in the case of Child F, the second feeding bag Letby is alleged to have tampered with came from the stock cupboard, not the pharmacy. There could be no expectation that this bag would ever be used, and the only reason that it was accessed was because there was a problem with an intravenous line into the infant. It is inconceivable that Letby could have foreseen this, and it makes absolutely no sense as a purported method of murder.

In the case of Child L, Professor Peter Hindmarsh conveyed a 'sticky insulin' theory to explain irregularities in results. Hindmarsh asserted that perhaps (this is hypothetical, of course) insulin from previously administered dextrose infusions became stuck to the inside of the infusion apparatus, and then magically became unstuck when Letby went off shift, so insulin continued to find its way into the system of Child L. This theory had to be proposed because the hospital was using bags with varying dextrose percentages which had to be mixed by the pharmacist before arriving on the ward, meaning there was no possibility of Letby spiking them in advance.

It would be generous to describe this as fanciful. There was a need to advance such a theory because Child L experienced hypoglycaemia (low blood sugar) in the absence of Letby, while having received a new bag straight from the pharmacy that Letby never had any contact with whatsoever. And the sticky insulin theory was not employed consistently.

As an example, Child F was hypoglycaemic for 17 hours. If we are to accept the 'sticky insulin' theory, it is reasonable to assume that, over such an extended period, the amount of insulin in the infant's TPN bag would become unavailable as the amount of insulin reduced over time as more of it became stuck to the inside of the bag. But the readings for Child F were notably stable throughout the day, which immediately contradicts Hindmarsh's theory.

Professor Wayne Jones was also sceptical about some of the figures used in court: "The expert witness for the prosecution, Hindmarsh, estimated that 10 units of insulin would be sufficient to contaminate the intravenous infusion bags, but this corresponds to only 0.1ml of Actrapid. This is a very tiny amount indeed. Why would a perpetrator not inject more insulin into the bags of dextrose?

"Administering medicinal insulin in such a diluted dosage form (0.1ml diluted with 500ml), compared with intramuscular injection of Actrapid taken from the vial, would probably not be pharmacologically active. But no experimental testing has been done on anything asserted in court."

It is quite feasible for bio-engineers to calculate the dilution, adsorption and decomposition effect of a specified quantity of insulin, and then calculate the net physiological effect on a subject. This has been demonstrated by Professor Geoff Chase and chemical engineer Helen Shannon whose contribution will be discussed later in this chapter. Experimental testing should have been conducted; this could easily have been organised by police with a competent laboratory. But as with so many things that could have been done, this never happened.

Despite the doubts that should already be apparent, Cheshire Police and the prosecution then extracted what they claimed to be a confession from Letby. She was told by both that the insulin poisoning had definitely occurred and so was unwilling to challenge this, instead asserting that she didn't know who had poisoned the infants but it certainly was not her – "someone tried to poison the babies but it wasn't me". This is often seized upon by those who are advocates for Letby's guilt, but, in reality, it is of negligible value.

Firstly, it was an unseemly blunder by Letby's defence to accept largely without challenge the notion that the insulin cases were based on sound scientific reasoning. Many experts have warned about potential problems with the insulin data, and yet this was largely ignored by the defence both before and during the court case. The jury heard nothing about any such doubts.

Furthermore, to put Letby in the position of being questioned about the insulin cases in court, even though she was patently unqualified to comment, is ludicrous. Letby even patiently explained her lack of credentials to the prosecution, not that this should have been necessary: "In general, I don't think a lot of the babies were cared for on the unit properly. I'm not a medical professional to know exactly what should and shouldn't have happened with those babies."

Neither Letby, nor anyone else in that courtroom, was in a position to agree that anybody had attempted to murder the babies with insulin. During cross-examination on 9 June 2023, Letby indicated that she had simply accepted blood test results that had been provided to her, which indicated that insulin had been administered exogenously. She also specifically stated that she had no notion of how the insulin levels of a blood sample are tested, and that she had never worked in any laboratory environment in which such testing takes place. No doubt, had Letby contested what she was told, she would have been criticised for this instead.

Yet the "concession", translated in the court and appeal proceedings as an "admission", was absolutely crucial in persuading the jury of her guilt. In his summing up, Judge James Goss cited "certain common features" between the two insulin cases and observed that the defendant was on duty for each event. If Goss was talking about the collapse of the baby this could be a mistake as Letby wasn't there at the time, but it could be he was referring to the alleged spiking of the bag.

It was also deeply unfair to put Letby in this position in the first place. Professor Carola Vinuesa noted that "many doctors themselves are not aware that these immunoassay-based insulin tests are not entirely reliable. So how can you expect a nurse to know this? Even Dewi Evans recently admitted not knowing that immunoassays can produce false positive results." Indeed, Dr Evans had told Dr Philip Hammond of *Private Eye*: "I didn't even know that there was more than one way of measuring insulin until I read the comments from Wayne Jones." This somewhat contrasts with proceedings in court on 30 November 2022 during which Dr Evans stated authoritatively that there was "only one explanation" for what he described as "astonishing" blood readings. "[Child F] had received insulin from some outside source." There was no doubt expressed by Dr Evans, even though he evidently knows very little about insulin or its testing.

Dr Thea Gumbert, an expert on juries and their behaviour, cited a phenomenon referred to as the 'white coat effect' as being significant here: "An expert can come in and pretty much persuade a jury by saying:

'Look, with high confidence, here's how I proved they did it.' But they also don't explain a lot of other things to jurors. They rarely introduce things like error rates, for instance. There is a lot of context that is often missing." In accordance with this, Professor Alan Wayne Jones told me that Letby had received "unwise" advice from her legal team in accepting the assertion that insulin poisoning had definitely occurred, and also suggested the fact that "forensic examination of Letby's computer and phone found no evidence she had searched for any information about insulin poisoning, or, for that matter, air embolism" was significant.

Central to the assertion that Letby administered insulin were readings derived from tests conducted by Liverpool Clinical Laboratories. In order to discuss these results, it is firstly necessary to establish an understanding of a substance called C-peptide. The body creates C-peptide, essentially a chain of amino acids, when the pancreas produces insulin. It is typically asserted that when insulin is injected or administered externally, sometimes referred to as 'exogenous' insulin, the C-peptide level is often much lower than the amount of insulin measured.

In court, the prosecution argued that readings reported by the laboratory in Liverpool could not have occurred naturally. Witnesses for the prosecution similarly testified that there was no other possible explanation – this had to be deliberate poisoning. Letby was told this herself by the police and then accused in court of injecting insulin into the feeding bags of two infants on the unit. The court did not hear from any witness who questioned the validity of these tests and figures.

The first key issue that the court failed to test, let alone settle, is whether the physiology of adults and neonates is the same. It should be fairly obvious that it is not, and yet what was discussed throughout the court case was conventional adult endocrinology. This fails to account for critical biological differences which have been shown to have a profound impact on the range of figures that are both possible and observable in premature infants.

This anatomical picture related to neonates was cited by Dr Shoo Lee, speaking at the press conference on 4 February 2025. Dr Lee noted that the standards for these readings and ratios cannot be applied to neonates in the same way as adults: "Preterm infants, and especially those with illness and drug treatments like antibiotics, have different normative standards compared to healthy adults and older children." Research conducted by Professor Geoff Chase found that exogenous insulin was unlikely to be the cause of hypoglycaemia in the infants, for several reasons. These include the fact that the C-peptide levels were not particularly low for a preterm infant; they were, in fact, around average, and also that the insulin to C-peptide ratio was within the expected range for critically ill preterm neonates that were suffering with infection and other clinical factors.

Chase also noted that the levels of blood glucose observed in the two infants were not unusual for any premature baby, and are frequently observed in preterm neonates who have not suffered insulin poisoning. In fact, the C-peptide result for Child L was well within the range expected for a healthy adult, let alone neonate, according to the Liverpool laboratory's own reference range, and this was the higher of the two readings.

This is significant because Chase is acknowledged as one of the world's foremost experts on the effect of insulin on preterm babies, having studied this topic for 17 years. His Google Scholar profile reveals that he has authored, co-authored or been cited in approximately 1,750 academic papers, of which around 250 directly involve insulin (there are hundreds more that are indirectly related). Professor Chase was described to me as being easily within the top 0.1% of academics in the world in terms of published work.

Professor Chase has also been working for many years on pioneering insulin sensor technology to enable improved testing for type 2 diabetes. He previously spoke with the BBC *File on 4* programme, and explained that "there are a range of other factors that could make those readings happen like that, given the range of variability that you can see in the neonatal physiology". Chemical engineer Helen Shannon works closely with Chase, and she similarly commented that there was "a degree of certainty presented in the case that is in no way justified by the level of uncertainty that we know about in neonatal physiology. This is a hugely variable topic. It is completely inappropriate to be that certain."

When Chase and Shannon applied their experience to an engineering model, they discovered that any such poisonings "would have needed much more insulin than the prosecution claimed". The prosecution asserted that only 1% of a vial of insulin would be required, whereas two of the world's foremost experts assert that between one-half and one entire vial of insulin would have been needed. Yet there is no record of any insulin going missing on the neonatal unit, and no such accusations were ever made in court. "There was no possibility to commit insulin poisoning as hypothesised in court," Shannon informed Sarah Knapton of *The Daily Telegraph*.

In April 2026, new research conducted by Chase and Shannon discovered that 40-45% of NICU infants experienced similar insulin to C-peptide ratios as those in the indictment cases. The experts noted that what appeared to be "impossible" ratios may be not only possible but "common" in neonates. This study is a meta-analysis, combining data from multiple independent scientific studies, each of which is published and peer-reviewed in its own right but none of which has previously been combined. The work of Chase and Shannon was further peer-reviewed by editor-in-chief of the *Journal of Diabetes Science and Technology*, Dr David Klonoff, considered a world-leading endocrinologist, as has been confirmed to me.

As the endocrinology system of a neonate is yet to become fully formed and developed, its insulin to C-peptide ratio differs significantly from adults. One academic paper from 2017 notes that neonates are especially vulnerable to hypoglycaemia due to their lack of metabolic reserves, limited glycogen and fat stores, an inability to generate new glucose, higher metabolic demands due to a relatively larger brain size and associated co-morbidities. The same paper estimates that 30-60% of these high-risk infants are hypoglycaemic and require immediate intervention. Clearance rates of insulin and C-peptide also tend to vary far more in preterm babies than in children or adults as critical organs, such as the liver, are often not fully functional. Another recent academic paper on insulin infusion in preterm infants notes that the level of C-peptide concentrations can be impacted by individual insulin sensitivity.

Preterm infants also often suffer with pancreatic insufficiency which, among other issues, impacts their production of insulin and C-peptide. It is also known that the insulin secretion of neonates is highly variable. Infants that are premature and born at lower than typical weights also have a tendency to exhibit insulin resistance. This means that even if exogenous insulin is administered at therapeutic rates, the production of endogenous (internal) insulin may not be suppressed as expected, which in the process affects C-peptide levels. There are many other factors and studies that also point to variability among individuals regarding C-peptide levels. One such paper from 2019 on preterm infants concluded that "exogenous insulin infusion suppressed the C-peptide concentration to individually different degrees. In addition, the effect of insulin infusion on…cells may be linked to individual insulin sensitivity, where a low insulin sensitivity resulted in a more pronounced decrease in C-peptide during insulin infusion."

Chase and Shannon observed that "insulin levels [in neonates] spanned 200 to 6,000 pmol/L (typical-to-extreme), and C-peptide levels remained within reported ranges". This explains how what can appear impossible divergence between insulin and C-peptide readings "may be common in NICU cohorts", and "should not be assumed indicative of exogenous insulin". In support of this, a 2017 study found that neonatal glucose-insulin handling is developmentally different from adults and evolved over time. In this study of 102 neonates, the insulin/C-peptide ratio was significantly affected by post-menstrual age.

In summary, neonate physiology is different even to other young children, let alone typical adult endocrinology. And the way that the bodies of premature infants respond to insulin is unpredictable, complex and highly dependent on individual circumstances. These are facts that the jury in the Lucy Letby case never heard once; in fact, the opposite impression, that there could be only one possible incriminating explanation, was conveyed to them repeatedly.

And this is just the beginning of the problems with the insulin cases. During my correspondence with Professor Alan Wayne Jones, he expressed his bemusement that "a person would give a poison (in this case insulin) mixed together with the antidote (glucose)", describing this as "baffling". Indeed, both infants that were allegedly poisoned with insulin survived, further calling into question why Letby would attempt such poisonings when she had already supposedly been successful with air and milk. Citing the use of glucose on the unit, Dr Shoo Lee also pointed out that, in relation to Child F, insulin had been administered in the wrong way – via repeated boluses (which are similar to large tablets) rather than "titrated continuous infusion in a careful way".

When Child F was tested and low readings were discovered, further boluses were injected, with less than two hours between each dose, described as "very frequent" by Dr Lee. The conclusion of insulin experts and neonatologists who have worked on the case for Letby's appeal was that the manner of glucose provided would cause insulin surges, and that all records indicate that the blood sugar of this infant was rising because intravenous infusions were restarted. The prosecution case was that sugar levels rose when the infusions were stopped; cited as plain wrong by experts that I spoke with.

Professor Matthew Johll was baffled by the glucose issue: "It simply doesn't make any sense. You don't even need medical training to know that insulin and sugar counteract one another. If Letby had used this methodology, she was a terrible poisoner – very small amounts being diluted highly, while administering it into the literal antidote! But because they decided to go down this improbable route, they have to keep piling the absurdities on top of each other."

Speaking at a press conference related to Letby's appeal on 16 December 2024, Dr Richard Taylor also cited glucose readings as being significant: "What was missed was an incredibly high blood glucose value, and that was completely inconsistent with the clinical findings on the baby, where bedside glucometer measurements were extremely low. And yet, the blood sample which was used to analyse the insulin actually read 999 millimoles a litre glucose". Dr Taylor explained this meant that glucose had been definitively "flagged" as being "high", and that this was "verified information that…was never even brought up in court". This 999 reading was in fact first discovered via blood test readings submitted to the Thirlwall Inquiry.

The 999 reading remains a major bone of contention. It is accepted that this reading is extraordinarily high, and yet it was not even revealed, let alone discussed or contextualised, during court proceedings. "It's just ridiculously high. It's stupidly high", Dr Richard Taylor asserted. "We have two stupidly high numbers; the high insulin number, which was the one that the experts focused on, and the high glucose, which was completely ignored". Indeed, this figure is indicative of the machine completing its analysis, but the result being impossible to report. The 999 reading is revealing something very important – the machine has measured an extremely high reading, but cannot report it back to a monitoring chemist.

Dr Taylor went on to explain the significance of this: "The most likely thing is that the sample was contaminated, and that's what led to the very high glucose value. This is not compelling evidence of murder. This is evidence of bad testing." An insulin expert explained to me that this explanation of 'contamination' could perhaps be more accurately described as the sample being compromised. If glucose and blood are drawn from the same line, glucose could easily become mixed in with the original blood sample, creating an erroneous result.

It is also illustrative to examine the two infants involved in the insulin allegations. Child F was premature, born at 29 weeks, low birth-weight, suffering with prolonged hypoglycaemia for 17 hours. Child F was the twin of Child E, and faced significantly heightened risk of complications and premature death. The mother of these twins endured a complicated pregnancy, during which the infants were diagnosed with twin-to-twin transfusion syndrome – a rare condition which occurs when identical twins share a placenta and grow unevenly as a consequence. Child E received an infusion of insulin due to associated nutrient deficiencies. Child F had respiratory distress syndrome and hyperglycaemia requiring insulin treatment, developing sepsis and hypoglycaemia during the early hours of his existence.

A panel of international experts convened by Dr Shoo Lee to study cases concluded that the hypoglycaemia of Child F began with sepsis, and was prolonged because the infant's IV bag infiltrated for several hours. Hypoglycaemia persisted in the child, and experts that assessed the case were critical of the fact that a higher infusion of glucose was required than that provided. The panel also provided some very technical information related to the infusion of dextrose, while pointing out that "since infusion bags were prepared in the pharmacy, stored in the unit, and changed at 12:00 hours, multiple infusion bags would have to be contaminated if there was insulin poisoning. The blood sugar rose after 19:00 hours, not because the infusion bag was changed, but because the dextrose was increased to 15%."

They further reported that "the insulin/C-Peptide (I/C) ratio does not prove exogenous insulin was administered because the C-peptide was not low for preterm infants (20-45 percentile), potassium levels were normal (insulin decreases potassium), antibodies can store insulin in the blood, glucose levels should be lower if exogenous insulin was used, the insulin/C-Peptide (I/C) ratio was within the expected range for preterm infants because insulin autoimmune antibodies (IAA) which are common in preterm infants bind to insulin and increase measured insulin levels. And the immunoassay test is unreliable because interference factors like sepsis and antibiotics can give false positive insulin readings."

There was a lot of fairly complex science provided by the panel in its preliminary report that was circulated publicly, let alone the enormously detailed full report. But some of the key points can be summarised thus:

- Child F suffered with prolonged hypoglycaemia due to sepsis, prematurity, borderline intrauterine growth restriction, lack of intravenous glucose when the long line infiltrated for a prolonged period of several hours and poor medical management of hypoglycaemia;
- The insulin level and ratio related to C-peptide are within the normal range for critically ill preterm infants that are receiving antibiotic treatment;
- Extensive swelling and induration (thickening and hardening of body tissue) was noted, indicating that infiltration had endured for a considerable period of time. Errors were made with IV lines, which meant that Child F did not receive adequate sugar;

- Child F did not receive dextrose for several hours, which is the likely reason for his hypoglycaemic state, particularly as the infant was fighting infection and had a higher glucose requirement;
- Mistakes were made with regard to the injection of boluses, which compounded the situation. This resulted in what Dr Lee termed a "yo-yo" pattern of rising and declining blood sugar. Dr Lee also described the mistakes made on the unit as a "very basic thing", and that "we teach all medical students not to do this";
- The document also discusses the rather implausible logistical scenario required for feeding bags on the unit to have been deliberately poisoned: "In order for this baby to have had insulin introduced into the bag, it would have to have been done multiple times, into multiple bags." It should be mentioned again that Letby wasn't even on duty when the feeding bags were hung out for the infants on the unit;
- It is noted that if all of the information available for Child F is used, "a very different conclusion" to that presented in court is inevitable.

Additionally, the fact that Child F was being treated for sepsis was discussed in court on 22-23 November. As has been established, sepsis was common, bordering on endemic, on the unit over the period of Letby's alleged crimes. The fact that this was a factor in the clinical outlook for Child F was not a secret, nor is the fact that sepsis can interfere with the immunoassay test used and contribute to falsely elevated readings. This phenomenon is documented in academic work, with a Japanese study from 2022 discussing the relationship between sepsis and hypoglycaemia. Various therapies related to pregnancy can also cause the mother to create antibodies to insulin which pass to the child, increasing measured insulin levels. When coupled with sepsis, this can have an enormous impact.

It must also be emphasised once more that both infants survived and neither exhibited symptoms of insulin poisoning such as seizure or heart arrhythmia. "The levels of insulin that they measured were so astronomically high that I would have not expected the child to recover," Dr Colin Ferguson told me. "And yet, both children did recover. You would have thought that this ought to have probably been a fatal event, particularly if administered externally as alleged." Similarly, another medic comment-ed that the levels of insulin measured in the two cases should have been "enough to put an adult male into a coma, yet both babies recovered rap-idly, and went home within a few days. There must be considerable doubt regarding the accuracy of results in these tests due to this element alone."

This leads into another important aspect of the insulin cases, namely problems associated with the testing methods used. The first thing to note about this is that test results had been received by a consultant at the CoCH in 2015, and nothing suspicious had been noted at the time. Indeed, speaking at the Thirlwall Inquiry on 7 October 2024, the an-onymised consultant, Dr ZA, indicated that the results were not surpris-ing, and "not that rare in neonates". Writing in *Private Eye*, Dr Philip Hammond observed that due to oversights from "the very people who most suspected [Letby], definitive forensic tests for insulin poisoning… were never done, and cannot now be done".

Everything that occurred in this investigation was retrospective, and since no blood samples had been stored, it was impossible to conduct further testing or check for other natural and genetic causes of what were eventually deemed suspicious figures. The investigation was based en-tirely on a form of test referred to as an immunoassay, which is reliant on antibodies. The validity and accuracy of the testing method was never queried, or even discussed, in court, but immunoassay tests are not de-signed for forensic use. This was not exactly a secret, as the test, which was performed at the Royal Liverpool University Hospital (RLUH), was described by this very institution as follows:

> *"Please note that the insulin assay performed at RLUH is not suitable for the investigation of factitious hypoglycaemia. If exogenous insulin administration is suspected as the cause of hypoglycaemia, please inform the laboratory so that the sample can be referred externally for analysis."*

This warning essentially acknowledges that the immunoassay used cannot identify virtually all forms of artificial insulin. If the defence had called a biochemist, they could have informed the court of the likely sample compromise for Child F and the healthy C-peptide level for Child L. This did not happen, and the jury heard no such explanation. It should also be noted that new research from Chase and Shannon is now available, whereas this didn't exist at the time of the trial.

The immunoassay test has a high rate of sensitivity but low specificity, meaning that it has a high false positive rate. Professor Richard Gill has pointed to repeat samples, further testing, the reporting of possible sources of error and potentially anomalous outcomes and the consultation of experts having not been conducted, and so "the tests should not have been accepted as forensic evidence".

Furthermore, the Forensic Science Regulator's statutory code came into effect on 2 October 2023, just six weeks after Letby's conviction. This new code would have been relevant during the trial, helping to ensure that credible scientific standards were required in the investigation. In line with this, insulin experts that I spoke with asserted that changes to the law are necessary, so that the determination of exogenous insulin is placed under the jurisdiction of the Forensic Science Regulator.

The weaknesses and problems associated with immunoassays have been firmly established; as one example, cross-reactivity with immunoassays can result in specificity issues. Pathologist Sacha Uljon, writing in *Advances in Clinical Chemistry*, noted that "immunoassays are often faulted for a phenomenon called cross-reactivity…Historically, cross-reactivity has been considered a negative attribute in an immunoassay because it can lead to false positive results." A 2023 study, published in the journal *JCEM Case Reports*, examined problems with immunoassay insulin interference and observed that "falsely elevated insulin levels" are possible with this method. Another 2019 paper explains that cross-reactivity with other drugs partly explains the high false positive rate that is associated with immunoassays. Other research points to systematic and random errors, consistent biases and unpredictable fluctuations in results. When combined, in this case, with more likely clinical explanations for the results, this must be considered seriously problematic.

The summary in this chapter only provides some of the uncontested scientific reasons why variation in insulin levels and C-peptide are possible, and why immunoassay is considered an unsatisfactory and unreliable mechanism for such an important judicial trial. This reality is reflected in the quality and quantity of experts who have felt obliged to criticise the standard of science presented to the jury.

When I spoke to Professor Alan Wayne Jones, he explained to me that his "background is in forensic toxicology and the analysis of abused drugs in biological specimens". In his speciality, "we consider that positive results obtained from immunoassay methods are 'presumptive positives', until these are verified by more specific analytical methods, such as liquid chromatography-mass spectrometry (LC-MS)".

This latter term refers to an established laboratory technique that separates, identifies and measures substances within a liquid sample. LC-MS is considered more specific and sensitive, and less prone to false positives and negatives. However, immunoassay is cheaper and faster, which could have been a motivating factor. Professor Wayne Jones told me that "if such verification is done in cases involving alleged drug abuse, then it most certainly should be required in an alleged murder trial". Professor Wayne Jones described this as his "principal objection to the insulin evidence in the Letby case", and was critical of the "acceptance at face value of positive immunoassay results, without any secondary testing being conducted to confirm possible cross-reactivity with look-a-like molecules, or other interferences and/or re-analysis of the plasma by LC-MS". The problem has been that courts have accepted this evidence, while exogenous insulin has been presented in the Letby case as the only possible interpretation of the results. This is now known to be untrue; in fact, considering the arcane and unlikely logistics, hypothetical nature of the allegations and the common incidence of similar figures in comparable subjects, poisoning is by far the least likely explanation.

Professor Wayne Jones had previously told the *New Yorker* that "insulin is not an easy substance to analyse, and you would need to analyse this at a forensic laboratory, where the routines are much more stringent regarding chain of custody, using modern forensic technology." He similarly commented during a Channel 5 documentary that "the analysis of insulin was done by an immunoassay method, and I don't think that is sufficient for use in a criminal prosecution. You need more robust methods of analysis to charge someone with administering insulin with malicious intent. People shouldn't accept that kind of flimsy analytical result. You really need to verify, by more robust methods, the result for use in a criminal prosecution."

During discussion with *The Daily Telegraph*, Professor Wayne Jones further asserted that the notion that such a high insulin level could have been derived from adding 0.1ml of insulin into a baby's feeding bag was "bordering on fantasy", and queried why the reliability of these figures and testing methods wasn't questioned during the trial, concluding that it would have been "more difficult for the jury to reach a guilty verdict, not just on the poisonings, but on any of the counts" if this had occurred. The view of Professor Wayne Jones has been further corroborated by a research paper he authored, which was published in the *Journal of Forensic and Legal Medicine* in 2023.

In a case involving nurse Colin Norris, Professor Matthew Johll contributed to a BBC documentary questioning the evidence used. Little has changed, and few lessons have been learned, in the intervening years that followed the 2008 conviction of Norris, as he explained at the time. "I think it's unconscionable to put a person on trial for murder with a presumptive test", Johll commented in 2015. "One little sample partially analysed, that's really where we're sitting at. With no supporting evidence, no injection marks, no signs of insulin depo, there's no witnesses, no empty syringe, there's no empty vial. There's nothing else connecting [Norris] to this case."

Professor Johll told me that the fundamental problem with the Letby case is that it relied on "a medical testing system that is designed for a very different purpose than the forensic science testing. At the heart of it is what is only a preliminary screening test. This wouldn't be relied on to convict a petty drug dealer, or disqualify an Olympic athlete, but it's being used to hand various nurses multiple life sentences." In the opinion of Professor Johll, the issue in court is a lack of awareness of how such testing works: "There is a distinction between medical and forensic testing.

A medical test, such as a COVID test, gets the results back quickly so that a diagnosis can be made. However, the cost of those quick medical testing results is that false positives can give inaccurate results in a small percentage of tests. The standard for testing in a forensic laboratory is much higher, as it should be when you are sentencing someone to prison for life." As an example of this, one study on the rapid antigen test for COVID-19 indicated that approximately 12% of results derived from the technique were likely to be incorrect.

Dr Adel Ismail, a retired consultant in clinical biochemistry and chemical endocrinology who was the head of an NHS pathology lab for 25 years, elaborated on these concerns in conversation with journalist Anouk Curry: "Of all the technologies we use in the lab for measurements, the one with the highest error rate is immunoassay. If there is the slightest doubt, we have to confirm the integrity and the veracity of the results. Without doing the follow-up tests, without confirming the results, then you are entering into the land of guessing." Dr Ismail also contributed to the BBC *File on 4* documentary on the Letby case, asserting that, "I wouldn't forward [these results] to the clinician, and definitely not in court, without verifying their veracity and integrity."

Professor Johll also cited this tendency for other substances to bind to the antibodies in immunoassays, and further explained how cross-reactivity is a well-established side-effect of this form of testing: "If you go to Google Scholar, and search for 'immunoassay', 'cross-reactivity', 'false positives', and so on, there are pages and pages of research articles going back 30 years on these topics. This is not new information, and that's part of my frustration. We know this is a flawed technique. We know that it is inherently flawed." One such study from 2015, the actual year of the supposed insulin poisonings, discovered that "detection of insulin analogues was highly variable and ranged from 0% to 140%", and observed that "physicians need to be aware of the limitation of laboratory methods to detect exogenous insulin".

Dr Nick Birse, a lecturer in mass spectrometry at Queen's University Belfast, has expressed doubts regarding the immunoassay, while Dr Charline Bottinelli, an insulin expert from the Laboratoire LAT Lumtox in France was also critical of the usage of immunoassay, noting that it "doesn't allow us to formally identify the type of insulin and to distinguish human insulin from synthetic analogues. A high level of insulin in blood could suggest exogenous (outside) administration, but also disease such as insulinoma." Dr Bottinelli further informed *The Daily Telegraph* that the levels of insulin for Child L were so elevated that it was "highly probable" that "severe hypoglycaemia and dramatic consequences" would have been expected. Finally, in the opinion of another insulin expert who spoke with Dr Philip Hammond, "the results are… conclusive: there is no evidence of insulin poisoning".

Hammond would later write in *Private Eye* of the enormous gulf in quality between reports written by the expert panel effectively acting in Letby's defence, and the original prosecution reports: "The prosecution reports are paltry affairs ranging from 2-15 pages. The new defence reports are 60 pages and 85 pages, extensively cross-referenced to the clinical records and the published literature, including new research evidence that has emerged since the trial."

"If we're going to put someone away for life in prison," Professor Matthew Johll commented, "let's take that blood sample and run the mass spectrometry data, and show that the exact molecular weight of insulin was present. This is not a secret, it's not obscure or obtuse. Let's do the requisite testing. I don't think that's too much to ask in exchange for somebody's life."

During my dialogue with Professor Carola Vinuesa, we discussed the insulin cases at some length. "Immunoassays are part of our day-to-day work in our laboratory," Professor Vinuesa explained, "so I am very familiar with the pitfalls of immunoassays, not merely for insulin testing but also in the broader sense where general principles and false positive results apply". I asked Professor Vinuesa how she had felt when she initially encountered the Letby case. "I cannot understand why the immunoassay test has not been repeated, and why the suspicion of exogenous insulin had not been confirmed by mass spectrometry."

When I queried why this was significant, Professor Vinuesa told me that "you should not convict someone on the basis of a test that is indirect". When I asked her to explain this further, she described this as a "basic principle" in both her field and related disciplines. "An immuno-assay does not directly measure insulin. It uses antibodies that normally bind insulin with high affinity, but they can also bind other substances non-specifically." As discussed previously, this binding aspect of the cas-es is critical. Mass spectrometry will detect insulin bound to antibodies; immunoassays will not.

This cavalcade of expert opinion and scientific evidence contrasts starkly with the way that insulin results were presented in court. Dr Anna Milan stated that "the only way you get a pattern like that is if insulin has been given to a patient". This must be considered an astound-ing assertion considering everything that has already been included in this chapter. Additionally, Dr Gwen Wark observed that the reports for Child L "met all required standards", and that she was "very confident in the accuracy and reliability" of the blood test analysis produced for the sample of Child F.

The terms 'reliability' and 'accuracy' used by Dr Wark have technical meanings, which would have been unknown to the jury, and probably the barristers and judge. 'Reliability' refers to whether the measurement results are reproducible when repeated. Regular programmes of testing are conducted on laboratory apparatus within the NHS, and this involves the preparation of identical samples which are sent to laboratories for results to be measured. The comment here simply means that the sample referenced is 'well within' the specifications of manufacturers, with con-centrations being neither too high nor low; essentially, optimal for the equipment. This has no relevance to the reliability of the test itself.

'Accuracy' means that if the sample is within the manufacturer's specifications then a high insulin reading means that the insulin level in the sample is high. However, if the sample, due to antibodies or other contaminants, does not fall with the specification of the manufacturer then the high insulin reading gives no indication regarding the nature of the insulin itself; i.e. whether it originated from an internal or external source. By falling within these criteria of being 'accurate' and 'reliable', the process had "met the required standards", as denoted by Dr Wark, but this is entirely irrelevant when it comes to assessing whether the tests actually demonstrated beyond reasonable doubt that synthetic insulin had been administered.

Of course, things may have moved on in the last 10 years but in 2013, Dr Wark co-authored a paper with Vincent Marks which seems to set out a different view than that presented in court. In that study, *Forensic aspects of insulin*, Marks and Wark noted that the role of insulin in the law can occasionally be open to question, and then asserted the following:

"This is especially true of situations in which insulin is suspected of having been used inappropriately or maliciously. The major differences between investigation of hypoglycaemia in clinical and forensic situations are that in the latter the history is often unreliable, appropriate samples for analysis were not collected, preserved or labelled correctly and analytical results are likely to be challenged on grounds of specificity, accuracy and interpretation. Immunoassay remains the mainstay of clinical investigation of hypoglycaemia but likely to become displaced by mass-spectrometry in the forensic situation especially now that human insulin is being replaced by synthetic insulin analogues for the treatment of diabetes."

In this instance, Dr Wark has co-authored a paper which concludes that immunoassay should be "displaced by mass-spectrometry in the forensic situation" as the former is prone to error, but when speaking in court this was never once even mentioned. In fact, after the court case was concluded, the primary prosecution witness, Dr Dewi Evans, didn't even know that there was more than one way of measuring insulin, let alone their relative accuracy! It is also important to note that there is no conceivable way that the jury can possibly question this information. If defence witnesses had appeared in court, the whole story could have been completely different.

It has been suggested to me that Dr Wark simply did not know about neonatal antibodies. This is not a criticism, as no one did at the time. It is likely that Dr Wark made implicit assumptions and, perhaps understandably, did not declare them, not least because she didn't fully understand neonatal antibody binding.

Professor Richard Gill told me that he had spoken with Wark's co-author Professor Vincent Marks "just a few weeks before he died". At the time, Dr Marks was receiving palliative care, but was still "so happy to talk about science". According to Gill, Professor Marks was "extraordinarily concerned" about the Letby case, and the insulin science that was used. Sadly, Professor Marks passed away in November 2023, and so couldn't play what would no doubt have been a valuable role in discourse around this issue.

As should be clear by now, supplementary testing should have been conducted on the insulin samples used in court. At the time that these samples were taken, it was customary to send insulin results to Guildford for checking, although Professor Carola Vinuesa informed me that immunoassays are now transported to Germany because "Guildford doesn't have the apparatus for doing liquid chromatography and tandem mass spectrometry". The requirement for follow-up testing is discussed in chapter 23 of the book *Substance Use and Addiction Research*, which describes the practice as a "first-line screening tool for drug testing". The meaning here is quite clear; immunoassay can be the first port of call, but certainly shouldn't be the last.

Furthermore, the procedure of sending samples to Guildford was well known. In her statement to the Thirlwall Inquiry, Heather Wilshaw-Jones, a Principal Clinical Scientist specialising in Biochemistry, explained that she was "involved in communicating insulin and C-peptide results to the CoCH". On 12 August 2015, Wilshaw-Jones "received and communicated results in relation to Child F to the CoCH". During this process, having flagged up the possibility of exogenous insulin, Wilshaw-Jones wrote the following comment, which must have been received by the CoCH: "Suggest send sample to Guildford for exogenous insulin".

This never happened. This is a fundamental failing, both in terms of the processes conducted at the time, and also the evidence that was presented in court. It cannot be said with any confidence that the figures and readings presented to the jury provide definitive proof of insulin being administered externally. The comments of Wilshaw-Jones in fact indicate that it is normal procedure to send samples to Guildford for exogenous insulin checks, and that the process can't possibly be considered complete until this has occurred. Indeed, in her statement to the Thirlwall Inquiry, Wilshaw-Jones explains that, "At the time, the insulin assay at Liverpool was not able to detect exogenous insulin, so a sample would need to be sent to another laboratory with the capability to do this". The situation cannot be made any plainer than that.

Professor Matthew Johll informed me that the United Kingdom and Ireland Association of Forensic Toxicologists (UKIAFT) "defines immunoassay as a screening method, and clearly states that it needs to be followed up". This is quite evident from the laboratory guidelines of the UKIAFT, which state that "presumptive screening tests such as immunoassay…must be appropriate and validated for the type of biological specimens being analysed. With regards to immunoassays used on whole blood, they must be appropriately validated for that purpose, especially if using post-mortem blood." Even the "use of a second immunoassay system to confirm another immunoassay is not regarded as acceptable, even if it is deemed to be a more specific assay," not that such a second assay test was actually conducted in the Letby case!

One final point is that this result was not deemed particularly significant at the time. It wasn't actioned by the CoCH, and it clearly wasn't an issue of any import to Wilshaw-Jones, as evidenced by the fact that she couldn't recall numerous details related to the test when questioned: "I can see that I phoned the results to the CoCH Biochemist at the CoCH. I do not recall the conversation or who I spoke to…I do not recall if myself or anyone else at Liverpool Clinical Laboratories took any additional action as a consequence of the test results…I do not know if the process for communicating or flagging results of insulin and C-peptide testing has been altered or improved since 2015-2016, as I no longer work at the trust." The clinician working on the sample did not flag this as an urgent result, indicating that the infant wasn't even noticeably unwell.

This impression is further cemented by the Thirlwall Inquiry witness statement of Sarah Davies, who was involved in the communication of test results related to Child L. Davies makes a number of important and illustrative comments which merit being fully recounted and analysed.

Davies firstly observes that "there is no evidence (telephone log) that Liverpool Clinical Laboratories were requested to expedite analysis on this sample," again confirming the impression that this wasn't treated urgently. There is then further discussion of the glucose aspect of the case: "Although a glucose result was not provided by the Chester Laboratory, and therefore full interpretation of the insulin and C-peptide results was not possible in Liverpool, I wanted to flag the results to the clinical team". Davies immediately explains that this was necessary "because the clinical details stated 'hypoglycaemia', and so I felt that the results may be inappropriate in this context and would need further clinical follow-up". If it isn't clear enough already, this once again confirms that additional testing was needed.

In her following statements, Davies expands on this: "It is not uncommon for clinical details to state 'hypoglycaemia' when the glucose is not low enough on that particular sample to be considered hypoglycaemic, which is why we need to check that the glucose measured at the same time is in the hypoglycaemic range rather than relying on the clinical details alone." In this passage, Davies reiterates the glucose issue, also observing that "the glucose was not available on specimens".

Next Davies moves on to the central point: "There was a requirement in our laboratory for all investigations for suspected exogenous insulin administration to be sent to Guildford, but there was no indication that this was suspected clinically from the clinical details on the sample we received or the telephone log of the conversation. No assessment of insulin or C-peptide assay interference was performed in our laboratory." This should immediately invalidate this sample being used for anything of the forensic importance of a court case involving murder. Had this test been performed at the time, antibodies may have been found. This should have been declared in court, but it was not.

If this initial statement is not clear enough, Davies then reiterates its meaning: "In other words, the C-peptide is lower than you would expect based on the insulin, and the reason for this would need further investigation." This 'further investigation' did not occur. Davies notes that the "ultimate responsibility for follow-up of results lies with the doctor that requests a test since they have the full clinical information. The laboratory can flag potentially abnormal results for more rapid review by the clinical team, and have a clinical advisory service that is available by telephone if interpretive support is required for any results." This unequivocally did not happen. Nurse shift leader at the CoCH, Belinda Williamson, also made it clear that nothing notable occurred at the time with regard to any readings. Williamson did "not recall discussing Child F's blood sugar readings with anyone", and did "not recall discussing Child L's blood sugar readings with anyone at the time".

The Thirlwall Inquiry seemingly ignored all of this information. But one would at least expect this to be communicated accurately to the court in the Letby case. However, not only was the impression conveyed that the insulin cases were irrefutably certain, erroneous statements were also made regarding testing. During court proceedings, Philip Astbury for the prosecution questioned Dr Anna Milan on Child F:

ASTBURY: Just one matter arising, doctor, with regard to Guildford. So I understand it, would Guildford assist with whether it was exogenous or not?
MILAN: No. The results dictate that it's exogenous. They would just help, if you were unsure of the source.
ASTBURY: So really, Guildford would have been deciding or assisting with exactly what type of exogenous insulin…
MILAN: Yes.
ASTBURY: Not whether it was exogenous or not?
MILAN: Correct.

No, it's *not* correct! Two representatives of Liverpool Clinical Laboratories have explicitly stated that this is incorrect. Numerous experts have indicated that there should have been further testing done, and that the sample cannot be confirmed as exogenous insulin without this. Royal Liverpool University Hospital even indicates clearly on the very test used that it "is not suitable for the investigation of factitious hypoglycaemia," and that "if exogenous insulin administration is suspected as the cause of hypoglycaemia, please inform the laboratory so that the sample can be referred externally for analysis". It could hardly be any clearer, and yet the court heard the complete opposite!

Having garnered all of this information, I quizzed Professor David Livermore on the hierarchy of responsibility in laboratories: "If you're running a laboratory, you get many 'typical' results and you can report these out confidently. But you also get the unusual. You should check these and, if they are reproducible, you have a duty to discuss them with the person who sent the sample. As an example, if my reference lab encountered some bacterium that was resistant to antibiotics to which we'd never seen resistance before, myself, or one of my senior colleagues, would phone the hospital lab that sent it and establish where the patient comes from, what was the history, and so on." This certainly didn't happen at the time that these tests were conducted, because the insulin cases were only discovered in 2018 by Dr Stephen Brearey, many months after the case had been referred to Cheshire Police (see "The Golden Thread" for more background).

"With the insulin cases, what I would like to know from that testing laboratory is what proportion of samples have ratios like that?" Professor Livermore explained. "Because if it's very rare, they should be on the phone; they shouldn't just be spitting out a standard report. Conversely, if they're common, but seem unlikely, then they should be looking at their assay.

"If one of my staff had not followed up on a grossly anomalous result, I would view it as a serious untoward incident. At the very least, I would have a chat with them and explain that this must be done in future. That's just competent management of a laboratory. It seems here that the report merely included a note to say that if exogenous insulin is suspected, another test should be done elsewhere by another method, and Chester didn't even follow up on that."

I then asked Professor Livermore whether the hospital or the laboratory should be considered responsible for escalating the matter. "Technically, it is the responsibility of the organisation looking after the patient – Chester in this case – but it's a pretty shoddy laboratory, in my opinion, that doesn't take action to ensure that it's done. And it comes back to my point of how common this sort of anomaly might be. You can run a laboratory like a production line – it spits out results, and nobody applies the least bit of thought to them, beyond stamping a few as anomalous. But that's not professional. You should always know the answer to how frequent such anomalies are, and whether they are real or test failures should be flagged up.

"As soon as insulin and C-peptide do not fall in the normal range that should be a red flag to the laboratory. Possibly something has gone wrong with their assay, which they need to look into. Is the test even suitable for neonates? Or possibly there's something unusual about this patient – perhaps there are genetic reasons? Could there be a contamination? It could be an error in testing, it could be an unsuitable test for a neonatal sample, or there could be exogenous insulin. These need to be distinguished. But all they did was to add a note saying that the sample should be sent to Guildford if exogenous insulin was suspected. And that wasn't done, probably because the infant recovered."

The account of Professor Livermore represents the inverse of what occurred at the CoCH. No follow-up tests were conducted. No blood samples were retained. Nothing was deemed unusual at the time, not least because Child F and Child L both survived. It was only 2-3 years later that this was actioned in any way. At that point, this was no longer a scientific matter, but instead a criminal investigation into murder. In a pattern that was repeated throughout the Letby case, the science here was fatally flawed, with superficial, and even completely incorrect, conclusions drawn from misleading and inadequate data.

There was also, critically, a third insulin case identified for which Letby was never charged. Dr Dewi Evans was bullish about Letby's guilt for this case, as he told Dr Philip Hammond of *Private Eye*: "There was a third insulin poisoning in November 2015. The insulin value was recorded as '>1000' and the C-peptide as '220' as handwritten entries in the notes. This is VERY abnormal. One expects the C-peptide to be 5-10 times the insulin value normally. Letby was most certainly on duty. She was the nurse who measured the six low glucose values, lowest of 1.0, when the baby was hypoglycaemic for nearly eight hours. The baby certainly survived and as far as I know is well."

Follow-up tests at Alder Hey hospital resulted in the baby being diagnosed with congenital hyperinsulinism. It is notable that neither of the infants in the Letby trial had similar follow-up tests for this condition. Of the three insulin cases, this third infant had the lowest blood sugar readings, and it was treated with the most seriousness at the CoCH, hence the fact that the baby was transferred to Alder Hey.

The evidence that this child was poisoned is, in fact, as strong as in the cases that were referred to court. The only difference is that the decision was made not to charge Letby on this case. Parents of other infants were told that Letby had harmed their infants, scarred for life on the basis of much less evidence; two obvious examples being Child K and the second tranche of cases that were rejected by the CPS. If decoupled insulin and C-peptide readings automatically mean exogenous insulin and deliberate poisoning then this infant should have been in the court case, which begs the question of why it was not. It seems that there are three possible reasons for this: the Alder Hey results contradicted the prosecution case, it was impossible to contrive a scenario in which Letby was on duty, or both.

As Dr Philip Hammond notes, the third insulin case demonstrates that "the pattern of blood results that the prosecution argued 'could only have happened with insulin poisoning' could also in fact happen with other conditions because the test concerned is not sufficiently accurate in neonates."

This is also the opinion of Professor Carola Vinuesa: "The third case was not presented to the jury because the high level of insulin proved to be endogenous insulin caused by a medical condition known as hyperinsulinism. The other two babies could not be retested because they were discharged. There are many reasons why abnormal results like those seen in the Letby case could arise for other reasons – the explanation could be medical for example hyperproinsulinemia, false positive results due to antibody interference, there could be pharmacy errors, or mislabelling. In other words, there are many different reasons why those results might occur other than the injection of exogenous insulin."

Professor Vinuesa further noted that false positive results in immunoassays are not particularly rare, and thus far more likely to occur than attempted murder by malicious administration of exogenous insulin. It is also worth noting that analysis of a 2020-23 dataset from the CoCH for insulin vs C-peptide blood test results discovered five other subjects that had test results similar to Child L.

The inconsistency of approach across the three insulin cases is stark; highly problematic from a medical and scientific perspective. The failure to conduct adequate, or indeed any, follow-up testing in the cases of Child F and Child L renders their results meaningless, particularly in the context of the third insulin case, which makes this failure all the more obvious. There are also question marks regarding the disclosure of evidence with the third insulin case, as uncalled defence witness Dr Michael Hall only learned of it when informed by Rachel Aviv of the *New Yorker*. One wonders why the police and prosecution, in particular, have apparently wanted to hide this case from public view.

As a reflection of this, a critical document regarding the third insulin test briefly appeared on the Thirlwall Inquiry website in February 2025. Dr Astha Soni, a paediatrician from the CoCH, had made a statement to Cheshire Police, indicating that the third infant was suffering with "congenital hyperinsulinism," with "transient hyperinsulinism" also possible. This diagnosis of naturally occurring excess insulin was supported by endocrine experts at Alder Hey. Yet this critical information was never disclosed to the defence. Lord Ken Macdonald KC, the former chief of the CPS, told David Rose and Cleuci de Oliveira that this was a failure of disclosure: "It sounds to me that the material you've found does meet that standard, and so should have been made available to Letby's defence."

Failures of disclosure are often cited as grounds for convictions to be appealed and overturned. Furthermore, the statement of Dr Soni (Thirlwall ref: INQ0102022) was rapidly removed from the Thirlwall Inquiry website shortly after publication, with no explanation given for this action. With new research also indicating that the supposedly damning insulin/C-peptide ratio is not actually incriminating but instead quite typical, this purported smoking gun suddenly seems rather tepid. There are many other infants similar to Child F and Child L that demonstrably produce similar figures entirely naturally, and it is now known that several such subjects were resident at the CoCH in the immediate aftermath.

Considering everything that has been recorded in this chapter, the comments of one medic who wished to remain anonymous seem particularly pertinent: "In my experience, strange and unusual blood tests come back regularly. And we just repeat them. It usually comes back totally normal, and no one has an explanation for the erroneous result". This assertion was almost perfectly mirrored by the anonymised Dr ZA, speaking at the Thirlwall Inquiry on 7 October 2024: "[The results were] something we saw not infrequently in neonates that would have slightly unexpected readings, and we would repeat them and they'd be okay." Note that they "would repeat them", and "they'd be okay." The problem here was that this time there was no repetition of testing because there were no concerns; in fact, by the time that the results were even flagged as being suspicious, this was impossible, as the samples no longer existed.

This lack of concern was not even slightly surprising, as Dr Shirley Bowles, a consultant chemical pathologist at the CoCH told the Thirlwall Inquiry just two days after the comments of Dr ZA that "we do get unusual results that we discuss with doctors quite regularly…It's not unusual to see results that are difficult to explain, or, unusual that you might want to talk to someone about." Of course, no such issues were ever communicated to the jury of laypersons, who don't know the first thing about insulin, laboratory testing or neonatal physiology.

Similar information has been used previously to convict other nurses. When I spoke with Professor Richard Gill, he pointed to the case of a nurse on remand in Birmingham, having been arrested in 2022, as being another possible insulin poisoning allegation: "She hasn't been charged, probably because the Birmingham police constabulary are sitting back to see what will happen with Lucy. But if you look at this statistically, there are around 750,000 registered nurses in the United Kingdom, and there are just over 30 serial killers in jail, of which six are nurses. So if you're a registered nurse, in an ostensibly caring profession, you're about 20 times more likely to be a serial killer. Is this really feasible?"

Readers should note that the narrative running right through the Thirlwall Inquiry has been that hospitals should refer similar spikes in deaths to that which occurred at the CoCH, and perhaps even considerably smaller spikes, to the police, and more rapidly than occurred in Letby's case. In short, this issue is far broader than Lucy Letby. This goes right to the heart of criminal justice, healthcare, state and government, and the fundamental functioning of these systems.

Asserting that spikes in deaths, supposedly suspicious incidents or even just the vague concerns of consultants, should almost automatically become a matter for the police is a chilling suggestion. The consequences of this could be nothing short of calamitous, particularly for nurses who are currently doing no more than diligently performing their tasks and duties, as was the case with Lucy Letby.

There are now several nurses in prison in the UK having been convicted of poisoning patients with insulin. In the case of Letby, this was treated as a matter of fact before the court case even began, with Letby being informed in police interviews that there had definitely been insulin poisonings. This is incompetent and unscientific, while running contrary to anything approaching an acceptable judicial process. It is, ultimately, completely indefensible.

The conviction of Lucy Letby was, at the very least, catalysed by the insulin cases. It was the closest that the prosecution came to a smoking gun. Yet it requires a series of events that are highly implausible; even the logistics alone are practically impossible. It is based on hypothetical assertions. There are no direct measurements and not even the most fanciful suggestion from the prosecution regarding how the insulin was accessed and used, or indeed in what quantity. There are also significant problems with how the figures cited in court as definitive proof were acquired.

And we now know that the data on which Letby was convicted is not only possible but demonstrably common in a cohort of infants with similar characteristics to those that were discussed in court. The prospect that the indirectly derived figures, with no audit trail or meaningful proof of insulin administration whatsoever, were poisonings is vanishingly small. This is particularly true when compared with the likelihood that these were simply infants demonstrating what are now understood to be not untypical insulin and C-peptide levels.

At this point, it is very clear that the so-called smoking gun has been extinguished. The broader question would be whether we, as a society, care about wrongful convictions and about erroneous science being used in court. And about scapegoats being targeted repeatedly because they offer a simple, perhaps even comforting, solution to deeper-rooted problems. This tendency has been dramatically evident in the fallacious prosecution of over 900 subpostmasters. If we continue down the precipitous path that we're on currently, it will become ever more obvious in the case of nurse convictions as well.

CHAPTER 12: OTHER INFANTS

This chapter will examine three examples that are outside of the typical allegations levelled at Lucy Letby, beginning with Child E. In this instance, the peculiar accusation was made that Letby attacked an infant with some indeterminate instrument and then stood around doing nothing. The case of Child E is particularly reliant on traumatic eyewitness testimony, which, even for this case, is unusually unreliable.

Before going into the background of this infant, there are some important anomalies to address. It is firstly notable that the mother of Child E told jurors that she was advised against a post-mortem. Doctors on the unit purportedly told the parents of Child E that any post-mortem would "not tell [them] very much". This was the decisive factor in any such examination never taking place, as the mother divulged that she did not ask for one "largely" because it was explained that there was "little point" in doing so. Usually, a post-mortem investigation would have been instrumental in understanding how the infant died.

Another important detail is that Letby herself called Dr David Harkness to assist with Child E, effectively immediately after delivering the supposed inflicted harm that was claimed in court. Letby was not the designated nurse for Child E, and she called Dr Harkness even though this could potentially have been incriminating – not really the actions of someone who had deliberately caused the alleged gastrointestinal tract damage. Dr Harkness also told the court that Letby was accompanied by another nurse when the sudden deterioration occurred. Furthermore, the court heard that doctors on the unit could have acted sooner to save the baby, while Letby broke down in uncontrollable tears, and court proceedings had to be interrupted, during discussion of Child E; again, hardly the conduct of a guilty person.

This pattern of Letby raising the alarm to alert doctors to incidents on the unit, or being the swiftest respondent, was repeated throughout. Letby either responded rapidly or raised the alarm with regard to incidents associated with Children A, B, C, D, E, G, I, M and O, while an email from Dr Ravi Jayaram indicates that she also raised the alarm in the case of Child K (discussed in "The Curious Case of Child K"). Letby wasn't on duty for Child F and Child L, and the hospital didn't flag these cases as concerning at the time, while she was not found guilty on charges relating to Child H, Child J and Child Q. Letby's primary 'offence' was responding quickly and diligently to incidents on the unit. There is a clear pattern of this throughout the court case. Further instances of Letby raising alarms were reported by Glen Owen in the *Mail on Sunday* on 17 August 2025. It should also be mentioned that Child E was yet another infant who was allegedly harmed via air embolism, with Dr Dewi Evans citing unusual purple patches on the abdomen.

Central to the case of Child E was a substantial amount of bleeding, which Dr Evans described as "significant haemorrhaging from the upper gastrointestinal tract", alleging that it had been caused by a "relatively rigid" object. In initial reports, Dr Evans had been "at a loss" to explain this haemorrhaging, before deciding that a nasogastric tube could have been thrust into the infant's stomach. He then later changed this view, not for the first time, instead suggesting that "there were a number of bits of equipment on a neonatal unit that are relatively rigid". This theory only appeared for the first time in a report written by Dr Evans dated 4 September 2022, just one month before the court case began. It seems to me that this was another case completely founded in the hypothetical. It is also interesting to note that Child E was receiving insulin, but Letby was not alleged to have poisoned him as with his twin, Child F; instead, she supposedly introduced yet another method of inflicted harm.

Child E was born at 29 weeks weighing 1,327g, factors that placed him at high risk of collapse and premature death. He had reverse end diastolic flow between himself and the placenta, meaning his body received less blood and oxygen than usual.

During his short life, Child E was stooled only once, on his fourth day, a worrying sign that should have prompted investigation for bowel obstruction. He passed only meconium, also concerning for mid-gut obstruction, and also possible gastric haemorrhage. Later, 16ml of bilious aspirate was withdrawn from his feeding tube, indicating milk was not passing through the gut. He also had fresh blood in an aspirate and suffered bloody vomit; this bleeding was largely ignored as intermittent, yet during compression there was active bleeding from his nose and mouth. An X-ray was taken and sent to Alder Hey, but it is not known if this was read, or if Alder Hey surgeons were informed.

Child E's clotting times were prolonged, meaning that he could not clot the bleed within a normal timeframe. He was not given blood until over two hours after the initial bleed, despite the unit holding emergency blood. The infant was also suspected to have necrotising enterocolitis. After his death, a consultant judged him high-risk and certified the cause as NEC and prematurity; pathologists' reviews did not contradict this until the involvement of Dr Evans. Dr Stephen Brearey later told Nigel Wenham of Cheshire Police that Child E was "displaying typical signs of NEC" and "as an isolated case, he would not have been considered suspicious".

Speaking in court, Dr Christopher Wood, who had been on a training placement at the CoCH, commented that there were "potential complications" for the twins from birth, agreeing that a neonate losing a significant quantity of blood would render the child immediately vulnerable. And a nurse who was anonymised for the trial agreed that Child E had numerous risk factors, while the fact that the infant was a twin meant that the "high-risk baby" was intrinsically "vulnerable to health complications".

It is not contested that Child E had suffered a large amount of bleeding, with Dr David Harkness observing in court that he had "never seen it in a baby, to this extent". The blood had come up through the baby's nasogastric tube, and when questioned further on this, Dr Harkness indicated that "it was 12 to 14ml, which for a baby is a substantial amount" – 10-12% of total volume, although even this appears to be a significant underestimation – and that a note made at the time indicated a gastrointestinal bleed was likely to be correct. Dr Harkness further noted that such a bleed is potentially serious for any infant. When asked by barrister Ben Myers whether it was a "very serious situation indeed", Dr Harkness conceded that this was "potentially" true. There was also some discussion regarding whether a blood transfusion should have taken place, with Myers indicating that the failure to consider this was a "serious mistake". This view was echoed by the panel assembled by Dr Shoo Lee, who asserted that an "emergency blood transfusion should have been given much earlier".

Dr Evans responded negatively to suggestions from Ben Myers that he had been "looking for something that could…support an allegation of deliberate harm that [Evans] must have known was not realistic", and "actively trying to find things that would support this allegation even when there is no evidential basis". Responding to this, Professor Colin Morley told me that "there was no evidence for the assertions of Dr Evans, and plenty pointing to common natural illness. For some reason, Dr Evans seems to think typical clinical signs all mean deliberate harm."

At the very culmination of discourse on Child E, the court heard that the infant had been at risk from the previously referenced NEC, a condition that is known to cause gastrointestinal bleeding. NEC was entered as the cause of death on the death certificate of Child E. The court heard that NEC was suspected throughout the lifespan of Child E, as voiced by the on-call consultant, and that the infant was treated for the condition via antibiotics, IV fluids and caffeine. "At the time I felt [Child E] had NEC which had led to his collapse and deterioration, so I discussed that with the coroner and we agreed for that to be put as [Child E's] cause of death", the consultant who had observed Child E informed the court.

There are several papers which point to the relationship between NEC and gastrointestinal bleeding in neonates, including one study from 2014 which highlights the severe impact of NEC on gastrointestinal morbidity. Further research from 2018 noted that NEC is particularly difficult to diagnose clinically, with bleeding in different gastrointestinal segments being a common feature. During court proceedings, the jury were also shown a chart which displayed five apnoea and bradycardia events for the infant, which are considered signs of NEC. A 2012 study explored the relationship between apnoea, desaturation and bradycardia and the development of necrotising enterocolitis in preterm infants. The discoloured stomach also seen in Child E is another recognised symptom, specifically indicative of a perforated bowel, which is often found in infants suffering with NEC, and discolouration is a typical sign of gastric perforation and bleeding. While NEC is a possibility for Child E, Professor Colin Morley believes that there are more likely natural explanations, given the clinical picture of the infant.

Child E was one of several infants in the case that pathologist Dr Jane Hawdon believed could have been saved with better care. Speaking at the Thirlwall Inquiry, Dr Hawdon observed that "the gastric bleed [of Child E] was significant", and "was the likely cause of the collapse". Dr Hawdon concluded that "gastric bleeds are sadly not unheard of in vulnerable and poorly babies", and that "isolated gastric bleeds in stressed babies, unfortunately, are not uncommon". Sepsis is another relevant aspect of this diagnosis, as it is known that this life-threatening condition can increase the risk of gastrointestinal bleeding. These factors collectively could have played a major role in the "catastrophic" levels of bleeding, as described in court, that were observed in Child E.

During court proceedings, Professor Sally Kinsey did not rule out the possibility that Child E suffered a gastrointestinal haemorrhage. But Dr Sandie Bohin asserted that "the bleeding may have made [Child E] unstable, but I don't think that is what caused his death". Dr Evans was similarly sure that there wasn't an innocent explanation for the bleeding, and that it must have been caused by inflicted trauma. "Gastric bleeding is not uncommon in sick premature infants", Professor Colin Morley observed. "There is no reason whatsoever to draw an extremely unlikely conclusion of inflicted trauma."

It seems odd that Evans and Bohin were so certain, considering the clinical picture of the child, and also the documented prominence of such bleeding in neonates. As an example, one study conducted in Finland found that approximately 20% of neonates suffered with gastrointestinal bleeding. And recent research published in *Frontiers in Pediatrics* found that 25% of all neonates admitted to eight different neonatal units experienced an episode of bleeding during their hospitalisation, with nearly half of these being categorised as major or severe. It is therefore hard to understand why the bleeding in Child E was essentially presented as being unprecedented and inexplicable in court.

It is also known that sepsis is a major risk factor for gastrointestinal bleeding, particularly in critically ill and vulnerable patients. The gut barrier can become compromised in sepsis, allowing bacteria and endotoxins to enter the bloodstream, worsening inflammation and mucosal (referring to the inner lining of organs) injury. Sepsis has been linked with the perforation of the bowel in numerous studies, including one that examined neonates. This also applies to NEC – for example, in *Intestinal perforation in very preterm neonates: risk factors and outcomes*, *Intestinal perforation in very-low-birth-weight infants with necrotising enterocolitis*, and *Necrotising enterocolitis complicated with perforation in extremely low birth-weight premature infants*.

There is considerable evidence pointing to major problems with bleeding in Child E, such as 15ml of blood being recorded in aspirates an hour after 16ml of bile-stained aspirates had been recorded. Shortly afterwards, a further 14ml of bloody vomit was recorded. Neonatal nurse Sloane Spade informed me that this was a "classic sign of intestinal bleeding, and a strong indication of either NEC, or major bowel tearing or perforation. The vomiting of fresh blood indicates that there was likely some early intestinal or stomach tearing." "GI [gastrointestinal] bleeding" was noted as a Datix incident by Lucy Letby herself on 4 August 2015. Spade also cited CPAP as being a major risk factor for Child E, directing me to a study which cited the abdominal distension seen in Child E as being characteristic of neonatal gastric perforation, along with vomit "which may be bilious or bloody in nature", both of which were observed in Child E.

Finally, there is also strong evidence suggesting a bowel obstruction in Child E as the infant only stooled once during his life. This is another risk factor associated with gastric perforation, while bilious aspirates and vomiting also point to this ailment. In accordance with this, one study from 2013 which analysed 16 neonates who were treated for gastrointestinal perforation over a three-year period identified intestinal obstruction as the cause of perforation in six cases, with four of these involving gastric perforation. As mentioned earlier, Spade further cited a delay in blood transfusion as being critical, especially as Child E had lost almost a quarter of his blood volume. This would be of grave seriousness, considering that gastric perforation has a mortality rate of 75% in neonates. The neonatal expert panel who reviewed the case notes for Child E later stated that even this 25% figure "was likely an underestimate because more was likely lost in the intestines".

Overall, there is considerable evidence for catastrophic bleeding in this premature infant, caused by a constellation of vulnerabilities and natural occurring factors. In court, Dr Evans claimed that "Child E had massive haemorrhaging from his upper gastrointestinal system and that is not something that occurs as a result of some kind of natural phenomenon."

Evans' final assertion is almost certainly incorrect. "Dr Evans stated that there is no natural phenomenon that can cause this kind of bleeding in a neonate, but there are causes that match the clinical picture of Child E", Spade commented. "There are natural explanations more common for his clinical picture, and Child E had risk factors that matched those for these natural explanations." Professor Colin Morley agreed, saying "Gastric haemorrhaging can certainly occur from natural causes; it is impossible for Dr Evans to rule this out."

Dr Michael Hall, who was standing by to give evidence at the trial, told me it was "likely" that Child E died due to gastrointestinal bleeding, and stated that there was "no good evidence" that Letby somehow caused damage with an indeterminate tool.

Commenting on the sad death of Child E, CoCH nurse Belinda Williamson observed that "any child being cared for in an NNU is at risk of a collapse, as if they were well, they would not be on an NNU. I did not feel that Child E's collapse and death was an unexpected event as during my career I have seen infants who appear stable collapse and die very quickly." This rapid deterioration was noted in Child E, and can be considered consistent with the catastrophic bleeding that is all too evident from the clinical picture.

On 3 April 2025, the summary report compiled by the panel of international experts concluded that Child E died from a massive gastrointestinal haemorrhage, due to either intrauterine hypoxia causing stomach or intestinal ulceration, or a congenital vascular lesion. The panel found no evidence of air embolism, and asserted that a post-mortem should have been requested.

Another infant who was deemed to have been destabilised in a quite unique fashion was Child G. This was a particularly premature baby, born at 23 weeks and six days, weighing just 535g. Even today the infant would have, at best, a 50-50 chance of survival; at the time of birth the likelihood was that Child G would not survive, even with optimal treatment on a high-performing unit, let alone an under-performing one. Dr Rachel Chang, who was on placement at the CoCH, asserted that Child G was "inherently extremely vulnerable" and said in a witness statement to the Thirlwall Inquiry she was not surprised by the infant's deterioration. Neonatal nurse Caroline Bennion likewise stated that "an extreme preterm baby like Child G had the capacity to become unwell very quickly".

Aside from this innate vulnerability, Child G suffered a catalogue of serious ailments – decreased lung capacity and chronic lung disease, hyaline membrane disease, bilateral pulmonary interstitial emphysema (a serious lung condition), hypoglycaemia, gastro-oesophageal reflux (stomach acid into the oesophagus), thrombocytopenia (low platelet count) and blood gases indicating sepsis. Dr Shoo Lee described the infant as having "a lot of chronic problems". After transfer to Arrowe Park, Child G was treated for infection; the infant's watery green stool pointed to likely gastroenteritis – "virtually certain gastroenteritis", Professor Colin Morley clarified.

There were also documented medical errors: delayed intubation, prolonged application of the DOPE acronym (ventilation guidance), and an episode when the baby was left behind a screen without a monitor on and suffered a cardiorespiratory event. The prosecution later accused Letby of deliberately tampering with the monitor, an accusation that is evidentially unsupported. An anonymous nurse told the court on 14 December 2022 that Dr John Gibbs and Dr David Harkness apologised for leaving Child G behind the screen and failing to turn the monitor on after the procedure.

Two episodes of projectile vomiting were cited in court as critical, but they were only two of numerous such episodes; Dr Shoo Lee cited several after transfer, while nurse Caroline Oakley said she could not "recall myself or anyone else present at the handover having any specific concerns about Child G's projectile vomiting and frequent collapses". Lucy Letby was not present, or even on duty, for most of these collapses.

The main concern with Child G is that Dr Evans stated the infant was supposedly destabilised via the deliberate overfeeding of milk: "In this case, the baby was compromised by receiving a large volume of milk to the stomach." It would be difficult to find support for this assertion from any qualified medic, but it should be noted that an earlier report of Dr Evans, which he read out in court, conceded that administering excess milk, and for that matter air, can occur accidentally.

This theory is dependent on speculative estimates of how much milk remained in the infant's stomach and how much was vomited – quantities that could not be measured – and then draws conclusions about aspiration that contradict the attendant nurse's own account. The theory also treats any supposed overfeeding as intentional rather than a far more likely accidental mechanism and ignores the practical logistics involved. This theory was revised several times during the court proceedings; indeed, the defence suggested that Dr Evans altered his testimony in real-time after hearing trial evidence. The cross-examination of both Dr Evans and Dr Bohin on this infant was less than convincing, with Evans even backing away from his own estimate when challenged.

"It's ridiculous", Professor Carola Vinuesa told me. "The attempts of Dr Evans to estimate the amount of milk left after vomiting, as occurred in court, were non-scientific and non-rigorous. I think it was appalling." In relation to milk allegations, neonatal nurse Sloane Spade noted that Child G was receiving Gaviscon, which delayed gastric emptying. Because the stomachs of premature babies empty more slowly, and the additional medications could make it even slower, more milk could be found in the stomach between feeds.

Dr Roger Norwich, echoing the words of a neonatologist quoted by *Private Eye*, referred to the hypothesis as "complete bollocks". "It's an extraordinary assertion. If too much milk had got into the stomach, the baby would have thrown it up. And how could he know that milk had been forcibly injected. He even admitted that his nonsense hypothesis could have been accidental! It's pure speculation. Total rubbish. You won't find anyone that agrees with that."

Michele Worden asserted that the milk hypothesis was "ludicrous", once again citing the logistics involved, and the fact that "babies would just puke the milk out. The whole thing is ludicrous. It's beyond ludicrous." Another experienced nurse also agreed that "if you give a baby too much milk, they're going to puke it out. They're actually more prone to blubbing it out through their noses and mouths." Another neonatal nurse was doubtful that the mechanism described in court was even possible. "The milk relies on gravity, not a pump, or anything like that. So there has to be some resistance, or the bag would just empty. If they're gravity-fed, that should tell you immediately that it would be very difficult to force things down with a tube than it is already being fed with gravity. And we know that babies aren't frequently overfed with milk because there aren't any known cases!"

Yet another neonatal nurse was doubtful that it was possible to force milk into an infant in the manner described in court and was equally sceptical that, "The mechanism proposed makes no sense. It's weird that they haven't looked at the actual practicalities." And another medic told me that the projectile vomiting was symptomatic of "an obstruction to the drainage of the stomach, which cannot be caused by a relatively small amount of milk".

The witness statement of Dr Alison Ventress, another doctor who was on a placement at the CoCH, was also dismissive of the notion that projective vomiting was significant: "Babies vomit frequently for many reasons, and the description of vomit is extremely subjective. I don't give much attention to how big or projectile the vomit is reported for a single vomit." Even Dr Stephen Brearey submitted a comment to the Thirlwall Inquiry indicating that he "had never heard of air or milk being forced into a baby's stomach before and it didn't cross my mind that this might have caused Child G's collapse".

Nurse Ailsa Simpson who was working on the neonatal unit at the time suggested a more mundane explanation for sickness in Child G: "I noticed that on the drug prescription reviewed in court during the criminal process, Child G had been given an oral medication of sodium chloride [salt] with her feed. Therefore, this could have been one of the causes of Child G's projectile vomiting." This wasn't even mentioned in court.

As should be clear by now, throughout the period referenced during the trial there was an array of factors which contributed to medical problems, collapses and deaths. And this applies, yet again, to Child G who was suffering with observed and documented sepsis. Nurse Christopher Booth wrote in his statement to the Thirlwall Inquiry: "The consensus was that Child G's condition and instability was a possible symptom of sepsis. Babies do vomit and so Child G's projectile vomiting did not cause me significant concern at the time. It is not unusual to encounter sepsis in infants, and it can manifest itself in many ways such as vomiting, abdominal distention, apnoea, metabolic acidosis among many others…At the time of these collapses and tragic deaths of Child[ren] G, I, N, O and P, I had no specific concerns, or considered a causal link between them. I felt that each infant had specific issues, be it prematurity, infection/sepsis and each episode could be explained logically." Child G was indeed treated for sepsis at Arrowe Park Hospital.

When Dr Shoo Lee provided the findings of international neonatal experts in February 2025, the panel explained that the vomiting and apnoea were the beginning of symptoms arising from infection. It was noted that vomiting and large watery stools, both observed in Child G, are very common in enterovirus infection. This virus can cause serious illnesses in neonates including sepsis, septic shock, meningitis and, sometimes, myocarditis. The panel also cited a catalogue of problems and issues relating to the care of Child G. In his earliest notes on Child G, Dr Evans noted "signs of infection". When he spoke in court, he repeatedly ruled out infection as being significant in the case of Child G.

When I asked Professor Colin Morley if the milk overfeeding theory had any basis whatsoever, he responded: "No. Next question, please."

The third and final infant to be addressed in this chapter is Child O. In this case, Dr Evans had suggested that Letby had damaged the child's liver by using "severe force". The idea that Letby "decided to punch this baby really hard" was described by Dr Philip Hammond as "the most compelling" part of this section of the trial. It is certainly an extraordinary accusation, not least because, once again, no such allegation was ever made with regard to any other infant in the case. Additionally, Child O was the infant Dr Dewi Evans determined had been deliberately harmed "immediately". Numerous paediatricians, neonatologists and pathologists have disagreed with Dr Evans' deliberate harm theory so it is difficult to work out how he came to this conclusion so rapidly.

Before assessing the clinical picture in this case, the 40-minute delay in the arrival of a consultant revealed during the Thirlwall Inquiry is particularly pertinent. It is precisely this sort of lack of medical attention that has been highlighted and criticised in previous chapters. With vulnerable neonates, every minute that passes can be the difference between survival and death.

Long before the expert panel assembled by Dr Shoo Lee had convened, other neonatologists had offered alternative explanations for the issues observed with Child O. Dr Philip Hammond cited three pathologists who had informed him that a subcapsular haematoma could have happened naturally during the birth. This condition results in an accumulation of blood beneath vital organs such as the lungs or kidneys. Pathologist Dr Jo McPartland had cited a "ruptured subcapsular haematoma of the liver", asserting that "the subcapsular haematoma is likely to have occurred as a consequence of hypoxia after the baby's collapse and deterioration". The opinion of Dr Martyn Pitman was consistent with this, citing "elevated heart rate, concerns with breathing and developing acidosis, which collectively point to the haematoma bursting, known as hemoperitoneum".

It is very difficult to understand how this verdict has been overturned in favour of a case note review by Dr Evans, whose conclusion requires an accusation of Letby, unwitnessed, to have physically struck an infant. Additionally, Dr Evans originally cited a deterioration occurring when Letby was off duty, during the early hours of 23 June 2016, and then later oddly decided that this collapse was not suspicious.

The panel of international experts later cited "inflicted blood trauma to the abdomen" which had caused "a ruptured subcapsular haematoma of the liver". This diagnosis was nothing new – not only had the pathologist drawn this conclusion but several clinical experts who spoke with Dr Philip Hammond had made the same assertion, crucially before the panel had even convened. And another neonatal pathologist made a blind assessment of the case notes from the Letby case, informing the *Tortoise Podcast* that a subcapsular haematoma was likely to be involved.

In addition, a leading perinatal pathologist told the BBC that Child O had died due to natural causes, concluding that "the way that the pathology was presented is not convincing to me". The pathologist pointed to a deficit in oxygen that preceded birth and suggested that trauma from the insertion of an umbilical catheter was a likely explanation for the phenomena discussed in court.

Dr Marnerides had likened the trauma involved to a road-traffic incident when speaking in court and asserted that an impact injury must have been involved. Questioned on this, Marnerides conceded that he used the reports of Dr Evans to assist in his conclusions. Experts who did see the clinical notes, aside from Dr Evans, have all drawn different conclusions which have all very closely correlated with one another. A pathologist who spoke to the BBC commented that the assertions made by Marnerides were impossible, as "unless a witness saw non-accidental injury occur, then you simply can't say [this]. To say that it is beyond reasonable doubt, and that this was not something natural, that this is a non-accidental injury, to put it bluntly, it's naïve…I have seen this sort of injury, but the prosecution expert must never have seen it."

Liver damage in young infants is also an observed and documented phenomenon. For example, one study examined preterm infants with a gestational age of less than 28 weeks and found that liver rupture is a complication that can be present which very few patients have survived. Another paper involving a much less vulnerable patient than a premature infant examined how cardiopulmonary resuscitation led to laceration of her liver. A third study discussed a life-threatening situation, described by the paper as a "massive upper gastrointestinal bleeding" in what was a non-premature and healthy baby, and another found examples of unusual liver haemorrhages in newborns.

Remember that it is not contested Child O was suffering with a ruptured liver. A report published in the *Journal of Clinical Medicine* in 2022 discovered hundreds of cases of precisely this sort of liver problem, all in newborn babies and all occurring naturally. The study noted that "premature infants face multiple complications", and specifically referenced respiratory distress syndrome, sepsis, necrotising enterocolitis and hypoglycaemia as being significant. It went on to observe that "subcapsular haematoma…usually occurs in preterm neonates, and it may be associated with birth trauma, cardiopulmonary resuscitation, sepsis, coagulopathies, maternal diseases and placental conditions. The above mechanisms can cause a simple liver laceration, or even a subcapsular haematoma, that can lead to hemoperitoneum [bleeding between the abdominal organs and the inner lining of the abdominal wall]. In some cases, the [haematoma] ruptures, leading to lethal massive abdominal haemorrhage, with non-specific clinical signs, which can be attributed to other clinical conditions, such as sepsis or intraventricular haemorrhage." In any infant, hemoperitoneum requires rapid identification and treatment, as it is immediately life-threatening, leading to inadequate blood flow, reduced blood pumping from the heart, organ dysfunction and death. It appears that such topics were not even touched upon during court proceedings or the Thirlwall Inquiry.

In citing a subcapsular haematoma, the panel of international experts noted that haemoglobin levels in Child O had halved due to the liver rupture, indicating that the infant had lost half of his blood – "a very major event". The panel also explained the mechanism which led to the haematoma, why this was likely to have been caused by a birth injury and why it could not have been an impact injury. It was also observed that "slow deterioration is characteristic" of acute collapses resulting from liver ruptures which runs contrary to the evidence of Dr Evans in court that the collapses were sudden. Mistakes with ventilation and intubation were also noted. "One of the main reasons that they're failing to resuscitate babies is that they're not ventilating them correctly", Professor Colin Morley asserted. "It's astonishing that Dr Evans had said in court that 'resuscitation efforts made on the unit were excellent'. They weren't! There was a strange blind faith that if something went wrong it was never the fault of doctors."

On the subject of mistakes, the second important aspect of Child O involved clinical errors made at the CoCH during the treatment of the infant. Examination of the clinical notes by the expert panel revealed an over-pressurisation of the infant's lungs during resuscitation, as well as the errant insertion of a needle into the right lobe of the liver which was the source of the laceration and parenchymal haematoma.

Senior coroner's officer, Stephanie Davies, who provided a critical report for Cheshire Police prior to their investigation, informed me that "there was no mention of this procedure whatsoever" in the notes she reviewed. "Blood was drawn, which is an immediate red flag for a medical error. I'm concerned that this procedure was not reported to the coroner. And because the coroner didn't know, it wasn't highlighted to the pathologist either. If this procedure contributed to the death, it should have resulted in an immediate inquest hearing", Davies explained. This is critically important, because Davies highlighted in her report that there were missing "jigsaw pieces" and these seem to have prompted further investigation from Cheshire Police. But she never knew about the aspiration procedure, nor the drawing of blood. Davies believes that Lucy Letby's conviction is a miscarriage of justice, and has written to Cheshire's senior coroner to express this view. "There was no mention of any such procedure when I reviewed the case. The coroner and pathologist should have further investigated this; instead, they were denied this information. If they'd known this, it may well have prevented the whole investigation from taking place."

The needle procedure is evident in a document from the Thirlwall

Inquiry which describes blood being drawn by Dr Stephen Brearey. This has been cited by neonatologists Dr Svilena Dimitrova and Dr Neil Aiton and is also referenced in the final report of the expert panel. Even expert witness Dr Sandie Bohin had concerns about "iatrogenic trauma secondary to attempts at decompressing the abdomen with a cannula".

A Level 2 Root Cause Analysis Investigation Report relating to Child O from 23 June 2016 had already recognised significant failings on the unit. The document referenced what can reasonably be considered a catalogue of medical errors:

- Presence of slight bilious aspirates not investigated;
- Members of the paediatric medical team omitted to keep contemporaneous records or indeed in some instances, any form of documentation whatsoever;
- No documentation of the request for commencement of antibiotic therapy;
- Consultant assistance with intubation not documented;
- No use of vasopressors and no changes made to airway support settings;
- No change to ventilator settings despite further deterioration in clinical condition;
- Potential congenital conditions were overlooked;
- The registrar left the ward to attend to clinical commitments elsewhere in the unit, resulting in a delay in attendance at collapse;
- There was a delay in the arrival of the consultant on call at a time when there was a critically ill patient on the neonatal unit.

It was therefore concluded that significant suboptimal care was relevant to the outcome of the infant which specifically involved failures in care to recognise problems and a failure to act appropriately. Considering that Letby was cleared of harming other infants in the case due to suboptimal care, what on earth occurred with Child O? How was this baby ever part of the court case in the first place?

When Dr Philip Hammond reported in *Private Eye* that he had seen a joint case report on Child O by two experienced, practising Level 3 neonatologists, it came as no surprise that the report "gives a clear explanation as to how and why the baby died, and the missed opportunities there were to save the baby's life. Most pertinently, according to these experts, the death has absolutely nothing to do with Lucy Letby." Furthermore, critical information regarding the needle insertion, a precipitous fall in haemoglobin and a botched ventilation was never communicated to the coroner at the time of death, or even the pathologist who reviewed the case some months later, possibly because those working on the unit never recognised their own errors.

Ironically, even though the contemporaneous records were, by the admission of the hospital itself, extremely poor, the problem with the aspiration was documented at the time. In the opinion of Dr Hammond, the reports prepared by the practicing neonatologists dismissing the conclusions of the court were of particularly high quality: "It is obvious how much time, effort and detailed analysis went into it." Can the same be said about the clinical evidence which appeared in court for Child O? Even the coroner, Nicholas Rheinberg, told the Thirlwall Inquiry that the results for Child O documented at the time "all seemed to be explicable". In my opinion, drawing on the opinion of others cited here, it is highly likely that no pathologist would conceivably have even considered an air embolism for this case, let alone claimed that Child O had been critically impacted by the deliberate injection of air.

The conclusion of the panel was that Child O had died from subcapsular liver haematoma caused by traumatic delivery, resulting in haemorrhage into the peritoneal cavity and profound shock. Additionally, several neonatologists and a pathologist have concluded that the demise of Child O was due to a subcapsular haematoma. The condition was also specifically cited by Dr Jane Hawdon in her post-mortem review report. Since that report, the cause of death has somehow transformed into Letby physically striking an infant which would most probably cause obvious abdominal bruising that was never observed, before causing deliberate harm with an indeterminate object with absolutely no supporting evidence for this whatsoever, and finally injecting air into the baby. Meanwhile, Dr Marnerides has made a definitive statement regarding injury resembling that caused in a road-traffic accident which has been opposed by other pathologists, and which no neonatal expert who has seen the notes agrees with.

Dr Evans claims to have taken both the conduct and conditions of the hospital and the clinical picture of the infants into consideration, but there is no evidence of this in court. In the case of Child O, given what is undeniable about the substandard care afforded to this poor infant who was suffering with life-threatening conditions, it is puzzling that Dr Evans did not appear to think they might have played a part in the child's death.

* * * *

This chapter concludes the section reviewing the medical and scientific information from the Lucy Letby case. Science will naturally seep into the remainder of the book as well, but the following chapters are focused on the circumstantial and anecdotal evidence that was used in court.

It is impossible for this account to be an exhaustive record of the Letby case and an enormous amount of evidence has been omitted out of sheer necessity. Nonetheless, in Chapters 4 to 6, the problems with the CoCH and its neonatal unit were firmly established. Having seen the court transcripts, such issues barely feature in the discussion of these infants. And the third chapter demonstrates that the public narrative which has since been communicated during the Thirlwall Inquiry regarding events behind the scenes at the hospital can be neatly flipped on its head. The idea that the consultants were bullied does not seem to reflect the actual situation on the unit; we need only examine documents from the Thirlwall Inquiry itself to understand this.

In Chapters 8 to 12 we have seen that the clinical picture of these infants was vastly different from how it was presented in court and the medical explanations provided by the prosecution were deeply flawed. Writing in *The Guardian*, Professor Neena Modi asserted that "the significance of crucial information from the medical records and post-mortem examinations was not recognised" in court. It is these two points which have resulted in so many healthcare professionals voicing their public concerns about the safety of Letby's conviction, and to the unprecedented formation of a panel of immense neonatal and paediatric expertise.

When interviewed by Sarah Knapton of *The Daily Telegraph*, Professor Geoff Chase, one of the world's foremost experts on the effects of insulin on preterm babies, criticised "the lack of consideration of well-known alternatives…the full story of this data for the insulin case and all its possibilities was not explored, and thus not presented to the jury." Professor Joanne Langley, head of the division of paediatric infectious diseases at Dalhousie University, "could not find evidence…to support the conclusions made by the trial experts". Dr Helmut Hummler, senior medical director at the European Foundation for Care of Newborn Infants, was "concerned that the available evidence based on the medical records was not adequately considered". Professor Mikael Norman, founder of the International Society of Evidence-Based Neonatology, was critical of two further cases. Professor Erik Skarsgard, of the University of British Columbia and director of the Canadian Paediatric Surgery Network, asserted that he "did not think the explanations suggested by the experts at trial were plausible". And Dr Tetsuya Isayama, head of division of neonatology, at Toyko's National Center for Child Health and Development, "did not find evidence for the conclusions of the trial experts that the cause of death was air injection".

It is important to reflect once more that, in addition to this exonerating medical evidence, no one has ever witnessed Lucy Letby doing anything harmful to an infant. The conviction of Letby is entirely reliant on hypotheses.

When Karen Rees was interviewed by the *Sunday Times* in February 2025, she, quite rightly, observed that "the one person that knows her nursing team is the manager or the unit manager – not a consultant that visits a couple of times a week. They know the strengths and weaknesses. I trusted Lucy's ward manager when she looked me in the eye and said 'she's [Letby] fantastic and she's right by the book, she does everything right.'" In the very same month, the Thirlwall Inquiry finally provided the public with the opportunity to view how Letby's nursing colleagues viewed her. Dozens of nurses had submitted statements to the inquiry, the publication of which was oddly delayed. None of them had suspected anything untoward. None of them had witnessed anything concerning. Several of them made explicit statements indicating that they believed Letby to be innocent.

We are told that the neonatal unit was on high alert because of the conduct of Lucy Letby. We are told that there were numerous red flags regarding Lucy Letby. We are told that nursing colleagues were suspicious of Lucy Letby. We are told that other nurses couldn't wait to remove Lucy Letby from the unit. However, the words of those who worked with her closely, and were most familiar with her practice, do not bear this out.

CHAPTER 13: SWIPE-CARD DATA FALLS APART

There are several curious aspects to the retrial associated with Child K and these will be fully assessed in the following chapter. But one of the most notable was surely the revelation that Cheshire Police used swipe-card data back-to-front in the original trial, logging entries as exits and exits as entries, while also using this data to place Lucy Letby in certain places at certain times.

As a consequence of this monumental blunder by Cheshire Police, the timeline was altered in the retrial for the attempted murder of Child K. As an example, in the first trial Nurse Joanne Williams was said to have left the ward at 3:47am, and Letby supposedly attacked the baby between this time and 3:50am. In the retrial, this was revised to Nurse Williams leaving the ward sometime around 3:30am, two other nurses (including Nurse Oakley, whose baby was also in Nursery 1) returning at 3:40am, and Dr Jayaram supposedly catching Letby "virtually red-handed" at some point between the conclusion of his phone call at 3:41am and the return of Nurse Williams at 3:47am.

It's not even been firmly established that Letby was ever alone in Nursery 1 during that period, and the account of Dr Ravi Jayaram, who was cross-examined during the retrial, shifted over time. At first, Jayaram couldn't recall if an alarm was sounding; later he was sure it was not. Joanne Williams, by contrast, was consistent throughout her interviews that the alarm was sounding when she returned.

The CPS was later forced to concede the swipe-card data error but, at the time of writing, has not been particularly forthcoming with further information when questioned. *The Daily Telegraph* also reported that the CPS had refused to confirm whether the data submitted from other doors in the unit was correct.

"We are confident the initial mislabelling of door swipe data had no meaningful impact on the prosecution", the CPS, unconvincingly, responded. "The defence did not deem the issue significant enough to include it in Letby's unsuccessful [request for leave to] appeal, and when the initial error was highlighted at Letby's retrial, it did not prevent a second jury finding her guilty." It's interesting that they are so apparently "confident" about this, because the CPS Code for Crown Prosecutors states in paragraph 4.8 that "prosecutors should consider whether there are any reasons to question the reliability of the evidence, including its accuracy or integrity". One might imagine that getting something completely the wrong way round would impact on its accuracy or integrity.

Slightly inconvenient for the CPS on this matter was the later revelation that bungled swipe-card data also affected eight other babies in the trial. This was discussed in *The Guardian* on 10 October 2024 with David Conn and Felicity Lawrence revealing that Cheshire Police had only realised their error in February of that year. Sadly, Cheshire Police couldn't comment on this due to their 'ongoing investigation'.

Aside from the errors in the swipe-card data, it's also important to consider the essential worthlessness of this as information. Swipe-cards are only as good as the data they generate. And the data they generate is woefully unreliable. I'm sure many people reading this account have been employed in workplaces with swipe-card systems. Did everyone always swipe their card in every single situation? No, of course not! So naturally, when I asked numerous nurses about this, they all immediately concluded that nurses would follow each other into rooms without swiping their cards with considerable regularity.

"When I'm busy, I've lost count of how many times I've left my security card in the locker room and borrowed someone else's card to access the room", one nurse told me. "I've also loaned my security card to others who have done the same." Radiographer Ashleigh Tavoulari also agreed that "card exchange is common", due to swipe-cards having been misplaced or even lost. Dr Margaret Ferguson informed me that "two or three nurses" will frequently "pile through" a door having only swiped one card, and Michele Worden confirmed that it's common to "hold the door open" in order for several nurses to walk through.

Immediately, this invalidates the dataset. And no one would understand this better than the prosecution in the Letby case, because on 18 May 2023, Nick Johnson KC had an exchange with Letby, during which the defendant was asked:

JOHNSON: So there are times when you've been on the neonatal unit when there is no trace of you having been there?
LETBY: There would be a trace because I would have had to swipe.

What was Johnson's response to this? That doesn't prove anything because colleagues could have held doors open for her. So when the swipe-card data places Letby in a certain place that is convenient for the prosecution, it is to be accepted without question. But when it places Letby in a position that exonerates her from wrongdoing, this cannot be trusted, precisely for the reason that many healthcare professionals have told me, namely that the dataset has no value in the first place because staff do not necessarily swipe all the time. One medic simply described the smart card data from the trial as "redundant and worthless".

But there's much more to come. Michele Worden informed me that swipe-cards were not brought into the CoCH to monitor the movement of staff. "In the early 1990s, a baby was kidnapped at Glan Clwyd Hospital. It was missing for several days. After that, it was decided that all units with babies must have swipe data. The swipe data is to stop Joe Public walking in; it was never, ever installed to say where a member of staff was. It's not even suitable for that purpose."

Former CoCH anaesthetist, Dr Fiona MacRae, explained to me that an expensive staff-monitoring scheme had been scrapped during her time of working at the hospital. "It was purported to have cost £12 million, and it was supposed to track staff at all times. The only problem was that it went to the BMA, and no one had even asked the staff for their consent, so it fell apart because the hospital didn't have the authority to track anyone."

Furthermore, there was an unmonitored route into the unit via a back staircase which makes it impossible for the prosecution, or anyone else, to know who was present at any given time, even if everyone had always prioritised utilising their swipe-cards in the middle of a medical emergency. Michele Worden confirmed that a keypad system was in operation which meant no data could be recorded. This was still in operation at the time of Letby's alleged crimes, which, as we know, nobody ever witnessed on an extremely busy neonatal unit.

Michele told me more about the back staircase. "It was used all the time by the nurses and the doctors. It ran up and down to the postnatal/transitional care wards, which came under the jurisdiction of the special care baby unit. You could have a nurse swipe into the neonatal unit, do some work in there, go up the back stairs to the postnatal ward, walk out of the postnatal ward, because there's no data out only data in, and be sat across the road in the pub when the data tells you that she's still in the neonatal unit."

Dr Murthy Saladi further confirmed the existence of this entrance during questioning at Thirlwall on Thursday 3 October 2024, while Dr Philip Hammond noted that "a clever murderer could use the backstairs all the time, do all their murders off duty and evade the spreadsheet and swipe-card data entirely. This makes the swipe-card data and the 'on-duty killer spreadsheet' even more worthless." One wonders if Cheshire Police were aware of this, although even if the back entrance did have a swipe-card portal this wouldn't have prevented the constabulary from accidentally reversing the data.

Then another swipe-card error emerged. TriedByStats produced a thorough analysis of Child N, based on court transcripts, which demonstrates that the prosecution case collapses under further scrutiny. Swipe-card data contradicts the information presented in court to such an extent that it "fundamentally breaks the prosecution timeline". This alters a key event in the case of the prosecution, meaning claims made that an infant cried for 30 minutes are defunct. There is then further evidence which indicates that Letby was not cot-side when the key events regarding Child B occurred, which further undermines that conviction and the quality of data provided in court.

Additionally, several months of swipe-card data were missing from the trial because the hospital didn't preserve it. This was confirmed by more than one source and also reported in *The Independent*. It is quite incredible that the prosecution relied on this spurious and incorrectly recorded data as a central pillar in its case.

On top of that, there are problems with telephone log times submitted in court. This has been discovered and flagged up by investigators working diligently on the case since the verdict. When the events surrounding Child E are examined in detail, the only rational conclusion is that calls made to Child E's father were an hour later than stated by Cheshire Police and the prosecution in court. This was critical because the mother of Child E stated that she witnessed blood around the face of the infant at approximately 9:00pm and according to the mother's phone records, she called her husband at 9:11pm. Notes made by Letby recorded this event as occurring at approximately 10:00pm, and the notes of Dr Harkness were recorded at 10:10pm, shortly after the doctor arrived.

The implication of this is that Letby had delayed calling the doctor for an hour, therefore allowing the child to suffer unnecessarily. Child E deteriorated again and the midwife was called at 11.30pm to bring the mother to the neonatal unit. The father was then also called, but there are conflicting accounts of the time at which this occurred.

According to the mother's call log, the midwife contacted the father at 10:52pm, requesting for his presence at the hospital. But clinical notes indicate that Child E didn't deteriorate until after 11:00pm and it was at 11:30pm that the midwife received a call from the neonatal unit indicating that they were preparing to intubate. Thus, the mother's recorded time of 10:52pm doesn't make sense, which is critical because statements to this effect were read out in court.

This discrepancy was pointed out by John Sweeney in his excellent podcast series with Edward Abel Smith on the Letby case and it was suggested that the only way to explain what may have happened is to compare Greenwich Mean Time (GMT) with British Summer Time (BST). Timings on the mother's phone were held in GMT but Child E's deterioration happened in August which was during BST. At this time of year, GMT is one hour behind BST so it's entirely possible that a phone call at 10:52pm GMT actually took place at 11:52pm BST, meaning that Letby's note at about 10pm is accurate.

This explanation would also make sense of the time when the midwife called the father – if the child hadn't collapsed until 11:30pm, it would have been impossible to call the father at 10:52pm, requesting him to attend the hospital. It is also important to note that the information on timings was not obtained by Cheshire Police, but by the mother of Child E and Child F via the perusal of mobile phone records. Another problem with the prosecution timings is that they require Letby to stand around doing nothing for over an hour while a child suffers a fatal gastrointestinal bleed and no one notices, which hardly seems plausible.

It should be remembered that this entire tapestry of Letby being in certain rooms at particular times was a key pillar of the entire prosecution case, consuming literally weeks of the trial. And yet so much of it is demonstrably incorrect. Furthermore, it doesn't really have any merit as evidence anyway. Swipe-card data is far too unreliable for numerous reasons discussed in this chapter. Information that is used to incriminate someone should never be included in a criminal trial, unless it is cast-iron. This is why DNA evidence is regarded so highly, precisely because of its reliability. The entire narrative that is based around swipe-card data and other specious information would have little foundation, even if Cheshire Police had managed to submit it correctly.

At this point, the Datix information used in the trial must also be discussed. Datix is an online system used by hospitals to report risks and incidents. Email correspondence dated 9 February 2016 from the CoCH outlines the importance of this system, stating that: "We must ensure a Datix is completed for all neonatal deaths or stillbirths", explaining that "It is better to have multiple Datix reports about the same event than to miss reporting an important incident."

When I spoke with healthcare professionals on the subject of Datix submissions, the common view was that doctors and consultants are often fairly resistant to this system. The implication is that it can effectively show them up. "Lucy was keen on filling in Datix", Dr Roger Norwich opined. "Karen Rees has said that Lucy did everything by the book – the Datix is another indication of that. It should have been seen favourably in court, not used against her, and this makes me suspicious that it was irking the consultants." Michele Worden corroborated this impression, stating that it was normal in hospitals for snide remarks to be made, but that "Lucy was very good at filling in Datix reports. And I think she was very good at reporting herself as well."

Another healthcare professional told me that the pattern of Datix submission indicated that Letby was "more honest than others. She was doing more Datix, she was calling for help, she had raised issues at the hospital. There are definitely incidents that formed part of this court case where she used her initiative to save babies. Why would you do that if your aim is to kill as many babies as possible? This whole part of the trial fits much more with someone who's very keen to improve the standard of service."

The logistics of filling in Datix reports could also be overlooked by anyone unfamiliar with a neonatal unit. Speaking about Datix submissions, one neonatal nurse told me that "by the time that I've done everything else, gone back in the office, and written it up on the computer, I can't remember what time I wrote on the card, so the times will probably not match up, more often than not. All these everyday things in the trial were painted as sort of some sinister plot. But it was really just run-of-the-mill stuff." Another neonatal nurse emphasised that "there often isn't time to fill in the Datix system. Nurses work beyond their shifts anyway. You're constantly fire-fighting. But doctors do not typically like Datix at all, particularly if it reflects poorly on them. Lucy's attitude towards Datix indicates both concern and care for her patients."

Everything we know about both the Datix system at the CoCH and the conduct of Letby indicates that she was particularly diligent when it came to Datix submission. Furthermore, Letby specifically did something that could be considered unfavourable by consultants at the hospital – she questioned them. This was explicitly mentioned by Eirian Powell during an interview with Dr Chris Green on 28 October 2016 which formed part of Letby's grievance procedure. "LL will question registrars or consultants and will call and say if she wants them to look at the baby now if she has any concerns. LL will Datix herself and even close colleagues", Powell explained. Another nurse made similar observations when speaking with former government minister Nadine Dorries: "[Lucy] even reported herself when she got something wrong, and I've never seen that before. No one could stop her filling in a complaint form; you wouldn't even try."

It's also important to note that the implication being made here, that consultants might not favour being essentially criticised by Datix entries, is not without foundation. An email exchange between Dr Stephen Brearey and Ian Harvey on 15 July 2016 sees Brearey state that he had "heard criticism of the risk and Datix reporting culture on the neonatal unit which I can only take as surrogate criticism from your department which is, at best, ill informed". But midwife Annemarie Lawrence cited a "difficult relationship" with Dr Brearey, and informed the Thirlwall Inquiry on 22 October 2024 that the consultant team "considered incident reporting to be punitive", rather than a healthy part of "lessons learned" to improve clinical practice.

The friction in the hierarchical structure of nurses and consultants is supported by Band 6 nurse Belinda Williamson who recalled that the unit manager, Eirian Powell, encouraged nurses to record problems "in writing if she felt it was necessary to have a record of the issue", while she also "encouraged the team to actively fill out Datix".

There is more support for the existence of cultural problems surrounding the reporting of issues at the CoCH. Annemarie Lawrence, the clinical governance lead at the hospital in 2016, told the Thirlwall Inquiry that consultants were not "open and transparent" about clinical problems in neonatology, asserting that the "consultant body" as a whole "stuck together" and conferred before reporting problems. "They wouldn't go against one another. So even if they thought somebody had made a clinical omission, rather than report it, they could have a conversation first, consultant to consultant." This was confirmed by the RCPCH report into the hospital, which noted that "there were several reports that the doctors will wait too long before escalating concerns about an infant". This suggests that there could have been issues for nurses on the unit who called the consultants into question, and Letby was one of the foremost candidates for this.

An NHS professional with decades of experience divulged that Datix "theoretically provides feedback and a learning opportunity. If staff are seemingly selective about what does and doesn't get reported, mistakes and bad practice are more likely to continue." But Dr Fiona MacRae told me that while Datix on the neonatal unit was intended to make a contribution towards "an open and transparent learning culture", in reality "it didn't do this at all. It was always a blame culture. Always."

While researching this book, I was fortunate to recruit the services of a neonatal nurse who examined every Datix submission from the CoCH that was publicly available. She told me: "There is a clear pattern of babies being left without antibiotics, fluids, surfactants to help their lungs not being given in time, long lines not being inserted correctly, plus countless issues with cannulation and ventilation. When you then add staff shortages and inexperience into the mix, you have a toxic recipe for disaster. It is clear to me as well that junior clinicians were reluctant to bleep or call consultants; there was an overwhelming culture of fear.

"The mothers' pre-existing medical conditions, labour delays, infections, multiple births and the complications that come with this are all swept under the carpet as well. All of these have influenced the conditions of infants at birth, not to mention their potential outcomes, but yet they are rarely mentioned.

"Reading through the documents was illuminating. There is no way that Lucy Letby should have been charged with any crime. She was a dedicated nurse, working multiple shifts and long hours. I believe that she cared very deeply for this unit, the babies and the families, which makes what has occurred even more tragic."

In fact, it was often Letby who noticed and noted signs of mottling and discolouration in the indictment infants, symptoms of circulatory issues that would later be incorrectly used against her in court. Letby made notes that explicitly referenced discolouration and/or mottling for

Children A, B, E, G, I, N, P and Q; over two thirds of the infants for which discolouration or mottling was deemed diagnostic in court.

Before making such extraordinary accusations as a hitherto dedicated nurse weaving an intricate web of falsified Datix entries, one would assume that the prosecution actually had some evidence. However, all of these allegations are based on, to give the most generous interpretation possible, pure supposition. There isn't an ounce of solid evidence backing up any one of them. These assertions fly in the face of all reason, considering that all actual available evidence points to Letby being the most diligent note-taker on the unit, while Judge James Goss noted in his summing up that "other nurses fail[ed] to complete some entries on charts". That is not intended to be a criticism of them; this is simply a highly pressurised, and often hectic, working environment. Also, in common with swipe-card data, the prosecution cited the Datix record evidentially when it supported their case, asserting it to be reliable, and then claimed, with no supporting evidence whatsoever, that Letby had created false entries when Datix contradicted their case.

It is also completely unreasonable to expect someone to remember what are often innocuous or obscure events from one of many working days that are quite similar, sometimes seven years after they occurred, and never make any mistakes or forget anything. That would be true in any circumstances but Letby had patently been through a highly traumatic experience, and had essentially suffered a breakdown quite recently. It wouldn't be particularly surprising if she wasn't firing on all cylinders. Incidentally, just to demonstrate how easy it is to make mistakes, remember that the police completely reversed swipe-card data in the original trial. Does this mean that this unseemly gaffe was held against Cheshire Police in perpetuity? Was any information gathered by Cheshire Police excluded from the court case? No, of course not. It was only Lucy Letby who was expected to be infallible.

There are two reasons I think the prosecution devoted so much time to this hotchpotch of nonsense. The first is that they didn't have any concrete evidence, and, in fact, had very little evidence of any value whatsoever. The prosecution was almost entirely based on the submissions of Dr Dewi Evans. The prosecution had very little of any solidity and therefore was obliged to construct something out of Evans' submissions. It is possible that the prosecution were quite happy that the trial lasted so long as it gave the impression there was lots of evidence against Letby; a 'no smoke without fire' strategy.

The second reason for devoting so much time to this was simply to create a narrative around the case. It is known that narratives tend to convince people more than facts. For example, a study published in the *Personality and Social Psychology Bulletin* noted that "stories are known to be powerful persuasive devices. Stories can capture attention, evoke emotion, and entrance listeners in a manner that reduces resistance to a message…stories persuade, at least in part, by disrupting the ability to evaluate facts, rather than just biasing a person to think positively."

As noted by the Royal Society, the United Kingdom's national academy of sciences, "the persuasive power of storytelling is well-recognised". This message was echoed by author Will Storr in an interview with the British Psychological Society, with Storr opining that "storytelling is your best weapon for convincing people…if you want to mislead people or sell them your one-eyed view of the world, then storytelling is the best way to do it". *Harvard Business Review* cited consultancy expert Nick Morgan, who commented that "facts and figures and all the rational things that we think are important…actually don't stick in our minds at all. Stories create 'sticky' memories by attaching emotions to things that happen."

This partly explains why one will still encounter people, particularly online, who remain steadfastly attached to the notion of Letby's guilt. They want to believe their opinion is predicated on 'facts and figures' because we all believe ourselves to be rational. But in reality, as Morgan has just outlined, their impression of the case is largely dictated by the attachment of emotions to events they've been told have occurred. And this is precisely the phenomenon that the prosecution was aiming for in court, hence why so much time was devoted to creating a narrative around the case and conveying emotional testimony to the jury.

One empirical study of the power of stories even concluded that judges and seasoned attorneys prefer story briefs rather than those built completely on logical arguments. These are considered persuasive to experienced lawyers and judges because they evoke emotional responses that make associated legal claims appear more credible. They are not alone in this – an academic study published in *Frontiers in Communication* noted that "narratives are persuasive because they are easier to understand". The study concludes that people are simply more readily "persuaded by information presented within a narrative".

Psychologist Dr Thea Gumbert offers a unique perspective on this topic, having written a PhD thesis on the behaviour of juries. Dr Gumbert also has extensive experience of working with clients in the criminal justice system, and has conducted over 1,200 psychological assessment reports for diagnostic and medico-legal purposes. Dr Gumbert explained to me that there is strong support for juries favouring the 'story model' of decision-making when forming an impression of court cases. She pointed to research published in the *Journal of Criminal Justice*, which notes that the story model is "widely regarded as the dominant explanation of juror-level decision making". The model focuses on the way that jurors construct trial evidence into a narrative that then informs their decisions, reconciling the different accounts by constructing an explanation in the form of a story, which is influenced not only by the evidence presented in the trial, but also by their general knowledge and life experiences.

"Jurors may initially construct and consider multiple stories, but one will usually emerge as the favoured narrative", Dr Gumbert informed me. "Studies have found that juries will organise evidence into narratives that rely on inferences which were not actually presented in the trial evidence. They use their pre-existing beliefs to construct these stories. It's been shown that if one side in a court case tells a story, and the other does not, there is a strong tendency to favour the storytelling side, regardless of the evidence presented.

"A lot of work has been done by two researchers called Pennington and Hastie, and they have found consistently that evidence is considered more persuasive by jurors when presented in a narrative format." The

Royal Society notes that "communicators wishing to inform and not persuade must always be very careful". The problem here is that the situation in court was the exact inverse of this; the prosecution wants to *persuade*, rather than *inform*.

By any reasonable assessment, the swipe-card data and Datix reporting included in the trial of Lucy Letby barely qualifies as submissible evidence, even if it was actually correct. It doesn't tell the court anything of significance, nor is it reliable. But it's not, in fact, supposed to do this; the jury was not intended to derive important facts or evidence from it. This part of the trial was a component of a broader narrative that the prosecution weaved around the case, hoping firstly to disguise the fact that they had little of any solidity, and secondly to emotionally convince the jury to buy into their story.

Once emotions have died down and it's possible to assess this dispassionately, it's clear that the enormous portion of the trial that was dedicated to 'who was in what room at what time' has no evidential value.

CHAPTER 14: THE CURIOUS CASE OF CHILD K

The original trial of Lucy Letby was troubling enough, but the subsequent retrial of Child K, in June and July 2024, careered far beyond being deeply unsatisfactory into the realm of the surreal. Initially, the jury had delivered no verdict on the attempted murder of Child K where Letby was alleged to have deliberately removed her breathing tube. Veteran journalist Peter Hitchens was one of many who questioned the legitimacy of this retrial. He noted in its aftermath that it was bordering on impossible for Letby to receive anything approaching a fair trial, considering the overwhelmingly negative media coverage that had already been directed at her, coupled with her 14 previous convictions.

When the retrial began, Judge James Goss informed the jury that they shouldn't make assumptions based on Letby's previous convictions, and that they were to assess this case purely based on the evidence presented in court. But the prosecution was then allowed to reference the convictions throughout the court case, without objection. It is hard to believe this didn't prejudice the jury who would have absorbed months of press coverage. And this press coverage, at the time, was almost universally scathing of Letby.

The jury for the retrial was expected to forget this while also being repeatedly reminded of it, but were denied the right to read the *New Yorker* article by Rachel Aviv which is frequently referenced in this book. Apparently, Aviv's work could have unfairly influenced the court proceedings. *The Guardian* described this invidious situation as "the elephant in the room".

The unequal attitude towards contempt of court was exemplified in October 2023 when the *British Medical Journal*, the UK's leading medical publication, published a comment from a retired British doctor cautioning against a "fixed view of certainty that justice has been done". In light of the new reporting restrictions, the journal removed the comment from its website "for legal reasons". At least six further editorials and comment articles, none of which challenged Letby's guilt, remained available on the website. The reporting restrictions that were instigated due to the retrial of Child K effectively gagged the press, delaying influential articles questioning the safety of Letby's conviction from Felicity Lawrence and David Conn in *The Guardian* and Sarah Knapton in *The Daily Telegraph*.

It's difficult to imagine how the jury could have forgotten about Letby's previous convictions while they were acting as jurors in a trial involving Lucy Letby. However, the Court of Appeal deduced that the jury was able to reach an entirely unprejudiced conclusion due to the "fade factor" which apparently meant that the jury would somehow forget about previous press coverage of the Lucy Letby case. "The Court of Appeal defends their procedure", Dr Thea Gumbert informed me. "That's what they do. That's the entire point of the law. There is no recourse to appeal under the law, just because of a small inconvenience like the jury being factually incorrect!"

The next chapter of this book will assess some of the eyewitness testimony that appeared in court. But the eyewitness account of Dr Ravi Jayaram was central to the retrial related to Child K and the ultimate conviction of Letby. There had originally been no verdict on this case, quite possibly because the evidence related to it was so spectacularly flimsy. It should be noted that babies at the CoCH received poor care generally, and that this had seemingly influenced the jury on some counts involved in the original case. Furthermore, Child K was the second most premature infant involved in the Letby case, born at 25 weeks gestation and whose life hung from a thread from the very moment of birth, being immediately resuscitated. At the time these events occurred, the chance of survival for Child K was doubtful.

Central to the case of Child K was the testimony and eyewitness account of consultant Dr Ravi Jayaram. The prosecution asserted that Dr Jayaram had caught Letby "virtually red-handed" in the process of harming Child K, although Jayaram never used this specific phrase himself.

Before we examine this in depth, it is worth pointing out the obvious – the phrase "virtually red-handed" is meaningless. Either someone is caught red-handed, or they haven't been caught at all. Nonetheless, as Letby was handed a life sentence almost entirely based on the words of Dr Jayaram, it is important for this case to be analysed.

The term 'standing over' was used to describe Letby's actions and demeanour on several occasions during the court case. This choice of phrasing implies something sinister, whereas Letby was actually observing infants in their incubators as a neonatal nurse should. In fact the word 'observing' would be more accurate because, as Letby explained during the trial, by standing over "doing nothing", she was simply following standard practice at the CoCH. In court it was noted that Dr Jayaram "could see Letby standing over Child K's incubator". This was unfairly presented as inappropriate behaviour in those circumstances.

One might recall that Karen Rees, the head of nursing for urgent care at the CoCH, commented that "Lucy Letby does everything by the book. She follows policy and procedure to the letter." This is what she was doing when observed by Jayaram. The court then witnessed the spectacle of the prosecution attempting to argue with Letby, before making the following assertion: "We say that in those circumstances the only reasonable thing for a nurse to do would be to call for help or use [equipment] to breathe for the child. The reason she was desaturating was because the breathing tube had become displaced and we suggest that the fact Lucy Letby was doing nothing and the alarms weren't sounding was because it was Lucy Letby, the convicted murderer, who had displaced the tube."

There are several problems with this:

1) The validity, or lack thereof, of catching someone 'virtually red-handed' as already explained.

2) Prosecutor Nick Johnson commented: "We say that…the only reasonable thing…to do…" Well, Letby was following standard procedure for the neonatal unit, which had been disseminated to her during her training. What else could she reasonably be expected to do?

During the court testimony of Mary Griffiths, the nurse stated that desaturations are not uncommon and can occur within seconds. As an example of this, a study of patient monitoring alarms on a neonatal intensive care unit found that there was a critical alarm every 3½ hours on average, and that over 60% of alarms related to oxygenation monitoring. Griffiths described the observation that Letby was engaged in as a "hands-off technique" for neonates, citing the fact that handling them could cause stress, hence why they are monitored electronically at all times.

3) It hasn't been satisfactorily established that the breathing tube was dislodged at the time, nor that it was dislodged deliberately, and certainly not the identity of the alleged person who had supposedly dislodged it. "It has never been shown where the endotracheal tube was", Professor Colin Morley told me. "This was a very small baby, and so the tip of the tube could have been at the larynx, or only just below it. There are no X-rays to show where it was when the baby was being ventilated. It can be difficult to secure an endotracheal tube, and they can easily be dislodged just by simply handling the baby or the baby moving. When Jayaram attended, the first thing he did was remove the tube. He should have looked to see where it was, or measured the expired carbon dioxide, and just pushed it in slightly. His management of the case was suboptimal, let alone is there any evidence to blame Lucy Letby."

4) Johnson went on to say: "We suggest…" Naturally, the prosecution must 'suggest'. Johnson can't say "we know", or even "we have evidence for this" because there isn't any evidence and no one saw anything.

5) Johnson manages to drop into his 'account' of what had allegedly occurred that Letby is a "convicted murderer".

The journalist Cleuci de Oliveira attended court for every day of the retrial and confirmed to me that the prosecution was quite relentless in this regard: "They repeated the previous convictions over and over and over. Every time something was going slightly awry for the prosecution, Nick Johnson would start saying: 'Lucy Letby, you were convicted previously, you murdered Child A (except that he was saying their real names), you tried to murder Child B, you murdered Child C', and kept going. He would go through the list, talking about the methods of murder, over and over and over." As an example, Johnson concluded his cross-examination of Letby on 9 June 2024 with the subtle closing gambit: "You are a murderer."

6) Endotracheal tubes can become detached accidentally. There are, in fact, endless resources online regarding what to do in such an instance. The only reason that Letby was even facing this allegation was that Dr Evans had deduced that the tube could have become detached accidentally, but that this was "probably" not the case. There is also evidence of incompetence on the unit; one example is a baby who died in 2014 after doctors mistakenly put a breathing tube into his gullet, rather than his trachea. There was even testimony provided in the trial that doctors had made repeated errors with this and similar equipment, perhaps partly due to the lack of experienced medics on the unit.

Nurse Mary Griffiths also agreed that a nurse can wait to see if a baby self-corrects when desaturating, paying attention to the skin colour of the infant as an additional observation. If the situation did not resolve, intervention would then become necessary. It should be noted that Griffiths was senior to Letby on the unit and is currently the ward manager at the CoCH. Despite this, an agreed statement to the court was provided by an unconnected nursing consultant, Elizabeth Morgan, who was not cross-examined in court. This statement suggested that it would not be normal practice, for an infant of this gestational age, to wait and see if a baby corrects. "Elizabeth Morgan is a paediatric nurse who is the head nurse at Great Ormond Street Children's Hospital," Michele Worden told me. "She was neonatally trained, but she's not worked clinically for at least 20 years." Meanwhile, Dr Michael Hall cited "nurses who would have been willing to speak in court and contradict what Dr Jayaram said about what nurses do, particularly with regard to responding to oxygen saturations. Every nurse I've spoken with has told me that what Lucy allegedly did is perfectly normal, and actually the correct thing to do."

When interviewing for this book, I spoke with numerous nurses, and they all agreed that this observational period would be perfectly normal and in no way suspicious. "When an alarm goes off, you hit a button, which is a bit like the snooze button on an alarm clock", Michele Worden explained. "You then stand at the end of the incubator and observe and assess the baby. To say that Lucy was stood there, not doing anything, I fundamentally dispute that. You must assess the baby before you put your hands in the incubator. Every time you do put your hands in that incubator, you are potentially introducing infection, which is a big thing with a premature and low-birth-weight infant."

In order to clarify, I asked Worden: "So could we say that, in fact, if you immediately responded, you immediately reached into the incubator, and you did that without this period of observation, that would be a serious mistake?" Worden replied: "Yes, it would, because these babies are so fragile. The whole ethos of neonatal nursing is minimal handling."

Another neonatal nurse explained that observation periods were essential "in order to see if a baby self-corrects. Often with neonates, oxygen levels dip, for example. But you don't immediately respond by handling the baby when there is an alarm." Julie Yates further corroborated that "it takes you a few seconds to look at the obvious. Why is the alarm going off? Has it become disconnected? What does the patient look like? What are the monitors telling you to do? Are they breathing? Is the tube blocked? And many other questions. The last thing you do is make a snap decision – you observe the infant first. Often, they will self-correct and start breathing spontaneously."

Finally, another neonatal nurse told me that "if you have a baby who is desaturating, meaning their pulse oximeter readings are going down, you check the readings firstly because they can be incorrect. For example, extra oxygen when not needed can cause damage to their lungs and their eyes. It's one of the tricky things in neonatology. And so we wait and see, and that assessment takes some time. You don't just immediately dive in there because an alarm has gone off."

It is also important to note that Child K was not Letby's designated infant. She was, in fact, responding to an alarm in the only rational and professional way possible. If Letby hadn't been attending to the baby, it would have been a dereliction of duty. And if Letby had responded rashly, immediately administering some form of treatment without assessing the situation first, this would have been inappropriate and unprofessional. She was engaging in the only appropriate course of action, but that didn't prevent her from being handed a life sentence.

When speaking with ITV, Jayaram said: "Lucy Letby was standing by the top of the incubator. She didn't have her hands in the incubator. What was she doing there? Was she just…she was just standing there." Jayaram's comment runs counter to what many nurses have told me regarding standard procedure when a baby desaturates. It appears to be another scenario whereby if Letby *did* have her hands in the incubator, then that would be held against her as well. Throughout the trial, Letby has faced the tricky predicament of always being in the wrong, regardless of which one of two diametrically opposed actions she engaged in.

Jayaram then concedes that "tubes become dislodged" (also referred to as 'extubation') which is reasonable as will be discussed shortly, but then makes the extraordinary assertion that "the only possibility was that that tube had to have been dislodged deliberately". This appears to run counter to what many nurses have told me about what the standard procedure would be.

Professor Colin Morley demonstrated how easy it is for tubes to become dislodged when speaking with the journalist Anouk Curry. "Accidental dislodgement is extremely common", Morley explained. The neonatologist was also at a loss to explain Jayaram's comments. "It doesn't make sense to me. We have all seen it frequently. The movement only has to be relatively small. If you are out by 1cm then suddenly the baby is extubated. Accidental extubation is common."

Professor Morley also told John Sweeney that claims made by the prosecution in court regarding the dislodging of tubes were "too simplistic", outlining that the incorrect insertion of tubes can play a major role in infant extubation. "If the tube is very close to the larynx, it's very easy for it to get dislodged by lifting the baby, turning the baby, moving the baby, and so it's something we see a lot." Morley also spoke about the evidence presented in court for Letby's guilt. "There was no evidence! She was just seen standing by the baby, and the baby was desaturating, which is what premature babies do, and without any evidence he subsequently said she must have dislodged the tube."

This accidental dislodgement of tubes is common knowledge in both paediatric and neonatal medicine with countless studies available to support this. Professor Colin Morley was astounded that anyone could assert that "small babies can't dislodge tubes on their own. Where have these people been? Tubes become dislodged all the time in nurseries, maternity wards and neonatal units. It's almost a daily occurrence." Professor Morley also queried whether "the endotracheal tube was even secured properly", observing that "securing tubes can be difficult; often dribbling causes problems. It doesn't take much movement at all – the baby's head being lifted or turned can cause the tube to become detached, particularly as the trachea is rather short in these tiny babies."

To me it seems a trifle odd that a paediatric doctor wouldn't know about this topic. It also seems that Dr Jayaram was able to locate an obscure paper from 1989 when researching air embolism, but he was unable to familiarise himself with the frequency of tube dislodgement, which is far easier to establish. Additionally, on 18 June 2024, Dr Srinivasarao Babarao informed those present that Child K had experienced "at least three accidental extubations".

Given the anecdotal and published evidence on the subject, it should not be surprising that neonatal experts told Dr Philip Hammond "accidental dislodgement of the endotracheal tube, possibly compounded by incorrect positioning and/or inadequate securing" was the most likely explanation, rather than deliberate tampering. CoCH nurse Joanne Williams who worked much more closely with these infants than Jayaram, also told the court that she was "certain" that "active" babies could dislodge their tubes, adding that Child K was definitely active. Another nurse, Caroline Oakley, also told the court of previous occasions where tubes had both slipped and been faulty.

"It should be noted as well that accidental extubations happen more often in premature babies. There are numerous biological reasons for this", Professor Carola Vinuesa informed me. Dr Roger Norwich added: "And also that tube, which was leaking like crazy and could not have been working properly, was the wrong size of tube for that baby. It was the wrong size because they couldn't get the right size in, as they weren't very good at intubating. So they put a small tube in, which was inadequate, and then the leak occurred."

"It's also important to measure carbon dioxide output", Professor Colin Morley continued. "If carbon dioxide is detected, the tube is in the trachea, but I've seen no evidence that such checks were conducted."

If we examine the court transcripts more thoroughly we see that the accuracy of Jayaram's recall is questionable. Jayaram firstly asserted that Nurse Joanne Williams had "left Lucy Letby babysitting". But Williams specifically told the court that "she does not remember asking anyone in particular to look after Child K in her absence".

The court then established that Letby was in Nursery 2 between 2:36am and 3:50am, while Child K was taken into Nursery 1. During this time two nurses, Caroline Oakley and Joanne Williams, were present in Nursery 1. Joanne Williams left the unit at 3:41am, at which point Jayaram claims that Letby "had to be looking after Child K". But the evidence points to these two designated nurses waiting for one another, before leaving the unit.

When I spoke to experienced nurse Julie Yates on this subject, she doubted that Letby was even present in Nursery 1. "With several other nurses, we analysed this case, and we put Caroline Oakley at the bedside, not Lucy, for a number of reasons. It would not be optimal for two nurses to leave an intensive care room at the same time. One would leave, and then when they came back, the other one would take over. You wouldn't leave a nurse from another room watching an intensive care room with the most vulnerable patient in the unit". Speaking at the retrial on 24 June 2024, Letby herself asserted that she hadn't been present in the nursery.

Jayaram then conceded in court that his own thoughts at the time could have been deemed "hysterical and completely irrational…because of this association [with Letby]". He then entered the unit, according to his own account, having not seen Caroline Oakley come into the room.

Michele Worden told me that there is a simple explanation for Jayaram's testimony: "Caroline Oakley who was in that nursery is very similar looking to Lucy. I worked with Caroline Oakley for many years. She's the same height as Lucy, she's blonde. It's the early hours of the morning, Ravi is perhaps a bit bleary eyed – it is extremely likely that this is a case of mistaken identity, particularly when you examine what was said in court."

There is further evidence for Jayaram's testimony being inaccurate. Joanne Williams has consistently stated that the alarms were going off in Nursery 1 at the time of the supposed harming of Child K. Conversely, Jayaram has changed his story. When questioned by police in 2018, he told them that he couldn't remember whether the alarm had sounded or not but then told the court that he was "absolutely certain" that alarms weren't going off, even though others that were present state the opposite. When asked in court about his previous comments, Dr Jayaram stated: "I don't know why I said that." Jayaram had previously told the police that Child K was sedated but later said that morphine was not running prior to the desaturation. As required by the botched swipe-card data, the prosecution also shifted the time of this desaturation between the original trial and the retrial.

When questioned in court, Letby had no recollection of these events and was accused by the prosecution of being a "liar". That seems unfair, considering that the prosecution's only form of evidence, by their own admission, was the cross-examination of Jayaram. He himself had absolutely no recollection of speaking with Joanne Williams, who told the court that she specifically spoke with Jayaram after the incident. The prosecution is therefore asking us to believe that Joanne Williams is incorrect about this incident which she specifically remembers, and instead accept Jayaram's version of events which he can't recall.

It has already become clear in this chapter that Jayaram's memory is rather haphazard. But one would certainly expect him to recall a telling incident which occurred in March 2014 when young Noah Robinson tragically passed away when just four days old at the CoCH following a litany of errors. Doctors at the hospital inserted a breathing tube into the infant's oesophagus, rather than the trachea. There were five independent indicators that the breathing tube was incorrectly placed, but the doctors, a junior registrar and a consultant, all failed to heed them.

Cheshire coroner Nicholas Rheinberg, who was also the coroner for several infants involved in the Letby case, was explicitly critical of the doctors when recording a verdict of misadventure, stating that there were "very considerable signs" that the tube was incorrectly positioned. Rheinberg also described the assumption made by medics at the time that equipment was faulty as "extraordinary". Signs of understaffing were also explicit; there was only one senior doctor on duty when Noah began to deteriorate on 22 March.

Further investigation from the journalist Cleuci de Oliveira unearthed the fact that Dr B, one of the so-called 'gang of four' consultants, had been the doctor reprimanded by the coroner at the inquiry into Noah's death, in which multiple failures with intubation were cited. It therefore seems rather unlikely that Dr Jayaram would not be aware of this, which begs the question of why he stated that Letby deliberately detaching the tube was the only possible explanation for this extubation, which, frankly, was a thoroughly bizarre statement anyway.

John Sweeney further wrote about the revelations surrounding Noah in the *Daily Mail*, noting something that may not hugely surprise readers at this point – the jury was told nothing of this in either the original trial or retrial. Similarly, Thirlwall managed to make precisely zero references to Noah Robinson, nor was his untimely death mentioned in any document submitted.

When the initial investigation into Noah took place, Letby was still employed by the CoCH. The mother of Noah noted that "staff shortages meant blood tests and X-rays were not assessed for seven hours and there was one doctor on duty who was splitting his time between the neonatal ward and the children's ward. The fact that his condition worsened on Saturday night and Sunday morning, when there were less senior staff on duty and the nearest specialist was 40 miles away at Alder Hey was [also] a factor." These are the exact issues highlighted earlier in this book, and yet, somehow, when the opportunity presented itself to blame absolutely everything on Letby, all of these more prosaic factors were suddenly jettisoned and forgotten about. We know for a fact, as confirmed by an experienced neonatologist from Arrowe Park tertiary hospital, that infants from the Letby case suffered, and even died, due to delays in transfer to more specialist care.

Why did the police rule out 'foul play' in Noah's case, but prosecute Letby on Child K? There is no evidence of deliberate harm in the case of Child K. It does appear that Cheshire Police are unable to consider the possibility that a doctor could possibly cause harm, but only too willing to jump to this conclusion when one particular nurse could be involved. When I spoke to Dr Fiona MacRae, she suggested that "if a nurse had been responsible for such glaring errors then a huge amount of trouble would have been thrown their way".

There remains no evidence that the Cheshire Constabulary ever felt any suspicion towards any doctor on the unit, nor that they ever engaged in any investigation of any doctors. They perhaps worked a little too closely with them.

I'm not suggesting that Noah Robinson's death was anything other than a tragic but avoidable accident. But please bear in mind there is as much evidence that Child K was deliberately harmed as Noah. In fact, in Noah's case a tube was inserted incorrectly on three separate occasions which directly resulted in his tragic passing. This coincides precisely with Child K, whose endotracheal tube was only inserted after what Dr Shoo Lee described as "three traumatic attempts" before being ventilated.

Allegations regarding the attempted murder of Child K are largely dependent on the testimony of Jayaram. It seems to me the only distinction is that in one case Cheshire Police have decided that a doctor couldn't possibly have deliberately harmed a baby, and in the other that a nurse simply must have engaged in malicious acts, because a doctor stated this was the case.

If you doubt these assertions, please note that the prosecuting barrister, Nick Johnson, indicated that the case of Child K should be decided by a single issue: "Do you believe Dr Jayaram saying what he saw? Do you believe he is telling you the truth about what he saw? And if you do, do you accept what we allege Lucy Letby was trying to do, bearing in mind what we have also proved?"

Letby's defence barrister noted at the retrial that if Jayaram's account "is not truthful or accurate then there is no safe basis for convicting Lucy Letby on this charge – on that point the defence and the prosecution are in agreement". Furthermore, if Jayaram seriously suspected Letby of committing a serious criminal offence, and had apparently seen something indicating this, why didn't he contact the police immediately? He said he "didn't question it at the time" – it's only after the fact that these eyewitness testimonies came to light – as there was "an element of fear of retribution from those people above". When it was put to him that he was happy for "this nurse to potentially go on killing", Jayaram claimed that "there is absolutely no precedent or training for us knowing how to deal with this".

If Jayaram had caught Letby *actually* red-handed, he would have known how to deal with it, and he would definitely have escalated it. Jayaram claimed again during the Thirlwall Inquiry that "the fear of not being believed" had prevented him from raising whatever it was that he saw. Jayaram was then asked whether he "was complying with [his] duty to public safety in keeping that quiet?" His response? "I'm not sure that I can answer that."

One of the neonatal nurses I interviewed was highly sceptical of the entire story related to reporting this incident: "What sort of environment does that hospital have to be for those doctors to feel like the rules don't apply to them? And that they don't have to phone the police when they're supposedly seeing someone attempting to murder a baby? That tells you everything you need to know about the culture on the unit. And he would have had training as well, because you get safeguarding training all the time, to the point where you get bored of it. And the threshold for reporting is so low. It's not like you have to do the investigation – you report it to somebody who does. If you suspect something, you report it. This is mandatory." Indeed, a safeguarding document from the CoCH submitted to the Thirlwall Inquiry baldly states that "it is simpler to lift the telephone than live with the regret of not doing so".

Every nurse I spoke with felt that if Letby was guilty of deliberately detaching a tube, the key should be thrown away as they all take their duty of candour extremely seriously. But, in common with all of the other eyewitness testimony that will be discussed in the following chapter, nothing even remotely incriminating was ever seen. "If a nurse has been hurting patients, throw the book at them – I want them out", a neonatal nurse practitioner told me. "The woman from Vanderbilt [this refers to RaDonda Vaught] – I am completely behind her prosecution, because she was so negligent and killed a patient because of that. But the more that I read about this case, the less that I find information which actually showed that Letby did something, and the more I was finding about medical mismanagement from those above her."

Jayaram then undermined his own testimony during the Thirlwall Inquiry. Firstly, it should be mentioned that Dr Christopher Green was clear in his testimony that Jayaram did not tell the grievance panel about allegedly walking in on Letby trying to murder Child K a few months earlier. *The Daily Telegraph* also noted this, outlining that Jayaram had told Dr Green during an interview that formed part of Letby's grievance procedure that there is "no objective evidence at all" to suggest that Letby had harmed babies, and that the "only concern raised about Lucy was she had been exposed to so many deaths" and this "might be traumatic for her". This second comment stands up to little scrutiny. Documents submitted to Thirlwall indicate beyond doubt that the consultants had suspicions that Letby was somehow implicated in deaths on the unit for over a year by this point. Dr Jayaram does not seem to have been the foremost communicator of this idea, but he was certainly aware of it, and thus his account here is plainly erroneous.

Jayaram also told Green on 11 November 2016 that the "only concerns raised were that we had a statistically significant rise in unexplained deaths and near misses and we didn't know why". While we know that Jayaram doesn't have the most sparkling memory, it does seem to have slipped his mind at this point that he's supposed to have seen Letby attempting to murder a baby. "He didn't mention its purported significance in any of the review meetings, nor the deep dive discussions", Dr

Margaret Ferguson noted. "He didn't mention it when the Royal College came to investigate, or the CQC, he failed to mention any of that for well over a year, but then it seems to become oddly emblazoned in his memory at some point."

Then Jayaram himself stated at Thirlwall that the deliberate dislodging of the tube "was the thought that went through my head", but that "in isolation it wouldn't even have crossed my mind". That is a clear indication that Jayaram's memory about what he saw is unreliable. If he could have seen it in isolation and suspected deliberate harm, or have indeed known this was the case, then there would have been no need for what he has already conceded was the 'hysterical' and 'completely irrational' association he had made with Letby. Anyone who witnesses malicious acts towards a baby will almost certainly remember them.

But even that's not the end of this matter. An email dated 4 May 2017 emerged in April 2025 which indicated that Dr Jayaram had initially suggested that Letby had called him for help. In that email, Dr Jayaram informed seven colleagues that he had specifically entered the nursery to check on Child K because Letby had raised the alarm, requesting assistance. Not only does this contradict what Jayaram stated in court but critically, this email was written only 11 days before he told Cheshire Police something *completely* different (see "Operation Hummingbird"). The email was not disclosed to the defence until September 2024, after Letby had been convicted of attempting to murder Child K.

In response to this the veteran MP, Sir David Davis, wrote to the Cheshire Constabulary requesting them to investigate Jayaram for perjury due to his apparently contradictory testimony. At the time of writing, over one year after Cheshire Police indicated that they would update on this matter "in due course", nothing more has been heard from them.

Considering all that has been discussed in this chapter, it is perhaps not hugely surprising that the retrial wasn't the finest hour of Dr Ravi Jayaram. "It struck me during the retrial that the strategy of the defence was to argue Letby's case in cross-examination", Cleuci de Oliveira recounted. "And Ben Myers was very intense and strong. He demolished Dr Jayaram, demolished him that day. I remember there was a 15-minute break, and everyone was supposed to leave. Jayaram was just sat there frozen, as if he couldn't move."

And what did Jayaram tell the parents of Child A and Child B on 10 February 2016? "When monitors alarm, it is a signal to the staff to look at them. They often alarm due to movement or poor contact. If an alarm goes off a member of staff may look up at the monitor and if it is clear it is a false reading or just a minor change then no action is necessarily needed. Usually, the first move would be to check the baby the monitor was attached to. For example an oxygen monitor may read low but if a baby is pink, or there is a poor trace on the monitor *then no action would be needed* [my emphasis]." Jayaram is providing exactly the same explanation countless nurses have given me – there is a period of observation when the nurse assesses what action is necessary and indeed if any action is needed. Even more significant is that he proffered this explanation just *one week* before the alleged incident related to Child K which occurred on 17 February 2016. Seven days later he would observe Letby doing exactly what he described, then he would forget about it for at least a year but possibly longer than this, never mentioning it when given numerous opportunities to do so; then he would suddenly realise that he'd witnessed Letby attempting to murder a baby.

To say this is an unsafe conviction would be a monumental understatement. This entire retrial was embarrassing for everyone involved with the criminal justice system, if they wish for it to have even the merest pretence of being objective. It could be said, more broadly, that it is a genuine national embarrassment. However, if there is one small saving grace for the criminal justice system, it was that the Court of Appeal verdict related to Child K was somewhat critical of Jayaram. The appeal was still rejected, that goes without saying. But it was noted in paragraph 19 of their verdict that the testimony of Jayaram was less than reliable: "In our judgment it is of some significance that the critical issue for the jury was whether they were sure of the evidence of Dr Jayaram. Legitimate criticism could be made of his evidence. Although he believed that Letby had deliberately dislodged the endotracheal tube, he had said nothing at the time nor for many months thereafter. There was an inconsistency between his evidence and the contemporaneous records."

The curious case of Child K was emblematic of a fundamental problem with the original trial. Proceedings became an absurd spectacle of "I said, you said", asking witnesses to recall obscure incidents that had occurred nearly a decade previously, and then citing this information as if it was gospel. By any reasonable measure, there is virtually no human being alive that would be able to recall these events with any degree of accuracy; this is simply beyond the capacity of memory. This entire portion of the trial, and what passed for evidence, can simply be the benign record of numerous colleagues going about their business on a normal working day.

This is evidenced by the fact that several nurses, not merely Letby, don't even recall precisely what they were doing, or even some of the alleged incidents. Let alone can they be expected to remember what room they were in, at what time, on one working day that is much like many others, and which had occurred six or seven years previously by the time the system managed to prosecute Letby. And that applies if the data was captured and presented accurately, which it was not.

In reality, the critical aspect of the Lucy Letby trial is, always has been, and always will be, whether or not crimes were actually committed, not who was in what room, at what time, or whether she was 'standing over' an infant when demonstrably correct to be doing so. Her guilt or otherwise should never, and cannot, be determined by whether or not she could precisely recall some innocuous incident that occurred seven years previously, and then holding it against her when she could not, particularly as she was being questioned at a time when she had been literally broken down to a shadow of her usual self. Letby, not unreasonably, told the court herself that she could not recall "from memory exactly what I was doing when", which would apply to anyone in the same circumstances.

This entire portion of the trial was designed with the sole intention of creating a narrative, which, as discussed in the previous chapter, would be easier for the jury to understand than facts. This theme also runs through the forthcoming chapters on eyewitness accounts and anecdotal evidence. As noted by a study published in the journal *Frontiers in Communication*, "Narratives are processed more easily than non-narratives, and when processing is eased, persuasion becomes more likely."

When one steps back and assesses the trial of Lucy Letby rationally, it is simplicity itself to conclude that so much included in both the original court case and the retrial has little evidential value. This would be concerning in any criminal case, let alone one with such grave consequences for the defendant. Furthermore, Letby has been handed a life sentence for the attempted murder of Child K, for which no evidence has been presented. It is doubtful that she was even in the room at the time of the alleged incident, the supposed event almost certainly didn't happen, the allegation is completely unsupported by evidence and the solitary witness, providing the sole evidence presented in court, has backtracked even on his phenomenally weak and unreliable testimony.

Everything points to this being a really obvious accidental extubation with no deliberate harm involved. When Dr Shoo Lee revealed the verdict of expert neonatologists on Child K, a catalogue of mistakes by clinicians was noted. Doctors at the CoCH used an incorrect type of endotracheal tube for the infant resulting in failed ventilation which led to gradual collapse. The verdict of Dr Lee was quite withering: "The consultant did not understand the basics of resuscitation, air leak and mechanical ventilation." Dr Lee also pointed to evidence that Letby had not tampered with alarms as had been alleged, citing the testimony of another nurse who had rushed in to help after becoming aware of alarms sounding in the nursery housing Child K.

Child K did sadly die, but this was not even remotely related to Letby. The child passed away at Arrowe Park Hospital several days after the supposed incident discussed in court. This was a chronically ill and premature infant; it is frankly utterly ridiculous to associate one particular collapse of this baby with deliberate extubation, without any credible evidence whatsoever.

Yet Lucy Letby was originally to have been charged with murdering Child K, despite quite evidently not being present at the time of the child's death. It was only at the eleventh hour during a hearing held at Manchester Crown Court on 10 June 2022 that the prosecution dropped its intention to accuse Letby of murdering a child who died in another hospital 18 miles away from Chester, three days after she had allegedly had contact with the baby which wasn't even satisfactorily established.

The title of this chapter describes the case of Child K as 'curious', but perhaps shambolic would be more accurate. "Should we really be happy with such a savage sentence on such questionable evidence?" the veteran journalist Peter Hitchens asked. The answer to that question is quite obvious.

CHAPTER 15: EYEWITNESS ACCOUNTS

One thing all parties can agree on is that no one witnessed Lucy Letby do anything to harm babies at the CoCH. No one contests this. Nonetheless, the prosecution did attempt to muddy the waters in this area by introducing some eyewitness evidence, which will be assessed in this chapter. Before discussing this, it is worth noting that nine doctors and nurses from the CoCH were afforded anonymity. Considering that this is only usually granted in exceptional circumstances, this degree of anonymity is rather puzzling.

Many commenters and observers of the Letby case have queried why CCTV cameras were not installed in the neonatal ward, which could have provided critical evidence. One neonatal nurse told *Private Eye* that she has asked for CCTV cameras to be installed on her unit to protect both her and colleagues from accusations of incompetence or murder should a spike of excess deaths occur. This sentiment has been reflected in a letter authored by the campaign group Nineteen Nurses which noted that "many of our colleagues are now terrified to continue working in the NHS as we believe that next time it could be one of us who are blamed for a failing system". This is obviously a very serious issue for an NHS system that is already stretched to breaking point.

Spikes in deaths are rather common, as has already been discussed earlier. As an example, in 2014-15 the CoCH was only twelfth in the league table of excess deaths. If cameras had been present on the ward at the Chester hospital, many suspect that there would never have been any murder inquiry as the evidence gleaned would rule this out immediately. The CoCH had experienced problems, controversy and deaths on the neonatal unit in previous years which could have hastened the need for CCTV. There was nothing particularly out of the ordinary about 2015 or

2016, and, as part of Letby's grievance procedure, Yvonne Griffiths told Dr Chris Green that she had "worked on the unit for 10 years…we have had equivalent deaths in previous years".

One of the most important eyewitness testimonies to appear in court involved Dr Sandie Bohin. Her testimony is particularly significant as it came from a doctor and is therefore likely to have been given credence by the jury. Bohin commented: "I remember the mother of one of the babies said she could hear in the corridor her child making a noise that a baby should never be making. That will be forever etched on her memory. To have a premature baby screaming is really unusual. What was described on the ward was babies screaming for up to 30 minutes. That is just unheard of. Somebody had done something to cause those babies extreme pain."

Bohin's account is problematical as it relies on eyewitness testimony from one of the parents of the deceased. None of the parents had reported anything untoward until they were approached by the police. It must be reiterated that no complaints about Letby, or anyone else, were made at the time – all of these accounts were recalled quite some time after the incidents. This poses problems immediately because, as has been well established, human memory is hugely unreliable.

Dr Bohin stated that the mother "could hear in the corridor her child making a noise that a baby should never be making". But there are numerous problems with this.

Firstly, Dr Bohin didn't witness this noise, but is now recounting it in court as evidence; she shouldn't even have been considered a witness.

Secondly, Dr Bohin is lending credence to the comment that the child should never be making this noise. As she wasn't there she doesn't know what noise was being made, so can't legitimately comment on this.

Thirdly, we don't know why the child was making the noise. Simply because the child is making an unpleasant noise, it does not automatically follow that someone had deliberately harmed the child.

Bohin then goes on to make the claim that a baby screaming for 30 minutes is "unheard of". Dr Roger Norwich commented: "She hasn't witnessed that noise, so that's the opinion of the parent, who, with respect, knows very little, and is, understandably, not exactly the most objective witness. It's meaningless." And Dr Colin Ferguson found it "extraordinary that nobody at the time prevented her from saying things like that. She's there to be providing professional evidence, not dealing with emotional hyperbole."

The comment that it is "really unusual" is more balanced; Bohin is acknowledging that this could occur. But then she asserts that it is unheard of for a baby to be in pain and screaming for 30 minutes, unless "somebody had done something to cause those babies extreme pain". This is a claim, from a doctor, which in my view has no rational merit. You cannot infer from a recounted recollection, which you have not corroborated, which describes circumstances that you have not witnessed, regarding infants that often feel and experience distress, that beyond all doubt a baby has been deliberately harmed.

"It's nonsense", Professor Colin Morley asserted. "I can't put it any kinder than that. Babies cry all the time, often loudly and vigorously. There is no way anyone could possibly, from that description, assert that this is evidence of deliberate harm."

I think there has been a disturbing tendency in the Letby case, and more broadly across a wider societal spectrum, to put doctors on an undeserved pedestal and simply trust their word. Let's be clear – doctors are people. They are simply people who have passed a university course. They are neither infallible, nor super-human. Any good doctor will readily admit this. That is, in fact, one of the defining qualities of a good doctor or scientific practitioner – openness to new data and alternative explanations.

In light of this, Bohin's testimony might have been given more credence than other witness testimony simply because she's a doctor. Questions have also been raised as to whether the anonymity given to some doctors would have been permitted if they had not been members of that profession.

On the topic of memory and its reliability, in 2023, the University of Sussex published research which demonstrated that "human memories are unreliable because we like stories with predictable endings.

Researchers found that the human tendency to construct complete storylines, with a clear beginning, middle and end, can lead us to misremember the conclusion of everyday events, and even 'remember' events that never happened. People often falsely recalled additional details about the expected outcome scenes [in our experiment], which filled the gap between the actual endpoint and its natural conclusion."

There is a very real danger that this is exactly what has occurred in the eyewitness accounts discussed in this chapter. Our memory is absolutely capable of filling in gaps to create 'closure', or more compelling narratives. Further research from the University of Amsterdam found that human memory may be unreliable after just a few seconds. "Even at the shortest term, our memory might not be fully reliable", Dr Marte Otten, the first author of the research from the University of Amsterdam, told *The Guardian*. "Particularly when we have strong expectations about how the world should be, when our memory starts fading a little bit – even after one and a half seconds, two seconds, three seconds – then we start filling in based on our expectations." The research paper notes that "expectations can reshape perceptual representations over short time scales, leading to what we refer to as short-term memory (STM) illusions."

It is known that trauma can have a significant impact on brain operation and the aspect of memory most commonly affected by psychological trauma is long-term memory. Missing memories, changes to memory and intensified memories are all known examples of the involuntary manipulation of long-term memory. Within the construct of long-term memory, trauma has been shown to alter both implicit and explicit memory.

Research shows that psychological trauma has great impact on physical aspects of the brains of patients to the point that it can have detrimental effects akin to actual physical brain damage, with even a reduced pre-frontal cortex observable in tests. In short, the memories of those who go through traumatic experiences can be seriously affected, which when combined with the unreliability of memory in the first place, naturally calls into question the reliability of completely uncorroborated eyewitness accounts. On the basis of this information, one could also assert that Letby's comments in court, where she often indicated that she couldn't recall or remember certain events, can be seen as honest testimony rather than deceit.

Problems with memory and recall are further reflected in other examples of eyewitness testimony related to the trial. The mother of Child E and Child F told the Thirlwall Inquiry that she had caught Letby "off guard". Well, actually she said: "I think I caught her off guard." The parent goes on to describe how Letby had failed to make eye contact, and was, according to her account, abrasive and dismissive. But the same mother also stated that Letby was "very attentive of me. Whenever she used to see me, she would hug me. She looked like every time she spoke to me, she was on the verge of tears, very upset. She was just as upset as me which, reflecting back on it now, is very odd behaviour."

It's worth remembering that Letby told the court that she found the death of Child E to be particularly traumatic. This can be deemed entirely believable, because she broke down in tears while discussing it during the trial on 5 May 2023, and court proceedings were interrupted. Letby recalled, as she wiped away tears with a tissue, how she had "found him a gown from the unit to be dressed in" because his parents didn't have clothes for him. In any normal circumstances, this would be viewed as the behaviour of someone who was generally saddened and empathetic, who had clearly engaged in an act of kindness because she felt sympathy for the parents. It is only through the prism of presumed guilt and trauma that such interpretations are made, and these are then recounted to the court and Thirlwall Inquiry as if they represent legitimate evidence.

"A lot of the evidence presented at trial by the prosecution was based on distant memories", the journalist Cleuci de Oliveira explained. "These are extremely traumatic circumstances, experienced by extremely traumatised witnesses, who have then had all manner of conversations with police and the prosecution. Not only have these appeared in court, but now Thirlwall is trying to shoehorn memories from the parents – which were, by their own admission, vague and uncertain – into the inquiry, and present them as fact. I have followed Thirlwall very closely and have seen what was not at all established information now being written into the public record as rock solid."

Cleuci cited the work of Professor Elizabeth Loftus, who had been profiled by Rachel Aviv in the *New Yorker*. The work of Professor Loftus has repeatedly demonstrated that false recollections can be inserted into subjects, in the process deliberately distorting their memories of events. Professor Loftus and her team of researchers have made people ardently believe in completely false scenarios, including certain experiences as children, teenagers and even the week before studies were conducted. There is no suggestion here that Cheshire Police have done this deliberately, but there is always a chance that false recollections can occur unknowingly, particularly when dealing with traumatised people.

This didn't prevent prosecutor Nick Johnson from declaring that the mother of Child E had caught Letby "red-handed", even though it is an uncontested fact that no one witnessed Letby doing anything untoward. This claim was inserted early in the closing statement of the prosecution, where it would have maximum impact. In my view, this categorical statement cannot be reconciled with the evidence.

Elsewhere, there are question marks regarding whether Letby has even been identified correctly. The father of Child C had reported that Letby made an inappropriate remark, but then later conceded that he wasn't "100% sure" it was her. "I think it could have been [Letby]", he concluded. Letby has always denied that this incident occurred, and that she was the nurse in question.

Should uncorroborated eyewitness evidence even be allowed in court, particularly when related to complex and nuanced events that occurred several years previously, and especially when it involves witnesses who are hugely involved emotionally and have no medical knowledge? What objective merit does such evidence really possess? Can it be considered remotely reliable?

Yet such was the determination of the prosecution to include emotive eyewitness testimony, even two grandmothers were allowed to provide statements. The first grandmother, of Child A and Child B, was asleep when key events took place, while the second, of Child O, admitted that she could not remember what had happened as she was too busy consoling the parents. This was deemed viable evidence, but, by contrast, Judge James Goss decided that the jury didn't need to hear about the RCPCH report.

And that's leaving aside the fact that we know, after all of this speculation and highly emotive discourse, no one has seen Letby do anything wrong. This supposedly vital eyewitness testimony comprised several days of the trial, and yet if witnesses were to be transparently straightforward about the case, it could have been concluded in mere seconds.

Professor Neena Modi told the *Doubt* podcast: "A court…should not be a place where emotion holds sway, but where facts and evidence hold sway. And that's an even more pertinent point when one considers the anguish of these families…what an agonising rollercoaster it must have been for them."

It should also be remembered that this is a busy neonatal unit, with staff and visitors coming and going regularly. The likelihood of no one ever seeing any malicious acts, considering the intricacy and repeated nature of the alleged inflicted harm, is phenomenally small. Yvonne Griffiths told Dr Chris Green that "lots of people were around" when Letby was alleged to have harmed infants.

The eyewitness accounts of nurses that worked on the unit often differed from the prosecution case. As one example, Child N was considered to have experienced a "sudden" deterioration by Dr Dewi Evans. The evidence provided in support of air embolism in this case by Dr Evans can only be described as baffling, being reliant on a self-correcting heart attack in a baby, which Evans openly conceded he had never encountered before, and the citation of an academic paper to support air embolism, but the only information that was gleaned from it was "the association between air embolus in these two cases and screaming". There was no X-ray or other evidence of air embolism whatsoever by Evans' own admission in court, and he required the submission of five separate reports to draw this conclusion. The screaming was deemed to be critical in the diagnosis, but Dr Evans overlooked this several times, again by his own admission. As discussed previously, swipe-card errors made by Cheshire Police also mean that it is doubtful the infant was even screaming for 30 minutes.

Nonetheless, even this hypothesis relied on this sudden collapse. But the account of nurse Jennifer Jones-Key, released by the Thirlwall Inquiry in February 2025, indicates that Child N had, in fact, been deteriorating steadily throughout the evening, prior to Letby's arrival on the unit: "In the early hours of the morning, Child N looked pale and mottled in colour…[the] abdomen was bloated and veiny. I notified the shift leader about Child N's deterioration, and I connected Child N to the full saturation monitoring. Child N was having desaturations, but no interventions were required…At 05:30am, Child N started to have more desaturations, IV fluids were commenced, the feeds were stopped and ambient oxygen was commenced in the incubator. At 07:15am, Lucy was in Nursery 3 as she had come to have a chat with me before commencing her shift." This directly contradicts the account of Dr Evans which relies on a rapid collapse, and yet it was never heard by either court or jury.

Speaking with John Sweeney, Dr Philip Hammond questioned why the voice of nurses had been so "marginalised" in Letby's case, noting that they had been warned against speaking up in the trial, and "largely written out of the Thirlwall Inquiry". Hammond noted that several senior nurses from the CoCH had spoken out, indicating that they never witnessed Letby harming any infant. "Neonatal nursing is not a solitary thing. You are grouped around. There's often one or two people there. It would be extraordinarily difficult to inject five syringes of air into a nasogastric tube to compress the lungs and then put air into the vein, into the umbilical catheter, and then punch the baby in the liver for good measure, without being observed." This is a prosaic observation, yet it was one that was never adequately discussed in court.

The previous chapter discussed narrative persuasion, a concept that was intrinsic to the entire basis for including the eyewitness accounts in court. Eyewitness testimony was another emotional component of the story for the jury to latch onto, rather than an objective, or even meaningful, form of evidence. Stories are powerful persuasive devices that capture attention, evoke emotion and "entrance listeners in a manner that reduces resistance to a message".

Wikipedia states quite plainly that any "person experiencing intense emotions tends to be more receptive to ideas and therefore more suggestible". This is reflected in published research, including a 2020 study in the journal *Cognitive Research: Principles and Implications*, which found that subjects of research were more susceptible to 'fake news' when in an emotional state. An extensive systematic review from 2022 concluded that "anger and greater cortisol response to stress may increase susceptibility to misinformation". Pioneering research by Green and Brock discovered that stories have the potential to change attitudes and opinions, even when the facts themselves are weak or inconclusive. There is even evidence that adults are more prone to suggestion than children, as they draw "links between items experienced and those already in memory".

This segment of the trial was one of several that appear to rely on emotion to convince the jury. The appeal to emotion may be why many members of the public remain adamant that Letby is guilty.

The work of psychologist Dr Thea Gumbert on juries and narratives has already been discussed, and another expert with a background in mental health and nursing was of the same opinion: "I think what a lot of people have done is bought into what is a compelling narrative. And that's what the prosecution did – they created a narrative for the jury." This interviewee went on to expand on some further issues related to memory. "There were times in the trial where Lucy couldn't remember something innocuous, which suggests she is innocent. If you're innocent, you don't necessarily remember, whereas if you're guilty you do remember, because you've got to keep your story straight."

Rachel Langdale KC put forward the view at the Thirlwall Inquiry that "medical or scientific evidence in a case should never be compartmentalised or examined in isolation from the wider canvas. Those who do this will be less likely to see the picture as a whole and in failing to see the picture as a whole, they may reach conclusions that are not only wrong but are speculative and damaging." I find it hard to agree. Facts matter. They matter far more than one's nebulous impression of something. It is a law of nature that if the constituent parts of something have no substance, the structure itself will inevitably collapse.

Ironically, BBC journalist Judith Moritz described observing the prosecution case in court as "like watching it build a house of cards".

It is difficult to disagree with that description.

CHAPTER 16: ANECDOTAL EVIDENCE USED IN COURT

As the trial of Lucy Letby unfolded between October 2022 and August 2023, those present in court and the general public, via media communications, were treated to an array of anecdotal evidence. Almost all of this was collated from police raids of both Letby's house in Chester and the home of her parents in Hereford.

The centrepiece of this evidence was a post-it note, written in an unstructured and somewhat garbled fashion, that the police and prosecution both claimed to be a confession note. It is impossible to know precisely what the impact of this note and associated claims had on the jury, but it can be assumed that it helped to paint a picture of a guilty party. The note has also significantly coloured public opinion – many casual observers of the case believe Letby to be guilty almost entirely on the basis of this note, and it is continually cited as irrefutable evidence of her guilt.

Attention paid to the note has been squarely focused on one sentence. Letby wrote in the note that she is "evil" and "I did this". Taken out of context, this may seem a rather damning confession. But when further analysis is undertaken, it becomes clear that this initial impression is misleading.

Letby states: "I killed them on purpose because I'm not good enough." This could easily be interpreted as saying: "I am responsible for the deaths of these babies because I am not a good enough nurse", as opposed to: "I deliberately killed these babies." It should also be noted that this "not good enough" phrase was used in the same context in text messages with the doctor with whom she was supposedly infatuated; the police and prosecution displayed these messages in court. Letby also explicitly repeated the "not good enough" phrase in capitals at the top of this note and underlined it.

When questioned on the note by police, Letby gave precisely this explanation, specifically referencing the "not good enough" comments. This was not something she was briefed to do by legal representatives, and her demeanour during police interviews was "calm, compliant and cooperative". In excerpts of police interviews after her arrest, Letby said: "I just wrote it because everything had got on top of me. It was when I'd not long found out I'd been removed from the unit and they were telling me my practice might be wrong, that I needed to read all my competencies – my practice *might not have been good enough*. I was blaming myself but not because I'd done something (but) because of the way people were making me feel."

"When bad things happen to patients, we often feel guilty", one neonatal nurse practitioner told me. "You feel that it's your fault. So if you've got someone who is being low-key blamed, they're going to feel more guilt. Every time I have a patient die, I feel terrible, and I go over every single thing. There is always a lot of guilt that you internalise as a caregiver."

Letby's defence barrister, Ben Myers KC, told the court: "You have seen the notes. They are full of distress, self-recrimination and anguish. They certainly do show a very distressed woman. Someone in a terrible state of anguish". Indeed, Letby also uses the following phrases:

"NOT GOOD ENOUGH"

"There are no words"

"I can't breathe"

"I can't focus"

"Kill myself right now"

"Overwhelming fear"

"NO HOPE"

"I'll never have children"

"I haven't done anything wrong"

"I'll never have children or marry"

"I'll never know what it's like to have a family"

"Slander"

"Discrimination"

"Victimisation"

"All getting too much"

"Taking over my life"

"Hate myself so much"

"Despair"

"PANIC"

"FEAR"

"LOST"

"I feel very alone + scared"

"What does the future hold?"

"How can I get through it?"

"I don't deserve to live"

"I don't deserve mum and dad"

"World is better off without me"

During the interviewing process for this book, I had a lengthy conversation with an expert in mental health, who also has nursing experience. She had many interesting thoughts about Letby's notes, beginning with the fact that they are "as ambiguous as is possible. They literally make contradictory statements, sometimes within the same sentence, and then the police have picked out the bits that suit them and completely ignored the rest. The only thing the post-it notes prove is that she worked for the NHS. I found it funny that they were cited as evidence."

The comments within the notes indicating innocence, despair, fear, misery and self-doubt considerably outweigh any supposed confession. This is clearly not a confession note, nor was it ever intended to be anything of this nature. This is the anguished soul-searching of a hugely damaged woman.

"The notes look exactly like a patient doing a cognitive behavioural therapy exercise", Dr Thea Gumbert told me. "Get it out of your head and on to paper. I think there are also significant similarities between this case and other miscarriages of justice – the scurrilous misinterpretation of diary evidence or journal evidence as confessions, when they're really not."

Dr Margaret Ferguson further informed me: "I have seen the writings of people who've been very distressed, and these notes look exactly like that. I also think Lucy may well have been reiterating allegations that were made about her, rather than saying that she'd done these things." Microbiologist, Professor David Livermore, had been alerted to problems with the Letby case by the presentation of notes in the popular press: "The first thing that really grabbed me was the so-called confession notes. I looked at them, and you can't read them from left to right like any normal document – they're random jottings of contradictory statements."

On 3 September 2024, *The Guardian* published an article indicating that the confession note had been written under the advice of counsellors. "Sources close to the case have told *The Guardian* that the head of occupational health and well-being from the CoCH, Kathryn de Beger, encouraged Letby to write down her feelings as a way of coping with extreme stress. Letby's Chester GP also advised her to write down thoughts she was struggling to process, according to these sources." This was later confirmed by Dr James Phillips, who wrote a substack post explaining that both he and Sir David Davis MP had been informed that Letby "had been advised to write down how the accusations were making her feel by counsellors, something that was not used in trial for unclear reasons".

Letby had given these precise explanations at the time when questioned by police, and the name of Kathryn de Beger is mentioned multiple times throughout the notes collected by Cheshire Police. This is not even confined to the green note that was primarily exhibited – Letby also wrote de Beger's name in another yellow note. An email from Eirian Powell to Stephen Brearey on 28 June 2016 informed him that Letby was being referred to occupational health as she was "upset" at having been removed from the unit, which Powell reiterated had been done purely "for her own well-being".

In her statement submitted to Thirlwall, de Beger herself commented that "at no time did Lucy tell me anything which required me to contact someone more senior in the hospital or the police". She also debunked another accusation made in court regarding the anniversary of babies in the case: "Lucy did ask for meetings with me on anniversaries of some of the babies' deaths as she was particularly distressed", but also expressed how much "more distressed and upset the parents must be feeling because they had lost their babies". De Beger concluded her statement by revealing that she still felt "privileged at being asked to support Lucy over such a lengthy period and to support Lucy over these very hard times for her".

During her interview at the Thirlwall Inquiry, de Beger observed that Letby felt the clear victim of bullying and discrimination on the unit: "[Lucy] has always told me that she'd done nothing wrong…why were people doing this to her? And why did the consultants hate her so much?…[There] was a plan to return her to the neonatal unit at the beginning of April and that had been paused, so she was very upset about that…She was very, very distressed, very confused about why she couldn't go back". The anguish Letby felt was also recalled by unit manager Karen Rees who held weekly meetings with Letby: "She was crying… very distressed every time we met her, saying, 'Why is this happening to me?…I am not going let them drive me out of the job that I love. I worked hard. I've done nothing wrong.' She cried in my arms on a weekly basis. It was harrowing."

Additionally, de Beger told Thirlwall that Letby was more concerned for the parents of the infants than herself, and that all of her conduct and comments were consistent with someone who felt no guilt and believed she had done nothing wrong. Letby, in fact, told de Beger repeatedly that she couldn't understand why accusations were being made against her, and was evidently very upset by the situation. This was consistent with testimony also provided at Thirlwall by Karen Rees.

It is clear that Letby was fully aware of the allegations being made against her and of the identity of those making them. During an interview with Cheshire Police following her first arrest on 3 July 2018, Letby told officers that she had "found out that" Dr Stephen Brearey and Dr Ravi Jayaram "were the ones who had raised concerns about myself being the common factor in the deaths, and they felt that I'd deliberately harmed them", despite the fact that Letby believed they'd always "had a good working relationship". Kathryn de Beger also named Brearey and Jayaram in her statement to Thirlwall, informing the inquiry that Letby "also talked often about the consultants involved; she couldn't understand why they were accusing her. She thought they must hate her so much to do this to her."

A bizarre claim was also made by hospital HR director Sue Hodkinson that Letby's father was making "agitated" calls to de Beger, and that this was "becoming increasingly difficult to manage". The accusation here was that John Letby was putting undue pressure on the hospital and de Beger. However, when interviewed during the inquiry, de Beger flatly denied this: "I do not recall any telephone calls with Letby's father." When barrister Andrew Bershadski pressed de Beger further, she told him: "I have no recollection of any telephone calls. I have no recollection of being harassed."

During the trial, no information was presented that would indicate to either the court or jury that Letby had ever been through any counselling sessions. It was never communicated that the name of de Beger appeared multiple times in the so-called confession note, and other notes presented to the court. This is, firstly, incomprehensible from a defence perspective. However, we also know that Cheshire Police were certainly aware, but there is no evidence they ever spoke with Kathryn de Beger, or bothered to acquire further background information on Letby's situation at the CoCH. Documents submitted to the Thirlwall Inquiry indicate de Beger informing Letby that her feelings "are normal in this very stressful situation, you will be feeling a mixture of thoughts and emotions, which again is all very normal". The court was denied this information, while an inordinate amount of effort was made to make Letby's conduct appear sinister. De Beger was also not asked about the note at the Thirlwall Inquiry.

Other notes that were displayed as evidence were similar in external appearance to the green post-it note, but the important thing to understand is that all of the other notes collected by the police are completely consistent with Letby's comments, and provide little evidence to support anything related to the prosecution case.

However, a blue post-it note discovered by Cheshire Police does merit further consideration. Unlike all of the other notes recovered during the numerous police raids on Letby's house, this one is quite calm in tone but contains some critical information. Letby has written "police naming me", and then in brackets "obviously no evidence, and would have been spoken to, but still upsetting". It is tricky to decipher the next paragraph perfectly, but it seems to say: "supporting me how they can but can't confirm 100% I didn't do anything (or anyone else) until it's finished mediation". The final paragraph reads: "OH [Occupational Health] lady, prepare tomorrow, might make me think of all the things I'm missing out on."

When this note is examined, it rapidly becomes clear why it has been barely referenced anywhere, while the police and prosecution focused on one isolated phrase in another note. This is not the note of someone who feels guilty; indeed, she states that there is "obviously no evidence" and refers to neither her nor "anyone else" having done anything wrong. The entire context of the note is related to her clinical work, and concerns that she may have made medical mistakes. There is no suggestion of any criminal element. In fact, Letby largely rules this out, not merely in relation to herself, but, critically, in relation to "anyone else" on the unit as well.

Would someone who knew herself to be guilty of harming babies have written a note to herself in which she, firstly, states that there's "obviously no evidence", and even links this to other people? If she knew that she'd committed the crimes, she would know that no one else had done anything, and there would thus be no need for any concern for them. The reason Letby has written there is "obviously no evidence" is because she believes herself to be innocent. Why does she believe herself to be innocent? Well, she is the only person who can know whether or not she is.

Across the notes presented in court, Letby has written, "I didn't do anything wrong", "We tried our best and it wasn't enough" and that there is "obviously no evidence" against her or anyone else, plus dozens of other statements that undermine the notes' status as confessions. And yet one statement, which was used elsewhere innocently, has been taken out of context and been cited as evidence that it's a confession note.

During their own promotional film, Cheshire Police conceded that the overwhelming majority of notes recovered during this operation consisted of completely mundane information which has absolutely no relevance to the case. Well, this also applies to the blue post-it note. In fact, this item is exculpatory. It demonstrates that, far from confessing, Letby believed in her own innocence which is absolutely consistent with every single other statement made by everyone else who worked with her. The blue post-it note confirms precisely what Letby has conveyed extensively when interviewed – she was concerned about her competence as a nurse, felt unfairly under suspicion and knew that there was "obviously no evidence" against her. There is no confession, so there is no confession note.

During my lengthy conversation with a creative writing professor who specialises in mental health, many salient points were made about the nature of the notes exhibited in court. "Think about the literal act of writing. What is significant about a post-it note? It's disposable. You write something down and throw it away. If I was going to sit down and confess my sins on paper, I would not use a post-it note, and even seemingly different pens, with further strong indication that this note wasn't written at one sitting.

"Another thing to think about is the actual form of what is written. If you saw a poem on a piece of paper, you would recognise immediately that it was a poem, purely from the shape. The same with a newspaper article. Different pieces of writing have different structures that we recognise. Lucy's note certainly does not look like coherent writing. And so the question is – what features does a confession have? Does Lucy's writing have those features? Also, any and all verifiable details are completely missing from these notes. They're simply an emotional outpouring.

"People place more significance on the notes because they're written down. If these were statements she had made in an off-hand way then they would be instantly forgotten. If I told my partner, "I could kill you", no one would take that seriously. But if I wrote that down, it can be interpreted completely differently. "I killed them because I'm not good enough" is exactly the sort of emotional remark that you might make as a nurse. You are also very much encouraged as a nurse to reflect and make notes. The picture that emerges from these notes is a very different one to that presented in court and initially reported in the media."

Senior coroner's officer Stephanie Davies provided a critical review prior to the Operation Hummingbird investigation but was not made aware of what she considered to be "highly subjective" material that "is not tangible forensic evidence". The notes were a catalyst in Davies questioning the verdict – "Is everything else in the case as obviously shaky as these notes?" – and she informed me that based on her Master's degree in forensic psychology, "If I had known about those notes, I would have questioned them immediately."

A psychiatrist told me that he was "cautious" when he first read about the notes. "I know from my experience as a psychiatrist that people can have all sorts of contradictory thoughts, especially in the context of a bereavement. There can be feelings of guilt, where there's no justification for being guilty. That's a normal part of the bereavement process. And there were other statements in the notes, that she felt slandered. You wouldn't expect those in someone who is actually guilty. Why would you say that? It doesn't make sense."

In September 2025, Professor Gísli Guðjónsson, considered the most authoritative voice globally on false confessions, joined the growing chorus of voices denouncing this item of evidence. Such was the concern of Guðjónsson, he resigned from his role at the National Crime Agency in order to assist with the Letby case. "The note reveals utter despair and bewilderment", Guðjónsson asserted, having been written when the neonatal nurse was in a "disturbed mental state and tormented by a maladaptive core belief – 'I'm not good enough.'" Guðjónsson concluded that the notes are "unreliable as evidence of a 'confession', or criminal intent, and should be treated with extreme caution". It's also worth pointing out that the work of Guðjónsson was instrumental in the exoneration of both the Birmingham Six and Guildford Four and his advocacy for Letby represents the effective torpedoing of any relevance that the 'confession' note could conceivably have possessed.

Various text messages were also presented by the prosecution during the trial. These were partly used to reference a rather fanciful theory that Letby had deliberately harmed babies in order to attract the attention of a doctor at the CoCH. Several messages were presented to the court in support of this, although the term 'support' is used here particularly loosely.

Firstly, possibly the most cited message was sent by Letby after a holiday, indicating that she was going back to work "with a bang" – the implication from the prosecution being that she would go back "with a bang" by killing babies. But even the most superficial analysis indicates that this is ludicrous. The phrase "with a bang" is unclear and commonly used and certainly cannot be taken to refer to something specific related to this case. Often it is used to indicate someone is refreshed and ready for their return to work or it could mean she was expecting a difficult day, unsurprising when one considers the context of the information that her friend had conveyed to her.

Additionally, it doesn't even make any sense to suggest that this message meant that Letby intended to harm babies, as why would she tell someone this? Elsewhere, she is painted as a cold, calculated killer who managed to evade detection according to the prosecution. But Letby also decided to tell her friend via text message that she would kill babies at work the next day? Does this really stand up to any scrutiny, or even the application of basic logic?

A lot of the news media focused on a "going commando" phrase used by a colleague during one text message exchange with the doctor that she was supposedly infatuated with but less emphasis was given to the statement that followed: "I don't flirt with him…certainly don't fancy him, just nice guy." Letby also told prosecutors during the trial that she "loved him as a friend, I was not in love with him". In fact, while the prosecution were arguing that Letby had supposedly deep romantic feelings for the doctor, these messages were enlarged on a big screen, and the message that they highlighted explicitly contradicted this assertion.

The prosecution even suggested that Letby was somehow wrong to call the doctor in question on an occasion when Child O had collapsed and required resuscitation – another occasion on which Letby behaved in the opposite way to someone who wished to harm babies. Nick Johnson's questioning attempted to get Letby to agree she called the doctor purely for attention:

JOHNSON: Were you trying to get his attention?
LETBY: Yes, I wanted him to help.
JOHNSON: But his personal attention?
LETBY: No. He was the registrar on the unit that day.
JOHNSON: Did you enjoy being in these crisis situations?
LETBY: No.

An NHS professional told me: "Lucy calls the registrar who was on call to a medical emergency, and Johnson tries to make it look like Lucy wants attention for herself. Every nurse in the country should be angry and terrified about this". A neonatal nurse bluntly added: "Lucy was simply doing her job. It is crazy. Completely outrageous."

The last known WhatsApp message collected by Cheshire Police was sent by Letby to a Royal College of Nursing representative, Hayley Griffiths, on 20 June 2017. "It's funny isn't it, I've had a really good couple of wks keeping busy doing things with friends etc and then today it's just hit me and I can't help but think of them and that [PD] they'll be celebrating a birthday with only 1 out of their 3 boys X". Other text message exchanges see colleagues being supportive towards Letby, praising her, and Letby discussing a holiday in Devon with her parents. In any normal circumstances, these would be seen as benign, even empathetic.

In their promotional film on the Operation Hummingbird investigation, Cheshire Police said the following: "So reading through her phone, it was remarkably normal for a lot of it. And it's not until you overlay the times and dates of some of the things that she's saying, in text messages or whatever WhatsApp messages, is that the timing of it, as well as what she said, that really you can pick up those patterns. And as an analyst, that's what you're trying to find – patterns to things. Reading through her phone, it was *remarkably normal* for a lot of it."

And the actual text messages that were used in court are also "remarkably normal". There is nothing unusual about them at all. It is only when read through the lens of presumed guilt, through which the entire case and investigation seem to have been viewed, that they have any meaning whatsoever. It is certainly implied in the film that this is precisely what the police have done. The risk of looking for patterns in things, particularly when there is a pre-determined impression, is that one can see patterns where nothing exists. If the search for 'patterns' is removed, the "back with a bang" message is completely innocent. She said "with a bang", and a baby died the next day – obviously this must mean that she was telling her friend that she was going to kill! What other possible explanation could there be for her choosing this stock phrase that has been used millions of times previously in a completely mundane context? Indeed, if the filter of presumed guilt is removed, none of the messages presented in court have any significance whatsoever, and this was a tiny percentage of those collected.

Cheshire Police also referenced a 'coded' diary they'd discovered at Letby's home. Even in their own promotional film on Operation Hummingbird, this was referenced rather apologetically, as if the police themselves recognised that their assertion would come apart at the seams under any form of examination. With regard to this so-called code, it can merely be stated that it has been revealed by nurses to be completely benign and normal practice, with experienced healthcare staff even providing explanations for the supposed murder code. "As an example, LD is simply an acronym for Long Day", one nurse told me. "There is no code in this diary at all, these are all nursing references that many nurses will have written down and will write down in the future." In fact, nurse Sophie Ellis used the acronym herself during a text messaging interaction with Letby: "Geez, four LDs in a row." Ellis was unknowingly referencing the very pages that Cheshire Police have since displayed to the world as supposedly containing a code known only to Letby herself.

"When I worked on the Kathleen Folbigg case, she had written extensive diaries, and these were used against her", Professor Carola Vinuesa told me. "And then psychiatrists and psychologists were invited to the second legal inquiry, and 10 of them, all independent from all over the world, said there was nothing even slightly incriminating in the diaries." Professor Richard Gill also informed me that notes and diaries had been used as evidence against wrongly convicted nurse Lucia de Berk.

Nursing handover sheets were also infamously discovered at Letby's property. These sheets essentially enable nursing teams to hand over responsibilities for patients from one team to another, particularly at the end of working shifts. Both the police and prosecution claim that Letby kept handover sheets as trophies, noting that some of the handover sheets contained details related to patients she was alleged to have harmed.

However, it has long since been well established, and was indeed discussed in the trial, that the vast majority of handover sheets found at Letby's house were completely unrelated to the case. There were 257 sheets found, and of these 236 were unrelated to the indictment infants, while only 12 corresponded with days when infants collapsed.

Additionally, the only sheet that was in any way treasured was her first ever handover sheet, which she kept in a keepsake box with a rose. This wasn't an argument made by Lucy Letby; the rose and keepsake box were raised by the prosecution in court, although this didn't prevent prosecutor Nick Johnson from arguing that a paper towel accidentally taken home in work clothing, and then found in a Morrisons carrier bag, was somehow a treasured souvenir of evil deeds. It is also notable that there were no handover sheets found for five of the 14 infants on which Letby was convicted, further weakening the notion that there was some sort of meaningful pattern involved.

When advancing their 'trophy' theory, Cheshire Police didn't readily mention that they found several of the handover sheets in a bin bag in Letby's garage, on the verge of being thrown in the rubbish. Not really the actions of someone who treasured those handover sheets as trophies. It was also asserted throughout the trial that there is no way that a nurse could innocently take home handover sheets, even though many nurses I have spoken to say it happens all the time.

Letby provided precisely this explanation, that she'd taken them home absent-mindedly by accident, during her police interviews. "They're just sheets that have inadvertently come home with me in my pocket. I've not emptied my pockets before coming home", Letby explained. The police completely ignored Letby's explanation and it seems that no effort was made to corroborate it.

When Letby was interviewed by Cheshire Police, transcripts indicate that she was thoroughly nonplussed by this topic:

Q: Do you have anything in your possession which relates to any of the allegations for which you've been arrested?

LETBY: What do you mean, sorry?

Q: Paperwork, medical records, anything?

LETBY: No. Not that I know of, no.

Q: Okay. Have you ever taken anything relating to the babies that we've discussed home?

LETBY: No. I don't know if…I might have sometimes taken handover sheets accidentally home with me.

Q: Okay.

LETBY: Not medical notes, no.

Q: No. Not just sticking to medical notes, anything relating to?

LETBY: I don't know specifically to them. I think sometimes I have brought handover sheets home, yes.

Q: Why? What's the purpose of that?

LETBY: Just inadvertently, they've just been left in my pocket.

Some rudimentary maths would also place the number of shifts Letby worked in her CoCH career at around 1,500, meaning that she didn't take sheets home for approximately 85% of her shifts. In that light, Letby's explanation, that she inadvertently sometimes took sheets home in her pocket, appears entirely plausible.

It can also be observed from this exchange that the police do not realise that handover sheets are not medical notes. "I think people have this idea that handover notes are medical files or something. But there is no private information even on them", an experienced nurse told me. A neonatal nurse confirmed that "handover sheets do not form part of the confidential medical record. They're just notes that the nurse will make to plan the shift ahead. It's essentially just a scrap of paper with any concerns that the nurses had from that shift previously."

Furthermore, several nurses told me that they had taken handover sheets home with them. "I've been there myself. The fact that you take something home from work, and then you've got it in your house, you don't want to take it back, but also you feel you can't throw it away because it's not really yours", one nurse informed me. A neonatal practitioner told me that, "You're not supposed to take report sheets out of the hospital, but they get in your pocket or bag, and you forget. Then when you discover them at home, you're not supposed to throw them in the trash, so then you forget to get rid of them. And then this repeats. I probably have a collection of report sheets in my closet right now. Many nurses will. It doesn't mean anything."

A third nurse told me that she hadn't worked in 10 years but was certain that there would be handover sheets in her house. Far from being anything of great significance, possessing handover sheets is commonplace among nurses. Even the most superficial investigation by Cheshire Police would have established this.

Cheshire Police would cite the handover sheets again in a Netflix documentary released in February 2026, this time claiming that the scraps of paper had been stored chronologically. Unfortunately, this stands up to little scrutiny, not least because it was agreed in court that multiple handover sheets had been found in different locations. The film also inferred that Letby had stored these 'chronological' handover sheets in a box marked "Keep", when, in reality, this box contained just five sheets; less than 2% of those recovered. The chronological claim wasn't used in court, had never been heard previously, and it's hard to understand why the sheets being stored chronologically would be significant anyway, even if it were true.

The next topic of concern was Facebook and Internet searches. This was unbelievably tenuous evidence, as it is known that Letby made thousands of Facebook searches for all manner of people, the overwhelming majority of which weren't remotely related to the case. In fact, there were

31 searches for names related to the case, compared with 2,287 for names not related to the case; i.e. searches related to the case constituted 1% of her total searches.

As an example of the unsatisfactory nature of this line of inquiry, at one point during the court proceedings, Letby was asked about searching for the parents of a baby who she is alleged to have harmed on Christmas Day, the implication being that this was somehow significant. But this was over two years after the child had died, with no evidence nor cross-examination to indicate that she had searched before then. The prosecution attempted to suggest that she'd derived some glee from the search and was wallowing in grief, but if this was the case then it would surely have made more sense for her to have searched in the immediate aftermath of the baby's death, which did not occur.

Letby's searches for families on social media was presented by the prosecution as stalking behaviour. Commenting in court, Nick Johnson for the prosecution asserted that, "The truth is, ladies and gentlemen, that Lucy Letby had a fascination with the babies she had murdered and attempted to murder, and with their families. She took pleasure in her murderous handiwork." These comments were later echoed by police. There is very little to support the idea that Letby had an "unhealthy obsession" with the babies she allegedly murdered; all of the evidence points to the perfectly normal concern of a nurse and empathic human. Equally, the prosecution have advanced no evidence that Letby "took pleasure in her murderous handiwork".

There is also no evidence that Letby ever made any searches for anything relating to the methods of murder. We know this because she was never asked about it. But why would Letby research them when she has written in her own notes, which the police used in court, there is "obviously no evidence" that she has done anything wrong? Why would someone who believed that have also searched for methods of murder?

"One thing that you find with people who are guilty, if they're being interviewed by the police, for example, is that they want to know how much you know", the aforementioned creative writing professor commented. "So where the note says that there is 'obviously no evidence' – if you'd committed crimes, you'd have the question in your head: 'Well, what do they know? What have they found out? What do they know about me?' This is the antithesis of that!"

When providing its verdict on Letby's application to appeal, the Court of Appeal acknowledged that she "provided explanations for the various strands of circumstantial evidence" and acknowledges that "only 21 of those [handover] sheets related to babies on the indictment". In fact, not only are there 'explanations' for this so-called circumstantial evidence, but in my opinion, it doesn't have any value in the first place. I believe Cheshire Police should have rapidly and emphatically drawn this conclusion. There will be more on this matter in the remaining chapters.

Cheshire Police knew that her Facebook searches related to the case were trivial. They were fully aware that most handover sheets were irrelevant and there was no evidence of Letby treasuring them, not least because she told them so. They could also have taken the time to discuss this matter further with experienced nurses, but there is no evidence that they did this. They should have known that her text messages were trivial. They should have been able to conclude that her notes aren't confessional, and even if they were unable to see this, they could have called in someone with professional qualifications to analyse them. They could have taken the time to locate and interview Kathryn de Beger, but they didn't.

It is sometimes stated by defenders of the prosecution case that debunking this anecdotal evidence has no value as it was somehow unimportant. Firstly, the fact that it was presented in court, repeatedly referenced and a significant amount of time was devoted to discussing it means, automatically, that it merits consideration. This evidence could have swayed the jury; it is impossible to say otherwise. Secondly, both the Court of Appeal and the CPS have cited anecdotal evidence as being key evidence in the case. The CPS continues to do so on its website. In its verdict, the Court of Appeal made the bizarre suggestion that the "conclusions" of Dr Evans were more valid because "he did so without knowing about other circumstantial evidence relied on by the prosecution in establishing guilt…including the applicant's Facebook searches…

and the "confession" in the note recovered from the applicant's home".

Thus, demonstrating the worthlessness of this material to readers cannot be dismissed as trivial, because the organisations that are primarily responsible for prosecuting and assessing this case consider it to be relevant, and even key, evidence. Nonetheless, the view of Dr James Phillips: "I think the rest of the evidence is irrelevant if the scientific and medical evidence collapses" is difficult to disagree with. The reality is that this material should never have been submitted to court in the first place, let alone should supposedly serious institutions still be citing it as critical.

This is perhaps why, in the complete absence of any evidence indicating that Letby actually committed crimes, or any eyewitness testimony of any value whatsoever, the prosecution instead fell back on whatever they could get their hands on, Nick Johnson telling the court that the "context is everything". *The Times* noted: "In other words, there was no one piece of evidence that proved Letby to be a killer beyond all reasonable doubt. Rather, guilt was evinced by a combination of interlocking, co-dependent facts."

This can only be described as an extraordinary situation. In order to hand down 15 whole life orders, the stiffest penal sentence issued to a woman in British history, not only was no concrete evidence required, but the judge also told the jury that it was not necessary for the prosecution to prove the precise manner in which Letby had acted, only that she had acted with murderous intent.

The wholly unsatisfactory process involved in the Letby trial has led to a fundamental error of logic. Many people believe there is a huge amount of evidence against Letby. But the *quantity* of evidence doesn't determine its merit; evidence must be assessed on its *qualitative* value. Police investigator Dr Steve Watts told the journalist John Sweeney that "They haven't found a smoking gun, [and] when you look at something in isolation and say that doesn't make somebody a murderer, when you add it to something else, it still doesn't make somebody a murderer. And when you add it to five other things, that doesn't make somebody a murderer."

It seems that many people, possibly including the jury, did not understand this, and simply believe that a 'lot' of evidence in quantitative terms is indicative of guilt, which is extremely troubling. Even more troubling is the fact that the officer leading the investigation, DS Paul Hughes, seemingly cannot understand this either:

"The amount of evidence we recovered from her home address was just not expected. Thousands and thousands of documents, many devices that led to downloads of half a million pages of information that we did not expect to find."

That's great, Paul, but when are you going to show us the *good* evidence from this process?

It seems to me that the prosecution simply battered the court over the head with this sheer weight of 'evidence' for 10 months until Letby was broken in the witness box and the jury had been beaten into submission. This seems wrong to me and is not a process that is likely to result in a safe verdict. The primary purpose of the criminal justice system is to prosecute those guilty of crimes and protect those from punishment who have not committed crimes. At the heart of this must be a process that seeks to identify the truth, but in no way did this investigation or trial even remotely resemble any such search. There is no better example of this than the so-called anecdotal evidence.

In the final section of this book, some critical elements of the trial will be examined before the police investigation is put under the microscope. But first we're going to hear from arguably the most important person in the entire case.

CHAPTER 17: THE EXPERT

The first thing that I wanted to ask Dr Shoo Lee was how he felt about this whole unlikely chapter in his decorated career. "It has been a very strange and unexpected experience," he told me from his home in Canada. "I was leading a quiet life, looking after my farm, and then an email dropped in my inbox from Richard Thomas – Lucy Letby's solicitor. I wasn't even sure if it was legitimate at first, but I began reading about this nurse who had been convicted, and seemingly by using my paper. I've never enjoyed medico-legal work, but I agreed to have a look at the evidence."

And what was the initial outcome of that? "I was concerned. More than concerned. The transcripts regarding skin discolourations were obviously incorrect. Claims were being made that were not what I had written. At that point, I felt duty bound to testify at the Court of Appeal". That initial leave to appeal was rejected, which left an unpleasant sensation lingering in the aftermath. "To put a woman in jail until she dies, based on wrong information, is a tragedy. I felt that I had to speak up because no one should be imprisoned based on incorrect information. But Lucy Letby's legal team told me that there was 'nowhere else to go'. I couldn't accept this. It's just morally wrong. It can't be allowed to happen."

The response of Dr Lee to this highly regrettable situation was to assemble an international panel of the highest level of neonatal expertise. "I am not aware of an instance where this quality and quantity of experts has come forward to challenge a conviction," Dr Lee informed me. So how had Dr Lee managed to bring together such a wealth of experience? "I'm well-known around the world, not only in Canada, because of my career. So when I contacted people, I chose some of the best institutions and the most experienced and reputable people, from North America, Canada, the United States, Europe, Asia and the UK."

Did Dr Lee encounter a lot of resistance? "Not at all. Most of the experts I approached agreed to help. There were very few who declined. And they're all doing this *pro bono*. They don't need any recognition or plaudits. They are already very well-known. It was also important that various sub-specialities were involved. So in addition to neonatologists on the panel, there is a paediatric surgeon, a paediatric pathologist with forensic expertise, a paediatric infectious disease expert, an insulin scientist and we also had a very senior obstetrician join us."

This latter point is particularly important, not least because Dr Dewi Evans informed Cheshire Police that no maternity input was needed, and thus the obstetric picture of the infants was never cited evidentially in court. When I corresponded with Dr Evans, he observed that the reasoning behind this was that "neonatal notes contain detailed maternity information". Did this apply to the neonatal notes from the CoCH, I asked Dr Lee. "Certainly not! The neonatal notes contained very little maternity information, and even missed critical information that would have been necessary for medically managing the babies. We frequently had to dig information out from other sources, in order to fill in the gaps.

"In fact, this was a major deficiency in the whole case," Dr Lee explained, echoing the words of obstetricians who have been mentioned earlier in the book. "The obstetric information was highly relevant in many cases. I should say as well that the medical notes of the babies contained very little information on their obstetric history. This is highly unfortunate; you must always have comprehensive information on the obstetrics and the antenatal condition and care. The fact that it's not in the NICU notes suggests that they did not have access to the antenatal notes for some reason, which strongly implies a systemic problem.

"As an example, the mother of Child A and Child B had antiphospholipid syndrome and gestational cholestasis, but the latter was not charted in the medical records. Child D should have been given antenatal antibiotics and this never happened. Child E had a twin-to-twin transfusion, with oligohydramnios, and the antenatal ultrasound showed small, dilated bowel loops with absent and reversed end diastolic flow. This is all very significant because it means that blood wasn't flowing to the baby appropriately. This is an emergency; blood was literally being sucked out of the baby during part of the cardiac cycle and this can cause ischaemia to the organs. It's life threatening.

"And Child O had a subcapsular haematoma. This is not caused by direct abdominal trauma, as claimed by Dr Evans; rather they are the result of traction or shear forces applied to the thin, fragile liver capsule through the hepatic ligaments, usually during delivery. And this child, who was the second of triplets, had an extremely rapid delivery, which is a well recognised cause of birth injury. Then there was another triplet who also had a subcapsular haematoma, and that infant survived. Birth injury is the most likely cause of the subcapsular haematoma in both of these triplets because the delivery was precipitate [rapid] in both cases. In fact, the hospital safety committee wrote to the obstetrician asking them to look at this – the email for this is in the Thirlwall Inquiry – noting that the haematoma could have been due to a perinatal injury, which is indeed the most likely cause."

I'd heard the explanations provided by Dr Lee many times previously. Time and again, qualified professionals had strongly questioned what they often deemed to be the arcane and poorly supported theories of Dr Evans. Nonetheless, I wanted to know more about the panel. No one could reasonably question their qualifications, but there have been suggestions that they were somehow lacking in impartiality, so I put this to Dr Lee.

"This is unfounded. Some of the top specialists from around the world are involved in this. From the UK, we have Professor Neena Modi, former president of the Royal College of Paediatrics and Child Health, Professor Marta Cohen, vice president of the Royal College of Pathology, and Professor Phil Bennett, who is the Director of the Institute of Reproductive and Developmental Biology, and a very senior obstetrician at Imperial College. These people have no need of money or recognition. They're doing it because, quite simply, it's the right thing to do. And the panel started from the assumption that if we found evidence of guilt then that would be published. If the panel had discovered that, it would have been the end of any appeal from Lucy Letby. But they found the opposite. They found no evidence of any murders."

There have been claims made by Dr Sandie Bohin in a *Daily Mail* podcast that the panel somehow didn't have access to all of the documents that were available to her, I informed Dr Lee. How would he respond to that? "Well, it's simply untrue. The International Expert Panel retrieved all medical records and transcripts, along with all of the reports from the prosecution witnesses. Additionally, we have seen new information from the Thirlwall Inquiry; we have, in fact, examined significantly more information than Dr Evans and Dr Bohin."

In the early part of our discussion, Dr Lee had already hinted at major problems within the CoCH. It was notable to me that so much of the court case was predicated on evidence provided by staff from the hospital, usually doctors, who claimed to have never seen anything of this nature before. Was that surprising to Dr Lee? "Yes it was. There could be a few explanations for this. Firstly, they may have been inexperienced doctors. They might not have seen, for example, the sort of discolourations that they encountered before. But on a Level 3 unit, we would see them all the time.

"During the appeal, I presented an example of a baby who had asphyxia at birth, and he had every single skin discolouration described in this case. Rachel Aviv from the *New Yorker* actually wrote to me and said that should have blown the whole argument out of the water immediately.

"Another possibility is a lack of monitoring. We know about the ward rounds on this unit. That can then lead to things not being properly recorded at the time. Then our memories can fail us. And I think all of these things are tied together. But, ultimately, what they often seemed to describe as unprecedented was, in fact, nothing out of the ordinary."

In the by now infamous February 2025 press conference, one of the headline-generating comments from Dr Lee was the assertion that the CoCH would be closed down if it was located in Canada. This cannot have been something that Dr Lee said lightly, so how bad was the situation on this neonatal unit? "Well, firstly we identified 25 major problems, which we have shared in our summary reports. These are not trivial things, they are serious issues. And then with regard to specific infants, in every case we found, not one, but multiple errors. Multiple repeated mistakes. And then we identified multiple reasons for those errors, processes not being conducted correctly, basic observations being missed, and so on. Yet somehow Dr Evans never picked out any one of these."

It was inevitable that our conversation would arrive at the topic of Dr Dewi Evans sooner or later. During a documentary aired on Channel 4 in September 2025, footage of Dr Lee had been shown to Dr Evans, during which Lee had questioned why Evans never cited any medical failings at the CoCH. As discussed in "Injection of Air Hypothesis", my own investigation discovered that the solitary thing Evans was able to cite, antibiotics in the case of Child D, was erroneous. When speaking in court, Evans had never volunteered this information, he had downplayed its significance, and even argued that Child D received exemplary treatment. This was despite the fact that in his initial notes for Child D, Evans had cited poor care on both 21 and 22 June, which somehow melted away in court. And this was the standalone example, from all of his five years of work and many hours in court, that Evans was able to cite of him criticising some aspect of care on the unit, and even this claim turned out to be a phantom!

What was Dr Lee's opinion on the work of Dr Evans? "It defies all logic", Dr Lee replied. "It contravened multiple principles of medicine. The first thing you should do is look for the most obvious explanation, not for some very remote, obscure cause. The second thing is that you must assess whether the disease or medical mismanagement can account for the death or injury. After that, then you consider other possibilities in your differential diagnosis list, to make sure you did not miss something. These are fundamental principles of medicine that all doctors should follow. I see no evidence that he did that. Instead, in this case the expert went looking for the most obscure methods of malfeasance, instead of the far more likely explanations related to natural causes or medical mismanagement."

Had Dr Lee been surprised when he encountered the allegations of air embolism? "Yes, not least because my paper is from 1989! I'm not sure there has ever been another scenario where someone has dug up a paper of that vintage, and then used it so prominently to support a conviction of this magnitude. And then used it incorrectly as well!"

Could Dr Lee walk me through the problems with the air embolism theory? "Well, firstly, I am one of the few people who *has* encountered a few cases. So there is that very rare grounding to begin with." In fact, Dr Lee is more pivotal in this field than this modest description suggests. The clinical sign of air embolism, the Lee sign, has been named after him, since his 1989 observation of previously undocumented skin discolouration in a newborn.

Had anything of this nature been present at the CoCH? "No. They were all either generalised or localised skin discolourations that would be expected in any baby that collapses. From all of the descriptions, from the trial transcripts and what was written in the medical records, I did not find anything that was even remotely convincing. In fact, skin discolouration is not automatically relevant, let alone important, in the diagnosis of air embolism. Air embolism results in a number of different presentations, and one of them *can* be skin discolouration. That doesn't mean that any skin discolouration is diagnostic of air embolism.

"There are three kinds of skin discolouration described with air embolism. The most important is the Lee sign, which appears as bright red blood vessels superimposed upon a cyanosed or blue background. This occurs because in air embolism, air bubbles can block the blood vessels, leading to circulatory collapse, resulting in a shortage of blood going to the skin and organs, and tissue hypoxia. This causes the skin to turn pale and then blue. Then, in air embolism, as the air bubbles travel through the blood vessels to the skin, the oxygen in the air bubbles oxygenate the red blood cells adjacent to the air bubbles. The red blood cells turn red, and this results in a pattern of red blood vessels spreading out from central to peripheral areas, resembling a tree. This lasts for just a few minutes because the oxygen in the red blood cells quickly diffuses out of the blood vessels into the surrounding tissue. The blood vessels then lose their red colouring, and the patterning disappears after a few minutes. This phenomenon I have described has never been seen in any other condition, nor can it be explained by any other condition. That's why it's diagnostic of air embolism, *if* you see it."

I asked Dr Lee to explain this further. "There are two other kinds of skin discolouration that have been described with air embolism – generalised skin discolouration and localised skin discolouration. Generalised skin discolouration essentially means that a large area of the body is discoloured in a uniform way. For example, when you go outside into the cold during winter without clothes, your whole body quickly turns pale or blue. It can also appear mottled, which is a pattern like a pinkish net over a pale background, due to some areas of the skin having a reduced blood supply. An example of localised skin discolouration is when you fall and hurt your knee, there can be a patch of localised skin discolouration, typically blue, purple, red or brown. Both generalised and localised skin discolourations can be caused by any number of conditions that lead to circulatory collapse and hypoxia, including sepsis, respiratory problems and asphyxia.

"In air embolism, skin discolourations are caused by circulatory collapse and hypoxia. When this happens, the blood vessels in the skin attempt to redistribute available blood by dilating and constricting – so some areas have less blood supply and will appear darker, and the patches can migrate and are transient. Actually, only 10% of air embolisms have reported skin discolourations. That is another reason to doubt the prosecution citing discolouration; this should only occur 10% of the time, and yet it's being cited in multiple consecutive cases. It's difficult to imagine that this is possible."

This final point of Dr Lee could even be considered an understatement. Discolouration and mottling were cited repeatedly throughout the court case as diagnostic factors – in 14 out of 15 air embolism collapses. Discolouration was also erroneously cited in other infants, but if one sticks to the cases for which it could conceivably be relevant then there was a phenomenally unlikely 93% prevalence across these collapses, compared with the 10% that would be expected. This is extraordinarily unlikely to happen. Something that should occur once or twice across 15 incidents very rarely happens 14 times; indeed the odds are astronomically high, trillions to one based on a simple study that I conducted. Essentially, for discolouration to occur across all of these infants, with the prevalence that it did, and for this to all be caused by air embolism, is virtually impossible.

Dr Evans should have known this because the information was included in the 1989 *Lee and Tanswell* paper that he used diagnostically, before later being updated and refined in a 2025 literature review. Defence barrister Ben Myers even cited the 11% figure for air embolism discolouration that was available at the time during the court case.

But this certainly isn't the only problem with the diagnosis of Dr Evans, as Dr Lee outlined: "Air embolism is a very specific diagnosis. So when Dr Evans states this was a diagnosis of exclusion that is fundamentally wrong. This should never be a diagnosis of exclusion. Never. You must have definitive proof, such as the Lee sign, or imaging at the time of the event in order to diagnose air embolism, which simply did not exist in these cases. Quite the opposite; the evidence cited, using my paper as the diagnostic source, was plainly wrong."

One can imagine what an enormous difference it would have made in the original trial for the jury to have heard this sort of forensic detail, particularly considering that the *Lee and Tanswell* paper was critically important. All of the injection of air cases could essentially be thrown out of court. Defence barrister Ben Myers described evidence from Evans as "treat[ing] a wide variety of cutaneous discolouration as diagnostic", which opinion Dr Lee said was "hitting the nail on the head". Approximately three quarters of the way through the original trial, Myers used this argument in an application of no case to answer, requesting multiple counts to be excluded from the case. It is now known that the arguments made by Myers were scientifically correct, but Judge James Goss rejected the application on 2 May 2023.

But that wasn't the end of the problems with the work of the prosecution witnesses, as Dr Lee explained: "Dr Evans has cited five criteria for diagnosing an air embolism. These are that the babies were stable, there was no medical explanation for collapse, the aforementioned skin discolouration, evidence of air in X-ray and that the infants didn't respond to resuscitation. So the first three of these can be discounted immediately. The babies were not stable, the panel has found a wealth of reasonable medical explanations for collapses and the discolouration evidence is plain wrong. That should automatically invalidate the diagnosis."

X-rays were not available for most infants in the indictment and, as discussed previously, in the case of Child C, Dr Evans had shifted the date of the cited collapse away from the date that an X-ray was actually available. But that wasn't the only issue with this supposed criterion for diagnosis. "Air in the great vessels on post-mortem was largely cited in relation to Child A," Dr Lee explained. "And in this infant, the X-ray was taken three days after death. This makes it untenable. You cannot use this for diagnosis because there are multiple reasons why the air can be present in the blood vessels. One of these is cardiopulmonary resuscitation. There is an excellent and comprehensive study which found that in 89% of cases, this did indeed introduce air." Dr Lee also referenced a study, primarily authored by Quisling, indicating that air can appear in the blood vessels within 25 minutes of death, rendering such post-mortem X-rays irrelevant diagnostically.

"Regarding resuscitation, Dr Evans claimed that it should be possible to resuscitate any infant. This is simply untrue," Dr Lee continued. "If it were true then no infants would pass away. If you're going to incarcerate someone in Britain every time an infant fails to be resuscitated in a hospital, you will need to build a lot more prisons!" I mentioned to him that there had been claims from prosecution witness Dr Sandie Bohin that all resuscitations performed at the CoCH on indictment infants had been of an acceptable standard. "Well, I should remind Dr Bohin that she actually criticised the resuscitation for Child H. This was a straightforward case of pneumothorax [collapsed lung]. The management and resuscitation was so confused and muddled, as Dr Bohin put it, that the infant ended up being transferred to a Level 3 unit. The expert who examined this case agreed with Dr Bohin, and told me that they had never encountered such a messed up resuscitation in their entire life.

"Child B was resuscitated and intubated three times, her vocal chords were red, swollen and inflamed. Eventually, they gave up and put her on CPAP. I don't think this can be described as good resuscitation. For Child C, one of the nurses had never done cardiac compressions before.

The medical registrar was called, he had three unsuccessful attempts at intubation before the consultant came. Then there was a 20-minute delay, during which there was marked respiratory and metabolic acidosis. In the case of Child D, this infant became pale and floppy at 12 minutes of life, needed bagging [manual ventilation], and the hospital didn't do a blood gas test or chest X-ray until four hours later. That is just unacceptable. And there are many other examples.

"So to claim that all of these resuscitations were optimal, or even acceptable, is untrue. Dr Evans never cited any of these obvious errors, while also claiming that every infant can be automatically resuscitated, and then he used this as his final criterion to diagnose air embolism. This is simply not tenable."

In common with many nurses I interviewed, Dr Lee is sceptical that the alleged attacks are logistically feasible. "After you introduce the air into the intravenous tubing, you then need to clear the air from this tubing by re-infusing fluid, and this takes time. If you don't do this, someone will notice air in the tubing. It is hard to believe that someone can introduce the amount of air required, via a small syringe, then re-infuse the line with fluid, with other people in close proximity, alarms potentially sounding, and then supposedly do this so many times without anyone suspecting anything."

I asked Dr Lee about the ability of Dr Evans to diagnose an embolism before he even knew about the discolouration, solely from the sudden collapse of an infant and failure to resuscitate. "This is totally ludicrous," Dr Lee responded. "Ultimately, air embolism should be at the very bottom of your differential diagnosis list. You shouldn't be, instead, deciding on it with absolutely no meaningful diagnostic criteria, and then shifting it to the top of the list. This is completely wrong."

At the time I spoke with Dr Lee, there had been claims published that the eminent neonatologist had somehow made mistakes in his research. Liz Hull and Caroline Cheetham discussed the issue on the *Daily Mail* podcast, and focused firstly on alleged errors related to two forms of air embolism – venous and arterial. Assertions were made that Dr Lee was wrong to have stated that air cannot cross internally from the venous to arterial circulation. I put these claims to Dr Lee.

"Air embolism is a condition in which air is introduced into the bloodstream, or the circulatory system, and that can block the blood vessels, leading to circulatory collapse and lack of oxygen in the tissues. Arterial air embolism is when air is introduced into the arteries, so that blocks the blood supply going to the organs and skin, because the arteries supply the organs and the skin with blood, causing circulatory collapse.

"Venous air embolism is when air is introduced into the veins, and the veins carry blood away from the organs and the skin. So this is potentially less dangerous because it is carrying blood away. And not only that, the blood first must go through the lungs before it is distributed to the rest of the body. And air bubbles tend to get filtered out in the lungs, and so they don't actually cross over into the arterial system.

"Newborn babies have a small opening in the heart that we call the foramen ovale, and also a small duct called the ductus arteriosus, that can remain patent for a few hours to a few days after birth, before closing spontaneously. And because there is this hole and duct, it is possible for air bubbles in the venous system to cross these holes into the arterial side of the heart and enter the arteries directly.

"However, these air bubbles have to travel against a pressure gradient, because of the arterial pressure. When you have your blood pressure taken, it will be 120 over 80 for example, with 120 being the arterial pressure and 80 being the venous pressure. So it's difficult to cross that pressure gradient. However, it's theoretically possible.

"Earlier we discussed the various types of skin discolouration, and how only the Lee sign is diagnostic of air embolism. If you look through the literature, it's very clear that venous air embolism cases have only described generalised skin discolourations. No cases of patchy skin discolourations have ever been described. You cannot therefore go to court and claim that patchy skin discolourations equal air embolism. It simply does not work.

"I never once said that air cannot move from the venous to the arterial system. In fact, I acknowledged that venous air can theoretically access the arterial systemic circulation through the patent foramen ovale in both my 1989 and 2025 papers. It is just that this is irrelevant to the findings, because of the phenomena that we have discussed."

There were also claims made in the same podcast that Dr Lee had excluded some research papers from his study. What was his response to this?

"There is a simple explanation for this. When you publish a paper, you have a limited amount of space to write your references. And in a paper containing 117 cases, it's not practical to have 117 references. Thus, 32 references were included in the main article, with other references placed into a supplementary reference list that was posted by the journal online. Unfortunately, the podcasters did not do their homework and did not look at the supplementary material; consequently they missed these references, all of which were included.

"There was one paper not included. This was a paper authored by Willis. But there was a good reason for this. We investigated this case in some depth. This was published several decades ago, when very little was known about air embolism. And it was believed at the time that this case involved venous air embolism that resulted in paraplegia and spinal injury, and injury to multiple organs with blood in the urine and stools.

"This would mean clinically that there either had to be a massive air embolism going to multiple organs, or there was a large bubble in the heart that blocked the blood supply coming out of the heart. And in either of those scenarios, one would expect the baby to have signs of circulatory collapse, and yet he was stable throughout, which would be very unlikely if there was such a massive air embolism.

"An alternative explanation is that there was thrombosis of a vascular malformation around the spine, resulting in spinal injury and paraplegia, with embolisation causing injury to other organs like the kidney and intestine. There was some corroborating evidence, in that the blood clotting time had increased. This doesn't happen in air embolism but it can happen in thrombosis, and furthermore, an ultrasound of the kidney discovered a clot in the left kidney. Unfortunately, the authors did not investigate for vascular malformation of the spine, so we can't be certain of this.

"Since we were unsure of the diagnosis, we chose to exclude that paper in the 1989 review. In the 2025 paper, the methodology was that we accepted all of the cases from the 1989 paper. We then conducted a literature review to look for new cases that were published after 1989, and then we added those. And that was stated clearly in the paper as well.

"The podcast also claimed that there was a recent case reported from Taiwan in November 2025 that showed the Lee sign in an infant with venous air embolism. That is incorrect. Without going into this in great depth, this is just another case of arterial air embolism with patchy skin discolouration. Again, this could have been confirmed very easily if they had read the paper carefully." Dr Lee indeed went into much more detail regarding this recent case when speaking with *The Sun* newspaper. So what would his concluding words be regarding the claims made in this podcast? "All of these supposed criticisms are wrong. It would, in fact, have been very easy to confirm this with minimal research."

I also discussed a couple of the other infants from the case with Dr Lee. In the case of Child E, Dr Lee pointed to the fact that, even in an adult, 20% blood loss will cause hypovolemic shock and collapse. "At this level of blood loss, with 25% blood loss at least, plus more likely lost down the intestine, the infant would collapse immediately. There was a very clear and obvious failure here with resuscitation and blood transfusion." What did Dr Lee think of Dr Sandie Bohin's claim that the infant hadn't died due to blood loss? "I cannot understand how she could say that."

Another critical infant was Child O, one of three triplets. In this case, Dr Lee cited serious suboptimal treatment, which was important, considering the details of the case. "These infants were born in rapid succession, one minute apart, increasing the chances of injury. And the hospital realised this, but the Thirlwall Inquiry never heard about this. It was only revealed in an email that was released recently." Dr Lee is referring to an email from Ruth Millward, Head of Risk and Patient Safety at the CoCH in 2016, who discussed "further review by obstetricians regarding delivery and possibility that the liver subcapsular haematoma (identified on PM) occurred in [the] perinatal period".

Dr Lee explained to me that "this kind of injury doesn't have a massive bleed right away. Because the liver has a capsule, the bleeding seeps out and accumulates over time, and it gets worse". So what were the mistakes made on the unit? "Firstly, this is a failure of diagnosis. And we come back to having inexperienced doctors working at the CoCH. In a Level 3 unit, the possibility of a haematoma would be at the forefront of any experienced neonatologist's mind."

Could this infant have been saved? "It's possible. Some haematomas will rupture and, sadly, death will result. But the critical thing is recognition and then appropriate management. We know that this hospital did not succeed when it came to recognition. We also know that they ventilated this infant at a pressure that was too high, putting increased pressure on the chest. This then effectively blocks the blood from returning to the heart. This makes a bad situation much worse.

"The haematoma, almost inevitably, ruptured. And then, to make things even worse, they inserted a needle into the abdomen because they thought it was abdominal distension from gastric distension, because they were bagging. This can result in air entering the stomach, but the answer to this is not to put a needle into the abdomen. It's to put a nasogastric tube into the stomach and suck the air out. You do not decompress gaseous distension of the stomach with a needle. You should also never put a needle into the abdomen without ultrasound guidance, as occurred here.

"There was a laceration in the liver that was reported by the pathologist, likely caused by this blind needle insertion. And the high ventilation pressure is a major factor in this because it pushed down the liver, making it more susceptible to injury. But the fundamental underlying problem was the haematoma from delivery and poor management. And the obstetric history is very relevant here, when you consider that two of the triplet infants had haematomas. So we need access to the obstetric notes in order to better understand what happened at delivery. But there is certainly a possibility that this infant could have been saved with better treatment."

My time with Dr Lee was drawing to a close, but there was still one essential thing that had to be put to him. Lucy Letby remains a convicted serial killer of babies. Overturning her conviction, regardless of which side of the fence you find yourself, must be considered a big deal. If Lucy Letby is exonerated, it would be a news story of nuclear impact. Did Dr Lee have any doubt about the conclusions of the panel? Was there a possibility that they were wrong? Could Lucy Letby conceivably be guilty?

Dr Lee addressed these questions with a calm assurance, and with words that will stay with me for the rest of my life:

"Anyone who reads the reports and still thinks that Lucy Letby is guilty should have their head examined."

CHAPTER 18: TRIAL AND RETRIAL PROCESS

There was much that was worrying and flawed about the trial of Lucy Letby. A fundamental problem that plagued both the trial and retrial was the assumption that almost every action of Letby had the worst possible intention, even when there was another interpretation that was more logical. As an example, the jury heard that Letby wanted to "garner sympathy" from colleagues when messaging them with concerns, rather than the more obvious explanation – she was genuinely upset about the death of babies and was seeking reassurance and emotional support.

This was but one of countless possible misrepresentations that was circulated during the trial. One of these, which is now widely believed by millions of people, is that Letby showed no emotion regarding the deaths of babies. In fact, the trial had to be interrupted because Letby broke down in tears when being questioned over Child E. She also cried when telling the police about the death of two triplets, and had previously broken down in tears on the unit, as the court was informed on 27 January 2023. The crying during the Child E testimony occurred just 12 days before prosecutor Nick Johnson accused Letby of not crying. At the time of Johnson's claim, the deaths of two triplet brothers were being discussed, but the court had already heard that Letby had cried during police questioning related to those infants.

The Court of Appeal repeated another accusation that was levelled at Letby in court: "She appeared to be fixated with being involved in events in the intensive care nursery and involved herself unnecessarily with babies who had been designated to other nurses." An obvious explanation is that Letby felt responsible as an experienced nurse on the unit, and was responding to emergencies in a way that she deemed appropriate.

The decision of Judge James Goss to exclude the RCPCH report of the CoCH neonatal unit was questionable at the very least. "The jury was left without a key third-party assessment of the unit", Sloane Spade asserted. "Conclusions about the hospital were backed by a report that actually visited and visualised the unit at the time of these incidents, but this was withheld from jurors. I really can't understand why." Similarly, Goss ruled that the grievance procedure was "not a matter that the court should get involved with", and consequently Letby's defence was denied the opportunity to explore this critical context.

It is interesting to note that every time Letby was accused of murder, the jury found her guilty. They did, however, find her not guilty of other charges in which babies did not die. This does suggest a typical flaw in human reasoning – a baby died, therefore there has to be an explanation for this, and the only explanation we've been given is that Letby killed them. When babies did not die, suddenly there could be another possible explanation.

"Juries often do not understand or follow the instructions that they're given during trials", jury expert Dr Thea Gumbert told me. "One of the mistakes they're very prone to making is reversing the onus of proof. No matter how much and how clearly they're told that the defendant does not have to prove their innocence, a lot of them still operate that way. There is tonnes of research that supports this."

Nick Johnson, lead prosecutor, argued in court that "in this extraordinary case, context is everything", the implication being that the broader canvas painted by the prosecution is somehow more significant than the actual facts. Dr James Phillips aired his view: "The safety of the conviction depends not just on each individual point of evidence and argument, but on how each relate to each other, which alters the confidence you have in each point. It is not apparent to me that anyone in the chain of events leading from Letby…possessed the skillset or perspective needed to detect catastrophically weak links in this web of evidential relationships. This required a scientifically trained mind looking holistically at how the parts relate, and this was conspicuously absent."

This, and the general wedging together of weak blocks of evidence, helps explain how Letby can be convicted and handed a life sentence in the case of Child K which arguably would not have reached court if it had been a standalone case. Indeed, this could apply to every infant in the trial. An array of "interlocking" arguments, to quote *The Times*, have been assembled, and it seems no one has stepped back to look at each case properly.

As an example, with reference to Child K, Dr Ravi Jayaram commented that, "If the incident had happened in isolation, I probably would have thought nothing more of it." He *did* think nothing of it at the time, reporting it to no one, taking no action and not mentioning it in the grievance procedure. Even in the meetings with Cheshire Police in May 2017, Jayaram conceded that there would have been no suspicion regarding certain infants without the coincidence of Letby being on duty.

Attempts to charge Lucy Letby with further murders and attempted murders floundered on 20 January 2026 when the CPS "concluded that the evidential test was not met in any of [the] cases" submitted by Cheshire Police. This prompted a surprisingly petulant response from Cheshire Police, in which the constabulary indicated their belief that "the evidence submitted met the CPS charging standard". Letby's barrister, Mark McDonald, reflected that Cheshire Police were "so invested" in further proving Letby's guilt "because they are seeing this case crumble".

Few neutral observers shared the opinion of Cheshire Police on these cases. A handful of alleged tube extubations related to infants in Liverpool, where Letby had been working on a placement, had featured prominently in this submission, and the BBC's *Panorama* had already taken something of a pummelling by seemingly offering tacit support for their credibility. When the dust settled, it became clear that the Liverpool cases involved four tubes falling out, with no eyewitness, no other evidence, no indication that any infant had been harmed and no meaningful indication that Letby was even cot-side or unsupervised.

Many believe that the decision of the CPS reflected the willingness of McDonald to unleash 31 experts on the court in the event of Letby being charged on these new cases. McDonald told *The Times*: "The defence can challenge that 'bad character' in a new trial and call evidence to say she's not guilty of that original case. I think [the CPS] know that and I'm sure that played on their mind as well. You could have a trial within a trial. You could have all this evidence being called to say she wasn't guilty."

This was not the first time that allegations were made against Letby which make little sense from a practical perspective when one considers what actually occurs on a neonatal unit. During the original court case, little consideration was given to the logistical likelihood of allegations made against Letby. For example, during the alleged murder of Child A, there were at least five staff members in the room. Letby has supposedly injected air into the umbilical venous catheter of this baby with all of these colleagues stood around her.

Experienced nurses have informed me that syringes are irradiated in sterile packaging. They are essentially wrapped in cellophane. So Letby would need to gain physical access to the syringe, without disturbing anyone, on what are usually extremely attentive units. She would need to remove the syringe from this packaging, while there was, according to court testimony, a nurse attending to another baby in a neighbouring incubator, while there are two doctors in the room, then draw the air up to make the injection, lift the lid of the incubator and reach into which one of the tubes that she supposedly used. She has to do this multiple times without being detected because there are serious question marks about how much air would need to be injected.

An advanced neonatal nurse practitioner who has been working on NICUs for 17 years told me that a "really large amount of air" would be required to "cause a significant air embolism". This would pose significant problems because this would require "more than usually just a small syringe". Another nurse with 18 years of experience agreed. "You're looking at perhaps one third of any air injected actually going where it's intended. It's not ergonomically, mechanically possible, let alone is it logistically feasible considering the number of people around her." A third nurse that I interviewed who has given up on her ambitions to be a neonatal nurse because of the Letby case said: "Neonatal units are busy units. You've got other nurses in there with you, doctors in there, parents walking in and out all the time on the unit, even during the night. The idea of being able to do this and go undetected – it's from fantasy land. The likelihood is non-existent."

Michele Worden further added: "You have to attach this 10ml syringe to the nasogastric tube, inject the air, remove the syringe, draw it up again. Some of the air would leak out of the top of the nasogastric tube during the process. The baby would naturally push this air out of its system. And then you've got to repeat that several times. And nobody in an intensive care unit sees you doing it. Ridiculous!"

Throughout the trial, numerous references were made to Letby being alone with infants at night, while they collapsed or died. A thematic review from the CoCH, again published in February 2016, notes that six babies from nine deaths reviewed collapsed between midnight and 4am. But the notion that there was a disproportionate number of deaths on the unit at night is poorly founded. There were 13 deaths on the unit during this period, and seven of them occurred between the hours of 8:20am and 7:05pm.

It has also frequently been asserted that deaths on the unit somehow 'followed' Lucy Letby from night to day when her shifts were reassigned. But Letby wasn't moved to day shifts until April 2016, after which only two of the 13 deaths on the unit actually occurred. These were Child O, in which there is strong evidence of medical error, and Child P, an infant suffering with a subcapsular haematoma (as was Child O). There are simply far more compelling medical reasons for the sad deaths of these infants than Letby changing shift patterns.

While the plausibility of vast swathes of the prosecution case went largely unchallenged, Letby's conduct was placed under the microscope to a degree that bordered on the ridiculous. One example of this was supposed lies that Letby told in court, which were related to critical matters such as whether or not she was wearing pyjamas, or if she owned a shredder.

The comment about her pyjamas passed by in a flash:

MYERS: And you were taken to a police station, is that right?
LETBY: In my pyjamas, yes.

The prosecution attempted to turn the tables and state that Letby lied about wearing pyjamas. However, when Netflix released a documentary on the Letby investigation in February 2026, it became evident that Letby *had* been arrested while wearing nightwear. In fact, one arrest involved the police barging into her bedroom at 6am while she was still in bed.

Another one of the alleged lies was when she was cross-examined about having mistakenly stated that she didn't own a shredder. During cross-examination, Letby said, not unreasonably, that she hadn't recalled this because it wasn't a significant item in her house. "Like the pieces of paper?" Nick Johnson retorted. Of course, Letby could have shredded this so-called 'evidence' with her shredder, had she wanted to cover it up. In fact, the prosecution even conceded that the paper "could have gone in the shredder" during the cross-examination of Letby, and Paul Hughes of Cheshire Police also acknowledged this during the Netflix film.

In another incident in court, Johnson accused Letby of lying about being cut off and isolated from friends on the neonatal unit. Letby had described her colleagues as "supportive", but that she had been told not to contact anyone on the unit. In response to this, Johnson accused her of telling a "sob story". But a statement submitted to the Thirlwall Inquiry in February 2025 by nurse Clare Bevan confirmed the account of Letby to be accurate. Bevan stated plainly that neonatal staff were told "not to have any contact" with Letby. Letby's tutor at the University of Chester, Ruth Sadik, further confirmed to me that Letby had confided in her: "I received this highly distressed phone call from Lucy, because she was really isolated at that time."

Can Lucy Letby really be legitimately accused of lying after 30 police interviews in which she cooperated endlessly, patiently answering question after question, without significant pause, giving entirely normal and plausible answers throughout, and never giving any indication of lying whatsoever, or even needing to search her memory for the answer to a question? If she knew the answer, she provided it immediately, and if she did not know the answer, she indicated this without commotion. Everything about her demeanour and answers indicates a commitment to telling the truth.

Conversely, there can be no better example of how ludicrous the prosecution cross-examination of Letby herself was at times:

JOHNSON: Do you dispute you were in the room at the time of the collapse?
LETBY: Yes, because I have no memory of that.
JOHNSON: Do you remember being born?
LETBY: No.
JOHNSON: Do you dispute being born?
LETBY: No.

Remember, these are supposed to be adults discussing extremely serious allegations that would result in the stiffest penal sentence that a woman has received in Britain since the abolition of the death penalty. It's easy to forget that when the discourse and level of argument plummets to the approximate level of an eight-year-old. Many would suggest that this is little more than bullying tactics from a highly experienced barrister, and there is a strong argument that Judge James Goss should have stepped in.

"In my view, the prosecution's interaction with Lucy was absolutely outrageous", Dr Margaret Ferguson asserted. "It was intimidatory and really quite abusive. And from her answers that I've read, she seemed to be sort of quietly speaking the truth, and yet it was deliberately distorted. I thought it was disgraceful." Stephen Phelps similarly asserted that the way Johnson questioned Letby was "absolutely disgraceful".

Another statement of the prosecution that could be criticised was the assertion that the mother of Child E and Child F "caught Lucy Letby red-handed". This claim was made by Johnson in his closing statement, without objection or intervention, despite the fact that it is agreed evidence that no one has ever seen Letby do anything harmful to an infant. It is hard to understand how this was allowed, and why there was no interruption from Judge Goss. Goss had also directed that the prosecution could deliver its whole case at once, rather than each baby being dealt with individually, as requested by the defence. This is believed by some to be influential in the decision not to call Dr Hall, meaning that Letby had no medical defence witnesses in court.

While Letby was expected to possess perfect recall of everything that has ever happened to her, those involved with the prosecution were allowed greater leeway: for example, Dr Evans misremembered events on numerous occasions; prosecuting barrister Nick Johnson was forced to concede that he'd accused Letby of lying in court, but was proved to be wrong, as he acknowledged himself; Dr Jayaram's memory was unreliable.

Events were recalled incorrectly, other recollections were inserted into the court case that we now know to be incorrect, the swipe-card data which was used by the prosecution was wrong, the existence of a back staircase renders this swipe-card data worthless anyway, there were cases and collapses being shifted around and in and out of the court case and the reliance on a shift chart was fundamentally flawed.

Uncertainty was an acknowledged element of the case against Letby. During the original trial, the judge told the jury that it was not necessary for the prosecution to prove the precise manner in which Letby had acted, only that she had acted with murderous intent. Such an instruction appears strange and unsatisfactory, considering the very specific allegations that were made against her and the degree to which some of these methods have since been criticised. The fact that Letby was found guilty of every murder suggests that this instruction might have been misconstrued; a baby died, therefore Letby must have acted with "murderous intent".

Dr James Phillips said: "If it had been clearly established that this cluster of deaths and collapses could only have occurred due to malign intent, maybe the instruction from the judge would be justified. But we know that's not the case. We're dealing with an unproven cluster of unexplained deaths, which then, of course, leaves open the enormous question of whether they were even harmed in the first place. It therefore seems hugely inappropriate that the judge stated the prosecution don't need to prove how the infants were harmed."

Private Eye spoke with one of the UK's top forensic pathologists regarding the post-mortems at the CoCH, and what initially emerges is an interesting explanation of the grey areas involved: "People often assume pathologists will have the definitive answer, but there are many uncertainties and shades of grey, and we tend to be fairly cautious in our pronouncements. Paediatric cases take science to the very limits. We use phrases like 'this feature raises the possibility of…' We have learned from past terrible injustices in criminal trials the dangers of declaring a sign is beyond doubt." Let's compare these views with comments made by Dr Evans when speaking with S4C News, aired on 29 August 2024: "Without a doubt, she was responsible for murdering the seven babies and without a doubt she was responsible for trying to kill a number of other babies."

Private Eye then went on to question the pathologist on the certainty that was displayed in court: "I can't say in this case, but my experience in court is that paediatric clinicians can be extremely hawkish and dogmatic on the stand. In one case I was involved in, a paediatrician argued that a child definitely had an infection on clinical grounds when there was simply no microbiological or PCR test evidence that they had. The jury sided with the paediatrician and the parent was deemed negligent for leaving a child when it had an infection.

"In general, the courts want an answer at all costs, even when there isn't one, and it's easy for a jury to be wooed by an expert with oodles of confidence, who presents very well and gives certain answers. You definitely need to hear both sides. All I can say about the Letby case is that it amazes me that she didn't have a battery of defence experts."

Professor Carola Vinuesa outlined some of the misconceptions about medicine and problems with the way that evidence was presented in this case. "Medicine isn't a crossword puzzle. It often doesn't have one simple, definitive answer. We're only learning now about how complex things are. There are about 10,000 rare genetic diseases, many of which are not even in textbooks and have only recently been discovered. Because of this, paediatricians would not be able to diagnose them without genetic testing. If a patient presents with an unusual constellation of symptoms, there can be any number of rare medical explanations, including genetic ones. Even today, we cannot explain all causes. Medicine is full of uncertainty."

This can be contrasted with the words of Dr Evans, who told *The Slow Newscast* podcast that, "Babies are simple things…there's not a lot that can go wrong with them." Professor David Livermore posed the following, not unreasonable, question to Dr Evans: "If babies are so simple, then why is there an entire specialty of neonatology?"

Twelve months earlier, Dr Evans had conceded that he himself could see no conceivable motive for Letby's alleged acts: "It's impossible to believe it, and I still can't believe it. I have no explanation why she would have done something like that."

While the law does not require a motive to convict, and this is absolutely fair, it is still something of a mystery why a woman who had dedicated her entire life to nursing, choosing this career path from a very early age, who had never shown anything other than total dedication to her profession, suddenly decided to start killing babies while exhibiting no signs of psychological disorder or deterioration. This was never adequately addressed in court. The prosecution was clearly aware that the absence of motive was a major flaw in their case and so attempted to fabricate something related to a relationship with a doctor. But this was not only wholly unconvincing – it wasn't even remotely demonstrated by any of the materials presented in court and has now been largely jettisoned. To this day, no one has a plausible motive or motivation for Letby to have committed any of the alleged crimes.

Even in light of the massive problems with the trial and judicial process outlined in this book, the jury still deliberated for 13 days without reaching a unanimous decision. The amount of time they spent suggests, by its very nature, that there was some doubt. And that was following an utterly one-sided court process in which Letby was barely afforded any defence. Imagine the level of doubt today, with all of the evidence that has since been publicised.

In such an important and high-profile case, with the most serious consequences possible for the defendant, it seems deeply unsatisfactory that Judge Goss allowed a majority verdict. This is not some partial perspective; the dangers are well established. In the wake of Andrew Malkinson's wrongful imprisonment, *The Guardian* was one of several publications to report on research which indicated that at least 56 miscarriages of justice have occurred in cases in England and Wales where the jury was split. In Letby's trial, 11 convictions were via a majority, and this occurred in a case during which one jury member retired. Other procedural concerns related to the jury were raised, and these are discussed extensively in the Court of Appeal verdict.

Despite the dizzying array of problems with the court case, there have still been efforts to defend the process, not least by the CPS. In the generic statement the organisation typically releases when questioned, the CPS states that "two juries have assessed the evidence and found Letby guilty". But the second jury only assessed the case of Child K, in a climate that was so unsatisfactory that it was inevitable that Letby would be found guilty.

Others have suggested that the defence could have called witnesses, and Letby didn't instruct them, so it's her own fault. This seems a trifle unfair. We cannot reasonably expect Letby to tell her own defence barrister how to defend her, even if she was at her most clear-headed, which would hardly be expected considering the ordeal that she'd endured even prior to her two-year incarceration and subsequent breakdown.

Not satisfied with that argument, other legal commenters have asserted that if Letby received a poor defence, this doesn't mean that the verdict isn't legitimate. It is true this doesn't illegitimise the verdict from a legal perspective but if the court and jury have not heard important evidence then it may well do from a moral, ethical and factual perspective. Protecting the court procedure and system from criticism does not matter. The job of courts is to convict those who are guilty beyond reasonable doubt. If there is reasonable doubt, particularly in a case of this magnitude, this should far outweigh any procedural sensitivities. Ultimately, guilty people should go to prison, and innocent people should be kept out of prison. If there is an innocent person in prison, the fact that this can be procedurally justified should carry no weight at all with any right-thinking person.

Commenting on the trial, a senior neonatologist told *Private Eye* that he was "deeply troubled" by the court process and evidence provided, and that "the cases all have much more plausible alternative explanations than those alleged". The medical expert went on to state that "on the basis of what I've seen, this conviction is wholly unsafe. It totally shakes my faith in the competence of the law." The author of the *Private Eye* article, Dr Philip Hammond, has requested for medics to come forward who explicitly support the guilty verdict. At the time of writing, this request remains unanswered. Very few medics have offered any support for the prosecution case, while dozens, if not hundreds, of credentialed professionals have been critical of it.

"Having been a juror in a past case, one of the biggest problems we encountered was not hearing the full story – we felt that there was critical information that we weren't allowed to hear. And the Letby case was plagued by this problem", TV producer Stephen Phelps told me. "Another issue was the bundling together of cases that we saw here. Why was this allowed? This laundry list of cases tended towards creating a miscarriage of justice because there was so much for the jury to consider. Why does the system not require them simply to pick the best of those cases? Presenting this string of cases to the jury prevents them from making a proper judgement on the facts of the case. In the end, they're overwhelmed."

Influential social media commentator, TriedByStats, who provided research for a BBC Radio 4 documentary on the Letby case backed this latter point. "This really didn't need to take 10 months. There are a lot of cases that are incredibly weak. Some of the collapses, like Child G and Child H, are just crazy. And Child K. There is almost no evidence." Dr Colin Ferguson asserted that this had been done "purposefully" because "each individual case on its own would not stand up". Dr Ferguson further explained that "the way it's been put together would have overwhelmed anybody's ability to think coherently about it. The length of the process must have been completely overwhelming for the jury, even though many of these cases are unbelievably weak."

Nonetheless, the Court of Appeal was so satisfied with the original trial process in Letby's case that it not only denied her the right to appeal, it also automatically disqualified all associated appeals. Yet we know that medical evidence has a troubling history in criminal cases. One study of 16 British miscarriage of justice cases since 1996, in which it was ultimately decided on appeal that no crime had been committed, found that 15 of them had featured poor or misleading medical testimony.

Lucy Letby's original trial failed to account for all of the points and criticisms contained in this chapter, and indeed the book as a whole, while the Court of Appeal dismissed them as inadmissible evidence. Cheshire Police continually refused to comment, citing an "ongoing investigation", and this position has not perceptibly changed since the investigation has been completed. The CPS has resorted to issuing a generic statement in response to criticism, which essentially says nothing.

The Thirlwall Inquiry has been deaf to issues at the hospital and problems with the court case, even though documents submitted to the inquiry have made these issues clear. Some of the references made by lawyers during Thirlwall have indicated, in my opinion, an extremely limited grasp of the context and specifics of the case.

When I searched for Dr Harold Shipman, I found nearly 30 different documents from Thirlwall referencing him hundreds of times. But there is no parallel between Shipman and Letby. Shipman was identified because he used the same *modus operandi* all the time, administering lethal doses of diamorphine. There was no laundry list of bizarre methods of murder, which experts decry as implausible, while never searching for any of them, as is the case with Letby. Secondly, Shipman had the clear opportunity to commit his crimes, facing none of the logistical difficulties that have been described in this chapter. It seems obvious to me that there is nothing the Thirlwall Inquiry could learn from dwelling on Shipman.

An important view on the rather weak circumstantial case used against Letby was provided by Gudrun Young KC when speaking with the BBC *File on 4* programme: "There's a danger in a circumstantial case of adding lots of different things together, which in and of themselves are actually quite evidentially weak. You might get eight pieces of evidence, but if each one of them is really weak, eight times zero is zero. It's not eight!"

One of the great myths of the Lucy Letby case is that there was an enormous amount of medical evidence in court but it is undermined by the reality. There were 136 days of court proceedings in the trial, only 13% of which was devoted to expert medical evidence, and approximately 90% of this expert evidence came from Evans and Bohin. The other six expert witnesses only collectively appeared in court on 11 of the 136 days, and many of these appearances were relatively fleeting.

Over half of the trial consists of various material from Cheshire Police, the accounts of parents and innumerable personnel from the CoCH exclaiming that they had no idea what was going on. This should perhaps not be surprising considering that the expert panel acting in Letby's defence made 25 broad criticisms of the hospital in their preview report, as well as finding many other specific faults, while arguably the most eminent neonatologist in Canadian history, Dr Shoo Lee, concluded that the CoCH neonatal unit should have been closed down.

Another issue brought up by Dr Lee during our conversation was the poor quality of medical notes from the CoCH: "The notes were very often incomplete, particularly with respect to the obstetric information. Critical information was frequently omitted. Antenatal notes should be automatically transferred to the neonatal unit. The fact that this information is not included in the neonatal notes suggests that the unit did not have access to it – a fundamental failing. But there are many other problems, multiple problems. There are multiple levels of deficiency. That's why I said, if this was a unit here in Canada, I would shut it down."

In short, it is clear that staff at the CoCH did not understand what was occurring with infants on the unit. But Letby should not have been convicted due to their failures.

The view of Dr James Phillips is that "the presentation and scrutiny of data and expert evidence at the trials was comprehensively flawed. The trial as conducted is so flawed that it is completely irrelevant that the jury found her guilty. Everything about this trial has the strong impression of an inevitable conclusion, which is unrelated to the evidence that is now emerging. The trial was set up to identify whether or not Lucy Letby murdered babies. But that is not the primary question. The primary question is, rather, what caused these babies to die?"

Systems frequently make mistakes. This is an inevitability in any system designed and operated by human beings which has occurred throughout history and will continue for as long as the human race endures. In the Letby case, there were many horrendous errors of practice and reasoning rendering the convictions almost automatically unsafe.

The trial of Lucy Letby may be one of those systemic mistakes, but a calamitous one. Based on medical evidence that is now available, it is overwhelmingly likely that there were no crimes ever committed at the CoCH. Lucy Letby has become entangled in an intransigent web of the UK's criminal justice system.

Perhaps the most chilling aspect of this is that Letby is far from the first. And if Britain as a nation is not courageous enough to meaningfully confront this reality, she definitely won't be the last.

CHAPTER 19: ARREST AND INVESTIGATION OF LUCY LETBY

These final chapters of the book will rewind to the lengthy prelude to one of the most significant court cases in British history. Before the trial, Lucy Letby was arrested on three separate occasions. On 3 July 2018, police arrested her on suspicion of eight counts of murder and six counts of attempted murder. She was bailed on 6 July 2018, rearrested on 10 June 2019 and bailed again on 13 June. On 10 November 2020, she was arrested for the final time and denied bail.

Had Dr Evans not walked into Blacon Police Station and stated "immediately" that infants had suffered inflicted harm, it is perfectly possible that the investigation would not have been taken any further as Cheshire Police stated explicitly, several times, that there was no evidence pointing to malfeasance.

Reflecting on this initial contact with Dr Evans, internal emails from Cheshire Police have a tone that seems almost excited. Detective Sergeant Adam Bolger gushes that: "We were certainly impressed with Dr Evans and he's clearly very interested in assisting us!" At this point, it would have been wise for Cheshire Police to seek, at the very least, a second opinion, but there is no evidence they ever did. Writing in *The Guardian*, neonatologist Professor Neena Modi asserted that had Cheshire Police "taken advice or had guidance available to them on how to assess the suitability of an 'expert', it is possible that they would have sought alternative opinions that could have reached different conclusions".

Cheshire Police came under considerable public criticism for the length of their investigation and the trauma that they'd caused Letby without charging her. Letby felt the sword of Damocles hanging over her for 1,970 days between the case being referred to Cheshire Police and the beginning of the trial – is it hugely surprising that she was in a troubled mental state by the time she was presented to one of the most high-profile court cases in British history? "Obviously, I've heard about suggestions that Lucy was suffering with anxiety, depression and PTSD. Everything I've read about her reaction is perfectly normal. She's been through a process of hell, really", a psychiatrist told me.

After her arrests, Letby was interviewed an incredible 30 times. The police do not make recordings of these interviews available, but from the excerpts that have been released, it can reasonably be inferred that none of the arguments Letby made during this process were ever taken into consideration. She was asked about the 'confession note', for example, and gave a perfectly plausible explanation – another instance sees Letby explain that she had "not intentionally" harmed any infants, "but I felt if I'd done something, if my practice wasn't good enough or people didn't think I'd done something in the right way".

Transcripts of police interviews indicate that Letby answered a multitude of questions on the so-called confession note, and on more than one occasion. Yet when Netflix broadcast a new film about the police investigation in February 2026 in collaboration with Cheshire Police, instances where Letby answered "no comment" to enquiries on the note were emphasised. A likely explanation for her declining to comment is Letby's solicitor recommending this because she had answered those questions during previous interviews. In fact, Letby was asked about the green post-it note at the culmination of her first interview on 3 July 2018. It was the very first question that Letby was asked and she answered at length.

The Netflix production appeared designed to imply that Letby frequently answered "no comment" and was evasive, whereas in the 166 pages of PDF transcripts available, she answers every single question asked. "Nine times out of 10, my guidance would be to avoid answering police questions anyway", former solicitor Lulu Minns, who represented many clients in police station interviews, told me. "In complex cases, I would often advise 'no comment' alongside handing in a written statement outlining the client's defence. Someone of exemplary character such as Lucy wants to answer the questions, but you certainly shouldn't answer questions over and over again especially on facts where an account has already been provided."

The full times and timings from Letby's police interviews have been made available, so it is known that between 3 and 5 July 2018, 10 and 12 June 2019, and 10 to 11 November 2020, Lucy Letby was interviewed for an extraordinary 22 hours and 54 minutes. In addition to the 1,374 minutes of questioning, Letby was afforded just 12 minutes of welfare interviews; thus, the questioning lasted 114 times longer than the welfare interviews.

It should also be noted that the police interviews that have been made public are, from the perspective of Cheshire Police, the most incriminating, with the highest standards of evidential support for the prosecution case, because they were the ones used in court. Considering that throughout the interviews, Letby patiently answers all of their questions, giving plausible and consistent answers, the veracity of which have since been confirmed by others, one again wonders what was in the police interviews that we haven't seen. It is impossible to say precisely as the police have declined to release them. But it is easy to imagine that we would have seen them by now if they supported the prosecution case in any meaningful way, after they cherry-picked what are likely to be the very few instances of Letby saying "no comment" from nearly 24 hours of police interviews.

It is clear from what Cheshire Police have been willing to release that the interviews were a one-sided process in which they attempted to recognise anything that could be used against Letby from her own words and jettisoned anything that contradicted their case. The most damning accusation of lying the prosecution was able to glean from these interviews was, as mentioned previously, the assertion that Letby didn't own a shredder. If they would like to disprove this, they are perfectly free to release all of their interviews, which would be recorded and part of the public record in many other countries.

In the promotional film the Cheshire Constabulary made about Operation Hummingbird, it is noted that "in effect, [Letby]'s a suspect, but she's also the key source of information. She knows more about this case than anyone else, because our evidence would suggest that she's been there." Now that a significant portion of the police interviews have been released, this view seems a little shaky. Cheshire Police didn't use these interviews as an objective fact-finding exercise – they used them to build a case against Letby. There is no evidence that the police who investigated this case and interviewed Letby ever took any of her explanations into consideration, as the prosecution case in court simply repeated all of the accusations from the police interviews, with none of the contextual explanations from Letby.

Some of the evidence used during the trial derived from police interviews was also based on a rather troubling methodology. Letby faced accusations in court that she must have poisoned babies with insulin, because she had agreed, during police interviews, there had definitely been an insulin poisoning. But this is entirely unfair and misleading. Letby was informed that there was no other possible result and so she was forced to agree, not being medically qualified to do otherwise, while stating unequivocally that she wasn't the poisoner. "All she is doing is saying: 'Well, if you tell me that's the case then it must be'," Stephen Phelps observed. "What else can she do?"

Defenders of the police investigation tend to claim that it has value because it was so protracted. Simply because something lasts for a long time does not lend it more credence or merit. Conversely, if something can be presented succinctly, with strong, irrefutable evidence, it is likely to be wrapped up quickly. The length of the police investigation and the poor quality of evidence recovered rather suggests that they were struggling to build a legitimate case, and they were, in fact, quite explicitly criticised for this at the time. Cheshire Police were certainly *persistent* in Letby's case and determined to charge her. Whether they were *thorough* is another matter entirely, particularly considering they made the most basic errors such as with the swipe-card data, which have now been conceded.

Dr Dewi Evans has provided an abundant treasure trove of commentary since the verdict in the Letby case was announced. Prominent among his contentions has been the assertion that statistics are unrelated to the Letby case. "The case had nothing to do with statistics. I'm not sure how many ways you can tell statisticians that the case had nothing to do with statistics", Dr Evans commented on 19 November 2024.

Detective Superintendent Nigel Wenham had been informed of a statistical coincidence related to Lucy Letby by independent chairwoman of the Child Death Overview Panel, Hayley Frame, in April 2017. Frame told the Thirlwall Inquiry that as soon as Wenham was told that one staff member was on shift for a series of baby collapses he concluded that it was "very much a matter for his officers". So the initial germ of an idea that this case should be investigated came directly from a statistical correlation that had never been investigated by statisticians. When presented with the opportunity to involve a statistician in the process, Professor Jane Hutton, the CPS advised against this and it was struck from the investigation.

Dr Evans, according to his own account, "told police that if you harm a baby, it will deteriorate there and then. So I also identified a time and date when each had probably been harmed and told them they needed to find out who was on duty. If they found the same person was there during lots of incidents, they'd have a suspect."

Professor Hutton has since become a critic of the prosecution case. "From what I know so far, I think the conviction is unsafe, and she should be allowed to appeal", Hutton told *Times Radio*. "The CPS knew that statistics could have been a major tool in favour of Lucy", Professor Richard Gill suggested, "because it would show that the number of supposedly suspicious events wasn't large when you take into account how many hours she worked there. It's that simple."

With regard to the issue of Professor Hutton, Colin George of BBC Studios noted that the CPS Code for Crown Prosecutors states in point 3.3 that "prosecutors cannot direct the police or other investigators". This is a critically important point. *The Guardian* had previously reported that "neither the initial engagement with Hutton nor the CPS instruction to the police to drop their line of inquiry into the 'validity of the statistical evidence in the case' were disclosed to Letby's defence team". This is not a trivial matter – in its own promotional film on Operation

Hummingbird, Detective Inspector Rob Woods makes the following comment: "Disclosure is absolutely vital to a fair trial. Because when you hear of jobs being thrown out of court, the vast majority of those will be because of mistakes or failings in disclosure. Often not deliberate, but mistakes or failings in disclosure is what causes big investigations to fall down."

It is hard to see how the actions of the CPS and Cheshire Police are appropriate here, and how this doesn't constitute a failure of disclosure. The same CPS Code for Crown Prosecutors states that the Full Code Test, which begins the assessment of a public prosecution, should only commence "when all outstanding reasonable lines of inquiry have been pursued". It would be fascinating to learn how all "reasonable lines of inquiry have been pursued" if the police have commissioned a statistical study, in a case which is overwhelmingly reliant on statistics in order to identify a suspect, the CPS advised them to cancel that study and Cheshire Police duly obliged. It appears plain that a "reasonable line of inquiry" had not been pursued.

Dr Steve Watts has decades of experience in such cases, including writing the national police guidelines on the investigation of deaths in healthcare settings, and has conducted a thorough review of the investigation from material available in the public domain. Dr Watts was exceedingly blunt in his assessment when speaking with the *Trials of Lucy Letby* podcast: "There has never been an occasion where I have been instructed by the CPS to do, or not do, anything. If I was given a direct instruction by the CPS, I would have flatly refused, and I would have reported them to the Director of Public Prosecutions or the Chief Crown Prosecutor." The involvement of Professor Hutton, and then its subsequent cancellation, should certainly have been disclosed to the defence.

When I spoke to Dr Watts, he cited what must surely be considered a major error in procedure. The CPS and police guidance on the investigation of deaths in healthcare settings now require that decisions in sensitive, serious and complex cases are referred to the CPS Serious Crime and Counter Terrorism Division (SCCTD). Prosecution guidance for the CPS explicitly cites that the SCCTD should be involved for "homicide allegations involving four or more victims" and "medical authorities such as NHS, NHS Trusts and hospitals". Dr Watts also recounted referring "multiple serious, sensitive and complex cases, including healthcare cases, to the Specialist Crime Division which was the forerunner of the SCCTD". The Letby investigation ticked both boxes and yet the regional CPS unit, Merseyside and Cheshire, made the charging decision. "It is likely, in my opinion, that if this had been referred to the appropriate CPS body that this case would never have gone to court," Dr Watts informed me, as indeed occurred in January 2026 after further cases were put before the CPS.

Meanwhile, those involved with the Thirlwall Inquiry have done their level best to stick their collective fingers in their ears, in an attempt to block out the cacophony of evidence contradicting the entire process. Despite this, it has been impossible to prevent some of the evidence gathered from seeping into the public discussion.

One example of this came from a witness statement presented to the Thirlwall Inquiry from Dr Veronika Jiraskova, a trainee doctor working in the paediatric team at the CoCH between August 2015 and February 2016. Jiraskova clearly hadn't been taken under the wing of the consultants, as she "found that the unit did not feel like a team that was working in a cohesive way, with some doctors disliking others…people were talking behind one another's backs and GP trainees were generally looked down at". As a consequence of this, Jiraskova was "completely unaware of the suspicions or concerns of others about the conduct of Letby" and had initially heard of the allegations via the media. Jiraskova went on to say that she has "great doubts" Letby "has committed the crimes that she denies".

It is notable, but unsurprising, that Jiraskova was not invited to actually speak at the inquiry. Dr James Phillips rightly stated that her remarks were "brave and heroic". Phillips went on to comment that "the Thirlwall Inquiry has turned out to be extremely useful for the defence of Lucy Letby, with the single biggest takeaway from it being the enormous volume of evidence that could and should have been used to defend her in court".

As the competence of Cheshire Police has been placed under the microscope, it seems that the constabulary has become increasingly sensitive to criticism, as exemplified by their response to a *Mail on Sunday* article by journalist Peter Hitchens. This storm in a teacup began when Hitchens asserted that "the Lucy Letby case has begun to stink like a neglected fridge in a student house". Hitchens expressed his "shock" that the "CPS and Cheshire Police had given a top-level briefing to journalists before the trial of Lucy Letby". This little known and selective briefing was held on Monday 3 October 2022 at Manchester Magistrates' Court, one week before the main trial began. Hitchens asserted, quite reasonably, that such briefings are held "in the hope of influencing the way certain issues are reported", and also divulged that no transcript or recording has been made available. The notion that this was an impartial briefing was rather sullied by the fact that no one from the defence was invited, as Hitchens himself noted.

In his next column, Hitchens outlined how the *Mail on Sunday* had received communication from the College of Policing, the National Police Chiefs' Council and the CPS suggesting that the newspaper print an article that was favourable to the police. The *Mail on Sunday* also received what Hitchens described as a "snappish email" declaring that simply writing an article containing incontestable facts was causing "disgust and dismay" among the police forces of England and Wales. "If this is how they behave towards Britain's biggest Sunday newspaper, what must they be like when dealing with a powerless citizen who has the nerve to disagree with their opinions?" Hitchens asked rhetorically. The National Police Chiefs' Council then, staggeringly, released an article attempting to debunk the criticism of Hitchens, seemingly with no understanding of how troubling the conduct of Cheshire Police had been.

It is worth noting that the Cheshire Constabulary is so fixated on public relations that it rapidly deletes all unfavourable comments on the YouTube video it posted for Operation Hummingbird. One can only hope that their response to actual crime is as swift. This blanket deletion occurs despite the fact that the social media policy for the Cheshire Constabulary cheerily states: "We welcome all questions and commentary, including constructive feedback."

Elsewhere, having posted over 48,200 times on X, on 8 December 2024 Cheshire Police suddenly ceased all posting on the platform. X does not allow account owners to delete comments; one wonders if Cheshire Police are concerned about being inundated with criticism. Hitchens later reported that Cheshire Police "have even complained about the way in which their conduct of the case is discussed on X". It is therefore clear that the constabulary continues to monitor the platform, although it has abandoned any pretence of providing updates on everyday policing. The constabulary then came under further criticism for arranging clandestine press conferences to brief carefully selected journalists before the court case was even concluded.

Hitchens later wrote in his *Mail on Sunday* column that the "police have grown too powerful and too scornful of the public they should serve". There is no apparent awareness from Cheshire Police or the CPS of their role, or that of a free press in a healthy society. They seemingly wish to interfere with perfectly legitimate journalism and reporting without apparently understanding why this is inappropriate, or indeed why their intervention should be considered concerning. "This thing with Peter Hitchens was disgusting", Stephen Phelps declared. "Everything about the way Cheshire Police went about this is dreadful."

News that Cheshire Police and the CPS had blocked the release of reports critical to Letby's appeal were anything but encouraging. Sarah Knapton and Cleuci de Oliveira reported for *The Daily Telegraph* that the CPS had denied defence barrister Mark McDonald access to revised reports authored by Dr Evans on Child C and submitted to the police in October 2024. The disclosure guidelines of the CPS itself state that "prosecutors must provide the defence with the schedules of all of the unused material and provide them with any material that undermines the case for the prosecution or assists the case for the accused" so it is hard to understand how this is allowable.

On 28 January 2025, Sir David Davis questioned the Justice Secretary, Shabana Mahmood, on delays in releasing information: "Can the Secretary of State explain to the House under what circumstances the police and CPS are allowed to deny access to evidence after a trial has concluded to a defence lawyer seeking to appeal, as has happened in the Lucy Letby case?"

In the immediate aftermath of the Letby trial, Senior Investigating Officer Paul Hughes made several statements which were somewhat lacking in objective analysis. Hughes firstly implied that Letby wanted the police to find evidence that was used against her in court, particularly the so-called confession note, saying: "She's intelligent and articulate, she did well on her scores [as a nurse], she was good at what she did when she wanted to do it correctly. You could see that in the way she wrote her hospital records. Furthermore, you could tell the way she intentionally misled doctors on hospital notes just how smart she was. To be able to mislead doctors into believing that a child was coming towards a collapse, to intentionally mislead clever doctors and colleagues. Did she want it [the note] found? Did she just want to write it down or did she just want to tell the world that she was evil, and she did this? Did she want the notoriety that she's got? Without telling us why, then the motive was right in front of us for us to find."

Hughes expanded on his speculation regarding why Letby had allegedly committed murders: "I don't think she went into nursing to kill children, but nursing gave her the opportunity to be around the most vulnerable in society. Once she saw what happened and the attention she received, that lit something inside of her that she continued with."

Why on earth would Letby want the police to find notes that they later used against her as incriminating evidence? Another possible explanation that has somehow evaded Hughes is simply that Letby didn't consider the notes significant, nor consider herself to be guilty. This is consistent with several statements in the notes, particularly her assertion that there is "obviously no evidence" against her.

Hughes also made the incredible claim that Letby enjoyed the process of the court case: "She clearly loves the attention, I think she loved the attention of a trial as well." In contrast, *The Guardian* was one of many outlets to report that the original trial was delayed due to Letby suffering from PTSD and having a breakdown which was so severe that she literally could not speak. On the first day of the trial, Letby's barrister, Ben Myers, told the judge that Letby was "incoherent, she can't speak properly". She had been diagnosed as having PTSD following her arrests. After two years in prison, she was moved to a new facility but she hadn't brought her medication with her. Any psychological stability she'd achieved, Myers said, had been "blown away." The start of the trial was consequently delayed for a week.

The *New Yorker* reported: "Letby, who now startled easily, was assessed by psychiatrists, and it was decided that she did not have to walk from the dock to the witness box and instead could be seated there before people came into the room." *The Guardian* said that in court Letby "cut an almost pitiable figure", her eyes darting "nervously towards any unexpected noise – a cough, a dropped pen, or when the female prison guard beside her shuffled in her seat". Furthermore, both the so-called confession note recovered by police, and a subsequent interview conducted by the Cheshire Constabulary, indicated that Letby had been suicidal. Asked by interviewing officers whether she had contemplated ending her own life, Letby answered plainly: "Yes…I just felt so isolated and alone."

There is no evidence that Letby was psychologically unusual or even behaving strangely at the time that her alleged crimes were committed and it is one issue many parties agree on, although Paul Hughes appears to be seeking some sort of motive or explanation for Letby's alleged behaviour. Hughes went on to make another observation on Letby's supposedly odd behaviour: "I'd be screaming and shouting. And where's the banging on the table?" Hughes asked, preposterously, about Letby's interviews in conversation with Liz Hull and Caroline Cheetham. "This was astonishingly naïve, because what he's saying is complete nonsense," Dr Steve Watts asserted. "He has no professional competence to draw any inference from someone's behaviour. How can anyone know how someone would or should behave when arrested for murder? And had Lucy banged on the table, would that have been interpreted positively anyway?"

Of course, investigating a case such as this must be a harrowing experience. In one of his comments to the media, Hughes stated that the team at Cheshire Police who were assigned the Letby case are "proud" of their investigation. I'm sure that's entirely true. I'm sure lots of people worked very hard on this investigation. I'm sure they went through some deeply emotional experiences. I'm certain they would have felt very great empathy and sympathy with the families involved, as we all do.

Unfortunately, that doesn't necessarily mean that they did a good job.

CHAPTER 20: OPERATION HUMMINGBIRD

On 2 May 2017 Tony Chambers, Chief Executive at the CoCH, wrote to Cheshire Police Chief Constable Simon Byrne, asking the constabulary to "conduct a forensic investigation into the circumstances surrounding the deaths [at the hospital] with a view to excluding any unnatural causes".

As we have seen earlier, at the time police were asked to investigate there was "no evidence other than coincidence". This was the case less than one month before Chambers made the referral on 3 April 2017. Stephen Cross, director of legal services and head of corporate affairs at the CoCH, had written: "In our view, there is no evidence to justify a criminal investigation." Shortly afterwards, on 13 April 2017, an "extraordinary board meeting" at the CoCH asserted that "neither the Royal College review or Dr Hawdon's review identified any criminal issues".

The April board meeting also noted that a further forensic review was preferable, which is exactly what should have occurred. There was no justification for a police referral and Cheshire Police have, by their own admission, no ability to perform any form of medical review. Although it is oddly comical to note that no one at the hospital seemed to know what this term constituted either – Sir Duncan Nichol, chairman of the board, conceded that "it is not yet known what the forensic review means", while the consultants "could not define what they felt was a forensic review".

Stephanie Davies was the Senior Coroner's Officer at Cheshire Police in 2017. She was asked to review several infants in the case after receiving a letter from Tony Chambers on 4 May 2017. Davies had worked on over 5,000 cases for Cheshire Police and was responsible for a team of officers. "My review has contributed to Operation Hummingbird starting in the first place", Davies told me "and so I have a duty to speak out."

Even at that early juncture, there seemed to be an undue haste with Davies given "just under three hours to conduct a review". Davies was asked to look at multiple deaths, "from the beginning of June 2015 to the end of June 2016", and all initially seemed normal. "On the surface, everything seemed natural, it was all natural causes", Davies told me. It was the case of Child O which prompted Davies to conclude that there were "missing jigsaw pieces", but the full picture of an errant cannula aspiration that caused bleeding was never provided.

Davies had been asked to attend an important strategic Gold Group meeting by top-ranking officers at Cheshire Police, during which then Assistant Chief Constable, Darren Martland, made what turned out to be a significant request to Davies. "He asked me: 'Before we confirm with the hospital that we're not investigating, can you confirm that the cause of deaths for these babies are explained? We need you to report to us by tomorrow morning.'"

The Davies review was crucial to the investigation. "Paul Hughes, who led Operation Hummingbird, told me that my review was one of the main reasons they decided to investigate", Davies informed me, and her statement to the Thirlwall Inquiry recounts her being "astounded by this". Davies has since asked the inquiry if she can update her statement, as she believes the conviction of Lucy Letby to be a miscarriage of justice, but has yet to receive a response.

When Cheshire Police convened to discuss their investigation, now given the name 'Operation Hummingbird', on 12 May 2017, it was clear that the investigation had stalled. "There is no specific allegation at this point to suggest a criminal act", the constabulary noted. "We do not have any reasonable grounds to suspect or believe that this may have been the case. At no point have the CoCH uncovered anything that would indicate a significant chance that there was an underlying criminal act… There is no direct allegation of any wrongdoing on the part of an individual(s) or significant negligence, which could potentially constitute a criminal offence. There is nothing to suggest this is the case."

In line with this, a preceding meeting held at the CoCH on 12 April 2017 heard Simon Medland KC repeatedly attempting to explain that the police essentially cannot investigate nothing: "The police can only sensibly investigate cases where there is – at the very least – reasonable grounds for suspecting that a criminal offence has been committed."

It is unlikely any further investigation would have taken place were it not for a meeting that took place shortly after Operation Hummingbird got under way on 15 May 2017. Paul Hughes and Nigel Wenham from Cheshire Police met with Dr Susie Holt from Alder Hey hospital, and Dr Stephen Brearey and Dr Ravi Jayaram from the CoCH. In an internal email dated 4 May 2017, Dr Jayaram mentioned that it would be important "for the police to have their interest piqued".

Ahead of this meeting, Ian Harvey had written to Margaret Kitching, a Regional Chief Nurse for the north of England who had been asked to liaise with the CoCH, to express his concern. Harvey observed that Cheshire Police were "minded not to hold an investigation – firstly they don't feel that there is evidence of criminal activity and secondly they are mindful of the effects on families". He then informed Kitching that "our paediatricians sent a document to them that was a listing of their concerns which was a very prejudiced view, effectively pointing the finger at one nurse…It does not contain anything new…despite the paediatricians' assertion that they haven't been listened to." And what was the justification for concern? "The nurse was present in all but one of the deaths", Brearey explained. The 'it's always Lucy' theory!

A document submitted to Thirlwall suggests that Letby was explicitly named by Brearey – "at that time the unit manager noticed that Lucy Letby was present at all three". This could be a typing error, and the consultants could have retained Letby's anonymity, simply referring to an unnamed nurse. It is impossible to know one way or another. What can be said with certainty is that Brearey and Jayaram identified Letby at the 15 May 2017 meeting, referencing her being withdrawn from the unit and her supposed constant presence at collapses. Cheshire Police were left in no doubt Brearey and Jayaram suspected a nurse, and indeed the identity of that nurse. "I think there is significant evidence of cognitive bias in the Operation Hummingbird investigation because of the way it began", the experienced police investigator Dr Steve Watts asserted.

At the very onset of the police investigation, Cheshire Police were told by the consultants that they suspected a nurse. Dr Brearey claimed Eirian Powell was the first person to mention this association although we know Powell wasn't even at the meeting where this supposedly occurred. Furthermore, no one else who was in attendance can recall this being mentioned.

There was an enormous danger of bias, and yet the police never questioned the consultants. They were never placed under any suspicion. Additionally, it becomes clear in the promotional film Cheshire Police made about Operation Hummingbird that they rapidly zoned in on Letby as the sole explanation for the spike in deaths on the unit, at the exclusion of any other factor. "My opinion was very quickly that, yes, there was something not right and, yes, the only obvious person was Lucy Letby", Darren Riley, a retired Detective Constable who was involved in the investigation helpfully commented during Cheshire Police's execrable film on Operation Hummingbird. This is literally the opposite of what Cheshire Police were asked to do, which was to "exclude unnatural causes".

During the conversation with Wenham on 15 May 2017, Dr Jayaram remembered that he had seen Letby potentially harming a child, saying: "I noticed the breathing tube had been dislodged". By this point, Dr Jayaram had been through endless internal processes, communicated with all manner of colleagues and management, there had been several medical reviews during which he interacted with the reviewers, there had been a grievance procedure related to Letby, he repeatedly cited his belief that the police should be called in, and yet this is the first time that Dr Jayaram mentioned the tube dislodgement theory.

Dr Jayaram had previously told ITV News that the night on which Letby allegedly attempted to murder Child K was "etched on my memory and will be in my nightmares forever"; a clip that was played in court during the retrial. According to Dr Jayaram, this was a traumatic experience that he will never forget, but it took him 453 days to mention it to anyone, during which period he extensively discussed what he had believed to be potential inflicted harm on the neonatal unit.

In the same conversation, the third insulin case, for which Letby was never charged, was also discussed. In relation to this, Dr Jayaram asserted that Alder Hey had been unable to explain the results from this infant. It is therefore, as discussed in "Insulin Cases" difficult to understand why this case was not part of the original indictment. This reinforces the impression that there was something associated with this infant that was fundamentally undermining for the prosecution case.

This is not the only instance where statements were made despite a lack of medical knowledge on the part of police officers. Dr Stephen Brearey commented that the "post-mortem does not explain why the babies suddenly collapsed and died". This could seem suspicious to Wenham and Hughes as they almost certainly did not know that many infant deaths are unexplained and more so for neonates.

Brearey also opined that "there seems to be a theme with multiple births…and the more stable infant being the one to collapse". The fact that twins and triplets are inherently more vulnerable than solitary infants was never explained to Wenham and Hughes. Throughout the conversation, frequent references were also made to unexplained collapses, and the nature of such collapses being predictable, a theme which was then reinforced by Dr Evans, for example writing in an email to police on 18 July 2017 that "premature babies tend not to 'just die'".

This assertion seemed to seep into the consciousness of Cheshire Police. "What we found out was in neonatal infants, it's very clear that they know when a baby's going to collapse and die, and parents are already prepared for that. And even on the outside chance of it being unexpected, it's always explainable", Hughes parroted in the Operation Hummingbird film. He has made similar comments on the record to various media outlets. It is already clear there was no tendency whatsoever for the police to question, or even corroborate, any of the claims made by Brearey and Jayaram.

In another part of the conversation, Brearey expressed his concern that the "survival rate for babies over 32 [weeks] is nearly 100%. For six of our babies to have died who were over 32 weeks to die [sic] is not right." It is notable that of these six babies, Letby was not charged in respect of three of them. Two of the remaining three infants were triplets, and the final one was Child D, who lost colour and became floppy in her father's arms within 12 minutes of birth and was suffering with pneumonia and serious respiratory problems. If anything was "not right" with Child D it was the failure of medics on the unit to respond adequately to palpable and alarming health concerns which were even voiced by the mother of the infant.

With the multiple medical reviews that had been conducted at this stage, the logical approach would have been to push for a multi-disciplinary review. Dr Brearey's desire for such a review had been recorded in notes made by Nigel Wenham. The stubborn insistence on police referral makes no sense as Cheshire Police, by their own admission, have no medical knowledge. They can't even question the erroneous and misleading assertions that were made during this discussion, and officers from Cheshire Police would uncritically repeat things they had been told by both the consultants and Dr Evans. Neonatologist Professor Neena Modi wrote in *The Guardian* that "standard procedure is to conduct a detailed case review involving all of the speciality disciplines involved…as well as independent clinicians with the requisite expertise", and that this was "one of the recommendations of an investigation of the CoCH neonatal service carried out by the Royal College of Paediatrics and Child Health in 2016".

When Dr Evans arrived on the scene, he suggested to Cheshire Police that they might not need to involve other medics. This is extraordinary, as, in documents seen by both myself and Dr Steve Watts, the NCA specifically advised Cheshire Police to enlist the assistance of multiple specialists. Sonya Baylis, who had previously worked alongside forensic pathologists for seven years at Guy's Hospital in London and was then instrumental in building the National Injuries Database – a resource that assists the NCA in helping investigators with the causation of injuries – informed Cheshire Police that they should seek out the following experts:

"Forensic and neonatal pathologists to review, jointly, the medical histories, etc…a forensic toxicologist and/or clinical pharmacologist to review the test results for all sampling conducted on the babies, etc…a nurse with experience of working in a special baby unit for neonatal births, etc…a medical expert with the experience of the working practices involved in a special baby unit for neonatal births, etc…an obstetrician to review the medical histories, test results, hospital notes/reports/scans, medication, etc."

Essentially, this is exactly the sort of panel that Dr Shoo Lee assembled, albeit the qualifications of that panel extend way beyond anything Cheshire Police could conceivably have brought together. "The NCA gave Cheshire Police very clear advice, to the Senior Investigating Officer in writing, that they needed a panel of relevant experts", Dr Watts explained. "This is very early in the inquiry, on 26 May 2017. And then on 28 June, the NCA followed up with a list of potential experts. So they have identified suitable people. And then that list is consolidated further still on 4 July. They're quite insistent that this is done properly. Then on 18 July, Dr Dewi Evans writes a lengthy letter to Operation Hummingbird, in which he essentially states that he doesn't need any additional expert opinion."

This is truly a staggering situation. "The best practice advice that the NCA were trying to provide Operation Hummingbird", Dr Watts told me "is the important concept of a panel where the individuals that comprise this come with their different expertise and disciplines, review the material separately, and come to a decision individually about the cause of death for an infant. And it's really troubling that Dr Evans has been allowed to work as an expert advisor, seemingly advising the police on what is needed, run the whole medical process that prompts the police to arrest Lucy Letby, and then appear as a witness in court."

When Paul Hughes appeared on the *Daily Mail* podcast on the Lucy Letby case, he revealed to Liz Hull and Caroline Cheetham that when Letby was first arrested, no medical expert had examined the case notes other than Dr Dewi Evans. It's very clear both from this discussion and the promotional Operation Hummingbird film that the constabulary had pretty much decided Letby was the only suspect. Additionally, on the subject of expert independence, Dr Sandie Bohin was handed the reports and conclusions of Evans, and other experts were similarly prompted, rather than examining the case notes themselves. Dr Andreas Marnerides conceded this in court and Bohin confirmed it in conversation with Hull and Cheetham.

As his work on the case has come under increasing scrutiny, Dr Evans has been keen to assert that he considered all possibilities at the hospital. But in his initial communications with Cheshire Police, he brushed away the possibility of infection, or even the need to investigate such possibilities: "One can identify evidence of infection which is common and haemorrhage via the usual tests, all easily available in baby units in 2015 and for the past couple of decades." Dr Evans is immediately rejecting the idea that infection could have been significant, as well as the need for any specialists in this area; it is hardly any wonder then that he discounted the possibility of infection contributing to collapse or death in every infant.

Dr Evans also insisted on two occasions that he didn't need to hear anything about the RCPCH review: "I would prefer NOT to receive the findings of any previous reviews or investigations." Although this may have been a legitimate attempt to carry out a blind investigation, that he also didn't speak to anyone from the CoCH means that he knew little about the context of the hospital or its neonatal unit.

In his notes, Dr Evans floats various hypothetical methods of potential malfeasance, such as "hand over mouth", "smothering", "intravenous", reflecting that they "would kill". Elsewhere, he suggests that "someone could have pushed the tube down". We also see Dr Evans deeming two cases that were never discussed in court as suspicious, whereas he had previously claimed that all of the cases he ruled out of the indictment were very obviously unsuspicious.

Dr Evans considered Child K to be entirely unsuspicious, yet Lucy Letby is currently serving a life sentence for attempting to murder this infant. With regard to Child H, Dr Evans acknowledged the pneumothorax cited by the expert panel, but then completely discounted it, oddly stating that infection was caused by the collapse. Contrary to his claims, there is no reference in the initial notes of Dr Evans to any collapse of Child C on 13 June. In fact, Dr Evans initially references a UV line falling out on 12 June as being suspicious; this was not even mentioned in the court case. Evans also confirmed that it is perfectly feasible to get air into an intravenous line by accident, but later universally ruled out any air being present in any of the cases inadvertently.

In the case of Child O, Dr Evans didn't even reference the subcapsular haematoma cited by pathologists, and suggested that an overnight period was relevant. This was later changed to a different collapse because Letby was not on duty at that time, essentially the same scenario as with Child C. Dr Evans was even prompted by Family Liaison Coordinator Janet Moore: "Is it the night shift for both the 22/23 June and 23/24 that are of interest?"

Dr Evans, among several "general questions for each baby", poses the following question: "Which room was the baby in for the time the nurse was on shift?" This implies Dr Evans had been told about "the nurse" whom Dr Brearey and Dr Jayaram had identified by this point. Dr Evans' job was to assess the medical condition of the infants. The police were supposed to be "excluding unnatural causes". The role of Dr Evans did not require him to seek the location of any medical staff.

When speaking at a meeting on 12 May 2017, Tony Chambers had told Cheshire Police that "the consultants have made their points, and they have been seen and not judged as sufficient to warrant a police led investigation, looking at how close it constitutes as a criminal act. There was a need to explore to ensure CoCH have not missed anything, but there is also a need to move on. It will become a GMC issue, likewise if the media are involved. This is for CoCH to manage appropriately." The meeting ended with Assistant Chief Constable Darren Martland agreeing that "there does not appear to be any evidence of a criminal wrongdoing from the reports and reviews, which would warrant a police led criminal investigation". Without the meeting between the police, Brearey and Jayaram the entire matter may have ended there. Dr Steve Watts concurs with this verdict: "It's clear that a hypothesis was taken forward from that 15 May meeting, and that there was very little, if anything, that ever occurred to challenge that hypothesis."

Dr Brearey was critical of the Hawdon review at the CoCH because it involved "one neonatologist [who] looked at case notes", yet this was exactly what Dr Evans did when he was called in. The difference was that, unlike Dr Jane Hawdon, Dr Evans wasn't a qualified neonatologist, he had been retired for a considerable period of time, he wasn't an experienced pathologist, he didn't examine the infants, he didn't directly liaise with anyone from the CoCH, he didn't take into account contextual factors related to the hospital and it is highly doubtful that Dr Hawdon has ever been told by a judge that medical evidence she presented was "worthless". Cheshire Police listened to the concerns of the consultants about a process, and then replicated in a considerably less credible way.

A pressing question for the consultants is why they didn't contact the CQC. The CQC is responsible for the regulation and inspection of health and social care providers. It would have been natural to involve the CQC who were far more qualified and connected to address the concerns of the consultants and arrange a multi-disciplinary review. Both Dr Brearey and Dr Jayaram expressed concern about the prospect of contacting the CQC – "this would be more whistleblowing", Brearey oddly remarked.

The CQC itself defines whistleblowing thus: "Whistleblowing is the term used when someone who works for an employer raises a concern about malpractice, risk (for example about patient safety), wrongdoing or possible illegality, which harms, or creates a risk of harm, to people who use the service, colleagues or the wider public.

"Ideally, such concerns should be dealt with by the employer. However, if the management have not dealt with those concerns by responding appropriately to them, perhaps by using the employer's own whistleblowing policy, or the worker does not feel confident that the management will deal with those concerns properly, they can instead make a disclosure to a 'prescribed body', such as a regulator like CQC."

What is the situation at the CoCH if not an incident that requires whistleblowing? It would even have been safer for the two medics to go down this route as the CQC guarantees anonymity and has documented policies and procedures for such scenarios, whereas this was clearly the first time that anyone from Cheshire Police had dealt with anything remotely resembling the situation at the CoCH. Eileen Chubb of Compassion in Care, a charity formed to offer support to whistle-blowers, told Sarah Knapton of *The Daily Telegraph* that "straightaway on day one as soon as the verdict came through we all said, 'these are not whistleblowers'".

Eileen told me that "very few whistleblowers retain their employment. They're either forced out, or they're sacked. None of the markers indicate that there was any whistleblowing here at all. The CQC are not perfect, I'm a critic of the CQC, but they are the first port of call for any healthcare whistleblower. While Brearey and Jayaram have acknowledged privately that they're not whistleblowers, they haven't done it nearly forcefully enough publicly. They have allowed a lot of things to be said in the media which are simply inaccurate."

The problems the police faced were succinctly illustrated by the fact that Paul Hughes was requested to "confirm factual accuracy and current status of the four deaths referred to in Dr J Hawdon's review". In the promotional film on Operation Hummingbird, Hughes speaks of being "presented with…effectively a number of reports written in medical jargon, that tried to explain why babies had collapsed, and why there was effectively a spike in numbers at the CoCH. For me, there were more questions than answers." It certainly sounds as if Hughes didn't understand them, yet he has been tasked with confirming the accuracy of reports authored by a highly regarded and credentialed neonatologist.

Above all else, throughout the initial discussion with Brearey and Jayaram, there is a trusting and empathic tone to the police correspondence. There is little evidence they ever questioned the consultants, let alone considered that they may have played some part in the infant deaths, either through errors, neglect, malpractice or inflicted harm. One document submitted to the Thirlwall Inquiry sees Cheshire Police essentially unquestioningly regurgitating every assumption and assertion made by the two consultants, while the details of 11 babies are redacted because they ultimately didn't feature in the case. It is already clear at this stage that everything possible was being thrown at Letby while no one else, including the consultants, seemed to be in the frame.

"The RCPCH review did not express any single causal factor", a minuted meeting from 12 May 2017 notes. "It expressed a range of things that collectively could be argued that this is an explanation. It would be an unsatisfactory outcome for the clinical team." Cheshire Police don't seem to understand that there may not be a 'single causal factor' for deaths on a neonatal unit. Even adults pass away for complex and nuanced reasons; there aren't always black and white explanations.

"At no point has anyone at the CoCH uncovered anything that would indicate a significant chance that there was an underlying criminal act, but the clinicians still feel it is unexplained", minutes from Operation Hummingbird note, indicating once more that this case was passed to the police with no evidence. As mentioned previously, the overarching problem has been that Cheshire Police have fundamentally misunderstood the medical concept of something being unexplained. The police disregarded contextual factors which were also downplayed by Brearey and Jayaram, then excluded entirely in the case note review of Dr Evans. Is it then surprising that such contextual factors barely feature in the trial of Lucy Letby? Cheshire Police simply do not understand that neonate deaths are frequently unexplained.

The speed with which the police changed their minds is incomprehensible. On 12 May 2017, they had no intention of investigating. Just three days later, on 15 May, they were suddenly convinced to investigate, apparently entirely based on one meeting with Brearey and Jayaram. There appears to have been no effort to understand more of the background; if they had, the police may have learnt about the grievance and the fact that Brearey and Jayaram had been required to apologise to Letby. Cheshire Police did interview Dr Christopher Green, who chaired the grievance procedure, in October 2019; the only material they have released from this is a small segment in which the interviewer evidently wants Green to reveal any incriminating information that he has on Letby.

The treatment of both Letby and patients at the CoCH had been so substandard that lawyer Ian Pace advised the hospital on 28 October 2016 the best case scenario would be Letby claiming constructive dismissal. Pace concluded that "the Trust would rather this than potential patient safety issues and the reputation impact this would have". This followed his 5 July 2016 email in which he noted that Letby "could bring a claim for constructive unfair dismissal if she decided to resign", a prospect that was reiterated by RCN representative Tony Millea in a September 2016 email to nursing manager Karen Rees, in which Millea cited "professional slander".

By 18 May 2017, the investigation had already been reported to *The Guardian* and this is where Dr Evans claimed to have first read about the case. "The initial investigation was moving forward sensibly, rationally and calmly. And then, within six days, suddenly it's been reported to the press. Why this happened, I have no idea", Dr Watts opined. Stephanie Davies was similarly nonplussed: "I don't know why there was such a rush. I don't know who made that decision, but it seems to me that carefully laying the foundation first would have been far more sensible. It's also concerning to me that the coroner had no active input, which I believe to be a big mistake." In fact, Nigel Wenham informed the Thirlwall Inquiry that the decision to launch the criminal investigation was made on 15 May, the same day that Wenham and Paul Hughes met with Brearey and Jayaram, and that visits to the families began the very next day.

Yet it is evident from their Operation Hummingbird promotional film, released six days after the verdict and two days after Letby was sentenced, that Cheshire Police became far too emotionally involved with the families. The first 35 seconds of the film are entirely dedicated to Cheshire Police expressing their desire to serve the families. "They deserve for us to have completely covered their case. And it is about them. And it is about their parents", one of many similar comments in the film observes. The families of those who tragically lost their infants were mentioned 33 times. Cheshire Police then tasked Family Liaison Officer Danielle Stonier with interviewing Lucy Letby in 2019 and 2020, long after she'd been integrated with the families.

The theme of emotional involvement permeates the entire presentation, with large portions of the film dedicated to playing on the heart strings of the audience. DC Michelle Birkett, for example, describes some of her discussions with bereaved families: "And then some of the families knew something was wrong, knew something wasn't right. I knew my child was not right." No such complaints were ever made against Letby, just as no one has ever seen her doing anything suspicious.

The film goes on to discuss the anecdotal evidence collected by police. As we know already, this was "remarkably normal", until, as one officer describes, "you overlay the times and dates" because "as an analyst, that's what you're trying to find – patterns to things." Later we are informed that Letby's diary contains "almost a code of coloured asterisks and various other things". It seems that Cheshire Police are oblivious to the danger of seeking such patterns, and also to the highly evident levels of confirmation bias in this investigation. "It's very easy to get confirmation bias if you think this has been caused by x," Professor Jane Hutton told BBC Radio 4. "It's very easy to see things that aren't otherwise there".

Did Cheshire Police speak to anyone qualified about this supposed code and purported patterns? It seems not. It appears that there has been no consultation with any other nurse regarding anything Letby has written, because Cheshire Police also don't seem to know that copious note-taking is common among nurses. "We didn't expect her to have kept to a catalogue year on year on year." "We thought that perhaps having been arrested, she might stop doing that, but…she had continued to write her thoughts and all sorts of processes about the investigation." All Letby has done by writing these notes was confirm that she is a trained nurse.

As the film continues, and any meaningful evidence remains conspicuous by its absence, one wonders what Cheshire Police did with the millions of pounds that was invested in investigating Operation Hummingbird. They did an admirable job of examining Letby's guttering, but did they actually ever bother to speak with anyone outside of their bubble? Did they seek expertise regarding areas of the investigation in which they had no prior knowledge? There is certainly very little evidence of this.

It seems instead that anything which could possibly be advanced, even as the most tenuous form of evidence, was viewed through the prism of Letby's assumed guilt. Information that could have contradicted this viewpoint was either ignored, downplayed or attributed with sinister motives, even in the absence of any real evidence. The officers involved don't seem to have any doubts whatsoever about the case; there is certainly no evidence of dissent presented in this so-called documentary.

Dr Steve Watts told *The Trials of Lucy Letby* podcast: "The problem is that at a very early stage, they accepted the evidence of one expert that the babies have been unlawfully killed or harmed, and they accepted the proposition that Lucy Letby was the person who'd done that. From that point on, there was confirmation bias, and the investigation moved from being an investigation of how these babies had died and become injured, and who might be responsible, to gathering evidence towards confirming the hypothesis that Lucy Letby had been the offender." The Criminal Procedure and Investigations Act 1996 requires "the investigator [to] pursue all reasonable lines of inquiry, whether these point towards or away from the suspect." It is extremely hard to believe that this occurred in Operation Hummingbird, which has prompted Dr Steve Watts and Sir David Davis to request critical decision logs and other documents from the investigation to be made public.

It seems that Cheshire Police rapidly concluded there was a potentially malign explanation for this spike in deaths. Paul Hughes commented that "by investigating that it could be anyone, it means we're not focused on one person." However, it doesn't seem to have registered that this phenomenon might not have been caused by "anyone" at all, and even if there was a human cause, it need not have been malicious.

For example, the original pathology reports have been abandoned in this investigation, and it seems that Cheshire Police never consulted the pathologists nor the other organisations that investigated the CoCH, not to mention any other medical body. They appear to have accepted the uncorroborated account of Dr Evans at face value. They allowed him to run the entire medical investigation, brush away the recommendations of the NCA and encouraged him to single-handedly build a case against Letby.

Dr James Phillips has explained how "institutions can struggle to deal with…how different pieces of scientific evidence relate to one another and alter each other's interpretation". He observed that "relatively little appeared to hinge" on the non-scientific evidence at the trial, and that the "case would collapse" as soon as "medical evidence was removed".

"One of the first things the police say in the Operation Hummingbird video is that they needed help as they didn't have the medical knowledge to conduct the investigation", Dr Phillips commented. "I hope in future, perhaps as an outcome of the inquiry-that-is-to-come, a proper body with the investigatory powers and scientific skills to conduct such an investigation is created. Probably as an extension of powers and responsibilities of an existing body." There certainly should have been a more stringent internal review at the CoCH, coupled with a forensic review operated by medical bodies. If this revealed nothing conclusive or incriminating, which applied to all previous medical investigations, then the consultants should have accepted the situation.

What has also become clear from the lamentable Netflix programme is that both Lucy Letby and her parents had contact with Cheshire Police well before the 15 May 2017 meeting with Brearey and Jayaram. John and Susan Letby met with Cheshire Police in March 2017, informing them of what they believed to be scapegoating of their daughter on the neonatal unit. Letby herself wrote to Cheshire Police, indicating her willingness to speak openly, as previously reflected in a discussion at the CoCH on 1 December 2016 in which Letby stated that she was "happy for the police to come", and that she had "nothing to hide".

What was Cheshire Police's response to this? Detective Superintendent Simon Blackwell claimed during the Netflix documentary that they had no choice other than to arrest Letby, even though she had made herself open to interview well over a year earlier. "He is talking nonsense", Dr Steve Watts informed me. "He was wrong in law. He was wrong in terms of police procedure. He was even wrong with regard to the Human Rights Act and European Convention on Human Rights. To say that the only thing you can do is to arrest somebody when you want to interview them about a serious offence is categorically wrong." Interestingly, Paul Hughes seemed to realise this himself as he spent some time discussing the decision to arrest Letby in the constabulary's own YouTube effort, describing it as "incredibly difficult". One wonders how something can be both an incredibly difficult decision, and also the only possible course of action.

Elsewhere, it is evident that there seems to have been a distinct absence of critical thinking. Simon Blackwell asserted that "to hear that there may be allegations of assault or concern at a hospital in our area was a huge thing. You don't often hear of multiple child/baby/infant deaths. They are extremely rare. One is rare enough as it is and tragic enough. But if you have a number of potential babies who have died, or have been harmed, it is absolutely hugely important."

Professor David Livermore told me that "even if you looked at all the deaths, including those that Letby wasn't charged with, they were still within the statistical bound of what the worst hospital might be in any year. The spike struck me as remarkably similar to things that I've seen when I worked for Public Health England and its predecessors – outbreaks in neonatal intensive care units, and general outbreaks of infection." Indeed, the reason that "you don't often hear" of such incidents is that they aren't usually referred to the police, they don't usually become newsworthy and they are dealt with internally as medical issues. That doesn't mean they don't occur with regularity; almost everyone working within the NHS will have encountered them. As a reminder, the CoCH was just one of 21 hospitals that were examined as part of the *Mothers and Babies: Reducing Risk through Audits and Confidential Enquires across the UK 2015 Report*. Spikes in deaths are not unusual, particularly among neonates, and especially at poorly performing hospitals.

The problem is that Cheshire Police have never considered this context, let alone investigated it, as their own comments make very clear: "When we got this, it's not a secret because it's been in the media and everything that Lucy Letby had been moved off the ward, and the deaths and collapses had stopped."

Everyone knew that Letby was the target from day one. It was "not a secret". She was practically identified by Dr Stephen Brearey when he met with representatives from the Cheshire Constabulary on 15 May 2017 before the investigation even began, at which point the Cheshire Constabulary performed their about-turn.

Dr Evans has stated that he had no idea Letby was involved, no names were mentioned, and even, rather implausibly, that he didn't know a crime had been committed. But the lead of the Cheshire Police investigation has stated that everyone knew Letby had been withdrawn from the unit, it had "been in the media", and also that the "deaths and collapses had stopped". I find it hard to believe anyone could argue that the investigation did not start out with a biased perspective and it is darkly funny that Cheshire Police don't seem to realise they fuelled that suspicion with their own PR.

Another indicator that Lucy Letby was the sole suspect from day one comes from the father of Child K, who told the Thirlwall Inquiry that "my wife received a phone call from the police in May 2017…she said she had had a phone call from the police and that there was an investigation on a nurse in Chester Hospital…the police came round in the evening to discuss further…we were just told that it was an investigation into a nurse in Chester Hospital." This again indicates that Operation Hummingbird, despite protestations from Cheshire Police, was never a broad-based examination into the CoCH. It was always solely focused on Letby.

From what we have been allowed to witness, Operation Hummingbird in no way resembles an investigation to "exclude unnatural causes" which is what Cheshire Police were asked to carry out.

"Major errors can happen in the intersection between science, technology and power", Dr James Phillips told me. "There needs to be more transparency with that process, and I think that for these kinds of very complex medical cases, there is a strong argument for having a specialised investigatory force. Because I don't think the kind of person that will be in that police force would exactly be world experts in every type of investigation. It would have been much better to have an external investigation by experts, which, in fact, they had already done!" Dr Steve Watts echoed this view: "I am starting to press for a dedicated unit, perhaps a Healthcare Incidents Investigation Branch, similar to the Air Accident Investigation Branch."

In short, Cheshire Police failed to conduct an investigation that adequately probed the context surrounding this not particularly unusual spike in deaths, and which uncovered the sort of information that is now public knowledge thanks to Dr Shoo Lee's panel of international experts. Dr Steve Watts expressed some of the failings of Cheshire Police:

"This investigation began from a position of confirmation bias and never recovered. This is clear from the Thirlwall Inquiry documents, and also from statements made by Nigel Wenham at the inquiry itself. He spoke about how powerful the consultants had been, and it's clear that he was emotionally involved by this." Based on his comments made at Thirlwall, it seems that Wenham's judgement was strangely clouded, speaking as he did of how the consultants wanted to be "listened to and believed", as if this is the job of the police. "He is clearly invested in what these doctors have stated, and he's recounting this in a high profile public inquiry, so he must have carefully considered what he said. All I can say is that if you believe unequivocally what people who walk into your police station are telling you, there are very obvious dangers for the objectivity of the investigation", Dr Watts concluded.

When I put it to Dr Watts that Cheshire Police had uncritically accepted the views of Brearey, Jayaram and Evans, he agreed and outlined another fundamental problem with the investigation. "There is a key principle that should underpin all investigations – ABC. *Assume nothing. Believe nobody. Check everything.* This is part of the basic training and guidance for investigators at all levels, and is cited within the ACPO Practice Advice on Core Investigative Doctrine. I am astonished that they managed to get themselves into the position of 'believing' the consultants, as Nigel Wenham put it, and also how it persisted."

Surely nothing could possibly happen to make things worse…

CHAPTER 21: THE GOLDEN THREAD

On 19 August 2023 in the aftermath of Lucy Letby's conviction, the *Observer* published an article in which the by now familiar figures of Dr Stephen Brearey and DS Paul Hughes were interviewed.

The article begins with Dr Brearey once again complaining about executives at the hospital, particularly comments made by Tony Chambers at a meeting on 4 July 2016 in which Chambers allegedly implied the deaths and collapses were due to poor care rather than deliberate harm. Chambers disputed Brearey's version of events, stating that it represented a "one-sided account of the meeting where what I said has been taken out of context…I also said that there were a significant number of factors to consider, including demand, acuity, clinical care, staffing and environment."

It is important once more to reiterate that the consultants never provided any evidence for their claims. When the case was passed to Cheshire Police, there was still no evidence. Yet during this period, Dr Brearey supposedly had a "drawer of doom", whose contents he refused to share with Karen Rees when this was requested. Genealogist Debbie Kennett described this on X as "inappropriate", whereas I would be inclined to say that it was churlish. Alongside acknowledged delays in reporting incidents, a picture emerges of a distinct lack of accountability and transparency.

Stuart Lythgoe, who was Director of Operations at the doctors' union HCSA, submitted a witness statement to the Thirlwall Inquiry in which he recounted that Dr Brearey was threatened by an unnamed medical director who had pointed out to him that Dr Brearey "had been working on the ward at the same time as Nurse Letby and, as such, he (Dr B) could be responsible for the deaths". This seems to be the only time this was ever suggested, and certainly there was no police investigation into any medical malpractice or mistakes.

The *Observer* article confirms what has already been established – there was no tangible evidence regarding Letby, and she was preparing her return to the neonatal unit in January 2017: "Letby had been just six days from returning to work on the neonatal unit."

A letter authored by Letby herself at that time describes the anguish that her "life was turned upside down". Letby asserts that "there has been a huge element of dishonesty throughout this process", which tallies precisely with the opinion of Dr Christopher Green that it was likely the consultants "had lied". Letby observes that she found "unsubstantiated comments" to be "extremely unprofessional", citing the remarks that Dr Stephen Brearey made about not caring whether or not Letby killed herself, or whether or not her elderly patients died. Letby not unreasonably asserts that "no individual and certainly no parent should have to hear something as distressing as this" and goes on to cite the "immense… detrimental effect this has had on me, my family, and potentially my future". Letby also reaffirmed that she remained "very passionate about and dedicated to Chester…and my return to where I belong".

In light of everything we know about the situation surrounding the CoCH, the response of the consultants when told that there would be a police investigation could be considered somewhat inappropriate. The *Observer* article continues: "[Dr Ravi Jayaram stated that] he 'could have punched the air' when Nigel Wenham listened to the consultants and said that their concerns were 'something that [the police] have to be involved with'." When speaking with ITV, Jayaram further claimed that the police accepted their explanation for the apparent spike in deaths within 10 minutes, again contradicting the claims of Cheshire Police that they kept an open mind to all possibilities.

An article published in *Vanity Fair*, for which Brearey was interviewed, describes how the police asked him to search the records of the twins and triplets involved in the case in an attempt to find something conclusive. That is how the insulin cases were established, although Dr Brearey is a little more sketchy on the details of the third insulin case which was excluded during the police investigations. Both Dr Brearey and the police were happy to go on the record with *Vanity Fair*, and thus apparently couldn't see any problem in the person who had reported Letby to the police cherry-picking evidence for them. The *Observer* takes up the story: "DS Paul Hughes, who led the investigation, told the *Observer* the information provided by Brearey and his colleagues had been 'the golden thread' for their inquiry."

For over two years, Dr Brearey was centrally involved with efforts to remove Letby from the unit, so much so that when Letby's grievance was upheld, Dr Green warned Brearey he should face disciplinary proceedings. Yet now we see Cheshire Police confirming that Brearey, a prime mover in getting Letby investigated, has become the golden thread in their investigation. The *Observer* goes on to corroborate in more depth the *Vanity Fair* article: "On the night before Valentine's Day in February 2018, nearly a year after police launched their investigation, Brearey was hunched over his computer screen when he spotted something unusual. He had been asked by detectives to review the care of siblings and twins on the unit and was looking at the records of a seven-day-old boy."

Let that sink in. Dr Stephen Brearey, who was instrumental in Letby being removed from the unit, who was hugely persistent in ensuring that the police became involved, who met with Cheshire Police on 15 May 2017 at a time when they had no intention of investigating any further and convinced them to launch an investigation, has now been "asked by detectives", some nine months later, to review cases related to Operation Hummingbird.

There are no circumstances in which any police body should allow someone who has been primarily involved in reporting an alleged criminal offence to then participate in its investigation. It is staggering that not only has this been permitted to take place, but also that no one from the Cheshire Constabulary appeared to be remotely concerned about it being reported to two separate media outlets. Indeed, DS Paul Hughes is perfectly happy to praise Brearey and Jayaram, telling the *Observer*: "They have been very brave in coming forward and they've put this ahead of their careers, in my view", [Hughes] said. "If it wasn't for their ongoing determination, would there have been more [murders]? I don't know.

It's difficult to answer or speculate on the future. But they've done well."

During an investigation interview conducted as part of Letby's grievance procedure on 17 October 2016, nurse Yvonne Griffiths stated that Brearey "wanted to grasp at anything that might be linked, to 'point the finger'". He would later be provided with the ideal opportunity to do this as the 'golden thread' in the police investigation, while Jayaram was also part of this process.

This is not something that Cheshire Police, Brearey or Jayaram have attempted to hide. Brearey told the Thirlwall Inquiry that he was asked to review the care of a number of babies in February 2018. A further indication of this was provided in the book, *Unmasking Lucy Letby*, in which Judith Moritz and Jonathan Coffey describe Brearey and Jayaram "passing any worrying cases on to the police". Even Brearey's statement to the Thirlwall Inquiry describes him being "asked to review the care of a number of babies". This again calls into question the way in which cases were selected, and it would be hugely surprising if they passed on any that Letby wasn't involved in.

Michele Worden informed me that "Steve Brearey drew up the roster chart with Eirian Powell. Eirian was very upset that, by the time it got to Alison Kelly, the doctors' names had been removed from it. Brearey cherry-picked the babies. There are seven deaths on that roster chart, but we know that there were 17 deaths. So the consultants are the accusers, they're the investigators, and then they're the main witnesses. I cannot think of any high profile case where you can be all three things."

When interviewed by Cheshire Police on 20 January 2020, Annette Weatherley told officers that the consultants had been "doing their own kind of investigation", during which "they decided it was her, she was the baby killer, they were openly talking about her as the baby killer, they went to the Trust, they said she's the baby killer, we don't want her on the unit". When Dr Jayaram met with Nigel Wenham on 15 May 2017, he stated that he and Dr Brearey "are not on a witch hunt". So what did Weatherley state about their campaign? "I felt it was a witch hunt". It should be noted that Annette Weatherley did not work at the CoCH; she chaired Letby's grievance panel and had never met Letby or the consultants prior to this. Her conclusion was simply the outcome of an independent inquiry.

Dr Watts also told me that Brearey and Jayaram's role in supporting the investigation was entirely inappropriate: "The consultants were significant witnesses in the case, and had all reasonable lines of enquiry been pursued, they might have been identified as potential suspects. They were clearly not independent to the extent required to act as expert advisors and reviewers for the investigation. This is a significant flaw in the investigation and a breach of the national guidance."

Operation Hummingbird was patently vulnerable to bias. Brearey and Jayaram knew that Lucy Letby was a suspect. Brearey was the one who named her and who had been suspicious of Letby for nearly three years at the point when Cheshire Police were using him in the investigation. How can he possibly investigate the case objectively?

But the plot thickens further still, when Dr Evans claimed that he identified the insulin cases. Evans divulged this when interviewed by Raj Persaud: "And then a little later, in 2018 I reviewed two more cases, and these were the insulin poisoning cases, and these had not been suspected by anyone before this, and it's only thanks to Cheshire Police's methodical way of looking at cases that both insulin poisonings were the second of a pair of twins, and they asked me: 'Look, just look at the notes. You know that we've not had any concerns about this, but let's look at the notes, just to cover all the options.'"

This same claim was made by the Court of Appeal: "In addition, it was pointed out that Dr Evans was the person who had identified that two of the babies had been poisoned by insulin (Baby F and Baby L). This was a matter which had eluded the treating medics and went to prove that someone was committing serious offences against babies in the unit; and it was particularly important independent evidence, bolstering Dr Evans' credibility and reliability."

This is important because both Cheshire Police and the consultants have claimed one thing, while the Court of Appeal and Dr Evans have claimed another, with the court being used to 'bolster' the credibility of Dr Evans. In fact, an email sent by the anonymised Dr ZA to Dr Brearey on 6 June 2017 already references "exogenous insulin" and "insulin levels done on neonates". This tallies with a statement from Dr Brearey, disclosed by prosecutor Philip Astbury, in which Brearey again stated that he "conducted a review of baby records" after a "request from Cheshire Police".

Elsewhere, we see other strange coincidences, such as both Dr Jayaram and Dr Evans citing the same obscure decades-old Canadian paper, and both advancing an obscure air embolism-related cause of death which hadn't been picked up by pathologists. And then when it came to the insulin cases, it's not clear whether Dr Brearey found them under instruction from the police, or whether Dr Evans located them, as stated by the Court of Appeal. It's hard to say because they have told several different stories to numerous different media outlets.

Cheshire Police were also aware that Letby had filed a grievance procedure against the CoCH and this simply should have been further investigated.

One final point is that Dr Dewi Evans has claimed on repeated occasions that he did not know the name of Lucy Letby when he compiled his initial reports. This may be correct – it is impossible to corroborate this definitively. But Evans wrote over 80 reports in total, and at least 25 of these were compiled between 2018 and 2022 after he *definitely* knew the name of Lucy Letby because her arrest had been publicised. In fact, Evans submitted a witness report to Cheshire Police on 3 July 2019, at which time Letby had already been arrested twice, while still writing further reports and changing diagnoses after this date.

The determination of Evans to convey the message he knew nothing of Letby has been curious, often making the assertion in response to an unrelated question. For example, during cross-examination on 7 March 2023, when asked about the rashes he had cited, Dr Evans instead replied: "I was not told anything about any suspect. I knew absolutely nothing." Judge James Goss then interrupted: "You have said this, Dr Evans. You've said it at least once, more than once."

Dr Steve Watts told me that fundamental errors had been made by Cheshire Police: "There were other potential hypotheses, and it was the police's job to progress the investigation on the basis of hypothesis testing. We know about the sewage now, about pseudomonas, the treatment of infants, the ward rounds, the medical errors, the staffing, the acuity, the risk that these babies presented, because several of them were very ill. And yet it seems that, at a very early stage, all possibilities other than malfeasance were excluded, and the entire investigation was devoted to proving this hypothesis. Cheshire Police should have examined these other factors, and I must say that it's essential that Mark McDonald and his team gain access to the documentation that demonstrates how the investigation was led, so that we can understand why other lines of inquiry were never pursued."

In April 2017, legal representative Corinne Slingo wrote to Director of People and Organisational Development, Sue Hodkinson, regarding what she believed to be valid "next steps" in dealing with problems on the unit. Slingo noted that "the neonatal unit mortality concern has now been investigated in a number of ways", which included Royal College and forensic pathology reviews, a review of each case by the medical director, an extensive HR investigation and continued liaison with the coroner. This is a truly fascinating document which is full of interesting insights, but perhaps the most intriguing is the assertion by Slingo that "a police investigation may need to consider corporate manslaughter issues…as well as exploring gross negligence manslaughter by individuals, and also the new offence of wilful neglect". Cheshire Police reportedly began an investigation into the issue in October 2023, but this seems to be far more focused on allegations of individuals being reluctant to report Letby to the police sooner rather than anything related to medical negligence or error. Could they have reported it sooner, considering that the police conceded when it was referred in May 2017 that there was "no evidence" of wrongdoing?

It seems to me impossible for any fair-minded and analytical person to be anything other than critical of the methodology and approach adopted in Operation Hummingbird, which fell catastrophically short of the standards that should be expected from an investigation of this importance. Stephanie Davies described the attitude of Cheshire Police as representing "blind faith in consultant paediatricians".

Fortunately, we know exactly what happened in this investigation from available documents. Dr Brearey and Dr Jayaram fed the dates to be investigated to the police in a document submitted to Cheshire Police on 10 May 2017 and they, to all intents and purposes, identified the suspect on 15 May. The police then restricted the investigation to those dates and there is no evidence that they investigated anyone else other than Lucy Letby. Brearey and Jayaram then selected cases for the police.

Cheshire Police fed the dates to Dr Evans on 28 June 2017, and then an email from Janet Moore to Sonya Baylis on 30 June encouraged Baylis to pass a summary of Operation Hummingbird onto him. Dr Evans examined only those dates, while making some curious comments inquiring about the location of "the nurse", which should be completely irrelevant to his medical investigation. Evans then told the police to go back and find out who was on duty for "lots of incidents". The police go back to Brearey and Jayaram. And Brearey and Jayaram tell them that Letby was on duty. It is the absolute epitome of a circuitous process that inevitably results in Letby being identified as the sole suspect.

The scale of this debacle prompted parliamentarian Sir David Davis to hold an adjournment debate on the Cheshire Police investigation of the CoCH on 26 March 2026, at which he outlined exhaustively the dizzying array of blunders they made. This prompted an extraordinary response from the Chief Constable of the Cheshire Constabulary Mark Roberts: he wrote back to Davis, in a letter shared with the *Daily Mail*, claiming to have "refuted" the Commons speech and calling on Davis to raise a point of order to correct his errors. The letter failed to address a single argument made in Parliament, and within 24 hours a withering response from Davis had thoroughly annihilated the claims of Roberts. The conduct of Roberts was described as "not very seemly" by prominent legal commentator Joshua Rozenberg. "It's not Roberts' job to be… annoyed by public criticism. His job is to investigate crimes, present evidence and ultimately to allow the courts to decide where truth lies and justice rests," Rozenberg added.

In summary, Operation Hummingbird involves a series of baffling and incomprehensible events and decisions that can collectively be described as indefensible.

SUMMARY

At the heart of the conviction of Lucy Letby is a story that, jarringly, makes absolutely no sense. These are the most sickening acts imaginable, allegedly committed by the most benign of people, someone who was even notably kind and caring. This is a massive red flag immediately because it is a conspicuous contradiction in terms.

There is no plausible motive nor feasible psychological explanation for Letby's supposed acts. No one has ever seen her doing anything wrong. The anecdotal evidence used in court was phenomenally weak. The statistical case on which the prosecution was built is fundamentally flawed. The court case was brim-full of eyewitness accounts that were specious and bereft of material or evidential value. The prosecution has erected, not merely one hypothesis, but an array of hypothetical events that are completely unprovable and then spun them into an overarching narrative intended to explain away their lack of evidential support. Often the prosecution even used evidence that is known to be incorrect.

And the scientific evidence presented in court has become increasingly dubious the more it has been placed under the microscope of examination. All of the cases on which Lucy Letby was convicted would have failed to reach court on their own merit, taken in isolation. The entire prosecution is based on bundling together these cases and relying on association and coincidence without statistical merit in order to secure verdicts that are hugely concerning for anyone who has assessed the evidence assiduously.

Letby was not afforded character witnesses in court, not least because those who were willing to speak in her favour were actively discouraged. Consequently, the court and jury never heard from the supporters of Letby at the CoCH, nor any of the context related to what happened to her on the unit. None of the previous reports regarding the CoCH, including the 2016 RCPCH report, were made available to the jury, nor were they mentioned in court. Judge James Goss similarly ruled Letby's grievance inadmissible.

The jury was not afforded any access to counsellor Kathryn de Beger who could have provided crucial context on the supposed confession notes presented in court. No professional analysis of these notes was sought by either the prosecution or defence; thus, the court never heard that all such analysis inevitably concludes that these notes are emphatically not confessional.

Pathologists and coroners who examined the infants involved in the court case were never cross-examined, nor were their conclusions discussed in court. It was not explained adequately, if at all, that primary prosecution witness Dr Dewi Evans had single-handedly disagreed with the conclusions of experienced coroners and pathologists. Yet the opinion of far more qualified and experienced experts was put to one side.

Organisational issues in the north west region were barely mentioned in court. The inadequate staffing situation at the hospital was never adequately conveyed to the jury, nor were any of the problems with monitoring and ward rounds. The jury weren't told that Cheshire Police had bungled large swathes of swipe-card data on which the prosecution case relied, and had, in fact, reversed this. They weren't informed that there was a staircase leading out of the neonatal unit which renders all of the swipe-card data completely worthless. In fact, the Cheshire Police investigation was shambolic, actively involving the accusers of Lucy Letby at the CoCH in the selection and investigation of cases.

There was no microbiologist in court to discuss the presence of the pseudomonas aeruginosa and stenotrophomonas maltophilia bacteria, and their dangers to vulnerable infants. There was similarly no discussion in court of the overwhelming evidence for sepsis on the neonatal unit; in fact, bizarrely, the jury was told that none of the infants showed any signs of infection at the time of collapse, which contradicts documented and publicly available medical records. Again, Dr Evans dismissed the need for infectious disease specialists, relying instead solely on his own expertise.

Dr Shoo Lee did not make an appearance in court which was a missed opportunity as he could have informed the jury that his co-authored paper, on which the diagnosis of air embolism was entirely based, had been completely misused. We know that Dr Evans has changed diagnoses that were used in court. He also altered some diagnoses during the court case itself (which of course he is allowed to do) and even the dates of key incidents, but the jury wouldn't have anticipated that he would continue to do so publicly after the trial was over. The statistical work of Professor Jane Hutton was never commissioned, nor did any other statisticians appear in court to challenge the flawed methodology used to identify a suspect.

It has been made incredibly difficult to obtain the entire court transcript of this court case. But what can be ascertained from what is available and court reporting is that the jury was never told about other deaths on the unit, nor was crucial context provided regarding deaths in previous years. It was asserted that deaths on the unit had ceased after Letby was reduced to a clerical role, and that her removal was critical. But the importance of the neonatal unit being downgraded after Letby was removed was never adequately contextualised in court. This was not only a critically important explanation but it had even been anticipated by legal representative Corinne Slingo. Similarly, the court was never told that Letby hadn't been removed due to suspicions about her conduct, but as a form of protection proffered by a supportive nursing team. There was no mention of the third insulin case in court; perhaps not surprisingly as it calls into question the entire prosecution case.

Lucy Letby was afforded no defence or character witnesses in court, and the reports prepared by Dr Michael Hall were never circulated among the jury. The court was therefore never told that the insulin testing used was highly flawed, and that it is certainly not an inevitability that babies were deliberately poisoned on the unit, as had been asserted. There was no examination of the differences between adult and neonatal endocrinology, and this was presented to the jury in a fashion that could be perceived as misleading and scientifically incorrect.

Jurors were never informed by experts of the unlikely nature of air embolism. They were never told that overfeeding babies with milk is an almost impossible method of murder. The jury never heard of the full circumstances regarding the sub-par care of, for example, Child D and Child E. The jury were not informed that the liver damage for Child O was likely caused by the medical blunders of doctors working at the CoCH.

And the true condition of the infants in the case was certainly never communicated to the jury. In this aspect of the trial, those assessing the case were given an utterly false impression of 'stable' infants who suddenly collapsed or died for no reason. Experts who have examined and commented on the case since have treated this with derision, and their medical evidence and expertise in court would have been critical. In my view, there is no way that a court case of this seriousness should be allowed to take place with experts for one side, and no experts for the other, unless the defendant intends to plead guilty. We now know beyond doubt that there are many experts ready to defend Letby; the system *must* facilitate such involvement, both in this case and in future, if it wishes to retain any degree of public support.

Instead of being furnished with all of this important context and vital information, the court was told that everything which occurred at the CoCH could be explained by the incorrectly recorded movements and both unseen and hypothetical actions of a hitherto dedicated and highly regarded nurse, who had no conceivable reason to harm any infant, and neither benefited from this in the slightest, nor demonstrated any psychological indication that she had done anything remotely resembling this. Furthermore, Letby has always unreservedly maintained her innocence, and all of her behaviour since being placed under suspicion has been consistent with that of an innocent person.

If it isn't clear by now, this is why many are critical of the conviction of Lucy Letby.

As has been emphasised in this book, once the lens of presumed guilt is removed, any examination of the circumstances at the CoCH has resulted in the prosecution case becoming ever weaker. This process of examination has certainly not revealed new evidence which would make the prosecution appear safer which would be expected if Letby was guilty. Everything that has emerged since the trial has called the verdict into ever sharper question, while no new evidence has come to light which buttresses the prosecution in any meaningful way. This is despite the fact that many people have engaged in forensic analysis of every aspect of this court case.

During the writing of this book, the spectre of an enormous crisis in maternity services loomed ever larger. This provided meaningful context to the failure at the CoCH, not least on 26 February 2026 when the release of an interim report into maternity and neonatal services made multiple criticisms. Among the more worrying finding was that "many families [felt] there had been a 'cover-up' and defensiveness from NHS Trusts", which could include "medical notes being amended or redacted". It does not require an enormous amount of imagination to see the relevance of this to the situation which has unfolded at the CoCH.

This has perhaps partly explained why no neonatal expert has come forward to support the conviction, despite repeated requests by Dr Philip Hammond; compare this to the calibre and quantity of those who question it. Meanwhile, the apparent conduct of those working on the neonatal unit seems to become ever more questionable as more is revealed. For example, the failure of CoCH consultants to immediately report cases to coroners so that the causes of death could be adequately investigated has been roundly criticised. The roles of Dr Stephen Brearey and Dr Ravi Jayaram, firstly as accusers, then being involved in the police investigation, before finally giving evidence in court against Letby has been examined thoroughly in this book, and certainly does not reflect favourably on anyone involved.

As public and media disquiet about the conviction has grown, the publication of final reporting from the Thirlwall Inquiry has been pushed back ever further. At the time of writing, it remains in hiatus, with no word on when the final report will be released. It is not particularly surprising that Lady Thirlwall finds herself in this predicament, considering that the whole ethos of the inquiry has been so obviously askew from day one. "The foundation of any inquiry should be a search for the truth. The

Thirlwall Inquiry has been the total opposite of that," Cleuci de Oliveira, who attended 12 days of the inquiry in person, told me. "You can't close the door to the potential truth because it's inconvenient! What's the point of having an inquiry in the first place? Inquiry lawyers would ask the most leading questions imaginable, and then try to steer the witness in that direction. And if the witness starts offering something that may veer from the path that the lawyer wants, they will cut the witness off."

Similar delays to Thirlwall are simply not acceptable in the case of Lucy Letby. She has been through a scarcely believable and harrowing ordeal. She was bullied at work, removed from the neonatal unit, had to endure constant suspicion while still working at the CoCH, had the job that she demonstrably loved, that had been her complete dedication in life, snatched away from her, and that career, which was her joy and passion, is now over for her whatever happens.

Then she was arrested by the police three times, on one occasion with burly male officers barging into her bedroom at the crack of dawn, interviewed 30 times, patiently cooperating throughout, nothing that she said in her defence was taken into account, while anything and everything was used against her, she was denied bail, and was then incarcerated for two years while she awaited trial. Just days before she was due to appear in court, she was forcibly moved from one prison to another, many of her personal belongings were lost, and she went into the court suffering from PTSD, reliant on medication, having had a borderline breakdown.

She then endured one of the most high-profile court cases in living memory, which lasted for nearly 10 months, knowing all the time that she could be found guilty and imprisoned indefinitely for the most heinous acts. Every second that she spent in that courtroom she knew that everyone was judging her, and some had already decided that she was guilty simply by association. She has furthermore been utterly castigated by the media.

But that's not enough. She was then afforded no defence witnesses in court, character witnesses were actively discouraged from appearing in her favour, she was sentenced to a full life order without any hope of parole, meaning that she would inevitably die in prison. She is being held as a Category A inmate in solitary confinement, under constant threat of retribution from fellow prisoners. She has been denied an appeal and then denied a second appeal, and was not allowed any representation at the Thirlwall Inquiry, while the inquiry has attempted to systematically discredit the reviews, post-mortems and pathology reports that exonerate her.

I pose this question rhetorically – isn't it about time that Lucy Letby was actually afforded the opportunity to defend herself?

The shifting public mood has been exemplified by the increasingly pro-Letby stance of *The Sun* newspaper. *The Sun* chose to devote its front page to an evidential review by Detective Superintendent Stuart Clifton on 29 January 2026 who concluded that "this is likely the greatest miscarriage of justice this century". In the immediate aftermath, a poll conducted by *The Sun* found that over 75% of respondents believed that Lucy Letby should be retried.

A rather sniffy attitude can often emanate from the insulated capstone that constitutes the judiciary. There has certainly been criticism of efforts to raise awareness of the deeply flawed nature of this conviction, as if those at the apex of justice in Britain still view it as *their* system in which they preside over *us*. I would therefore like to remind them of some illustrative words from Thomas Bingham. At the time of his death in 2010, Bingham was described by the former President of the Supreme Court of the United Kingdom, Nicholas Phillips, as "one of the two great legal figures of my lifetime in the law". On page 22 of his book *The Rule of Law*, Bingham comments on defences against injustice, making the following critical comment:

> *"The judges are not, of course, the only guardians of the rule of law, perhaps not even the most important. Parliamentary and public opinion, informed by the media, should be alert to detect and scrutinise any infringement."*

Thus, no one should apologise for highlighting the plight of Letby, nor the debacle that has led to it. One can only imagine the brutal psychological toll on Letby herself. One gentleman who perhaps can envisage this is Michael O'Brien, one of three men wrongfully convicted for the murder of a Cardiff newsagent in July 1988. O'Brien was later exonerated, but the scars of that time remain, as he explained to me when we met: "I was suicidal. I didn't want to live anymore. I felt that my whole world had been shattered into pieces. When I was released on remand by the police, I was utterly traumatised. I ended up in a mental hospital for two days. All of my core beliefs had been obliterated. I cut myself, making my arms bleed. I just wanted to let the pain out."

Unquestionably, Michael is one of the bravest people that I've ever met, and he made it clear to me that he wouldn't allow himself to be viewed as a victim. But he also recounted the long-term consequences of his experience: "Every day is still a struggle. I'm not going to tell you that I don't still suffer with PTSD. I do. I see psychiatrists every month. I will be on medication for the rest of my life. I take tablets for depression and anxiety. Without them, I can't get out of bed. That's how bad the psychological damage has been. I still have nightmares. I still have flashbacks. I have seen and experienced horrific things. They don't go away."

Michael O'Brien was imprisoned for 11 years before being exonerated. Andrew Malkinson served all 17 years of his wrongful sentence for rape, and had three appeals rejected. The Birmingham Six were incarcerated for 16 years. The Guildford Four served 14 years before being exonerated. Peter Sullivan had 38 years, virtually half of the average lifespan, and the majority of his adult life, taken away. Such life-destroying timeframes cannot be repeated again in the case of Lucy Letby, particularly as dozens of mainstream publications have now reported that this is a likely miscarriage of justice, and five of the biggest national newspapers, *The Daily Telegraph*, the *Guardian*, the *Daily Mail*, *The Sun* and the *Mail on Sunday* have all called for this case to be resolved rapidly. At the time of writing, Letby has spent six Christmases in prison. This is already far too many.

This is not purely about justice. It is not merely about a young woman inexorably becoming a middle-aged woman, her life dripping steadily away in the harshest conditions imaginable, while having done nothing wrong. It is, fundamentally, about patient safety. It is about whether NHS institutions will be held to account. It is about whether the police are considered too big to fail, and whether their most serious mistakes can be publicly scrutinised.

And it is about the ability of the criminal justice system to reflect on its own failings, when it would be more convenient to blame a scapegoat. There is one unequivocal truth at the heart of this book, and it is one that cannot and must not be ignored, if even the merest scrap of public faith in the criminal justice system is to be retained. The conviction of Lucy Letby is chronically unsafe. It cannot be allowed to stand. And with this in mind, I will afford the final words to Dr Michael Hall, who observed the entire prosecution case in court:

"My opinion is that the verdicts on all infants are unsafe. And if they're unsafe, I think the conviction should be quashed".

ACKNOWLEDGEMENTS

I would firstly like to thank Dr James Phillips for his unwavering support. I also owe an immense debt of gratitude to my research assistant Marian Kensler.

I also acknowledge the contribution of all those who have been interviewed, engaged in correspondence, and/or assisted with fact-checking. These are as follows: Professor John Ashton, Eileen Chubb, Dr Allan Corder, Stephanie Davies, Cleuci de Oliveira, Dr Peter Donnelly, Dr Colin Ferguson, Dr Margaret Ferguson, Dr Thea Gumbert, Professor Richard Gill, Dr Michael Hall, Professor Jane Hutton, Professor Matthew Johll, Professor Alan Wayne Jones, Dr Shoo Lee, Professor David Livermore, Dr Fiona MacRae, Lulu Minns, Dr Jonathan Moore, Professor Colin Morley, Jayne Nickalls, Kate Nickalls, Dr Roger Norwich, Michael O'Brien, Professor John O'Quigley, Stephen Phelps, Dr Martyn Pitman, Ruth Sadik, Sloane Spade, Ashleigh Tavoulari, Stephen TriedByStats, Professor Carola Vinuesa, Dr Steve Watts, Dr Keith Wilkinson, Dr Ron Winter, Michele Worden, Julie Yates and Amber Zaman.

It can be difficult for those currently working in certain professions to go on the record in relation to this case. The conviction of Lucy Letby has also created something of a climate of fear in nursing, and this makes it particularly difficult for nurses to speak freely. I am therefore hugely thankful for the time and expertise of the many professionals who spoke to me anonymously. This encompassed eight nurses, a nursing practitioner, three expert witnesses, a statistician, a PhD in creative writing, two psychiatrists, a microbiologist and four further medics.

Additionally, I would like to express my most sincere thanks to everyone involved with all of the online groups with which I've been affiliated. You have been an unending source of information, expertise and encouragement. I could not be more grateful for your assistance.
Christopher Morris, July 2026

INDEX

BETWEEN THE LIES

The debut novel from award-winning journalist and broadcaster,
Louise Tickle

When it comes to families, is anyone a reliable witness?
Cherry Magraw can never forget the date her mother and brother were killed – the night of her ninth birthday. When her father was jailed for their murders, she lost everyone she loved.

Twenty years later, Cherry is a freelance journalist investigating domestic abuse and the secret world of the family courts, when she gets a letter from her father – still in prison for the killings – which contains a startling request.

From that point on, her past becomes entangled with her work, dismantling everything Cherry thought she knew about her family tragedy and plunging her into a dangerous game of cat and mouse. Will her history cloud her judgement about another desperate family? And how far will she go to save someone else's children?

About the author
Louise Tickle is an award-winning journalist and broadcaster who specialises in reporting on domestic abuse, family courts and child protection. *Between the Lies* is her first novel.

"This book is brilliant: gripping, powerful and one of the best thrillers I've ever read – I could not put it down."
Victoria Derbyshire

SANCTUARY

Sometimes the only refuge is escape

Alex Donovan, a young refugee lawyer, is in crisis.

His boss has relegated him to humdrum corporate case work, not the cut and thrust of immigration appeals he loves. Helping desperate clients reach safety is what makes being a lawyer bearable.

Meanwhile, the woman he adores, hotshot immigration barrister Amy, is increasingly distant.

So Alex sets out on a quest, to regain the confidence of his boss, his old job and the affection of Amy. As life imitates art, will he succeed?

About the author

Tom Gaisford is an immigration and asylum barrister and a freelance contributor to The Independent, The Tablet and Open Democracy.

This is his debut novel.

"Gaisford's insider knowledge makes his cleverly constructed legal thriller a compulsive and genuinely enlightening read."
Suzi Feay, former literary editor and literary critic for The Guardian and The Financial Times

BETTER CALL LOUIS
Adventures in the media jungle

Better Call Louis is a rare chance to see behind the scenes of over thirty years of landmark scandals through the eyes of one of the UK's leading media lawyers, Louis Charalambous.

The now infamous Bashir/Diana interview. Persuading Amber Heard to be a witness against Johnny Depp. Winning damages for Robert Murat, falsely suspected in the disappearance of Madeleine McCann. "Plebgate". Defending the journalist who exposed the wrongful convictions of the Birmingham Six.

Louis was in the thick of all these stories and many more, taking him on a journey from the High Court and Downing Street here to the Middle East, Los Angeles, Portugal and Strasbourg.

His unique vantage point at the heart of these affairs makes Louis the perfect guide to what really happens in this often shadowy world of deadlines, ultimatums, hubris and power.

About the author

Louis Charalambous has been working with newspapers, journalists and in the libel courts for years both as an external adviser for a string of newspapers and TV channels and acting privately. His background, working his way up from the foothills of the profession, fires his sense of justice and desire to protect the innocent.

THE GREAT POST OFFICE COVER-UP

The *Great Post Office Cover-Up* reveals for the first time the full story behind the largest miscarriage of justice the nation has ever seen. Building on *The Great Post Office Scandal*, freelance journalist and broadcaster, Nick Wallis, uses the fresh evidence uncovered by the statutory inquiry and Nick's own journalism to chronicle the legal obstruction and embedded cultural attitudes that led one of the nation's most respected institutions to become a byword for corporate callousness and incompetence. Along the way, he recounts hitherto untold stories of the human cost of their actions.

The scandal sparked national outrage in January 2024 when the ITV drama, *Mr Bates vs The Post Office* was broadcast, but we now know that was not the full story. With the statutory inquiry over, *The Great Post Office Cover-Up* stands as the definitive account of one of the darkest episodes of modern British history.

About the author

Nick Wallis is an award-winning freelance journalist and broadcaster. He has worked with the BBC, Private Eye and ITN. His Radio 4 series on the Post Office scandal has been nominated for national awards. He also acted as series consultant for the ITV drama, Mr Bates vs The Post Office.

Publication due Autumn/Winter 2026.

A VERY BRITISH BANKING SCANDAL

The shocking stories of how our high street banks broke hundreds of family businesses

Imagine. You are running a growing business. You go to your high street bank for a loan. The bank agrees, only too willing to offer you a very attractive interest rate. Then, suddenly, the promised low-interest rate rockets, alongside added fees and hidden charges. You are no longer a valued customer for the bank, instead they now have an agenda to seize your assets to help the bank plug its own financial hole. You're told your business is failing.

The next step is to sell off your assets including your home. You face ruin. Your family life is shattered. You may even contemplate suicide. You feel stitched-up but when you try to fight back, you find the police, the regulators and the courts are of no help. The bank insists it's all legal and it has bottomless funds for an army of expensive lawyers. Inquiries set up by the Government in response to your claims of unfairness and fraud begin to look like a cover-up.

A Very British Banking Scandal reveals the human stories of thousands who suffered a fate like this after the banks were bailed out in 2009. Former BBC Correspondents Steve Brodie and Emily Buchanan have spent years following the fate of business owners whose lives have been destroyed.

Publication due Autumn/Winter 2026.

COMING SOON FROM CINTO PRESS

TAINTED LOVE

A policeman's wife dies in an unexplained fall from her flat. As journalist Cherry Magraw digs deeper, whistleblowing, corruption and her own past are exposed in this gripping crime thriller.

The second Cherry Magraw novel picks up the story from her near death clifftop chase in *Between The Lies*. Recurring themes of deceit and domestic abuse remain at the heart of Cherry's fearless reporting, this time leading her into the centre of the very organisation that should be policing the crime.

Publication due September 2026.